JESUS
the Phoenician

KARIM EL KOUSSA

SUNBURY
PRESS

Mechanicsburg, Pennsylvania   USA

Published by Sunbury Press, Inc.
50 West Main Street
Mechanicsburg, Pennsylvania 17055

SUNBURY PRESS

www.sunburypress.com

For information about special discounts for bulk purchases, please contact Sunbury Press Orders Dept. at (855) 338-8359 or orders@sunburypress.com.

To request one of our authors for speaking engagements or book signings, please contact Sunbury Press Publicity Dept. at publicity@sunburypress.com.

ISBN: 978-1-62006-578-5 (Hardcover)
ISBN: 978-1-62006-281-4 (Trade Paperback)
ISBN: 978-1-62006-282-1 (Mobipocket)
ISBN: 978-1-62006-283-8 (ePub)

Library of Congress Control Number: 2015934924

FIRST SUNBURY PRESS HARDCOVER EDITION: March 2015

Product of the United States of America
0 1 1 2 3 5 8 13 21 34 55

Set in Bookman Old Style
Designed by Lawrence Knorr
Cover by Karim el Koussa
Edited by Jennifer Melendrez

Continue the Enlightenment!

My work is a mixture of Religion, History, Philosophy, Spirituality and Esoteric inner insights. Life itself is nothing but a deep hidden insight, emerging out of the Mind of God, a Journey, which I am trying to discover - a strange, yet magnificent Journey inside the Human Life.

It has always been a query of the Human mind to know and comprehend the world we are living in and the world that lies beyond. Philosophy, Religion, and Science have been the Knights that have fought the great battle; the lifting of the veil of the unknown.

Humanity, however, has been embedded in a labyrinth, one that very few escape. This liberation that we're all seeking as Human Beings, does not occur through the belief in Philosophical, Religious and Scientific "Dogmas", & I repeat "Dogmas", but rather through the free will and the in-depth implication with & into their Esoteric hidden side - with & into OUR inner Spirituality.

As Above so Below, echoed in the ears of the wise. These few Initiates recognized in man the Microcosm of the Macrocosm. It is upon each one of us to seek the Individual Consciousness, thus to be able to commune a Collective one.

It is now the age of the Homo-Cosmicus. So Meditate on the Human Potential of Becoming Cosmic.

Karim El Koussa
Lebanese Author

Also By Karim El Koussa

The PHOENICIAN Code:
Unveiling the Secrets of the Holy Grail
Religious Mystery (Christianity)/Fiction Thriller
—Sunbury Press, USA

PYTHAGORAS the Mathemagician
Historical Fiction/Philosophical novel
—Sunbury Press, USA
—Winner of the Saiid Akl Prize
for the Lebanese Edition
—Dec. 19, 2001
—Receiver of two Official Citations
for the first American Edition
—Oct. 17, 2005

Table of Contents

Introduction 1

Part I
Etymology of the Savior's Name 17
The Great Annunciation 32
The Family of Jesus 43

Part II
The Geographical Region: Mt. Carmel & Bet-Lahem of
Galilee 84
The Historical Evidence of Jesus the Galilean 105
The Galilean Disciples of Jesus 133

Part III
The Cultural and Religious Entourage at the Time of
Jesus 154
The Hypothetical Jesus the Jew Fails to Prove Himself
Once Again 191
Which God and What Temple? 209

Part IV
The Extra-New Testament Sources 243
The Church New Testament 252
The Religion and Theology of Jesus the Phoenician
....289

Epilogue 309

Appendix 311

Acknowledgments

I would like first to acknowledge a very special and extraordinary person, Father Dr. Youssef Yammine for the many helpful sessions granted for the realization of the novel—*The Phoenician Code*—that preceded this academic work and for the few details he put forward into this book itself. It was Fr. Yammine who opened my eyes to the ultimate reality that enabled me to understand the true identity of Jesus Christ.

I should like to express my indebtedness to Dr. Eddy Dib for his valuable comments and advice.

In addition, I also owe a great debt to all friends and acquaintances who have helped me write this book and have supported me, each in his/her own different way, and who wish to remain anonymous.

I am also grateful to Mr. Lawrence Knorr, the publisher, who has given me another great opportunity to publish my third book in the USA. A special thanks also goes to the staff at Sunbury Press.

I should also express my appreciation to Mercury Content (part of Quantum Group) for the impressive cover design.

And last but not least, I would like to show my candid gratitude to my growing readers around the world.

Karim El Koussa
Ehden, March 17, 2013

Introduction

After the release of the controversial thriller, *The Phoenician Code,* by Sunbury Press Inc. in October 2011, which has been listed in the top ten in the Sunbury Press Best Selling List for three consecutive months, I began to receive a lot of questions and feedback from my readers all over the world concerning the contents of the novel, since it reveals on so many levels, say, historical geographical, theological, and religious, the non-Jewish identity of the Christian Son of God and Savior, Jesus Christ.

The meeting with the publisher in Harrisburg, PA, during my 2011 US book signing tour concluded that I should work on a companion book to the novel that would only contain historical proofs to the theory in question. Hence, we came up with the title, *Jesus the Phoenician.*

Although the novel describes without any shred of doubt and with great historical and archeological certainties the myths and legends behind the Old Testament and the Biblical Israel, relying on important works penned by the British scholar, Thomas L. Thompson (*The Mythic Past: Biblical Archaeology and the Myth of Israel,* Basic Books, 1999), Jewish archaeologist, Israel Finkelstein and Jewish historian, Neil Asher Silberman (*The Bible Unearthed: Archaeology's new vision of Ancient Israel and the Origin of its Sacred Texts,* Touchstone, 2002), British professor, Keith W. Whitelam, (*The Invention of Ancient Israel: The Silencing of Palestinian History,* Routledge, 1996) and others, we decided not to include all facts in the new book. Yet, I will briefly expose a few things regarding the Jewish origin, religion, and the temple in Part III. We only want to focus now on the true hidden identity of Jesus Christ, also known in the New Testament as "Immanuel," which literally means "El with us," "God with us." To be more precise on this, it is in Matthew (1:23), where we find this important quote "Behold, the virgin shall be with child, and shall bring forth a son. They shall call his name Immanuel, which means God with us."

A simple proof, to start with at this point in the introduction, is the fact that Ēl, or Al, was and has always been considered as the Most High God of the Canaano-Phoenicians, with an adjective form of "Ēl-Alyon," literally translated into "Ēl the Most High." On his baptism, Jesus was called Immanuel, therefore, according to Matthew's—conscious or unconscious, deliberate or non-deliberate—decree, Jesus became the divine holder of the spirit of Al through baptism.

In fact, evidence relating to the non-Jewishness of Jesus is not new at all. It has been recorded or noted by many writers ever since the story of Jesus began, ever since the Divine Annunciation was given to the Virgin Lady Maryām by the Angel Gabriel. Since the early days of Christianity until today, many theologians, thinkers, and writers thought out of the box and presented proof denying the identity of Jesus the Jew.

I shall do so again in this book, as many who have preceded me, by following systematically the Table of Contents here provided with great faith and logical analysis, hoping to create a reasonable doubt in the mind of the readers, asking them three main questions:

1. Have you ever thought that Jesus could not be of Jewish origin while meticulously researching and comparing the gods and the scriptures provided and presented in the pages of the two books, the Old Testament and the New Testament?
2. Could it be possible that Jesus was not Jewish and hence of a different origin?
3. What does that mean to the faithful?

As a matter of fact, I never considered myself a historian simply because I'm not. I don't have a degree in history, or theology—hence I'm not a theologian, either. I'm a writer, a thinker, and a Christian, but not a blind Christian who believes without proof. Let's say I'm like Thomas, one of the Disciples of Jesus who was described in the New Testament as "Doubting Thomas." We have seen him in John[1], saying that unless he could see the nail marks in Jesus' hands and the gash of the spear in His side he would not believe. But Thomas became certain of the reality of Jesus by doubting what he was asked to believe blindly, and yet he became a man of devotion and his doubts turned into faith.

I had no doubts like Thomas in that sense concerning the spiritual, supernatural, and divine character of Jesus, but my doubts grew bigger concerning the historicity of the New Testament, precisely the four Gospels of Matthew, Mark, Luke, and John, in portraying the life of Jesus. The more I read and examined the New Testament, the more I came to understand that the text holds within its pages great contradiction. The thinker

---

1 John 20:25.

and faithful in me began to wonder. I mean, it almost sounds as if there were two Christs: one Galilean-Phoenician and the other Jewish. This constitutes a conflict in itself since a Galilean is not Jewish and a Jew is not Galilean. Hence the clear name given to Galilee in the Biblical text as *Gelil Haggoyim*, which is translated into "Circle of the Gentiles."

Following that logic, the more we study the New Testament, the more we notice these discrepancies regarding the identity of Christ. In an even clearer statement, we read in Matthew (21:10-11), "When he had come into Jerusalem, all the city was stirred up, saying, Who is this? The multitudes said, This is the prophet Jesus, from Nazareth of Galilee."

It is traditionally accepted that Matthew, who was a tax collector or a publican[2] as presented by The King James Version of the New Testament, addressed his gospel to the Jews in the Aramaic or Hebrew language—probably being the most learned of the Disciples to present to the world an account of the teaching of Immanu-Ēl, the Nazorean Master, in an attempt to make them understand the words of Jesus of Nazareth of the "Circle of Gentiles" and believe in him.

Knowing Jesus

To know Jesus well, we should comprehend the socio-religious environment that existed more than two thousand years back in order to write about him in an objective method with yet growing doubts in my mind concerning the historical accounts narrated by the four Gospels accepted by the Church, Matthew, Mark, Luke, and John, and their portrayal of his life in the New Testament. Therefore, I decided to study them even more than just reading and taking them for granted as if they were descended upon us immediately from the mouth of God—upon me, a faithful Christian.

Aside from the four gospels endorsed by the Church, there are many other documents narrating the story of Jesus that we should take into consideration herein, and which were not accepted in the Biblical Canon but are available nowadays. They are called *Apocrypha*, which means "hidden." We know for a fact that some were written by Gnostics who were divided into two branches: the dualists and non-dualists. The non-dualists were Christians and their stories about Jesus Christ were spiritual. The Gospel of the Magdalene, the Gospel of Philip, the Gospel of

---

2 From the Latin, *Publicanus*, which means "someone engaged in public service including handling public money."

Thomas, the Gospel of Bartholomew, the Gospel of James, and the Gospel of Marcion are cogent examples. The dualists, on the other hand, pretended to be Christians and claimed to know the true story of Christ. In fact, their tales closely resemble the story written by the Jews in the Talmud. This is known as the *Panthera* issue. They are better termed as Judeo-Christians. Many other narratives existed, written by different people, like the *Quelle* documents, the earliest of all, most probably issued by the Galileans, and are, to a certain degree, similar to those of the non-dualist Christian Gnostics. There are many, many others, too.

In addition to that, we should not forget the early sources that mentioned Jesus outside the traditional accepted gospels and Apocrypha. Works by the Romano-Jewish historian Flavius Josephus (37 AD–100 AD); the Roman Magistrate, Pliny the Younger (61 AD–112 AD); Roman historians, Tacitus (56 AD–117 AD) and Suetonius (69/72 AD to after 130 AD) are to be treated here. Along with that, we shall also tackle works by the Church First Historian, Eusebius of Caesaria (260/263 AD–339/340 AD). But let us first have a look at the four gospels.

The Gospels

The first three gospels, called *Synoptics*, those of Matthew, Mark, and Luke, could have been written between the years 60–64 AD and 80–85 AD. We cannot know exactly which one was penned before the other, and there have been many speculations and theories in that concern. We know for sure that the fourth gospel, the one attributed to John, and which is extremely different from the other three, could have been written around 100 AD, but some suggest that it could have been done almost fifty years later, in 150 AD.

Matthew: The Gospel of Matthew appears to have been written around the years 80–90 AD. Some say it's the second to be penned, but it could be the third, after that of Luke. It is well known that this gospel was mainly addressed to the Jews, as we have just seen above. Matthew tried to present the life and works of Jesus as an achievement of Divine Promises given by God to the people of Israel, in a well sewn plot portraying Jesus in the image of David, the Jewish king, being born in the Bethlehem of Judea where David was born. But, he never stopped weaving delicately, meticulously, and purposely ciphering important information that would undoubtedly suggest otherwise, like the two quotes from Matthew (1:23; 21:10-16) mentioned a few paragraphs before. There are plenty of examples here. We will come to know about them as we proceed.

Mark: The Gospel of Mark appears to have been penned sometime between 64 and 70 AD and is considered by many specialists as the first among the four gospels to be written. Hence, it is viewed as the closest to reality and the most authorized to describe the events that occurred with Jesus in their utmost truth. Mark focused on presenting Jesus as the Son of God, receiving Divine Blessings and incarnating the Holy Authority from his Father in Heaven. Although it seems to a certain extent that the text rejuvenates the memories and the teachings of the Apostle Peter, written in short, incomplete, chaotic accounts missing chronological details but better in its description of little details, it appears to be in perfect coordination with the Gospel of Matthew, which is based on long discourses and written in a totally different language. Yet, profoundly distinct one from the other, they give the feeling that the authors, who do not resemble each other in character or in discipline, had the chance to look at each other's work before writing their own. In that case, and if we consider the time each one was written as per the specialists' study and deduction, we could simply conclude that the Gospel of Matthew could be an Aramaic or Hebrew quasi-copy of the Gospel of Mark written in Greek—although the Matthew version that was canonized in the body of the New Testament was written in Koine Greek.

Luke: The Gospel of Luke showed Jesus in a universal manner by affirming the foundation of the Divine Goodwill that he held deep in his heart, a message of Love and Peace offered by God the Father to all the faithful humanity anytime and everywhere. This exceptional Synoptic narration appears to have been written sometime between the years 80 and 85 AD, most probably after the siege of Jerusalem in 70 AD by the Roman Army led by Emperor Titus. However, many authors from the 2nd century AD believe it was penned by some Syrian physician from the ancient city of Antioch who used to accompany Paul during his travels, and that is Luke himself. Others think that the Acts of the Apostles and the Gospel of Luke were done by the same person. This Synoptic seems to be well in order and very well written, though with certain little chronological and topographical errors, but in perfect unity resembling a biographical work, having the disciplined and liberal character of its author, who might have accessed the other two gospels and other writings of pseudo-Gnostic nature when penning it. Luke was a devoted disciple to Christ who wrote for the Gentiles in Greek tongue, for he didn't know any Hebrew except perhaps a little bit. Although he tried to portray Jesus as accomplishing all the Jewish rites, maybe mirroring the Gospel of Matthew in that concern, he seems to have omitted all the Hebrew definitions like the word *Rabbi* and didn't cite any of the words of Jesus in that language. And that is so, because Jesus definitely spoke Aramaic in his everyday life, not Hebrew, and Luke knew that for certain. At any rate, his Acts of the Apostles seems to mention many of the words spoken by Jesus that appear to be authentic yet are not available in the Synoptics.

John: The Gospel of John differs totally from the previous three, except perhaps only for the description of the Last Supper and the Passion of the Christ, two essential events carved into the minds and hearts of the Apostles. It has probably been analyzed the most and was judged by many as not being the work of the Apostle John, but instead an imaginable text written in allegorical form and thus not historic. Others believe quite the opposite, declaring that it is indeed the work of John in its entirety, its contents are factual events, and the discourses are the true words of Jesus. Opinions differ on whether John wrote it all or if it was edited by his disciples and whether the words spoken by Jesus are truly his or came from the fertile mind of the author of the text. Whatever the case or the views of the specialists, the Gospel of John seems to be the most powerful, the most spiritual, and the most inspiring of them all, especially in its esoteric approach of understanding the Divine Will that leads the way to Salvation. To John, Jesus is the Way, and the Truth, and the Life; no one comes to the Father but through Him. There was no doubt in the minds of early prominent fathers of the Church, such as Theophilus[3] and Irenaeus[4], that this metaphysical work was indeed the work of John. It is certain that although it differs greatly from the so called "Judaic" Gospel of Matthew in many ways[5], it became sometime in the middle of the 2nd century AD the cornerstone in the constitution of the Christian dogma and religion, after it appears that it was first adopted by a few circles

---

3 Patriarch or Bishop of Antioch (c. 170 AD).

4 St. Irenaeus (2nd century AD), an apologist, whose writings have left a profound impact on the early development of Christian theology. He was once a hearer of Polycarp, who in turn was a disciple of John the Evangelist; he later became a Bishop of Lugdunum in Gaul (now Lyon, France, and part of the Roman Empire back then).

5 An example of such is when the word Jew(s) is somehow equivalent to an *enemy of Jesus*, greatly exposed in John 8:19-47. There is resemblance to such a feeling in Paul's (accused of anti-Semitism) Letter to the Hebrews and others.

of non-dualist Christian Gnostics. With John's Gospel (90 AD–100 AD), the Book of Revelation/Apocalypse (c. 96 AD), and the three epistles attributed to him (c. 99 AD), a new spirit blows and a different perception of the Divine flows in the air. John's Gospel uses mystic language not to be compared with any of the three Synoptics, where the author puts in the mouth of Jesus discourses of different nature and doctrine—words such as the Way, the Truth, the Life, the Light, the World—a religious style that has nothing Hebrew in it, nothing Jewish, as the *Quelle* documents also suggest. It is undoubtedly the work of a profound Galilean.

Before going through the other ancient sources that mention Jesus Christ, something tackled in Chapter 10, we must first examine the veracity of the four traditional gospels just cited, which include lots of contradictions in the same texts and with each other. The Gospel of John is not the only one that lacks some form of historical authenticity; in fact, all other three gospels have historical flaws as well. There is nothing absolutely certain in history, especially ancient history, due to the fact that we lack the live testimony of the people who watched the events unfold in front of them and of those who lived during the time things happened to narrate to us the facts as they were. In addition, the lack of archaeological proof could also play a part in doubting the historicity of a certain event occurring in ancient history, and hence not taking it for granted, as it has been given to us since thousands of years ago.

The Paradox of Jesus' Genealogy

Having said that, if we take for example the genealogy of Jesus mentioned only in Matthew (1:1-17) and Luke (3:23-38), we find two different unmatched genealogies. Both of them, Matthew (2:1) and Luke (2:4-6), state that Jesus was born in Bethlehem of Judea, an event not mentioned in the other two gospels—a very important issue that I will tackle and strongly debate for accuracy all through the following pages of the book.

The first genealogy, that of Matthew, starts with Abraham, continues with David, and ends with Jesus, describing Joseph, the husband of Mary and the father of Jesus, as the son of Jacob, son of Matthan. This genealogy lists fourteen generations from Abraham to David, another fourteen from David to the time the Hebrews entered Babylon, as per the Old Testament, and another fourteen from the time they left Babylon to Christ. However, our concern here is neither with the Biblical founders of Israel, nor with Biblical Israel, the legitimacy of whom and which we strongly question in the course of history. Instead, we concern ourselves with the historical Jesus, who is deliberately portrayed here by Matthew as a Jew, and we have given the reason why it is so.

The second genealogy, that of Luke, starts with Jesus, "as was supposed," son of Joseph, son of Heli or Eli, son of Matthat, and ends with Adam, son of God, passing by Abraham, Cainan, son of Arphaxad, Enoch, and Kenan, father of Mahalalel and son of Enosh. This genealogy is so important, but before analyzing the beginning of this list, since Joseph the father of Jesus cannot be the son of Jacob (in Matthew) and also the son of Heli (in Luke), let us first have a look at the essential names that are not listed in Matthew.

Cainan is a variant of the name *Kenan* in the generations of the first man, *Adam*, included in the lists of antediluvian human patriarchs[6]. This Cainan, son of Arphaxad, as per the genealogy of Luke, is present in the Septuagint and Samaritan versions of both the Book of Genesis and the Book of Jubilees, but many modern Biblical interpreters, basically Judeo-Christian scholars, believed it to be an error, mainly on the basis of his omission from the Masoretic Text, or what is known as the authoritative Hebrew text of the Jewish Bible. In the Apocryphal Book of Jubilees, Cainan was mentioned as a boy who was instructed by his father to read; a learned man he became, finding mysterious inscriptions concerning the science and wisdom of astrology carved on the rocks. These inscriptions belonged to former generations, taught by the Watchers, who had rebelled against God before the deluge.

We have similar story in the Book of Enoch (Enosh), a work that seems to be not older than 150 BC, maybe a copy of an older original lost work, and which the Apostle Luke, who related Jesus to Enoch in his list, probably knew its significance and the importance of the man (or men) who would probably transmit it from mouths to ears all throughout the years until it was written. Enoch is not at all Hebrew, but a Canaano-Phoenician prophet and seer of vision who received his Initiation directly from God, Ēl, on Mt. Hermon in Phoenicia, known today as Jabal Al Sheikh in Lebanon. No wonder the names of the angels mentioned in the Book of Enoch, considered an Apocrypha, are extremely connected to their state and functions. The suffix of each high ranking angel's name, or the great majority of them, is "el," "Ēl," meaning "God the Most High," Ēl-Ēlyon, the Canaano-Phoenician God. Even Archangels such as Gabriel, (Kabbir-el, "Strength or Great Power of Ēl"), Michael (Manka-el, "Who is like Ēl"), Raphael

---

6 They were not Hebrew as the Torah wants us to believe.

(Raphaat-el, "Compassion of Ēl"), etc., are great examples of that and assure once again their Aramaic origin.

Proceeding with that in mind, we find that Enoch's direct disciple (or son) was Canaan, Cainan, or Kenan, son of *Enosh.* Hence, the existence of Cainan or Kenan in the genealogical list of Luke is not at all an error for the honest scholars but a direct link intended or not intended by the Apostle Luke to relate Jesus to Canaan (Kena'an), the father of the Canaanites. In addition, there is no doubt that Enoch is Phenok, the father of the Phoenicians. Historical and geographical books describe the Phoenicians as being the native people of ancient Greater Lebanon. In truth, the Phoenicians settled along the coastal cities and some major parts of the inlands, Lebanon in particular, some western parts of Syria, Palestine, northwestern Jordan, Israel, and even the Al-Arish area in Egypt. We will investigate more on who the Canaanite/Phoenicians were in Chapter 7, but for now, it is important to know that "Phoenicians" and "Canaanites" are the same people. Canaanites were the Phoenicians living up in the mountains. Phoenicians were the Canaanites living along the coastal cities. It is not surprising though after we have tackled the issue in its proper way and its rightful historical context to find that the name of Cainan was omitted from the Hebrew text, and the consequent general rejection of him by historians is quite understandable coming from Judeo-Christian scholars.

Let us now continue the analysis and start examining the first sentence of the list arranged by Luke. Some Biblical scholars, from as early as John of Damascus (8th century AD) and Martin Luther (16th century AD), considered the words "as was supposed" a parenthetical note, explaining that Luke intended to call Jesus a son of Eli, and that Eli or Heli was actually the maternal grandfather of Jesus, so Luke was actually tracing the ancestry of Jesus according to the flesh through Mary. Hence, they have suggested that the Luke genealogy is not to be taken as that of Joseph but of Mary, claiming that it was of a preference at the time to drop women's names out of the list, hence it could not be read as Joseph son of Eli but rather Joseph son-in-law of Heli, the father of Mary[7].

Now, since these explanations are mere suppositions offered by Judeo-Christian scholars, let us consider something else: let's say that the words "as was supposed" are a parenthetical note, with the Apostle Luke actually calling Jesus a son of Ēli. This

---

7 The most celebrated names given to Maryām's parents are those of Joachim and Anna, found in the Apocryphal Gospel of James (probably of the 2nd century AD).

consideration works all ways, and I mean for Jesus, Joseph, and Mary. In fact, I shall propose the following logical explanation that very few seem to have dared to tackle or to have seen.

Jesus is the son of Joseph, son of Ēli. Joseph is his earthly or adoptive father and Ēli or Ēl is his Divine Father, for he was called in Matthew (1:23), "Immanu-el," meaning "El with us," as we have seen earlier.

Jesus is the son of Joseph, son of Ēli. Joseph is also the son of Ēli or Ēl, being himself a priest of the God the Most High, Ēl, through his affiliation to the Ashayas, a religious group very much different from the Essens or the Qumran Community who were, in fact, Orthodox Jews. The Ashayas, Asayas, or "healers"— mentioned later in the text—lived among the Phoenicians and some other groups inhabiting the areas of Mt. Carmel and Galilee. They believed in the God Ēl, and wore medallions inscribed with the name "Al," as if embodying the fact that they were Phoenicians, at least in faith. However, should we humanize the Archangel[8] Gabri-el sent from God Ēl to Nazareth, in Galilee, at the hour of Annunciation of the Birth of Jesus to Mary, he would then be deciphered as "Kabbir-el," or "one of the Greatest who serves the God Ēl."

Jesus is the son of Mary, daughter of Ēli. Mary is the daughter of Ēli or Ēl, being herself a virgin prepared in the ancient Phoenician temple at the top of Mt. Carmel, an important fact we will focus on in the coming chapters.

Eli, Eli

Of course, when Jesus was suffering on the Cross for humanity's sake, he neither called upon his so-called grandfather Heli (the alleged father of Mary) nor the prophet Elijah, but Ēli, Ēl, the God the Most High, his Father who is in Heaven. The reference to that appears in both Matthew (27:46):

> And about the ninth hour, Jesus cried out with a loud voice and said, Eloi Eloi lama sabachthani! My God, my God, why have you forsaken me?

and Mark (15:34):

---

8 Archangel is higher than Angel, yet both are messengers from God, and are pronounced as *Melki* for the first and *Malak* for the second in the Aramaic language.

And at the ninth hour, Jesus cried out with a loud voice, saying, Eloi Eloi lama sabachthani! My God, my God, why have you forsaken me?

Again, this is another flaw of the New Testament, a wrong translation into Greek from the original Aramaic words of Jesus on the Cross, or perhaps another intentional attempt to link Jesus' words spoken here to a Psalm (22:1) in the Old Testament. Yet, whatever was the effort to mislead the Christian reader and faithful, it fails, for it is clearly felt in the heart, mind, and spirit of Christians that the God the Father of the New Testament is absolutely different from the deity that appears in the Old Testament. One of the reasons behind this book is to explain and show the differences between the two Gods.

At any rate, the Lamsa Bible, (based on the Aramaic *Peshitta*, sometimes argued to be the original New Testament), has a different interpretation of Jesus' cry at the moment of crucifixion. The interpretation goes:

And about (at) the ninth hour, Jesus cried out with a loud voice, (saying) and said, Ēli, Ēli, lemana shabakthani! My God, my God, for this I was spared!

This interpretation is more logical and goes well with the understanding of who Jesus was and what his mission was here on earth. Of course, the Father would not have forsaken his Son (only son), who bowed his head and surrendered his last breath saying, "It is finished." Jesus Christ called his God, Ēl, his Father, in whose warm hands he committed his Spirit and rested everlastingly.

"It is finished," said Jesus. What was accomplished by his Crucifixion was his destiny that had been long planned by the Divine Will. Indeed, many a time, Jesus was attacked by his enemies in an attempt to kill him, and in different places though mainly around Jerusalem, but he was always spared, kept alive for this particular moment, which the Apostle John referred to in John (13:31-32) during the Last Supper, "So, when he had gone out[9], Jesus said, 'Now the Son of Man is glorified, and God is glorified in Him. If God is glorified in Him, God will also glorify Him in Himself, and glorify Him immediately.'" This deep and aesthetic incantation of glorification by the Son to the Father

---

9 Judas Iscariot leaving the room fast after being discovered of his plan to betray Jesus and deliver him to the Guardians of the Jewish Temple to crucify him.

appears also prior to the crossing of the Kidron Valley with his disciples and entering a grove of olive trees, in John (17:1), "Jesus spoke these words, lifted up His eyes to heaven, and said: 'Father, the hour has come. Glorify Your Son, that Your Son also may glorify You.'" Also in John (17:5), "And now, O Father, glorify Me together with Yourself, with the glory which I had with You before the world was." The Son of Man never felt that his Father left him; on the contrary, he wanted to be glorified on the Altar of Life—a moment when He would take the sins of humanity (from the first man to the last) with him to the Cross and purify it with every drop of his sacred blood.

Another interpretation that matches perfectly the latter could be written as follows:

> And about (at) the ninth hour, Jesus cried out with a loud voice, (saying) and said, Ēli, Ēloi, lamash (lemana) baktani (bachthani)! My God, my God, how much have you praised (glorified) me!

And so it happened that at this delicate and great moment of praise and glorification; Jesus did not call his Father by the name YHWH, simply because the Jewish God was not Jesus' Father. It is obvious for those who are willing to see the Truth. We will come to that important theological notion as we proceed.

Other Historical Flaws

There are many historical flaws in the New Testament that could be added here after being carefully considered and meticulously analyzed, for example the birthday of Jesus Christ and his age when he died. Corrections concerning that are made by the Church. Both Luke and Matthew wrote that Jesus was born before the death of Herod the Great, the Roman Client King of Judea who lived between 73/74 BC and 4 BC. The Church recently accepted the idea that Jesus could have been born before 0 BC, sometime between 6 BC and 4 BC, whereas some historians and Biblical scholars place the date between 7 BC and 2 BC.

According to Luke (3:23), Jesus started his ministry at the age of thirty and continued for around three years before he died at the age of thirty-three, but in John (8:57-59), the Jews in Judea wondered about him. "Then said the Jews unto him, Thou art not yet fifty years old, and hast thou seen Abraham? Jesus said unto them, Verily, verily, I say unto you, Before Abraham was, I am. Then took they up stones to cast at him: but Jesus hid himself, and went out of the temple, going through the midst of them, and so passed by."

Indeed, Christ was older than Abraham[10], the Jewish Patriarch, not in physical terms, of course, but in religious knowledge, since Jesus' ministry and theology precedes the Jewish religion by thousands of years. In addition, the "Word that became flesh and dwelt among us," mentioned in the opening of the Gospel of John, is to the faithful, older than the beginning of manifested time itself, because "the Word was with God, and the Word was God."

Thirty-three or fifty, we don't actually know Jesus' exact age when he died, but it seems that Irenaeus, the Church father we mentioned earlier, affirms in his work[11] what he claimed to be an "Apostolic Tradition," that Jesus' Crucifixion and Death could have happened sometime between the ages of forty-one and fifty.

One more note before we move into the following chapters: the Church, mainly Western Christianity, adopted 25 December as the birthday of Jesus Christ by early-to-mid 4th century AD, a date later adopted by Eastern Churches, except for the Armenian Apostolic and Catholic churches who celebrate it on January 6 in connection with the Epiphany. As a matter of fact, there are many explanations concerning the date for Christmas, since in the earliest centuries of Christianity there was no special day of the year that was associated with the birth of Jesus. However, as speculation rose, Christians proposed December 25 to be the date for that celebration after being confused by the many different dates previously suggested, such as: January 2, March 25/28, April 18/19, May 28/29, and November 17/20. But why did they settle on December 25?

It may have initially been chosen to match the exact day, nine months after March 25, the date Christians believe Jesus to have been conceived (the Feast of Annunciation)—a belief greatly supported by Pope Benedict XVI. It could also have been chosen in correspondence with the Sun, a cosmic symbol for a cosmic event, which might have inspired the Church leaders in Rome to elect the Southern Solstice (Roman Winter Solstice), December 25, as the birthday[12] of Christ. They were most certainly aware that Romans called this day the "birthday" of *Sol Invictus*, but it seems to have been too little of a detail to concern them back then. Or

---

10 There are no historical proofs of Abraham's existence outside the Old Testament.

11 Irenaeus, *Against Heresies*, Book 2, Chapter 22:4-6.

12 It corresponds with the Roman solar holiday *Dies Natalis Solis Invicti*, as per the Julian calendar, created in 45 BC under Julius Caesar.

was it a deliberate placement of this date for Christmas to end the Roman festival to the Sun? Yet, on the contrary, it has been argued by a few specialists, like William J. Tighe, Associate Professor of History at Muhlenberg College in Allentown, Pennsylvania, that the Emperor Aurelian (214/215 AD–275 AD), who in 274 AD, almost one year before he died, instituted the holiday of the Birth of the Unconquered Sun (*Sol Invictus*, "Invincible Sun") in an attempt to give Roman significance to a date already important for Christians living in Rome. In truth, the date seems to have no religious importance in the Roman, so-called "pagan" festal calendar before Aurelian's time, nor did the official cult of the sun-god, known to a number of ancient civilizations and called "pagan" by the rising force of Christianity, play an important role in Rome before him.

At any rate, the cult of the Sun surely received the full support of the emperors well after Aurelian, but the habit of representing *Sol Invictus* on coins, as it was the case with the consecutive emperors, came to an end in 323 AD with Constantine the Great (272 AD–337 AD), a Roman Emperor from 306 AD to 337 AD, also known as Constantine I. He was known, too, as St. Constantine for being the first Roman emperor to convert to Christianity, making it the official religion of Rome. However, the cult of *Sol Invictus* may have resurfaced later on in the 4th and 5th century AD but on a very minor scale.

Whether Christ was born on December 25 or March 25, in winter or in spring, doesn't really matter to the faithful. What matters is his historical birth that changed the world with his Word. What matters to me, a Lebanese Christian of Canaanite/Phoenician descent, is the Truth that has been meticulously manipulated and powerfully tarnished by Judeo-Christian Biblical scholars throughout the years. Thus, I will try to be objective, as much as possible, in revealing and presenting the geographical, historical, theological, and religious revolutionary ideas and information herein.

Although my novel, *The Phoenician Code*, introduced to readers a fraternity of believers whom I called the Society of Keepers—Keepers of the Word—and which I described as a physically nonexistent movement in the real sense of the word, a non-organized entity, there are an ever increasing number of people in the world today who believe that the message and life of Jesus Christ portrayed in the New Testament was nothing but a religious, spiritual, and social revolution against the God of the Old Testament. As a matter of fact, that would be the exact reason for the Crucifixion, which eventually led to the Glorious Resurrection of the Son of God—the real aim of the Divinity of Jesus Christ.

I think it was this very belief felt and practiced by the true Christian faithful that strongly compelled Martin Luther to write in his profound book[13], "Therefore, the Promises of God belong to the New Testament. Indeed, they are the New Testament."

I shall end this introduction with a quote from the New Testament that I have always admired and often wondered about in its implicit and explicit meanings. It is found in John (14:23-24), and reads as follows:

> If a man loves me, he will keep my word, and my Father will love him, and we will come to him, and make our home with him. He who does not love me, does not keep my words; and the word, which you hear, is not mine but the Father's who sent me.

---

13 Luther, Martin. *On Christian Liberty*, page 26.

Part I

The Christian Lord

His Names, Conception, and Family

Chapter 1

Etymology of the Savior's Name

Many titles, nicknames, and names have been attributed to the Christian Savior in the New Testament: Son of Man, a title he always loved; Son of God (the Father), a title he felt belonged to him; Son of David, a descent he always seemed to have refuted; and King of the Jews, a post he often rejected, as is clearly shown in his answer to Pilate during his trial as described in John (18:36), "Jesus answered, My Kingdom is not of this world. If my Kingdom were of this world, then my servants would fight, that I would not be delivered to the Jews. But now my Kingdom is not from here." This is a two-fold answer with two meanings: one spiritual, the other material. This vital issue mentioned in John (18:33-37) will be addressed later on in the book.

Let us now have a look at the five most important names or nicknames given to the Christian Savior in the New Testament, and let us professionally analyze each one of them and their sources of origin. Other than being defined as Galilean, and we shall know why as we proceed further, the first name that appears on the list is *Immanuel*; the second, *Jesus*; the third, *Nazarene*; the fourth, *Messiah*; and the last one is *Christos*.

There is no doubt that Jesus was called Galilean, not only because he was not a Jew, but because he was definitely born in Galilee as cited in Matthew (21:11), raised in Galilee, and lived all his life in Galilee, moving from one village to another during his ministry. He also spent most of his time visiting neighboring Phoenicia, precisely the region of Tyre and Sidon, as per the New Testament, in Matthew (15:21), Mark (7:24), and Luke (6:17), while traveling a few times to Judea only to preach the God of Love. No wonder why we find in John (7:41), the following interesting quote, "Others said, 'This is the Christ.' But some said, shall Christ come out of Galilee?" This very question is a solid confirmation from John that Christ was a Galilean. He added[14], "They answered him, 'Are you also from Galilee? Search and see that no prophet has arisen out of Galilee.'"

---

14 John 7:52.

To Jews, back then, at the time of Christ, Galilee, *Gelil-Haggoyim*[15], was described as the "Galilee of the Nations" or "Circles of the Gentiles." We have seen that citation in the introduction and it is stated in Matthew (4:15). That surname came from the certainty that Galilee was inhabited only by Gentiles, and therefore, non-Jews! We shall see in the following chapters that Jews in Galilee, if there were any at the time of Jesus, and this is a very, very slim supposition, would have formed an extremely closed group. For in fact, historically speaking, Galilee was a place swarming with people from many different nations, Canaano-Phoenicians, Aramaens, Romans, Greeks, perhaps a few Buddhist missionaries, and others, hence, "Galilee of the Nations." It has also been ascertained that the many nations inhabiting the region of Galilee did not speak Hebrew, except maybe for the very tiny Jewish community that may have lived there during the time of Jesus. In general, Galileans spoke Aramaic.

From this, we objectively conclude that "Jesus the Galilean" means "Jesus the non-Jew," but what about the other names given to the Christian Savior? Let us investigate them one by one.

Immanuel

It is very clear that the name "Immanuel," composed of two words, "Immanu," which means "with us" and "Ēl" meaning "God," has Canaano-Phoenician-Aramaic roots. The name appears in Isaiah (7:14), in the Old Testament, "Therefore, the Lord himself shall give you a sign: Behold a virgin shall conceive, and bear a son, and shall call his name *Immanuel*" (italics mine). It also appears in Matthew (1:23), in the New Testament, "Behold, the virgin shall be with child, and bear a Son, and they shall call His name *Immanuel*, which is translated, God with us" (italics mine).

Analysis: The reader may wonder why the prophet Isaiah and the Apostle Matthew, both of Jewish origin—as the Judeo-Christian tradition has it—opted to give an Aramaic name to the Child of Prophecy that would become the Savior of the Chosen Jewish People having a suffix "el," "Ēl," related to "Ēl-Ēlyon," the Canaano-Phoenician Most High God. It is definitely a legitimate question to ask, but what the usual reader fails to realize, due to his blind attachment to the Judeo-Christian tradition, is that both Isaiah and Matthew could well have not been Jewish, and hence,

---

15 The term *Haggoyim* refers to Canaanites in Judges 4:2,13,16 of the Old Testament.

the prophecy Isaiah predicted and the assertion Matthew followed, actually copes with a prophecy related to a different people—the Galilean-Phoenicians.

Logically speaking, if both Isaiah and Matthew were of Jewish origin, they would have at least named the Divine Savior, whose manifestation or incarnation here on earth they had been waiting on for ages, by a Jewish name, or even yet, by adding the suffix "yhwh" to "Immanu," making his name look like Immanu-yhwh, Immanuyhwh, translated as, "YHWH with us."

The true identity of Matthew will be exposed in the chapter related to the Galilean disciples of Jesus. As for now, let's have a quick look at who could have actually been Isaiah. It seems that Isaiah was not originally a Jewish prophet; nor was his book a Jewish book, claimed to have been written around the year 500 BC. Most likely, it was copied and manipulated to appear Jewish by Jewish scribes during the process of writing their Old Testament and was later interpolated by the Church fathers to link it with the prophecy of Matthew and consider it a Jewish Christian tradition, as we shall see that trend being practiced in Chapter 10. Yet, this book may well have been rooted in Galilee with the Ashayas sometime between the 4th and 3rd century BC and considered sacred to the Phoenicians, Galileans, and the Ashayas, who strongly opposed the Judeans settling in the land at the time. One cannot ignore the similarities between Isaiah, spelled in Hebrew as Yeshayahu, and the Aramaic Yāwshaya or Ashaya. Hence, the real name of the prophet Isaiah could well be Ashaya, a purely Aramaic name. It is the same as the Syriac Asaya, which means healer in Greek. On him, Jerome wrote[16]:

And then adding this, that it is being spoken not only by a Prophet, but by an Evangelist. For thus all the mysteries of Christ and the Church are pursued to clarity, so that you would not think them to be prophesied of the future, but they covered the history of things past.

At any rate, the Ashayas most probably formed a group of people who lived and prospered in both Mt. Carmel and Galilee. They were also known as the Essenes, accurately, Galilean Essenes, and were not similar in any way to the other Essens who appeared by the Dead Sea and were known as the Qumran Community, who were Orthodox Jews, also in continuous struggle with the Judeans.

---

16 Jerome, *The Prologue to the Prophet Isaiah.*

In short, the Ashayas were "healers," and so was Immanuel, undoubtedly one of them, and their ascetic religious ideas profoundly influenced their social way of life. The Book of Ashaya could then be a Galilean book, and the same stands for the Q Source, which we will tackle later on. These two books talked about Galilean Prophecy and Prophets.

Jesus

It is not at all clear that the Aramaic name *Yeshu* corresponding to the Greek *Iesous* or *Iezos*, which has been translated into English as Jesus, is in any way similar to the name Yeshua, *yēšūă'* in Hebrew, which has been considered as a common alternative shorter form of the Hebrew Biblical name *Yehoshua*, in reference to "Joshua the son of Nun," "Joshua the High Priest," and other priests as well, called Jeshua, along the narration of the Old Testament, mainly of the post-exilic period, especially in Ezra, Nehemiah, Chronicles, and accordingly, used among Jews of the Second Temple Period (between 530 BC and 70 AD). It was also found in the Dead Sea Scrolls (between 150 BC and 70 AD) by the Orthodox Jews of the Qumran Community, also known as the Essens. However, the name "Jesus" in reference to the Christian Savior did not appear in the Old Testament in the form of prediction as it occurred with the name Immanuel in Isaiah. It seems to have only appeared in Luke (2:21) in the New Testament, "And when eight days were accomplished for the circumcising of the child, his name was called JESUS, which was so named of the angel before he was conceived in the womb."

Analysis: The name Yehoshua being the alternative form of Yeshua (which is a verbal derivative from the act of "to rescue," "to deliver," or "to save" in Hebrew) is a composed name of two words, "Yeho" which means "Yahweh" or "Jehovah," and "shua" meaning "a saving cry." Thus Yehoshua would be translated into "YHWH is a saving cry," or "YHWH saves." This explanation is greatly accepted and mostly preferred by Judeo-Christians who believe that Jesus is the son of the Jewish God, YHWH. By doing that, they follow the traditional teaching of the New Testament that describes Jesus as living in a Jewish milieu, reading from the Hebrew Bible at the Temple and debating with the Pharisees over some of the interpretations of the Hebrew tradition.

It is important to note that the Hebrew language is a mixture of both an Aramaic dialect and an Akkadian-Babylonian idiom, yet, the Aramaic itself is a direct descendant vernacular from the

Canaano-Phoenician language, and that's why many modern scholars typically argue that the word "Hebrew" in the New Testament refers to "Aramaic." Indeed it does, and that being said, I believe that the real name of Jesus is of Aramaic origin of two words "Yāw" and "shu," hence, "Yāwshu," meaning, "May YĀW saves." It could thus be identical to the other Aramaic form of "Yeshu" or "Ye'shu." In fact, "Yāw" appears to be mentioned as the god of Rivers and Sea in the ancient Canaano-Phoenician city of Ugarit. "Yāw" or "Yeuo" is like "Yam," the god of the Sea, and mentioned as one of the Elohim (or sons of Ēl), hence, the name Immanuel, "Ēl with us," which was given to Jesus by Matthew and, as we have seen, is a legitimate correspondent to the Yāwshu form of the name. It all fits well, and it is perfectly logical to relate the Canaano-Phoenician god of the Sea to Galilean-Phoenicians, a people known to be greatly connected with the Sea and the art of fishing, since the Disciples of Yāwshu (Yeshu) were described as fisherman in the New Testament. At any rate, names including words such as "Yehi" or "Yehaw" were in use by Canaano-Phoenician kings, like the 10th or 8th century BC King of Byblos, Yehi-Milk (King Yehi), and Yehaw-Milk (King Yehaw), another Byblos King of the 5th-4th century BC.

Both the Old Syriac Bible (sometime between 170 AD and 200 AD), based on the Syriac language, a dialect or a group of dialects of the eastern Aramaic, and the Peshitta (sometime between 426 AD and 464 AD), based on the Aramaic language, always use the pronunciation "Yeshu" in reference to Jesus in its Aramaic-Syriac form instead of the Hebrew "Yeshua" or "Yehoshua." It is still used even today in the West Syriac liturgy, known as Syro-Antiochene Rite, whereas the East Syriac liturgy, known as Assyro-Chaldean Rite, has rendered the pronunciation of the name as "Išô." The Islamic Tradition, moreover, holds the name "Isa," son of Maryam, for Jesus, who was indeed the promised Nabi (Prophet) and Masih (Messiah).

It was most probably the distinction of the Aramaic name Yeshu or Yāwshu from the Hebrew name of Yehoshua or Yeshua (Joshua), that made Clement of Alexandria[17] and Cyril of Jerusalem[18] consider the Greek form, *Iesous* (or *Iezos* from "Iaso" or "Ieso" the Greek goddess of healing), to be the original name of

---

17 Clement of Alexandria (c. 150 AD–215 AD), also known as Titus Flavius Clemens, a convert to Christianity from pagan origin, who became one of the most famous Christian theologians, regarded as a Church father, and venerated as a saint in Orthodox Christianity, Eastern Catholicism, and Anglicanism, revered at some point in history in the Roman Catholic Church, but his teachings were strongly suppressed in 1586 by Pope Sixtus V due to rising concerns about his orthodoxy.

Jesus[19], meaning "the healer[20]." They even went far enough to declare and interpret it as a true Greek name and not simply a transliteration of Hebrew. And that would make sense as to why the Hebrew name Joshua does not appear in the Slavonian (of Slavonia) Bibles when referring to Jesus, but instead, we find the name *Iessus Navin*. In addition, Eusebius, the Roman historian mentioned in the introduction, connected the name to the Greek root meaning "to heal" thus making it a variant of Jason, a purely Greek analogy of Jesus, meaning "healer[21]." This interpretation of "healer" is also mentioned in the Gospel of Bartholomew after he (the Apostle) finishes praying to the Lord God, the Father, the King, to save the sinners. It reads[22] as follows (italics mine):

> When he had thus prayed, Jesus said unto him: Bartholomew, my Father did name me Christ, that I might come down upon earth and anoint every man that cometh unto me with the oil of life: and he did call me *Jesus* that I might *heal* every sin of them that know not ... and give unto men the truth of God.

In fact, the act of healing is not at all strange in the vibrant life of Jesus, for many times he appeared healing and curing people from their sins and illnesses, as portrayed in the New Testament. Thus, the explanation given by Jesus to Bartholomew, and the interpretation made by the two Church theologians just mentioned, along with the relation made by Eusebius, is the conclusion we determine and choose for the correct name of Jesus. However, there is a minor difference with yet another important notion: not ignoring the power of water in the act of healing for the ancients, Yāwshu could then be understood as "May YĀW heals." Hence, the Greek *Iesous* could well be a derivation from the Aramaic *Ieschou, Yeshu,* or *Yāwshu,* which in turn could be derived from *Ashaya* or *Asaya* in Syriac (Aramaic) explaining the derivation for the name, "Essenes," meaning "therapeut" in Greek[23]. Here again, we reach the same conclusion

18 Cyril of Jerusalem (c. 313 AD–386 AD), most probably born and raised in Caesarea of Palestine, one of the most distinguished theologians of the early Church, highly respected by the Palestinian Christian Community, venerated as a saint by the Roman Catholic and Eastern Orthodox Churches, along with the Anglican Holy Communion, and declared a Doctor of the Church by Pope Leo XIII in 1883.
19 Clement of Alexandria, *Paedagogus*, Book 3, Chapter 12.
20 Cyril of Jerusalem, *Catechetical Lectures*, Lecture 10:13.
21 Eusebius, *Demonstratio Evangelica*, Book 4, Chapter 10.
22 Bartholomew 4:65.
23 Schuré, Edouard, *Les Grands Initiés*, Page 438.

that links Jesus to the very special group of healers cited just above—a religious group that lived among the Phoenicians in the areas of Mt. Carmel and Galilee who believed in the God Ēl, wearing beautifully crafted medallions on their chests with the name "Al" clearly inscribed, embodying the religious fact that they were Phoenicians.

Nazarene

There has been no doubt among scholars that the word Nazarene or Nazorean is very different from Nazareth, in Galilee, the very well known city the New Testament presented as the primary place where Jesus grew up, hence, the title, "Jesus of Nazareth," mentioned in all the four gospels and the Acts of the Apostles. We find it in Matthew (21:10-11):

When he had come into Jerusalem, all the city was stirred up, saying, Who is this? The multitudes said, This is the prophet Jesus, from Nazareth of Galilee.

In Mark (16:6):

And he saith unto them, Be not affrighted: Ye seek Jesus of Nazareth, which was crucified: he is risen; he is not here: behold the place where they laid him.

In Luke (24:19-20):

And He said to them, 'What things?' So they said to Him, 'The things concerning Jesus of Nazareth,' who was a Prophet mighty in deed and word before God and all the people, and how the chief priests and our rulers delivered Him to be condemned to death, and crucified Him.

In John (18:3-5):

Then Judas, having received a detachment [of troops], and officers from the chief priests and Pharisees, came there with lanterns, torches, and weapons. Jesus therefore, knowing all things that would come upon Him, went forward and said to them, 'Whom are you seeking?' They answered Him, 'Jesus of Nazareth.' Jesus said to them, 'I am [He].' And Judas, who betrayed Him, also stood with them.

And in Acts (10:36-39):

> The word which [God] sent to the children of Israel, preaching peace through Jesus Christ—He is Lord of all—that word you know, which was proclaimed throughout all Judea, and began from Galilee after the baptism which John preached: how God anointed Jesus of Nazareth with the Holy Spirit and with power, who went about doing good and healing all who were oppressed by the devil, for God was with Him. And we are witnesses of all things which He did both in the land of the Jews and in Jerusalem, whom they slew and hanged on a tree.

Analysis: It seems that historical research and the science of archaeology have proven that the town of Nazareth was not in existence at the time of Jesus, but rather built in a later period, sometime around the 3rd century AD. These findings entice us to think of what was really meant by Jesus of Nazareth in the New Testament. But, since the four gospels were written well before the foundation of Nazareth, then the error of mentioning Nazareth as a town could not be their fault because they certainly knew that Nazareth didn't exist. It could be a typing error in the process of copying and translating the word from its original Aramaic source into Greek, or it could be that the four Apostles meant something else, and that indeed what they had in mind for a Nazarene or Nazorean is something else. Or yet, it could be a later alteration of the word "Nazarene" to "Nazareth" during the collection of the Church New Testament in the 4th century AD, almost one century after the foundation of the town of Nazareth.

The answer to this new riddle, however, is not hidden outside the New Testament, but within its pages for sure. It is found in Matthew (2:22-23):

> ... Having been warned by God in a dream, he (Joseph, Jesus' father) withdrew into the region of Galilee, and came and lived in a city called Nazareth; that it might be fulfilled which was spoken by the prophets: He will be called a Nazarene.

The term "Nazarene" as cited above was used in the traditional and New King James Version (KJV and New KJV) of the New Testament only once. Some other versions of the New Testament, like the New Living Translation (NLT), the American Standard Version (ASV), the New American Standard Bible (NASB), and the Young's Literal Translation (YLT), seem to have chosen to replace Jesus of Nazareth with Jesus the Nazarene in many different citations that relate Jesus with Nazareth. In addition, it appears that the New International Version (NIV) not only did that but also mentioned Paul as a Nazarene, too. It is found in Acts (24:5) at the time when Paul was being judged. We read, "We have found this man to be a troublemaker, stirring up riots among the Jews all over the world. He is a ringleader of the Nazarene sect."

Striking as it may sound, why did Matthew say that Jesus would be called a Nazarene as a fulfillment to the prophecy spoken by the Jewish prophets? And why did Luke, author of the Acts, mention Paul as a Nazarene? These are issues to be treated, most appropriately, as we proceed.

All we need to know now is that the word Nazarene is an Aramaic word. "Nazarene" is a term that comes from the Canaano-Phoenician word *Nazir* or *Nazar*. It is given to someone who leaves everything behind and consecrates his life by taking a solemn vow to God, or who was chosen to be consecrated by his faithful parents to Ēl, and this is definitely a Canaano-Phoenician habit. The term "Nazar" or "Natzar" would simply mean "to keep (the word), to observe (the divine)," whereas the term "Nazir" would mean "to sanctify (the sacred), to consecrate (the self)." A Nazarene would therefore be "a man who had been sacredly chosen by the Divine Will to consecrate himself for keeping the word of God in his heart, mind, and spirit." In short, a "Saint," in Christian theology, and "Son of God," in the religious terminology of the New Testament.

We undoubtedly believe that the name Nazarene given to Jesus made him neither a mainstream Jew, nor even an Orthodox Jew, or a member of the Qumran Community, known as the Essens, as some have claimed. He instead was an adept of the Ashayan or Asayan society—a healer. After his baptism by John, Jesus became a Nazarene in the ritualistic sense of the word. Among the very few members that were counted within the Nazarene-Ashayas were Paul, John (Yāwhanan) the Baptist, and Mary (Maryām) Magdalene. They all knew at once that Yāwshu was the Meshiha and followed him faithfully ever since.

In fact, the *Quelle*, the Q Source, still considered the earliest text on Jesus, was carried by a group already established in Galilee and always in conflict with Jews everywhere, especially in Jerusalem. This group is none other than the Nazarenes, characteristically defined as the ascetic branch of the Ashayas, long established in Mt. Carmel and Galilee. It is most probably because of that name given to Jesus and the ascetic group he belonged to that Christians were known all over the world by the name of Al-Nassara, Nazoreans, or simply, Nazarenes.

Messiah

It is indeed important to know that the term "Messiah" appeared once in the King James Version (KJV) of the Old Testament in Daniel (9:25-26), and once as "Anointed" in Psalm (2:2), then three times in the New King James Version (NKJV), one time in the Old Testament, again in Daniel, and twice in the New Testament in John (1:41; 4:25), but it appeared many times in the New Living Translation (NLT) of the New Testament in reference to Jesus. We read in Matthew (22:42-46):

> What do you think about the Messiah? Whose son is he? They replied, 'He is the son of David.' Jesus responded, 'Then why does David, speaking under the inspiration of the Spirit, call the Messiah 'my Lord'? For David said, The LORD said to my Lord, Sit in the place of honor at my right hand until I humble your enemies beneath your feet. Since David called the Messiah 'my Lord,' how can the Messiah be his son?' No one could answer him. And after that, no one dared to ask him any more questions.

In Mark (1:1):

> This is the Good News about Jesus the Messiah, the Son of God. It began.

In Luke (3:15):

> Everyone was expecting the Messiah to come soon, and they were eager to know whether John might be the Messiah.

In John (4:25):

> The woman said, 'I know the Messiah is coming—the one who is called Christ. When he comes, he will explain everything to us.

In Acts (4:26):

> The kings of the earth prepared for battle; the rulers gathered together against the LORD and against his Messiah.

Analysis: The name "Messiah," known in Hebrew as *Mashiah* or *Moshiah, Māšîāḥ*, "the anointed (one)," from "Mashach" ("the act of anointing"), is a term used in the Old Testament to specifically portray sacred places, kings and High Priests, who were traditionally anointed with holy anointing oil as described in one of the books of Moses, Exodus (30:22-25):

> Moreover the LORD spoke to Moses, saying: Also take for yourself quality spices—five hundred [shekels] of liquid myrrh, half as much sweet-smelling cinnamon (two hundred and fifty [shekels]), two hundred and fifty [shekels] of sweet-smelling cane, five hundred [shekels] of cassia, according to the shekel of the sanctuary, and a hint of olive oil. And you shall make from these a holy anointing oil, an ointment compounded according to the art of the perfumer. It shall be a holy anointing oil.

The Old Testament presents some of the Hebrew leaders, whether of religious stature like Aaron, or political stature such as David, as being anointed with the sacred oil described in Exodus, even Cyrus the Great (Cyrus II, the King of Persia), though not a Hebrew, is mentioned as "God's anointed" (Mashiah) in Isaiah (45:1), the book we believe was manipulated to appear Jewish: "Thus saith the Lord to his anointed, to Cyrus, whose right hand I have holden, to subdue nations before me ..."

Although in Jewish theology, the term "Mashiah" came into existence to refer to priests being anointed with the sacred oil in a ceremonial ritual, it is extremely evident that its use was mainly practiced on past and future Jewish kings from the Davidic line who would be "anointed" with the holy anointing oil in a religious ceremony that would allow them, under the watching eyes of YHWH, to rule the Jewish people during the Messianic Age. Hence, in Hebrew custom, the Mashiah is often referred to as *Mélekh ha-Mashíaḥ*, which means "the anointed king."

It is very clear that the citation "King of the Jews" in relation to Jesus the Mashiah was mentioned by the four gospels, and we believe it was an attempt by the Apostles to connect Jesus with the Jewish Kingship of David Lineage. Yet, we know very well that the Jews strongly refuted Jesus to be Son of David (no Jewish lineage), that he had no relation with their God Yahweh[24] (no Jewish priesthood), and that he was not to be called "King of the Jews" (no Jewish kingship), as revealed in John (19:21):

---

24 This is clearly exposed in their description of Jesus and his life in the *Sepher-Toledoth-Yeshu*, which we shall discuss later on.

"Therefore the chief priests of the Jews said to Pilate, 'Do not write, The King of the Jews ...'" In fact, that was a false claim, as shown in Matthew (27:37), Mark (15:26), and Luke (23:38), "And the inscription of His accusation was written above: THE KING OF THE JEWS." Truth be told, if the Jews had at any time considered Jesus as one of them, they would not have delivered him to the Roman governor to be crucified in the first place and would have certainly chosen to liberate him when Pilate offered them the chance to do so—but, they chose Barabbas. In fact, if Jesus was truly a Jewish prophet, he would have found a place for himself in the Old Testament, which was not completed for the Jews until the very end of the 1st century AD.

However, not only did the Jews refute Jesus to be one of them, he also refuted the idea of being one of them in many ways. He obviously rejected the notion of being the Son of David, the Mashiah of YHWH, as we have seen earlier in Matthew (22:42-46), Mark (12:35-37), and Luke (20:41-44). He also never claimed himself to be the King of the Jews, especially during his discourse with Pilate, as per John (18:33-36), when Pilate entered the Praetorium again, called Jesus, and said to Him, "Are You the King of the Jews?" To which Jesus answered him, "Are you speaking for yourself about this, or did others tell you this concerning Me?" Jesus' answer here is so evident. What he was accused of as King of the Jews was mere a claim. Then, Pilate answered, "Am I a Jew? Your own nation and the chief priests have delivered You to me. What have You done?" Again, Jesus answered, "My kingdom is not of this world. If My kingdom were of this world, My servants would fight, so that I should not be delivered to the Jews; but now My kingdom is not from here." Again, Jesus' reply here is a complete negation of the charge leveled against him. His statement that his kingdom is not from here but from somewhere else has double meaning as we shall see later on.

We undoubtedly conclude that Jesus Christ would not fit in any way possible the characteristic of the Mélekh ha-Mashíaḥ, "the anointed Jewish king (and prophet)," but on the contrary, as revealed in Matthew (21:10-11) and John (7:41), "Others said, He is the Messiah. Still others said, But he can't be! Will the Messiah come from Galilee?" Of course not. The Jewish Mashiah would not come from Galilee, yet, certainly, the Meshiha, "the anointed one," as spoken in Aramaic, and prophesied by the Canaanite/Phoenicians, had already come from Galilee, the Land of the Gentiles, the Land of Canaan-Phoenicia, the Circle of the Most High God Ēl-Alyon. That Ēl-Alyon is different from the

Hebrew YHWH and Highest, is established beyond a doubt and we shall explain that further on.

At any rate, we must understand that the practice of anointment, from Meshih[25], was not at all an exclusive Jewish practice and did not actually start with them. References of anointment are first made to the Hittites, and scholars believed it was a Hittite custom before becoming a Jewish one. Yet, more in-depth studies show that the practice was well established and observed as a sacred rite for kings and High Priests as "God's Anointed one" in both Canaan-Phoenicia and Egypt. In a letter sent to Pharaoh Thutmosis III found in the Tell el-Amarna Letters[26], we read about a certain man named Taku who was made king and anointed by the Pharaoh. Even the Pharaoh himself is depicted being anointed by Horus, the sun god, and by Thot-Tautus, the god of wisdom. The act of Baptism with water practiced by John the Baptist, and later on by Christianity, is an evolved ceremonial rite from pouring sacred perfumed oil to clear running water, the element of life, though it might mirror the symbolic depiction of the stream of Ankhs, symbol of the Nile (water) and life, over the head of the Anointed Pharaoh in Ancient Egypt. Knowing that Egyptians and Phoenicians had close religious and ceremonial relations, we find that in the heart of the mountain of Gebel (Byblos), inside the bursting grotto of Afqa where the River Adon (Adonis) had its source, that such a rite of Baptism by water was practiced by Phoenician priests.

Christos

There is no doubt at all that the term "Christ" in reference to Jesus has been mentioned in almost all the books of the New Testament, from the Gospel of Matthew to the Book of Revelation. However, we will only mention a few quotations, starting with Matthew (16:16):

Simon Peter answered and said, You are the Christ, the Son of the living God.

In Mark (1:1):

---

25 The act of anointing a person as in a religious rite by pouring perfumed sacred oil over his head.

26 Tell el-Amarna Letters are clay tablets of mostly diplomatic nature between the Egyptian administration and its delegates in the lands of Canaan and Amurru (Amorites) during the reign of the Egyptian Empire.

The beginning of the gospel of Jesus Christ, the Son of God.

In Luke (24:46):

Then He said to them, Thus it is written, and thus it was necessary for the Christ to suffer and to rise from the dead the third day.

In John (4:42):

Then they said to the woman, Now we believe, not because of what you said, for we ourselves have heard [Him] and we know that this is indeed the Christ, the Savior of the world.

In Acts (4:10):

Let it be known to you all, and to all the people of Israel, that by the name of Jesus Christ of Nazareth, whom you crucified, whom God raised from the dead, by Him this man stands here before you whole.

Analysis: There is not much to analyze here since it has been clearly stated that the term "Christos," *Khristós*, or *Krestos*, is in fact the Greek translation from the Aramaic *Meshiha* or the Hebrew *Machiah*, and has the same meaning to the followers and believers of Jesus who became known as Christians as mentioned in Acts (11:26):

And when he had found him, he brought him to Antioch. So it was that for a whole year they assembled with the church and taught a great many people. And the disciples were first called Christians in Antioch.

However, it is a known fact that the first believers in Jesus were the Galileans, who had a prophecy about the coming of the Meshiha, the Savior, as inspired in the Q Source. It was originally the case in the Phoenician theology that talks about the coming of Adon, where the Savior died for them and was resurrected for their salvation. It is identical to the life of Jesus as narrated in the New Testament from Divine Conception to Glorious Resurrection. The similarities are striking and cannot be missed. This is a very important issue that we will definitely highlight later in the book. For this religious and theological reason, it became obvious that this Jesus had always been rejected by most of the Jews—in the accepted Canonical Gospels by the Church—as being their Messiah.

In short, there is no conclusion better than saying that the Galilean-Phoenicians believed that *Ieschou*, the Nazarene, was indeed the *Meshiha*, or the *Christos* they had been waiting for a long time to incarnate and live with them as the Son of the God Ēl-Alyon, having Immanuel as his name.

Or, let's say it in a more elaborate way—

Yāwshu (Jesus) is the son of the Canaano-Phoenician Most High God Ēl-Alyon, being the Son of the Virgin Lady Maryām[27] by the Divine Will of the Lord, who blessed this conception of a child that would be named Immanuel. He would live among us as "God Ēl with us," a Nazarene, sacredly chosen to consecrate himself for keeping the word of God in his heart, mind, and spirit, healing the human race from its many errors and sins. He is the Galilean *Meshiha* (Messiah) who would anoint the people—who believed in him, his mother, and Father, and who believed in the Great Message he came to deliver, Love and Peace—with sacred water[28], the purest form of what is considered as the origin of life here on earth. He is the *Khristós* (Christ) who came and had himself crucified on the altar of life so that we may be clean and have life abundantly.

He is the Good Shepherd.

---

27 Maryām is the original Aramaic form for Mary. It was a very common name for females in the land of Canaan-Phoenicia. We shall explain the etymology of the name in Chapter 3.

28 It is called the "oil of life"—in the Gospel of Bartholomew 4:65 as we have seen before—by which Christ will anoint every man that cometh unto him. He was named Christ by the Father, that he may come down upon earth and do that.

Chapter 2

The Great Annunciation

Although divine annunciations by higher beings to virgins have been recorded in history to have preceded the coming of saviors[29], no one other than the Apostle Luke, in the accepted Canonical Christian texts, mentions the Great Annunciation of the Birth of the Savior, Jesus, to the Virgin, Maryām, by the Archangel Gabriel (Gabri-el) sent from God the Highest to Nazareth, in Galilee.

Let's have a close look now at the Great Annunciation cited at the beginning of the narration of the Apostle who considered Jesus to be the son of Ēli in his genealogy. According to Luke (1:26-38):

Now in the sixth month[30] the angel Gabriel was sent by God to a city of Galilee named Nazareth[31], to a virgin betrothed to a man whose name was Joseph, of the house of David. The virgin's name [was] Mary. And having come in, the angel said to her, 'Rejoice, highly favored [one], the Lord [is] with you; blessed [are] you among women!' But when she saw [him], she was troubled at his saying, and considered what manner of greeting this was. Then the angel said to her, 'Do not be afraid, Mary, for you have found favor with God. And behold, you will conceive in your womb and bring forth a Son, and shall call His name JESUS. He will be great, and will be called the Son of the Highest; and the Lord God will give Him the throne of

---

29 It has been recorded in the religious history of some parts of the world that divine saviors were conceived by virgin ladies and were delivered though virgin births. Examples of such appeared in ancient India, Krishna and Buddha; ancient Phoenicia-Greece, Pythagoras; and others could be cited, as well.

30 Six month after the conception of John (the Baptist) by Elizabeth as per the New Testament. Christians believe the date to be March 25, a special day when Jesus was conceived (the Feast of Annunciation)—a belief greatly supported by Pope Benedict XVI.

31 We have seen earlier that Nazareth, as a city, was not in existence at the time of Jesus, but rather built in a later period, sometime around the 3rd century AD. For Nazareth to be called a city in the text, it would have been written or interpolated during the period that followed its foundation.

His father David. And He will reign over the house of Jacob forever, and of His kingdom there will be no end.' Then Mary said to the angel, 'How can this be, since I do not know a man?' And the angel answered and said to her, '[The] Holy Spirit will come upon you, and the power of the Highest will overshadow you; therefore, also, that Holy One who is to be born will be called the Son of God. Now indeed, Elizabeth your relative has also conceived a son in her old age; and this is now the sixth month for her who was called barren. For with God nothing will be impossible.' Then Mary said, 'Behold the maidservant of the Lord! Let it be done to me according to your word.' And the angel departed from her.

The description from Luke literally portrays how the Archangel (or Angel) Gabriel (Kabbir-Ēl) appeared to Mary and revealed to her the Great Destiny she would undertake as bearer of the Son of the Highest[32], though she had not known a man; the Holy Spirit would come upon her and she would deliver the Son of God who would be called Jesus. However, it does not show where the divine appearance took place. Was it in her house when she was awake? Was it a vision? Or in her dreams during deep sleep? Or was it somewhere else? The text is unclear.

And no other text, in what are considered Apocryphal works, mentions this unique encounter with the Archangel except for two: the *Infancy Gospel of James*[33] and the Gospel of Bartholomew[34]. The Apostle James specifies the location of the Annunciation and describes well how Mary met with the Angel after leaving the Temple of the Lord[35] with Joseph, who was appointed by the High Priest to take her into his own possession after the signs worked for his favor. We read in James (11:1-9):

---

32 The Highest or the Most High could only be Ēl, since Yahweh was never considered "the Highest."

33 We will investigate the Gospel of James in the following chapter, especially the relationship of Mary to the Temple.

34 The Gospel of Bartholomew, known also as the Questions of Bartholomew, is the "Lost Gospel," as some scholars have suggested. Some say it is an authentic work written around the 2nd century AD; others believe it was penned later on, sometime around the 6th century AD. It could be considered as one of the non-dualist Christian Gnostic works, thus a Christian Apocrypha, like the Gospel of Thomas, for example. However, Bartholomew considered Jesus as the Lord and talked about his Crucifixion and Resurrection, a belief system the Church New Testament highly endorsed. As for the person of Bartholomew, we will introduce him to the reader in Chapter 6.

35 Both James and Bartholomew mention Mary (Maryām), a woman, and her connection to the Temple.

And she took the cup and went out to fill it with water. Suddenly, a voice said to her, Rejoice, blessed one. The Lord is with you. You are blessed among women. And Mary looked around to the right and the left to see where this voice came from. And trembling she went into her house. Setting down the cup, she took the purple thread and sat down on the chair and spun it. Suddenly, an angel stood before her saying, Do not be afraid Mary. You have found grace before the Lord of all. You will conceive from his word. Upon hearing this, however, Mary was distraught, saying to herself, If I conceive from the Lord God who lives, will I also conceive as all women conceive? And the Angel of the Lord said, Not like that, Mary. For the power of God will come over you. Thus, the holy one who is born will be called son of the Most High. And you will call his name Jesus, for he will save his people from their sins[36]. And Mary said, See, I am the servant of the Lord before him. Let it happen to me according to what you say.

The Annunciation is very similar to what we have in Luke in terms of the Holy Visitation of the Angel and his dialogue with Mary, but the location that Luke didn't reveal appears with James to have been in two relatively close places. The first was probably by a fountain where she was filing the cup with water. When she heard a voice that made her tremble she ran into her house. The second place was inside the house; the voice she heard before turned out to be that of an angel, who stood now before her.

Although the scene of the Great Annunciation is now more complete than that of Luke, the Gospel of Bartholomew could even be more accurate and helpful than the previous two, at least, from this author's point of view. In his second chapter, Bartholomew describes how he approached Peter, Andrew, and John, and told them to ask Mary how she had conceived Jesus. We can find this in Bartholomew (2:1-5):

Now the apostles were in the place [Cherubim, Cheltoura, Chritir] with Mary. And Bartholomew came and said unto Peter and Andrew and John: Let us ask her that is highly favoured how she conceived the incomprehensible, or how she bare him that cannot be carried, or how she brought forth so much greatness. But they doubted to ask her. Bartholomew therefore said unto Peter: Thou that art the chief, and my teacher, draw near and ask her. But Peter said to John: Thou

36 Again, here Christ is called Jesus because he is the Savior and Healer.

art a virgin and undefiled (and beloved) and thou must ask her. And as they all doubted and disputed, Bartholomew came near unto her with a cheerful countenance and said to her: Thou that art highly favoured, the tabernacle of the Most High, unblemished we, even all the apostles, ask thee (or All the apostles have sent me to ask thee) to tell us how thou didst conceive the incomprehensible, or how thou didst bear him that cannot be carried, or how thou didst bring forth so much greatness. But Mary said unto them: Ask me not (or Do ye indeed ask me) concerning this mystery. If I should begin to tell you, fire will issue forth out of my mouth and consume all the world.

The text shows that they never gave up asking her to reveal the greatest mystery of all times, and she, who was not anymore able to hide it from the Apostles her son had already chosen to continue his legacy, could not refuse their request any longer. She told them to stand up in prayer, and that's what truly happened. Then the Virgin Lady stood up in firm position before the four disciples, Peter, Andrew, John, and Bartholomew, spreading out her hands in adoration towards the heaven and began to pray. When she finished her prayer, she invited the Apostles to sit down on the ground. It is now, here, where she decided to reveal to them what had really occurred to her.

Not only does Bartholomew reveal the Great Annunciation to Mary as it appeared in both Luke and James, but he also shows where it happened. In fact, the locality described here along with the ritual mentioned at the hour of Annunciation is of great importance to us. Let's first have a look at the text before going through a thorough analysis, and I quote from Bartholomew (2:15-22):

And when they had so done she began to say: When I abode in the temple of God and received my food from an angel, on a certain day there appeared unto me one in the likeness of an angel, but his face was incomprehensible, and he had not in his hand bread or a cup, as did the angel which came to me aforetime. And straightway the robe (veil) of the temple was rent and there was a very great earthquake, and I fell upon the earth, for I was not able to endure the sight of him. But he put his hand beneath me and raised me up, and I looked up into heaven and there came a cloud of dew and sprinkled me from the head to the feet, and he wiped me with his robe. And said unto me: Hail, thou that art highly favoured, the chosen vessel, grace inexhaustible. And he smote his garment upon the right hand and there came a very great loaf, and he set it upon the altar of the temple and did eat of it first himself, and gave unto me also. And again he smote his garment upon the left hand and there came a very great cup full of wine: and he set it upon the altar of the temple and did drink of it first himself, and gave also unto me. And I beheld and saw the bread and the cup whole as they were. And he said unto me: Yet three years, and I will send my word unto thee and then [thou] shalt conceive my (or a) son, and through him shall the whole creation be saved. Peace be unto thee, my beloved, and my peace shall be with thee continually. And when he had so said he vanished away from mine eyes, and the temple was restored as it had been before. And as she was saying this, fire issued out of her mouth; and the world was at the point to come to an end: but Jesus appeared quickly (Lat. 2, and laid his hand upon her mouth) and said unto Mary: Utter not this mystery, or this day my whole creation will come to an end (Lat. 2, and the flame from her mouth ceased). And the apostles were taken with fear lest haply the Lord should be wroth with them.

It is interesting to learn that St. Bartholomew reveals clearly in his gospel, as we have just read, that Mary was in fact in the Temple of God when she received the visitation from the Angel or from one in the likeness of an angel. The scene of Mary being visited by an angel while she was in a temple has been the subject of paintings by many well-known Renaissance European artists[37]. This notion by itself is a revolution, since we know by heart and knowledge that Jewish women were not at all accepted in the Circle of Priesthood and were not at all allowed to enter the temple for any reason. Only (male) priests entered the temple, and only the High Priest entered the Holy of Holies.

In addition, the Qumran Community, who appeared by the Dead Sea at the time of Jesus, formed a closed religious community that strongly rebuked the mainstream Jewish Law of the time. They were Orthodox Jews who refused to live in Jewish territory, taking the caves by the Dead Sea as their homes. Always being in conflict with the sacerdotal community of Jerusalem could be the reason why some believe that Jesus was a prominent

---

37 Artists like the Italians Fra Angelico (c. 1395 AD–1455 AD) and Melozzo Da Forli (c. 1438 AD–1494 AD) whose painting is still exhibited at the Pantheon in Rome; the early Netherlandish painter, Jean Hay (c. 1475 AD–1505 AD), and many others.

member of the Qumran Community along with John the Baptist, probably because of their strong rejection of the Judaic system as a whole. But, in fact, to portray either of them as Orthodox Jews or Jewish Essens is absolutely wrong, simply because they were both important members of the Galilean Essenes or Ashayas. The differences between the two groups[38] will be thoroughly explained in proceeding chapters. At any rate, history shows that the Qumran Community consisted of only males—a male group, choosing and encouraging celibacy in order to engage in ritual purity, and consecrating their lives to spiritual awareness. Hence, this group had strict rigid laws where women were not allowed to be around them[39].

Since Orthodox Jews of the Qumran Community rejected women in general, then Mary had no place with them, and if Mary was Jewish of the mainstream societies, she could not have been allowed to enter the temple. Yet, as we see, Mary was in the Temple of God when she had the encounter with the Angel. This very fact by itself proves that Mary was not Jewish.

It has been well recorded throughout history that women were not only allowed to enter the Temple but even reside as goddesses and priestesses in both the Canaano-Phoenician and Egyptian civilizations. The well known Phoenician Goddess Astarte is mirrored in Egypt as Isis, but there is a whole group of them in both religious systems. The image of Mary with her infant son Jesus is undoubtedly similar to the image of Isis with her infant son Horus. The titles, "Queen of Heaven," or "Virgin Lady," given to Mary by Christians have also been given to Anat, the mother of Adon. As a matter of fact, Ashirai (Asherah)—the Mother-Goddess of the Phoenicians, was in fact the Virgin Lady Anat herself—the Queen of Heaven.

There is no doubt that Mary could not belong to the Jewish community, as we have seen, had in fact her origin been rooted in the Canaano-Phoenician culture. Whether Christianity intended to picture Mary as Anat or not, the fact remains that Mary (Maryām) entered the Temple of God as was custom in all of the

---

38 We will elaborate more on that point, particularly in Part III, and reveal the many important differences that existed between the Ashayas or Galilean Essenes and the Qumran Community or Jewish Essens.

39 The Dead Sea scrolls show that the law within the Qumran Community was very strict towards women, whom they considered impure. They deemed women selfish creatures, hypocrites, and unreliable. They never trusted or respected them. They were hesitant and careful about marriage due to the danger of infidelity. The Ashayas, on the other hand, respected women greatly. Jesus had many female disciples and followers like Mary Magdalene, the most famous among them.

Land of Canaan-Phoenicia. In fact, tradition has it, especially in Gebel[40], that families brought their children to be blessed in the temples. Therefore, the priestess of Ēl would bless the female children in the Temple of Astarte, whereas the priests of Al would consecrate the male children in the Temple of Adon. Later on, if chosen by the Divine Will, or desired and wished by their own free will, those anointed boys and girls might choose to serve the sanctuary at a younger or older age.

Hence, it is very reasonable to believe that Maryām (Mary) was blessed as a baby, probably at her first birthday, in one of the temples dedicated to a female goddess, and then began to visit the temple on a regular basis when she was a child until a certain age, and later, as Luke and Bartholomew describe, was chosen to bear the Child of Prophecy. However, there remains another issue to be tackled here: Which temple and where?

We will come to prove in the coming chapter that Maryām, the Mother of Jesus, could not have originated from Kafar Cana[41] (or Kfar Kanna as shown in the map) in Galilee, a few kilometers away from Nazareth, but instead came from the small Lebanese Village of Cana or Kana, close to Sūr (Tyre). Yet both villages, Kfar Kanna and Cana (Kana) were indeed part of the city of Sūr back at the time of Jesus.

Now, since Maryām originated from Kana of Lebanon and was most probably raised there as a child until a certain age, she would have undoubtedly visited and prayed in one or more temples dedicated to one or more Canaano-Phoenician goddesses, say, Anat (Anath), Astarte (Ashtarte), Ashirai (Asherah), Ba'alat (Lady of ...) in the surrounding region of Sūr (Tyre) and Saydoun (Sidon). Therefore, the encounter she had with the angel at a later period could have happened in one of these temples. But if we are to fully and literally consider the narration of Bartholomew, Maryām was in the Temple of God—not the Temple of a goddess. That being said, it will surely lead us to look at the Ashayas or Galilean Essenes, who seem to have built temples where both men and women could visit at the same time to worship the deity.

---

40 "Gebel" (Geb-Ēl, "Sacred Land of Ēl") is the old Hamito-Semitic word for Byblos, one of the most famous coastal cities in all Phoenicia, perhaps the oldest, and believed to have been founded in the early ages of the formation of the world by the Most High God, Ēl, himself.

41 In his book, *Vie de Jesus*, page 157, the French historian, philosopher, and writer, (Joseph) Ernest Renan (1823–1892), states that Mary was probably from the Galilean village of Cana, known as Kfar Kanna. We, however, doubt that, and consider his statement half wrong. Although he believes Mary was Galilean, he simply confused the two Canas. We shall explain and give proof in the coming chapters.

History shows that in the region of Galilee and Mt. Carmel, this mysterious religious group of healers, the Ashayas, lived alike with the Phoenicians and believed in the God Ēl, as we have seen before. In the *Guide de Mt. Carmel*, published in Jerusalem in 1946, we read that the first Church in devotion to Mary rose near the grotto of Mt. Carmel. Some say the grotto was changed into a chapel. Others say it was probably built from the stones of a temple dedicated to Ashirai—the Mother-Goddess of the Phoenicians, the Virgin Lady Anat herself—the Queen of Heaven, as we have noted above, foreseeing Maryām as Virgin and Queen of Heaven.

Hence, we come to understand that there is a strong presence for the veneration of Mary or Maryām in Mt. Carmel, and she, like her husband-companion, her son, and the majority of his disciples, was of the Phoenician-Ashayas, wearing a medallion on her chest inscribed with the name of the God the Most High El. The special visitation by the Archangel or Angel Gabri-el is a clear indication of the religious system to which she was adept—a very unique and pure lady; a maiden chosen to bear the Child of Prophecy[42].

It is also of great significance to note that both Phoenician and Ashayan hermits became Christians after being properly prepared, ever since the day of the Whitsuntide. Hence, Mt. Carmel[43]—cradle of the monastic life—became a place for the veneration of the Virgin Mary and a sanctuary of the spiritual contemplative life that has characterized the Carmelite Order ever since its foundation.

Bartholomew's revelation doesn't actually end here, but it continues to surprise us even more, mainly when the Apostle gives us the voice of Mary, describing that she was in the presence of an angel, or one in the likeness of an angel, performing one of the most sacred ritual of all times: the ritual of Bread and Wine.

---

42 Edgar Cayce, one of the well-known American visionaries, psychics, and mystics of the 20th century is said to have revealed in a book about himself, *L'univers D'Edgar Cayce*, page 321-322, written by the French journalist, writer and specialist in *Caycein* philosophy, Dorothée Koechlin De Bizemont, that on the top of Mt. Carmel, was erected an Essenian Temple, which was the religious center of the Fraternity. In this Temple, Mary, the Mother of Jesus, was instructed and prepared by the Priests of the Essenes. Although Edgar Cayce is not to be considered an academic source, it is worth noting what he saw in one of his visions concerning Mary and her Initiation on Mt. Carmel. It is most likely this Temple of God that Bartholomew referred to in his Gospel.

43 Mt. Carmel is situated near Galilee and was part of Phoenicia at the time of Jesus. It has always been one of the most important places for meditation and spiritual evolution. We will elaborate more on its significance further on.

Should we humanize the Angel or the Archangel Gabriel (Gabri-Ēl), into a likeness of his own, we could envision the possibility that Maryām was in front of one of the High Priests of the God the Most High Ēl, a Kabbir-el (Kabbir-Ēl) who serves in the Temple, performing this special sacred sacrificial ritual holding the great loaf of bread with his right hand before setting it upon the altar of the Temple, eating from it first and giving Mary to eat, and then holding the cup of wine with his left hand before setting it upon the altar, drinking from it first and giving Mary to drink, too[44].

This is striking indeed because the sacred ritual of Bread and Wine[45] is purely a Canaano-Phoenician religious ceremony first performed and practiced by Milki-Sedek (Melkisedek or Melchizedek), king and High Priest of Jerusalem[46]. It is clearly noted during the Last Supper[47] mentioned by the three Apostles[48], except for John, that this ritual was well alive in the heart, mind, and spirit of Christ. This is what has been written in Luke (22:14-20):

---

44 The ritual of Bread and Wine was immediately put in practice by Christians ever since Jesus Christ performed it during the Last Supper. It was practiced in homes and later in secret places such as caves and underground cells when Christians became persecuted by the Romans. It remained secret until the 4th century AD when Christianity became the official religion of the Roman Empire at the time of Constantine and the construction of churches began. However, we have a tradition in Lebanon that the first Christian Church in the world was built sometime around 54 AD in the city of Tyre.

45 It was even mentioned in the Old Testament, in Genesis 14:18, "Then Melchizedek king of Salem brought out bread and wine; he [was] the priest of God Most High."

46 Jerusalem is a derivation from the word "Ur-Shalim," the city of Šalim—the son of Ēl. As a matter of fact, Šalim or Shalim was the god of dusk for the Canaano-Phoenicians. As for Ēl, or Ēl-Ēlyon, Ēloi, or the High Ēl, He represented the very First Light of Creation, and the sun is but His reflection. The High Priest, Milki-Sedek, built the Temple in the city of Jebus, founded earlier by the Canaanite-Phoenician Amorite/Jebusite tribe. He later called it the Place of Shalim (Šalim) or Ur-Shalim, which is Jerusalem.

47 The scene at the Last Supper where Jesus Christ served Bread and Wine to his Disciples as a ritual of spiritual bond between him and them and between Heaven and Earth seems to have a quasi-resemblance to the Messianic Banquet of the Qumran Community. We will though elaborate more on the differences in the context as per the findings of the Dead Sea Scrolls in Chapter 8.

48 It is found in Matthew 26:26-29, Mark 14:22-25 (identical to Matthew), and Luke 22:14-20. John probably didn't mention the ritual because he focused on showing the humbleness of the Lord who rose from supper, laid aside his garments, and began to wash and wipe his disciples' feet (John 13:4-5). This act was only mentioned by John.

When the hour had come, He sat down, and the twelve apostles with Him. Then He said to them, With [fervent] desire I have desired to eat this Passover with you before I suffer; for I say to you, I will no longer eat of it until it is fulfilled in the kingdom of God. Then He took the cup, and gave thanks, and said, Take this and divide [it] among yourselves; for I say to you, I will not drink of the fruit of the vine until the kingdom of God comes. And He took bread, gave thanks and broke [it], and gave [it] to them, saying, This is My body which is given for you; do this in remembrance of Me. Likewise He also [took] the cup after supper, saying, This cup [is] the new covenant in My blood, which is shed for you.

It becomes evident though when we read more from the New Testament that Jesus Christ performed and practiced this ritual at the Last Supper in remembrance of Milki-Sedek. The connotation appears in St. Paul's Letters to the Hebrews[49], where he described Christ not as a priest after the Law of Carnal Commandment of Aaron (the brother of Moses), but spoke about the clear declaration of Jesus Christ on the House of Prayer, and declared him a High Priest of God the Most High, Ēl, after the power of an endless life: "Thou art a priest forever after the order of Melki-Sedek[50]." This is a straightforward declaration from Paul of one spiritual priesthood that linked Jesus to Milki-Sedek.

Hence, referring to Mt. Carmel with its Canaano-Phoenician name—the Generous Vine of the God Ēl, as we shall see later on—and to Bethlehem as Bet(h)-Lahem—meaning the House of Bread, as will be explained later—makes us deeply think about the most important Phoenician religious ritual of all time: that of Bread and Wine, performed by Milki-Sedek and Yāwshu.

Not only would the lifestyle and the everyday teachings of Jesus Christ appear to us as being greatly influenced or deeply rooted in the Canaano-Phoenician religious and theological

49 Hebrews 5:6-10; 6:20; 7:11, 15-17, 21. Hebrews 7:11, "Therefore, if perfection were through the Levitical priesthood (for under it the people received the law), what further need [was there] that another priest should rise according to the order of Melchizedek, and not be called according to the order of Aaron?"

50 In Canaan-Phoenicia, the High Priest—Milki-Sedek, himself a direct adept of Enoch-Thor—preached the belief in the Universal God Al-Elyon, the Most High. Throughout history people considered Milki-Sedek to be Enoch himself, but he was not. The Milki-Sedek of St. Paul—meaning "my King is Righteous" was indeed a direct adept of the ancient Canaano-Phoenician-Egyptian Fraternity, a monotheistic religious community that began first to function as an esoteric theological circle of priests in Phoenicia before it was later adopted by Egyptian priests, venerating Enoch-Thor as Thot-Taautus.

system[51], but both geographical studies[52] and historical accounts[53] also present ample evidence of his non-Jewish roots. The more readers turn the pages of this revealing book, the more they will undoubtedly learn and discover that the man who changed the world had his life's story manipulated by the Judeo-Christian civilization.

---

51 We will keenly expose Jesus' religious and theological backgrounds as we proceed, mainly in Part III.
52 We will objectively observe in Chapter 4 the geographical region of both Galilee and Mt. Carmel where the Birth, Life, and Ministry of Jesus took place.
53 We shall present all the historical evidence of the existence of Jesus the Galilean in Chapter 5.

Chapter 3

The Family of Jesus

The first thing that comes in mind when we tackle the issue of the family of Jesus would be his parents, the Virgin Lady Maryām and his adoptive father Joseph[54]. Then, we investigate his grandparents (as described in the Apocryphal Gospel of James and the Canonical Gospels of Luke and Matthew), his great aunts and uncles (if he had any we can trace back) from both sides of his parents, his brothers and sisters or half-brothers and half-sisters (as some biblical scholars have suggested), and lastly, his cousins.

His Parents

---

54 There is no mention of Joseph in Islam, however, the Quran always refers to Isa Ben Maryam, Jesus son of Mary, whom they consider a great prophet, and greatly honors his mother. The Jewish Talmud, on the other hand, spoke of Joseph and Mary in a different and disrespectful manner. The *Sepher-Toledoth-Yeshu*, probably written by the Rabbis, narrates that in the era of the Second Temple, at the time of King Herod II, there lived a Jewish man of the House of David by the name of Joseph Ben Pandera, and his beautiful wife, called Myriam (Marie). Joseph had a neighbor, by the name of Yohanan, an impious outlaw and adulterous man who lusted after Joseph's wife. One night, in the month of Nissan (April), Joseph left home at midnight to perform his religious studies. Yohanan, spotting him leaving home, entered the house, and found Marie sleeping. He forced himself on her. In the darkness, Myriam assumed him to be her husband, driven crazy by his desire to sleep with her, despite being on her menstrual period. Early the next morning, when her husband returned home, she reprimanded him for his wild deed of the night before. Joseph at once suspected Yohanan; a man accustomed to frequent prostitutes (as stated in the Talmud). The story carried on that Marie got pregnant and Jesus was born—a bastard son of Yohanan, the impious man, and Myriam, a woman of sin! Joseph, her husband, who could not tolerate the impact of humiliation and shame, left Jerusalem for Babylon. Yet, in another version of the four documents, we find that Jesus or Joshua was a bastardized son of Joseph of Panthera or Pandera—a roman soldier, an impious man, who committed adultery with Marie or Myriam—a virgin—originally betrothed to a young man by the name of Yohanan. These documents were later known as the Gospel of the Ghetto.

We have seen in the previous chapter that Maryām[55] (Mary) originated from the Galilean Kana of Lebanon and we shall elaborate on that fact as we proceed, but let us first have a look at Jesus' earthly father. The New Testament reveals through the Gospel of Matthew (13:55) that Joseph was a carpenter. It says (speaking of Jesus), "Is not this the carpenter's son? Is not his mother called Mary?" Whereas Mark (6:3) shows that Jesus, and not Joseph, was a carpenter, thus we read, "Is not this the carpenter, the son of Mary ..." However, it is very well known in the old days, at the time of Jesus, and even now in some places, that fathers and sons often share the same profession, for the father usually teaches his son his own profession. But in fact, Joseph was Jesus' adoptive father; his real father was the God Ēl. Jesus is then a carpenter through Joseph and a Divine Being through the Father.

The trade of a carpenter is not something to be taken lightly, for it shows that the carpenter is a man that measures things correctly and turn disordered pieces of wood into shapes (like chairs, tables, etc.) orderly managed and strongly tied together exposing the beauty of the artist. Yet, the carpenter trade was not only cited in the New Testament, but also in the Old Testament, particularly in Isaiah (7:14), the book we believe was manipulated to appear Jewish, and one of the reasons is its concurrency with Matthew (1:23) in regards to the Virgin bearing a Son who shall be called Immanuel.

In Isaiah 44:13 (Ashaya), the carpenter is described as an architect with all the necessary tools for his work such as the rule and compass. Here how it reads:

> The carpenter stretcheth out [his] rule; he marketh it out with a line; he fitteth it with planes, and he marketh it out with the compass, and maketh it after the figure of a man, according to the beauty of a man; that it may remain in the house.

So, Joseph was described as a carpenter in the New Testament, but let us investigate if he had another profession. Was he a priest of the Most High Ēl? The New Testament shows that not only Mary had an encounter with the Angel as we have

---

55 The Aramaic Maryām, a reputed female name in Canaan-Phoenicia, is in fact a composed name of two words, "Mort-Yām," and it means "Lady of the Sea." The word "Mort" or "Mart" means "Lady" and the word "Yām" or "Yamm" means "Water or Sea." The "Lady of the Sea" has been given as a title to the goddess Astarte (Ashtarte) by the Phoenician seafarers who always sought her protection during their travels across seas and oceans.

seen in the previous chapter, but Joseph[56] as well, though in a dream, and at least two times as mentioned in Matthew. The first one (2:13) reads:

And when they were departed, behold, the angel of the Lord appeareth to Joseph in a dream, saying, Arise, and take the young child and his mother, and flee into Egypt, and be thou there until I bring thee word: for Herod will seek the young child to destroy him.

Did the Angel of God really appear to Joseph in a dream, or did the historical event occur in a different way? Before we analyze the possibility of an encounter between Joseph and the Angel, let us first examine the historicity of the fleeing of Joseph and his family to Egypt as a preemptive action against Herod's desire to kill the young child.

First, the story of Herod killing the young children because he was afraid of the prophecy that said that a King of the Jews and Savior would be born and thus endanger his rule over Judea[57] is not a historical event to be taken seriously. In fact, it's a myth and may bear resemblance to the story of Moses being hidden in a basket and thrown in a river[58] because of the Pharaoh's desire to

---

56 The majority of Biblical scholars, as traditionally thought, believe that Joseph is a Hebrew name written as Yosef or Yôsēp composed of two words, "Yô" and "Sēp ," which means, "May Yahweh add." We, however, believe that the name is of Aramaic origin of two words "Yāw" and "Sēp ," hence, "Yawsēp ," meaning, "May YĀW add." In fact, "Yāw" appeared to be cited as the god of Rivers and Sea in the Canaano-Phoenician city of Ugarit. "Yāw" or "Yeuo" is like "Yam" the god of the Sea and mentioned as one of the Elohim (or sons of Ēl). It is believed that the Hebrew name "Yose" is derived from the Aramaic Yāwse or Yase and it is etymologically linked to Yāwsēp , Yosef or Joseph. Thus, it is perfectly logical to relate the Canaano-Phoenician god of the Sea to Galilean-Phoenicians, known to be greatly connected with the Sea and the art of fishing. The disciples of Yāwshu (Yeshu, Ye'shu) or Iesous, were described as fisherman in the New Testament.

57 Matthew 2:1-3, "Now after Jesus was born in Bethlehem of Judea in the days of Herod the king, behold, wise men from the East came to Jerusalem, saying, Where is He who has been born King of the Jews? For we have seen His star in the East and have come to worship Him. When Herod the king heard [this], he was troubled, and all Jerusalem with him."

58 Exodus 1:22, "So Pharaoh commanded all his people, saying, Every son who is born you shall cast into the river, and every daughter you shall save alive." And also in Exodus 2:1-3, "And a man of the house of Levi went and took [as wife] a daughter of Levi. So the woman conceived and bore a son. And when she saw that he [was] a beautiful [child], she hid him three months. But when she could no longer hide him, she took an ark of bulrushes for him, daubed it with asphalt and pitch, put the child in it, and

kill him, he, the little baby prophet who could endanger his rule when he grew up and became a leader and liberator of his people out of Egypt[59]. However, the Biblical story of Moses has no historical proof since archeologists and historians have not found any concrete clues outside the narration of the Old Testament. In fact, the life of Moses, the prophet and spiritual father of the Jews, was a copy, created on the image of two important figures that appeared in the ancient history of both Akkad and Egypt. We will tackle this issue in more detail in Part III.

Second, the fleeing of Joseph and his family, consisting of his wife and his young child, all the way from Judea—as per the New Testament—or Galilee—as per us—to Egypt has no logical explanation and no rational support. Such a long travel at the time would have needed considerable preparation and effort, something that we don't believe was accessible to the Galilean family. We are inclined to think that this verse from Matthew is a Biblical approach that ties Joseph the adoptive father of Jesus and his fleeing to Egypt to the well known Jewish personality by the same name that appeared in the Old Testament fleeing to Egypt as well[60]. Although, we believe that such an event of the Old Testament has no historical credibility at all.

At any rate, if such avoidance of an anticipated event had been historically taken by Joseph and his family after being warned by the Angel of God of Herod's factual desire to kill the baby Jesus, it couldn't be but an escape plan proposed by the Galilean-Asayan High Priest[61] of Ēl for a feasible journey from Galilee to Mt. Carmel or Gebel. Of course, no one outside the circle of the Ashayas would know that the word "Egypt" used in Matthew would either mean Mt. Carmel or Gebel.

There are in fact two main intellectual social and religious Orders in the world today, and both are significantly old and go back thousands of years. The authentic and older one is the Great White Fraternity that originated with Enoch-Taautus himself, the founder of the First Religion. It began as a Phoenician-Egyptian monotheistic fraternity that sought with anchored faith the resurrection of the self to its higher level and believed in the

---

laid [it] in the reeds by the river's bank."

59 The enslavement of Jews in Egypt has no historical proof whatsoever.

60 It is found in Genesis 39:1-2, "Now Joseph had been taken down to Egypt. And Potiphar, an officer of Pharaoh, captain of the guard, an Egyptian, bought him from the Ishmaelites who had taken him down there. The LORD was with Joseph, and he was a successful man; and he was in the house of his master the Egyptian."

61 Joseph the foster father of Jesus could be an important priest or the High Priest of the Temple of the God Ēl in Galilee and Mt. Carmel.

immortality of the spirit. Monotheism lay at the foundational core of the theological concept of the Great White Fraternity. In Phoenicia, the High Priest—Milki-Sedek, himself a direct adept of Enoch-Thor—preached the belief in the Universal God Al-Ēlyon, the Most High. Canaano-Phoenician kings like Ahiram of Gebel and Hiram of Tyre profoundly believed in the God Al as the One, and pledged to Enoch-Thor. In Egypt, Pharaoh Akhenaton preached Aton as being the Universal God, and his predecessor, Pharaoh Thutmose III, keenly adopted this unique concept. Both Al and Aton represented the first Light of Creation, symbolized by the Sun.

It is not exactly known when Phoenicians started to believe in the One High God Ēl, yet, this new concept of monotheism entered Egypt as a Mystery School with Thutmose III or *Thut-Mosis*, "Initiate of Thut,"[62] and eventually appeared with Akhenaton as a religious reform. Thutmose III (c. 1505 BC–1450 BC) proved to be the most erudite Pharaoh among all Pharaohs who ever ruled in Egypt. He established a great empire in Asia—a name given to the Land of Canaan—which expanded even beyond the Euphrates. During the many expeditions and military campaigns he led through Asia, he acquired a high interest in the Asiatic gods, with a particular focal point in monotheism—already established in Phoenicia.

Among the many locations he occupied in Phoenicia, Mt. Carmel presented the most suitable place for Initiation. In his annals, he referred to this particular place as the "Sacred Island." The name "Carmel," as we shall see in the following chapter, derives from the Phoenician word, *Krm-el*, the "Generous Vine of Ēl." It means the "Spiritual offering of Ēl." As we have seen earlier, Phoenician priests built two temples at the top of Mt. Carmel; one dedicated to Ēl (Baal) and the other to Ashirai (Anat), the Mother Goddess, destroyed later during one of the many invasions of Thutmose III.

It was there, on Mt. Carmel, where Thutmose III encountered some Phoenician Enochian priests, direct adepts of Enoch, the seer of Mt. Hermon. After watching them worshipping the One Most High God Al, he was incited by the idea of monotheism, as he weighed it against the over seven-hundred city-gods worshipped in Egypt. In a spark of genius, he speculated the possibility and benefits of combining all major Egyptian gods into One Supreme Being. In consequence of this revelation, he built a new religious centre—a school of Initiation—on some of the ruins

---

62 Thut or *Thot* is Thor. He is Enoch-Taautus-Hermes himself, the founder of the First Religion.

of the Temple of Ashirai (Asherah). This school immediately found ground all around the surrounding areas of Mt. Carmel, such as Galilee and the Dead Sea. It then entered Egypt as a Phoenician-Egyptian monotheistic fraternity, known some time later as the Great White Fraternity. This relationship between Canaan-Phoenicia and Egypt persisted for a long time, and therefore, Memphis and Gebel subsisted as twin religious cities.

A bit over a hundred years later, monotheism emerged in Egypt with Pharaoh Amenhotep IV (c. 1370 BC–1350 BC)—the religious reformer known as Akhenaton. It surfaced precisely in his religious city: Akhetaton, Horizon of Aton. His father, Amenhotep III, was the son of Thutmose IV, who took for a spouse the Phoenician queen, Tia, a believer in the One God Ēl. Thutmose IV was the son of Amenhotep II, the offspring of our famous Pharaoh Thutmose III. And so, in the footsteps of his father, Amenhotep III married a Phoenician queen, Tiy, also, of course, a believer of the One God Ēl.

Hence, after this brief historical exposé, we undoubtedly conclude that the monotheistic relationship between both Canaan-Phoenicia and Egypt was also a strong religious family tie. And apparently during the rule of Akhenaton, their belief led to the laying of the very last stone in the foundation of the Great White Fraternity. As Memphis stood for the religious twin city of Gebel, so did Akhetaton to Mt. Carmel.

Although the sacred Temples of Gebel in Canaan-Phoenicia had great religious, spiritual, and historical connections with the Temples of Memphis in Egypt, we believe that Joseph, his wife, and son, could have had actually found refuge either in one of the Geblite Temples or in one of the Temples of Mt. Carmel, if the story of Herod is historically correct. We have seen in the previous chapter (in footnote 42) how Edgar Cayce's vision revealed that on the top of Mt. Carmel was erected an Essenian Temple, which was the religious center of the fraternity, and that in this Temple, Mary, the Mother of Jesus, was instructed and prepared by the Priests of the Essenes. Now, one may ask: What is the connection between the Essenes of Galilee and Mt. Carmel at the time of Jesus and the Phoenician-Egyptian Great White Fraternity of the past? The answer to this question resides in the fact that there appeared in the course of history very few religions and fraternities that were in direct affiliation with the Great White Fraternity.

Like the Hermetists, Pythagoreans, and the Therapeuts of the Egyptian desert, the Asayas (or the Galilean Essenes who we believe were the writers of some of the ancient scrolls of the Dead

Sea, mainly attributed to the Jewish Essens), with their ascetic Nazarene branch of Mt. Carmel and Galilee, were affiliated to that fraternity. Along with them appear the Christians and some of the non-dualist Christian Gnostics, few Alchemists of the Hermetic tradition, several Theosophists, and the Anthroposophists who believe that Christianity is a unique spiritual system for the evolution of humanity and that without Christ humanity might well bring about its own destruction. Adding, of course, the Rosicrucians, who seek to accomplish the Great Work by identifying Christ as the Philosopher's Stone.

Undoubtedly, this historical approach makes us well understand the Second Visitation of the Angel to Joseph. It is described in Matthew (2:19-23) as follows:

Now when Herod was dead, behold, an angel of the Lord appeared in a dream to Joseph in Egypt, saying, Arise, take the young Child and His mother, and go to the land of Israel, for those who sought the young Child's life are dead. Then he arose, took the young Child and His mother, and came into the land of Israel. But when he heard that Archelaus was reigning over Judea instead of his father Herod, he was afraid to go there. And being warned by God in a dream, he turned aside into the region of Galilee. And he came and dwelt in a city called Nazareth, that it might be fulfilled which was spoken by the prophets, He shall be called a Nazarene.

Of course, the journey from the Sacred Island or Mt. Carmel (the allegorical word for Egypt) to Israel after the death of Herod couldn't have happened or wouldn't have happened since Joseph and his family had nothing to do in Israel. Their journey would then have taken them back to Galilee from whence they came in the first place, so that it might be fulfilled that which was spoken by the prophets (Phoenician-Asayan prophets), that he (*Iesous*) shall be called a Nazarene, which was the Ashayan ascetic and therapeutic branch of Galilee and Mt. Carmel.

His Grandparents

We have seen earlier in the introduction that the genealogy of Jesus mentioned in Matthew (1:1-17), ends with Jesus, describing Joseph, the husband of Mary and the father of Jesus, as the son of Jacob. However, the second genealogy, that of Luke (3:23-38), which contradicts the first in terms of the fatherhood of Joseph, starts with Jesus, "as was supposed," son of Joseph, son of Heli or Eli. This is totally misleading since Joseph, the father of Jesus, cannot be the son of Jacob (in Matthew) and also the son of Heli (in Luke), and we have seen that some Biblical scholars, from as early as John of Damascus to Martin Luther, have considered the words "as was supposed" to be a parenthetical note, explaining that Luke intended to call Jesus a son of Eli, and that Eli or Heli is actually the maternal grandfather of Jesus. So Luke was actually tracing the ancestry of Jesus not according to Joseph but rather according to the flesh through Mary, claiming that it was of a preference at the time to drop women's name out of the list, hence it could not be read as Joseph son of Eli but rather, Joseph son-in-law of Heli, who is the father of Mary.

Now, since this explanation is mere assumption given by the Judeo-Christian community, which I found irrational, I, on the other hand, considered that Mary's parents were called Joachim and Anna, names accepted by the Church, although it was found in the Apocryphal[63] Gospel of James[64] (probably of the 2nd century AD), that the words "as was supposed" are indeed a parenthetical note, with the Apostle Luke actually calling Jesus a son of Ēli. A logical explanation that very few seemed to have dared to tackle yet works all ways, and I mean, for Jesus, Joseph, and Mary, and can be summarized as follows:

Jesus is the son of Joseph, son of Ēli, and is also the son of Mary, daughter of Ēli. Joseph is his earthly (adoptive father), and Ēli or Ēl is his divine father, for he was called *Immanu-el*[65], "Ēl with us." Joseph is also the son of Ēli or Ēl, being himself a High Priest or priest of the God the Most High, Ēl, through his affiliation to the Asayas—the Healers. Joseph's priestly name could well have been Kabbir-el (Gabriel), one of the greatest who serves the God Ēl, after humanizing the Archangel Gabriel sent from God Ēl to Galilee, at the hour of Annunciation of the Birth of Jesus to Maryām, a virgin being prepared in the ancient Phoenician-Ashayan Temple at the top of Mt. Carmel.

---

63 The Church actually doesn't approve Apocryphal works but it surely considers the names of Joachim and Anna, found in the Gospel of James as the true names of the Virgin Lady's parents. It also approved, later on, the Divine Ascension of Mary into heaven found in another Apocrypha, the Gospel of Ascension.

64 James the brother (or half-brother) of Jesus, if taking the New Testament in a literal manner, in both, Matthew 13:55 and Mark 6:3, and according to many Biblical scholars. We, however, believe James was his cousin as we shall see in this chapter and in Chapter 6.

65 Matthew 1:23.

Undoubtedly, that would surely lead us now to talk about that special spiritual preparation found in religious texts other than the revelations of the American visionary Edgar Cayce. Hence, in the Gospel of James (c. 145 AD–150 AD), Joachim and Anna were pictured as the only couple in Israel that had not conceived a child. Described as coming from the tribe of Judah, and descending from the family of King David, both were very old, yet the Lord heard their prayers as he heard before them the prayers of the Patriarch Abraham and his wife Sarah[66], and gave them a child by the name of Isaac in their last days.

In James (2:1), we find Anna mourning and lamenting greatly for two reasons, saying, "I lament that I am a widow and I lament that I am childless." Yet, it would be difficult for us to understand that she could have reasonably considered herself a widow while she was the wife of Joachim, who was still alive. Unless she was not the wife of Joachim, but of someone else (Ēli, as per the genealogy of Luke). "Joachim," which sounds to be a Hebrew name, as the Biblical tradition has shown, could have originally been an Aramaic name[67], or in the worst case scenario, a Hebrew addition to the original text, as might be the case to all Hebrew connotations used in the work at hand[68]. "Anna," on the other hand, could well be a name derived from the Canaano-Phoenician name of the Goddess Anat[69].

---

66 There is no historical proof for the existence of the Hebrew Patriarch Abraham and his wife Sarah in historical records outside the Old Testament. Some say that Abraham and Sarah are copies of the Hindu divinities Brahma and Sarasvati.

67 The name Joachim as it appears in the Gospel of James is of Hebrew origin, *Yehô-yāqîm*, and means "he whom YHWH has set up," but it could also be a derivation from the Aramaic name, *Yāw-yāqîm*, composed of two words "Yāw" and "Yāqîm." Yāw appeared as the god of Rivers and Sea in the Canaano-Phoenician city of Ugarit, hence, the name *Yaw-yāqîm* would mean "he whom YĀW has set up firm." It is thus very logical to give such a name to the father of Maryām since we know that Galilean-Phoenicians were greatly connected to the Sea and fishing, as we have previously stated. Remember the words *Yehi* or *Yehaw* that had been used in the names given to the two Canaano-Phoenician Kings of Byblos, the 10th or 8th century BC King, Yehi-Milk (King Yehi), and Yehaw-Milk (King Yehaw) of the 5th-4th century BC.

68 Eminent scholars have stated that the work could well be pseudoepigraphical, which means, a work not written by the person it is attributed to. The claim that James could not be the author is half-established, and that conclusion is thoroughly based on the style of the language used in the text. The fact that the unknown author depicts some activities as Jewish customs of the time, most probably, rather undoubtedly, did not exist ever. What is remarkable, however, is the depiction of Phoenician custom.

At any rate, when we continue reading from the Protoevangelium of James (3:3), we hear Anna saying, "I am reviled and they treat me with contempt and cast me out of the temple of the Lord my God." This sentence by itself cannot be true, since we know that Jewish tradition never accepted women in the temple. Yet, it might prove something else, since Anna then said (4:2), "As the Lord God lives, whether I give birth to either a male or a female child, I will bring it as an offering to the Lord my God and it will be a servant to Him all the days of its life." A female child as an offering to the Lord God to serve Him has proven to be not a Jewish custom at all, but rather a Canaano-Phoenician-Galilean (Gentile) tradition, as we have seen before.

James (5) then describes Anna giving birth to a female child that she called Mary, and next, (James 6), she swore when Mary was six months old, that she would take her to the Temple of the Lord. This was followed by the blessings of the priests and High Priests of the child at her first birthday, an event that probably occurred inside a temple and which could not have actually happened in a Jewish temple, but instead in one of the Canaano-Phoenician temples we have mentioned in the previous chapter. Thus, this blessing could have correctly and historically taken place in a temple dedicated to one of the goddesses, Anat, Astarte, Ashirai, or the Ba'alat, in the surrounding region of Tyre and Sidon.

James (7) relates that Mary was taken up to the Temple of the Lord[70] at the age of three as promised by her mother and approved by her father to be consecrated there and be of service to God. "And her parents went down," adds James (8:1), "marveling at and praising and glorifying the Lord God because the child had not turned back to look at them." And the text continues

---

69 If we are going to combine Anna as the mother of Maryām with Ēli as her father, per the explanation given to Luke's genealogy, we would then decipher her parents' names as being given after the Canaano-Phoenician Goddess Anat and the God Ēl. Hence, Maryām could well be defined as the daughter of Anat and Ēl.

70 We believe that Mary's parents took the child up to the Temple at Mt. Carmel as was the habit of the Canaano-Phoenician-Galileans. There is no sacred mountain for such a consecration of a child, especially a female, or even to host a temple for the Hebrew God, in all of Judea. As a reminder to what has been said earlier, we have related that in the *Guide de Mt. Carmel*, the first Church rose near the grotto of Mt. Carmel in devotion to Mary, or the grotto was changed into a chapel, or was probably built from the stones of a Temple dedicated to Ashirai (Asherah)—the Mother-Goddess of the Phoenicians, the Virgin Lady Anat herself—the Queen of Heaven, and that is undoubtedly a forecast of Maryām as Virgin and Queen of Heaven in Christianity.

beautifully in the following sentence, "While Mary was in the temple of the Lord, she was fed like a dove and received food from the hand of an angel."

A long time seems to have passed before the priests met to talk about the fate of Mary, as James (8:3-4) reveals, "When she turned twelve, a group of priests took counsel together, saying, Look, Mary has been in the temple of the Lord twelve years[71]. What should we do about her now, so that she does not defile[72] the sanctuary of the Lord our God?"

Following that, the text shows that Joseph, for whom the signs worked in his favor, took Mary into his own keeping as the High Priest reasoned. James (9:7) says, "And the high priest said, 'Joseph! Joseph! You have been chosen by lot to take the virgin into your own keeping.'" But when Joseph refused the idea because he was old and had sons, the high priest seems to have frightened him. It worked, for we then read (9:11-12), "Fearing God, Joseph took her into his own possession. And he said to her, Mary, I took you from the temple of the Lord and now I bring you into my house. I am going out to build houses[73], but I will come back to you. The Lord will protect you."

The next chapter continues in stating that after meeting with the priests at the Temple of the Lord, the High Priest asked his servants to bring the virgins to him. It says in James (10:2-6), "And the high priest said, Call the pure virgins from the tribe of David to me. And the servants went out and sought and found seven virgins. And the high priest remembered that the child Mary was from the tribe of David[74] and was pure before God. So the servants went out and got her. And they brought the women into the temple of the Lord[75]."

---

71 If she had actually entered the temple when she was three and was now twelve, she would then have been there in the temple for nine years, not twelve as the text shows.

72 How can a child of twelve, a virgin, defile the temple of the Lord? Such concept is refused within the Canaano-Phoenician-Galilean tradition but accepted in Jewish tradition since a woman is looked upon as soulless and sinful since her birth.

73 Joseph is described here as a builder of houses, more specifically, not a carpenter as the New Testament suggests in Matthew 13:55.

74 She could not have been from the seed of David as the Christian tradition claims. Both Ernest Renan and Jacques Duquesne are affirmative in that concern as they have repeatedly proven that Jesus was not of the House of David. If he is not by blood, then she is not either. Besides, we strongly believe that Maryām was a Phoenician virgin from the Lebanese village of Kana.

75 The text tries to show that there were some form of consecrated temple virgins in Judaism, a practice similar to the Canaano-Phoenician sacred

What the text suggests concerning virgins being consecrated in a Jewish temple is undoubtedly fictional. This practice could not have existed in mainstream Judaism, and not even within the outside Judaic cultures of the Qumran Community or the alike secluded Jewish groups. And once more, we come to realize that the text at hand, like all other Biblical and extra-Biblical texts, has been manipulated in the manner to cast out Gentile tradition and practices and impregnate them as being Jewish all in the hope to eliminate any relation Jesus and his family originally had with the Gentiles of Galilee, precisely, the Canaano-Phoenician-Galileans.

However, this attempt is destined to fail because scholars, and I mean respected ones, are aware now more than ever of the truth that has been tarnished all through the past years. This book is a solemn peaceful whisper in the ears of Christians and others who are in awe and admiration of the persona of Jesus Christ that we have all been fooled about by Judeo-Christian propagandists.

Continuing one sentence further on into the Gospel of James (10:7-8), we read, "And the high priest said, Cast lots to see who will spin the gold and the pure and the linen and the silk and the violet and the scarlet and the true purple threads. And Mary was appointed by lot to the true purple and scarlet threads."

Indeed, the Virgin Maryām seemed to have been chosen to spin the true purple and scarlet thread right before the Great Annunciation of the Angel of God who first spoke to her by the fountain of water and then appeared to her inside her house as we have seen in the previous chapter (11:1-9). Perhaps it was after all a slip of the tongue by the author of this text! Mary was appointed to spin the true purple and scarlet threads like her own people. One may ask: Who were known in the whole ancient world as the artist-inventors and fabricators of fine true purple clothes? The answer is simple: the Phoenicians.

And how amazing it would be for her to receive the Visitation of the Messenger of God announcing her Holy Fate to bear in her womb the Son of the Most High after that probable slip of the tongue? Or was it a code, written by the author of this particular gospel—an extra-biblical code—to be deciphered, later on?

---

rituals of the virgins in the Temples of the Goddesses or as it appears to be in existence later on with the virgins (*Parthenos* is the general use of the word) in the Greek temple of Artemis, who was known to be a virgin Goddess herself, and also, in the type of Vestal Virgins in Rome. To be more accurate, this is Gentile practice, or "pagan," as some would like to call it. It was most surely practiced by all the related groups in Galilee, and most precisely by the Asayas or the Essenes of Galilee and Mt. Carmel.

As we turn the page into the next chapter, we read (James 12:1-2), "And she made the purple and the scarlet thread and carried it to the high priest. And taking it, the high priest blessed her and said, Mary, God has magnified your name. You will be called blessed among all the generations of the earth."

This is another proof that relates Mary or Maryām to the Phoenicians: her making the true purple and scarlet thread. In his praised book, *History of Phoenicia*, British author George Rawlinson, describes that Phoenician High Priests used to wear Purple Robes in their ceremonies[76]. Thus, meeting with the High Priest, most probably in the temple, carrying with her the purple and scarlet thread, shows the preparations for making the purple robes. He blessed her among all the generations of the earth, for God had magnified her name.

Immediately after that, we read (James 12:3-5), "Then, Mary went gladly to her cousin Elizabeth. And she knocked at the door and when Elizabeth heard, she threw down her scarlet thread and ran to the door and opened it for her. And she blessed her and said, Where have you come to me from? Why should the mother of my Lord come to me? See how the child in me leaps and blesses you."

Again, the text clearly shows that her cousin Elizabeth had been spinning the scarlet thread when Mary knocked at her door. It is logical to believe that since Maryām was of Phoenician origin, then her cousin Elizabeth[77] would be Phoenician, too, not Jewish of the tribe of Aaron as the New Testament suggests[78]. Her connection to the Phoenicians is also evident in the text with the scarlet thread. But what about her husband, Zacharias? Was he Jewish? It seems that his name suggests otherwise[79].

---

76 Rawlinson, George, *History of Phoenicia*, iBooks, page 261-262.

77 The name Elizabeth or Elisabeth is definitely derived from the Aramaic *Ēli-sh-beth* meaning "the Just before the God Ēl" or "the peaceful dwelling of the God Ēl." The Hebrew explanation of the name Elizabeth is *Elisāba* or *Eli-Sheva* is "My God has sworn." Yet, the Jewish God is not Ēl but Jehovah.

78 According to Luke, as in James, Mary was a cousin of Elizabeth. It is described in Luke 1:36, "And, behold, thy cousin Elisabeth, she hath also conceived a son (John the Baptist) in her old age: and this is the sixth month with her, who was called barren." And it is in Luke 1:5 where we learn who Elizabeth was: "There was in the days of Herod, the king of Judaea, a certain priest named Zacharias (Zechariah) of the course (priestly division) of Abia (Abijah): and his wife was of the daughters of Aaron (lineage of Aaron, the brother of Moses as per the Old Testament and so of the tribe of Levi) and her name was Elisabeth."

79 According to L.A. Waddell, in his book, *The Phoenician Origin of Britons, Scots, and Anglo-Saxons*, page 273-274, Zacharias (the father of John the Baptist) was a fire priest, offering fire incense in the temple in the course of

Then, James (12:7-9) shows Mary spending three months with her cousin, probably during her first three months of pregnancy, and that she was sixteen years old when she conceived from the Lord. Her sixth month of pregnancy after returning home from her stay at her cousin's was a shock to Joseph, as mentioned in James (13 & 14), since he had not known her and was surprised that she was now pregnant, as he took her as a virgin from the Temple of the Lord. He didn't know that his wife Maryām, who was the purest of all, had conceived with the Lord and this very fact frightened him, but his fear soon disappeared as the Angel of God in his dreams comforted him[80].

Later on, James (17) stated that there was an order[81] from the Roman Emperor Augustus to register how many people were in Bethlehem of Judea, and describes the trip on the donkey that Joseph took from his house with his wife and his two sons from a different woman, as the text shows that he had not yet registered. The text determines no clear area where his house was located, but it gives a certain idea that almost in the middle of the journey the area looked like a desert. However, it was there, somewhere in the deserted area, that Joseph had actually found an appropriate shelter for his wife after taking her off the donkey because the child was pushing from within her. Time to deliver.[82] In fact, the

---

Abia, as mentioned in Luke 1:5. To Waddell, he was presumably a Gentile, not Jewish, whose name has no meaning in Hebrew, but it is a derivation of the Sumer title *Sakhar* and *Sakar*, which means "water-libator," thus "Baptist." If Zacharias (Zachariah) had actually enacted the ritual of fire incense, it could be due to the logical perception that Gentile Sun-Priests actually existed in the Temple of Mt. Moriah at Jerusalem. In fact, the name Mt. Moriah is recognized as Mount of the Morias or Amorites, and that precise Temple, long before the occupation of Jerusalem by David and its rebuilding by Solomon (as per the Old Testament, which will certainly differ from archeological and historical realities that deny the existence of both David and Solomon and might consider the Hebrew occupation of Jerusalem to have happened after the decree written by Cyrus II in the 6th century BC) was a famous temple dedicated to the Sun by the Amorites, a Canaanite tribe, or to the Higher Light, Él, by the Jebusite, also a Canaanite tribe.

80 James 14:5-6, "And night overtook him. And suddenly an angel of the Lord appeared to him in a dream, saying, Do not fear this child. For the child in her is from the Holy Spirit. She will bear a son for you and you will call his name Jesus. For he will save his people from their sins."

81 Many scholars throughout history doubt this order was in accordance with historical facts.

82 The text describes that almost in the middle of their journey from their point of departure, which is unknown, to their destination, which is stated as Bethlehem of Judea, that Joseph took his wife off the donkey because the child was pushing from within her and time had come for her to deliver in a shelter he just found. This statement by itself shows that the delivery did not

safe haven he discovered was clearly described (18:1), "And he found a cave and led her there and stationed his sons to watch her."

This cave by itself is certainly around the village of the Galilean Bet-Lahem. If the family took off from the house of Maryām, which we believe was in the Lebanese Kana where the miracle of Wine was enacted, or, from the house of Joseph, which could also be located somewhere in the region of Tyre or Sidon, then halfway to Bethlehem of Judea, as the text shows, could well be the cave herein mentioned in the Bet-Lahem of Galilee, which we believe was located at the foot of Mt. Carmel—a mountain full of caves used for many purposes from meditations to prayers, even shelters, by the adepts of the Galilean and Carmelite Essenes, better termed as the Asayas.

If the family took off from the so-called Nazareth of Galilee, which was not built at the time of Jesus, in the direction of Bethlehem of Judea, then halfway could only be the region of Samaria. This is a doomed hypothesis, since there is not any known religious or historical tradition that supports such a claim. Besides, Jesus had to have been born in one of the two proposed Bethlehems; yet, the Bethlehem of Judea fails again to be the birthplace of Jesus during this journey. Geography doesn't lie.

At any rate, after Joseph placed his wife in the cave, the text continues in James (18:2), "... while he went to find a Hebrew midwife in the land of Bethlehem." Yet, the author seems to have played on words in the next two paragraphs, and it reads as follows (18:3-11):

> Then, Joseph wandered, but he did not wander. And I looked up to the peak of the sky and saw it standing still and I looked up into the air. With utter astonishment I saw it, even the birds of the sky were not moving. And I looked at the ground and saw a bowl lying there and workers reclining. And their hands were in the bowl. And chewing, they were not chewing. And picking food up, they were not picking it up. And putting food in their mouths, they were not putting it in their mouths. Rather, all their faces were looking up.
>
> And I saw sheep being driven, but the sheep were standing still. And the shepherd lifted up his hand to strike them, but his hand remained above them. And I saw the rushing current of the river and I saw goats and their mouths resting in the

---

happen in Bethlehem of Judea, but somewhere else, almost halfway on the road to Bethlehem.

water, but they were not drinking. And suddenly everything was replaced by the ordinary course of events.

These two paragraphs are very clear in their style and description as if the author was trying to show and tell us that Joseph didn't actually go anywhere, but stood still, there by the cave. And this is supported by what comes next (19:1), "And I saw a woman coming down from the mountain and she said to me, Man, where are you going?" And continues (19:5), "Then, she said, And who is giving birth in the cave?"

It is evident to determine that this woman Joseph met by the cave was a person belonging to the Carmelite Ashayas and coming down from the top of Mt. Carmel. And to add more clarity to the situation, Joseph answers (19:8), "And I said to her, She is Mary, the one who was raised in the temple." First, this temple cited here is a confirmation of the one built by the Asayas at the top of Mt. Carmel, which we have spoken about before. Second, the woman probably knew Mary because she was raised in the temple, as inferred from Joseph's reply.

After hearing that Mary was not yet Joseph's wife, since she did not know him, but a virgin that carried a fetus from the Holy Spirit (19:9), the woman decided to come with Joseph and see her waiting in the cave. And suddenly she appeared to be the midwife who would help her deliver as it shows (19:12-14), "So the midwife went with him. And they stood near the cave and a dark cloud was hovering over the cave. And the midwife said, My soul glorifies this day, for today my eyes have seen a miracle: salvation has come to Israel[83]."

Moments later, the gospel continues to expose the birth of the child and it reads (19:15-16) as thus:

And immediately, the cloud withdrew from the cave and a great light appeared in the cave so that their eyes could not bear it. And a little while later the same light withdrew until an infant appeared. And he came and took the breast of his mother, Mary.

---

83 There are in fact two meanings for the word Israel that we shall propose an explanation for in Chapter 7, however, it is important to know, as for now, that one meaning is related to the Canaano-Phoenicians' religious concept of being themselves "Isra-Ēl" or "family of Ēl" and the other meaning is connected to the Hebrews and their conflict with the God Ēl as per the Old Testament and their choice of adopting YHWH as their national deity.

The text tries to show that the event of the birth was of divine and miraculous nature as if the midwife had not actually helped Maryām in the process of delivering the child to the world.

Then, the text mentions a person by the name of Salome, well recognized by the midwife who called her by the name and imparted to her the new miracle that had just happened (19:18). Many biblical scholars believe that Salome mentioned herein is the same Salome mentioned in the Canonical text as one of the women who appeared in the life of Jesus, or better say, one of his few female Disciples. Her name was shown twice in the Gospel of Mark alongside Mary Magdalene and Mary the mother of James the Less and of Joses[84]. Of course, Salome and the women cited in the New Testament were with Jesus ever since he started his ministry in Galilee. Yet, those three appear again in the next chapter of Mark as being the special ones who came to the tomb after the Crucifixion of Jesus to anoint his body but didn't find him for he had risen from the dead[85].

Later on, the James text proves once more that all this—the event that led to the birth of Jesus—happened not at all in Judea but of course in Bet-Lahem of Galilee, as we have proved earlier. It is shown (21:1), "Now, Joseph was about to depart to Judea when there a great commotion in Bethlehem of Judea." This, by itself, clearly proves that Joseph had not departed either to Judea or to Bethlehem of Judea before and during the Birth of Christ.

At any rate, the text continues on, showing how the astrologers had come to pay homage to the child who had been born "King of the Jews," after seeing his star in the East, and how Herod the Great had heard of this birth and decided to investigate if the birth had really happened and where. We read about him sending his servants to the astrologers to learn about the divine sign they saw concerning the newborn king, so that he may come and worship him as he told them, but, really so that he could take action against him. He then sent his executioners with a mission to destroy all the infants that were two years old or younger after he had been tricked by the astrologers. A similar story has been narrated in the Church New Testament by Matthew (2:1-3).

---

84 Mark 15:40-41, "There were also women looking on from afar, among whom were Mary Magdalene, Mary the mother of James the Less and of Joses, and Salome, who also followed Him and ministered to Him when He was in Galilee, and many other women who came up with Him to Jerusalem."
85 Mark 16:1-2, "Now when the Sabbath was past, Mary Magdalene, Mary [the mother] of James, and Salome bought spices, that they might come and anoint Him. Very early in the morning, on the first [day] of the week, they came to the tomb when the sun had risen."

The text ends with a testimony of James declaring that he wrote this history when there was unrest in Jerusalem, at the time Herod died, and that was after his servants had murdered Zachariah, the father of John (the Baptist)—a child who was also sought by Herod who was afraid that he might be the Messiah that was destined to rule Israel. Hence, one more thing is worth mentioning here before we end our study of the Gospel of James: the account of the safety measures that had been taken by both Maryām and her cousin Ēli-sh-beth, and which appears in James (22:3-9) as follows:

> And when Mary heard that all the children were being destroyed, she was afraid and took the child and wrapped him up and put him in a stall of cows. And when Elizabeth heard that John was being sought, she took him and headed for the hills. And she looked around to find where she could hide him, but there was not any good place. Then, as Elizabeth sighed, she said with a loud voice, Mountain of God, take me, a mother with her child. For Elizabeth was too afraid to go up higher. And at once, the mountain split open and received her. And there was light shining through the mountain to her. For an angel of the Lord was with them, guarding them.

The text is very clear in its description of the place where both women found refuge after Herod's massacre of the little ones (if this event should be believed, historically). It was indeed in one of the temples at Mt. Carmel, the headquarters of the great religious and spiritual group—the Asayas.

Great Aunts and Great Uncles

Now, some have suggested that Ēli-sh-beth was not in fact the cousin of Maryām but her aunt, who the Virgin came to visit and serve during her pregnancy. Christians as well as Muslims regard Elizabeth as an important religious figure for mainly two reasons: first, her conception at an old age by the will and power of God, and second, her delivery of a great prophet, John the Baptist (*Yāwhanan* in Aramaic), who appeared to have prepared the way[86] for Jesus Christ before baptizing him by the River Jordan. And during the Rite of Baptism that he was enacting to the multitude that gathered near him, in expectation that he might well be the

---

86 Luke 7:26-27, "But what did you go out to see? A prophet? Yes, I say to you, and more than a prophet. This is [he] of whom it is written: Behold, I send My messenger before Your face, Who will prepare Your way before You."

Christ they had been waiting for[87], John revealed something of great importance about Jesus being the one chosen from the beginning to become what he was in reality: the Elected One of the Nazarenes[88]. In fact, his revelation appears not only in both Mark (1:8) and Luke (3:16), but also in Matthew (3:11), "I indeed baptize you with water unto repentance, but He who is coming after me is mightier than I, whose sandals I am not worthy to carry. He will baptize you with the Holy Spirit and fire."

Hence, it was not coincidental or by any chance erroneous terminology used by the Apostle Matthew when he called Jesus a Nazarene as a fulfillment to the prophecy spoken by the prophets[89]—and certainly Phoenician-Galilean-Ashayan prophets, not at all Jewish. Thus, as a quick reminder, we have learned what the word "Nazarene" means, in Chapter 2. The Canaano-Phoenician word "Nazir" or *Nazar* (*Natzar*) is given to someone who leaves everything behind and consecrates his life by taking a solemn vow to God, the Father, or had been chosen to be consecrated by his faithful parents to Ēl, the Most High— definitely a Canaano-Phoenician habit.

At any rate, if Ēlishbeth was the aunt of Maryām from her mother's side, then she would be the sister of Anna, her mother. And if this is so, then both Anna and Ēlishbeth are the sisters of Yāwsēp̄ of Rameh (Joseph of Arimathea) as stated in the many semi-legends surrounding his life, and we would consider him the uncle of Maryām; there are always some truths in popular stories[90]. We have already investigated the most probable derivation of the name Anna from the Phoenician name of the Goddess Anat, and considered the Phoenician roots of Ēlishbeth as per the logical analysis of the genealogical lines within the Holy Family, along with her image of spinning the scarlet thread in the Gospel of James as part of her know-how of the Canaano-Phoenician habit.

Now, investigating the true origin of their supposed brother, Joseph of Rameh (or Ramah), would shed more light about their strong familial relation with Phoenician DNA, but first, let us consider the New Testament. All four canonical texts mention Joseph in a very similar way and represent him as an important

87 Luke 3:15.
88 Adepts of the ascetic branch of the Asayas that counted among them John the Baptist, Mary Magdalene, Jesus, Paul, and a few others. They all knew at once that Jesus was the *Christos* and followed him faithfully ever since.
89 Matthew 2:22-23.
90 There is in fact much more to Joseph of Rameh than in the Canonical texts at hand. A whole bunch of other stories have indeed grown up around him, mainly originated from Britain.

man within the circle of Jesus, not only because he was the man who took the body of Jesus off of the cross to bury him—and that would be the work of a man of respect and power to be able to convince Pilate—but also because he was one of the secret disciples of Jesus.

Starting with Matthew[91], he considered Joseph a rich man from Arimathea, a disciple of Jesus who went to Pilate and asked for his body to bury him in a new tomb in the rock. Mark[92] mentions Joseph as a prominent council member, who was himself waiting for the Kingdom of God, coming to Pilate and asking for the body of Jesus to entomb him in the same way. As for Luke[93], he considered him a counsellor, a good man and just, who also waited for the Kingdom of God, went to Pilate, and asked him for the body of Jesus to lay him similarly. And John[94] looked at him as a secret disciple of Jesus, who went to Pilate and asked him if he could take away his body to place him in a new tomb in the nearby garden with the help of Nicodemus.

---

91 Matthew 27:57-60, "Now when evening had come, there came a rich man from Arimathea, named Joseph, who himself had also become a disciple of Jesus. This man went to Pilate and asked for the body of Jesus. Then Pilate commanded the body to be given to him. When Joseph had taken the body, he wrapped it in a clean linen cloth, and laid it in his new tomb which he had hewn out of the rock; and he rolled a large stone against the door of the tomb, and departed."

92 Mark 15:43-46, "Joseph of Arimathea, a prominent council member, who was himself waiting for the kingdom of God, coming and taking courage, went in to Pilate and asked for the body of Jesus. Pilate marveled that He was already dead; and summoning the centurion, he asked him if He had been dead for some time. So when he found out from the centurion, he granted the body to Joseph. Then he bought fine linen, took Him down, and wrapped Him in the linen. And he laid Him in a tomb which had been hewn out of the rock, and rolled a stone against the door of the tomb."

93 Luke 23:50-53, "Now behold, [there was] a man named Joseph, a council member, a good and just man. He had not consented to their decision and deed. [He was] from Arimathea, a city of the Jews, who himself was also waiting for the kingdom of God. This man went to Pilate and asked for the body of Jesus. Then he took it down, wrapped it in linen, and laid it in a tomb [that was] hewn out of the rock, where no one had ever lain before."

94 John 19:38-42, "After this, Joseph of Arimathea, being a disciple of Jesus, but secretly, for fear of the Jews, asked Pilate that he might take away the body of Jesus; and Pilate gave [him] permission. So he came and took the body of Jesus. And Nicodemus, who at first came to Jesus by night, also came, bringing a mixture of myrrh and aloes, about a hundred pounds. Then they took the body of Jesus, and bound it in strips of linen with the spices, as the custom of the Jews is to bury. Now in the place where He was crucified there was a garden, and in the garden a new tomb in which no one had yet been laid. So there they laid Jesus, because of the Jews' Preparation [Day], for the tomb was nearby."

So, to portray Joseph of Arimathea in one sentence after summarizing what came in the tongues of the four Apostles, Joseph would then appear to be a famous council member of probably the Sanhedrin with important political power and richness, yet a good and just man in wait for the Kingdom of God, who enjoyed a secret discipleship of Jesus and after the crucifixion took care of the body.

But if Joseph was indeed the great uncle of Jesus, then there is more to the text we have in the New Testament. According to the Talmud, Joseph of Arimathea was an uncle of Mary, being the younger brother of her father. Other genealogists, probably of less credibility than that of the Talmud in that matter, describe him as being the uncle of Joseph, the adoptive father of Jesus. This is a very slim supposition. Whatever may be the truth of his relationship to Jesus, he remained his great uncle and was regarded as a successful merchant who gained his wealth from the tin trade that existed between Cornwall in Britain and Phoenicia in many British tales.

What came in the Talmud and other British sources is indeed extremely beneficial to us. Going north, out of Galilee and inside the adjacent Phoenicia, as per all the four maps presented herein, stood another important location that we should consider very well in our study. It is the city of Arimathea, from where Joseph originated. Now, the investigative mind in all of us wonders where could Arimathea be located on the map ...

Only the Book of Luke mentions that Arimathea was a city of the Jews, but apart from that there is no place called Arimathea in recorded history. Many hypotheses have been given by Biblical scholars throughout the years. Some have suggested that it was another name for the Old Testament town of Ramathaim-Zophim, identified today with the modern locality of Neby Samwil (prophet Samuel), and located about four to five miles in the northwest of Jerusalem, the birthplace of Samuel (1Samuel 1:1), usually called Ramah[95] (later Ramathaim) where their house was[96]. (Biblically,

---

95 1Samuel 1:19
96 The event and the names of the characters in 1Samuel 1 describing a certain woman called Hannah (unable to give birth but her prayers to the Lord during one of their pilgrimages at the Temple made that happen), and Elkanah, her husband who loved her, always beside her, and Eli the priest there, are identical to the story of Anna (who was childless but the Lord listened to her prayers) and Joachim her husband (in the Gospel of James) who loved her and Eli her husband (in the Gospel of Luke). In the Samuel event, the name Ramah appeared to be the place where their house was. Could that very same name represent the place where the house of the family of Maryām was?

this area was known as the land of the tribe of Ephraim.) Others may have identified it with Ramlah or Ramleh, in Central Israel, west of Jerusalem, probably founded sometime around the years 707 AD–716 AD by the Arabs after their conquest of the region. (This area was known as the land of the tribe of Dan in the Jewish Bible.) Still others believe it was Ramah that was identified today with modern Er-Ram, situated about eight kilometers north of the city of Jerusalem. (This area was biblically known as the land of the tribe of Benjamin[97].)

Yet, there are still other places by the same name, at least four, to be considered, since we agree that the right name of this city, as known at the time of Jesus, was Rameh or Ramah. Fortunately though, it is not hard to find where the four places having the same name are located, and so, if we look at Map 1 at the end of the book, we will surely find them. One of them could be identified with the modern Palestinian city of Ramallah in the West Bank, north of Jerusalem. Another one could also be found in Samaria. (This area was known as the land of the tribe of Manasseh in the Hebrew Bible.)

However, what the Biblical scholars and archaeologists have probably forgotten or may have purposely neglected, is the fact that there were two places by the name of Rameh (Ramah) in the region of Galilee-Phoenicia. One of them is just on the Galilean-Phoenician border. (Biblically, this area was known as the land of the tribe of Naphtali.) The other is farther north, and to be more accurate, it still exists, even today, in Lebanon, as per Map 2 (Nr.52) very close to Kana (Cana)—the place from which Maryām, the mother of Yāwshu came, and it was there where he performed his first miracle. (This area was Biblically known as the land of the tribe of Asher). As a matter of fact, we undoubtedly believe that this is the Rameh from which Joseph originated. It is located twenty-one kilometers south of Sūr, encircled in green, and only nine kilometers from Kana, encircled in blue, also in Map 2 (Nr.53), and this is precisely the location that concerns us now in this geographical exposé part of the book.

So, if both Anna and Ēlishbeth were the sisters of Yāwsēp̄, then they shall be considered as having originated from Rameh itself. If, on the other hand, Yāwsēp̄ was the brother of Maryām's father, as mentioned in the Talmud, then he would be the brother of Yāw-yāqîm (Joachim) as stated in the Gospel of James, or the brother of Ēli, mentioned in the genealogy of the Apostle Luke— the theorized father of Maryām, as we have seen earlier. Ēli would then be considered as having originated from Rameh, as well.

---

97 Matthew 2:18

Inquiring more on Joseph of Rameh, the mysterious man—the great uncle who played an important role in Jesus' life—would definitely lead us to clearly expose the true identity of this man as we elaborate herein about his life and profession. The proposition declared by the Talmud about Joseph as being Maryām's uncle[98], and what has been thereafter revealed by early British historical sources about Joseph making fortune as an international merchant of tin, a secret trade that existed between Cornwall in Britain and Phoenicia in the Mediterranean[99], is indeed very interesting.

If the Talmud, the ancient tradition of the Eastern Church and the Harlein manuscripts are accurate, which we believe they are, and since we have proved the relation of Joseph to Rameh in Tyre, then it will undoubtedly reveal his Canaano-Phoenician origin. In addition, if the British sources are correct, then Joseph of Rameh could have been a wealthy Phoenician merchant who owned a large fleet of Phoenician ships and ran the tin trade for the Roman Empire between the Land of Tin—known in the old days as Bar-Tanak, the Phoenician name for Britain[100]—and Phoenicia.

---

98 In his book, *The Traditions of Glastonbury*, page 19, author E. Raymon Capt wrote, "Ancient traditions, in the Eastern Church, assert that Joseph was the great-uncle of Jesus. This is confirmed by the Jewish Talmud which has Joseph as the younger brother of the father of Mary and thus was her uncle and a great-uncle to Jesus. The Harlein Manuscripts (in the British Museum—38-59 f, 193 b) further supports this claim that Joseph of Arimathea was uncle to the Blessed Mary. It also adds he had a daughter, Anna, calling her 'consobrina' or cousin of Mary."

99 Ibid., page 23-36, the author presents proof concerning Joseph's profession as a worldwide international trader of tin in the British Isles. This very fact of tin trade between the British Isles and Phoenicia has been proven by many other authors along the history of Britain. At any rate, E. Raymond Capt adds to his discoveries valuable information he found in the works of British historians to successfully prove that Joseph was the man in charge of the Romans' mining affairs in Britain. Historical records show that the Phoenicians possessed a secret reservoir of tin in Britain ever since the 6th century BC; some say, even earlier. They owned mines in Cornwall, west of England, and all across Ireland and Gaul (France), to Marseilles. Strabo, the well known Greek geographer, historian, and philosopher, a contemporary to Joseph of Rameh, lived between 64/63 BC to 24/25 AD, believed that the tin trade with Britain was highly profitable to Phoenician traders. It seemed to him and many others before and after him that the Phoenicians completely controlled the tin trade while keeping their sources totally secret. Accordingly, they used to bring it home or trade it around both the Mediterranean and the Aegean Seas.

100 It is said that the word "Britain" comes from the term *Prutani*, given to the Celts by the Romans. We, however, believe that the Phoenicians gave to Britain the name *Bar-Tanak*, meaning the Land of Tin, *Britannica*. In his book, *The Phoenician Origin of Britons, Scots, and Anglo-Saxons*, page 52-59,

According to St. Jerome's (347 AD–420 AD) works of translations, most notably for his translation of the Bible, the Old and the New Testament, into Latin: the *Vulgate*, Joseph was given an official title by the Romans, "Nobilis Decurio." Such a title, of course, would not have been given unless Joseph was looked upon as "a Roman citizen of some standing." This title has been confirmed by Maelgwyn of Llandaff (c. 450 AD), Rabanus Maurus, (c. 776 AD–856 AD), and Cardinal Baronius (c. 1538 AD–1607 AD), four important sources we will come to mention in due time. At any rate, the Latin word "Decurion" is translated into "deacon," a term that could well describe an ecclesiastical officer in the Christian church and could also denote a town Councilor, a Senator[101], or a Minister, perhaps of mines, for the Roman Empire, having a direct access to Pilate himself. Such a strong connection with the Romans allowed Joseph to obtain the body of Jesus while on the Cross, although we know that according to the Roman laws, the crucified body must stay on the cross to disintegrate by itself[102]. Yet with all the determination he had, Joseph had the authority to bury him in his garden. Of course, Pilate knew Jesus was not a Jew.

Since we have proven that Maryām was from Kana and that her uncle was from Rameh, which is only nine kilometers away from Kana, we propose that Yāwsēp̄ was indeed a counselor, though not of the Sanhedrin[103]—as explained in the footnotes of the New Testament—but rather, an honorable one, of the Ashayas —a good and just man awaiting the Kingdom of God. And so, what came in the Canonical text concerning the Burial of Jesus, in all four gospels, Matthew (27:57-60), Mark (15:43-46), Luke (23:50-53), and John (19:38-42), is surely interesting. After Pilate conceded to the wish and demand of Joseph, who appealed to him

---

L.A Waddel believes the name for Britain or Britannia was originated from *Barati* (Barat), the Phoenician Goddess of the Sea. Barati, Barat, or Brut could be the ancient form for Beirut, the Lebanese capital.

101 He is Joseph the Senator, as per the work of Mâr Solomon, the Nestorian bishop or Metropolitan of al-Basrah (Iraq), in the 13th century AD, and whose work we will mention soon.

102 Markale, Jean, *L'enigme du Saint Graal*, page 81.

103 The Sanhedrin were the 71 elders that formed the supreme council of the Jewish people, mainly composed of scribes, lawyers, and men of experience and knowledge in the Jewish Law. It was the Sanhedrin that put Jesus on trial and condemned him to death. There is no way Joseph of Rameh could have been a member of the Sanhedrin, and the notion mentioned in Luke 23:51 that "He had not consented to their (the Sanhedrin's) decision and deed", surely proves he had not attended the Sanhedrin trial of Jesus due to the fact that he was Phoenician-Asayan, not Jewish.

secretly, "for fear of the Jews" (for fear he would be assassinated), he, Jesus' great uncle, the closest person of authority in the house to have responsibility for the young Jesus after the death of his father, took the body down from the Cross, wrapped it in a clean white linen cloth[104], and placed it inside a tomb—within a garden—which he had carved in a rock[105]. Joseph made sure that Jesus would rest in an unscathed new tomb. He then rolled a big stone to the door of the sepulcher to seal it before he departed.

The contribution of Joseph to Christianity and his strong relation to the New Faith does not end here, by burying his nephew, nor does his life end as a well known tin trader between the Great Phoenicia and Britain. There is indeed more about this enigmatic person in the many British tales that we will come to discover and learn about later.

After the Burial of Jesus Christ and his Glorious Resurrection after three days[106], he congregated with his Disciples for some time before he ultimately Ascended to Heaven, as Canonical texts and few other Apocryphal works, like that of Bartholomew[107], suggest. Then, the holy mission of spreading the Word of Jesus officially began[108], and thus, among the many nations and countries that received the Gospel was Britain, and it happened through Joseph of Ramah.

This historical fact—not legend—was not mentioned by the Apostles of the New Testament, though it was cited by a few writers shortly after, as some have cited Joseph as the leader of

---

104 Wrapping the body in a clean white-linen cloth is certainly an Ashayan method used in the rite of burial, similar to the Pythagorean style of burying the dead, not Jewish.

105 This burial procedure is unerringly a Canaano-Phoenician custom; they were reputed for making tombs in such a manner.

106 The Resurrection of Jesus after three days has been mentioned in both Matthew 27:63 and Mark 8:31. Yet, Jesus also spoke in allegory of the Temple of God (that he was) being destroyed and rebuilt after three days, and this is cited in Matthew 26:61, Mark 14:58, and John 2:19, "Jesus answered and said to them, Destroy this temple, and in three days I will raise it up." The concept of resurrection is not at all Jewish, but rather Canaano-Phoenician and Egyptian. The Resurrection of both Adon and Osiris are great examples of such belief, and the precise Resurrection of the Phoenix (the legendary bird and symbol of Phoenicia) from its ashes after three days is an ancient religious projection of the Resurrection of Jesus.

107 Other than his gospel we mentioned earlier, Bartholomew wrote what is known as *The Book Of The Resurrection of Christ*. It is hard to give a precise date when the book was produced, but suggestions are made from the 2nd (most favorably) to the 5th century AD.

108 Luke 10:3-5, "Go your way; behold, I send you out as lambs among wolves. Carry neither money bag, knapsack, nor sandals; and greet no one along the road. But whatever house you enter, first say, Peace to this house."

the Christian group who arrived in Britain. The earliest source we come to notice talking about the arrival of the first Christians (or Nazarenes) to the Land of Tin was Tertullian[109] (c. 155/160 AD–222/225 AD), who seemed to have ignored or most likely hidden the information that tells how the Gospel had arrived there before his time. However, in his book, *Adversus Judaeos* (*An Answer to the Jews*), considered to be Dogmatic, he officially suggests that Britain had indeed received and thus accepted the words of Jesus when he was still alive, though he gives the feeling that it reached Britain way before his time by using the words, "subjugated to Christ," a socio-religious transformation from the earliest Celtic tradition to Christianity that did not happen overnight. Tertullian wrote[110] on *The Question Whether Christ Be Come Taken Up*:

> ... For upon whom else have the universal nations believed, but upon the Christ who is already come? For whom have the nations believed—Parthians, Medes, Elamites, and they who inhabit Mesopotamia, Armenia, Phrygia, Cappadocia, and they who dwell in Pontus, and Asia, and Pamphylia, tarriers in Egypt, and inhabiters of the region of Africa which is beyond Cyrene, Romans and sojourners, yes, and in Jerusalem Jews, and all other nations; as, for instance, by this time, the varied races of the Gaetulians, and manifold confines of the Moors, all the limits of the Spains, and the diverse nations of the Gauls, and the haunts of the Britons—inaccessible to the Romans, but subjugated to Christ, and of the Sarmatians, and Dacians, and Germans, and Scythians, and of many remote nations, and of provinces and islands many, to us unknown, and which we can scarce enumerate?

Contemporary to Tertullian, Hippolytus Romanus[111] (c. 170 AD–236 AD) seems to have put the names to the unknown seventy Disciples mentioned in Luke[112], and whom Christ sent

---

109 Tertullian is the anglicized form of Quintus Septimius Florens Tertullianus. Called "the father of Latin Christianity" by some, and "the founder of Western theology" by others, Tertullian stood as one of the earliest Christian authors. From Carthage, he was most probably the first to produce a whole collection of Latin Christian literature and was considered a remarkable Christian apologist and a polemicist against heresy.
110 Tertullian, *Adversus Judaeos* (An Answer to the Jews), Chapter 7.
111 Hippolytus Romanus (of Rome), probably born in Rome, and most likely a disciple of Irenaeus was known to have been one of the most erudite theologians and historians of the Christian world.
112 Luke 10:1, "After these things the Lord appointed seventy others also, and sent them two by two before His face into every city and place where He Himself was about to go."

forth to spread his Word of Love and Peace. The seventy (or seventy two) Disciples or Apostles mentioned in Luke are cited as twelve (the traditional known twelve Disciples of Jesus) in both Mark[113] and Matthew[114]. Among the seventy Apostles of Hippolytus, appears the name of a certain Aristobulus[115], as Bishop of Britain (Aristobulus of Britannia), and most probably the first bishop in Roman Britain who preached and died there. However, there is no mention either of Joseph or of his connection to Britain in this list. It is very probable that Hippolytus only put the names of the Apostles who were *sent* by Jesus as suggested in Luke, whereas Joseph, the great uncle, who knew Britain well before the birth of Jesus, could have travelled *according to his own will* to Britain to preach the words of his Divine nephew.

Of course, some later inspired authors like the English biographer and novelist, Reverend Sabine Baring-Gould[116] (1834 AD–1924 AD), ascribed to Joseph of Arimathea the profession of a merchant of tin having a strong connection with Britain due to his business association with the tin mines of Cornwall. Reverend C.C. Dobson[117] and author Glynn S. Lewis[118], both even suggested that Joseph had actually brought Jesus with him in some of the travels he made to the Land of Tin, and that would most likely have happened during the mysterious lost age of Jesus between 12 and 33, where the New Testament fails to give accounts of his life during that period.

---

113 Mark 6:7, "And He called the twelve to [Himself], and began to send them out two [by] two, and gave them power over unclean spirits."
114 Matthew 10:1, "And when He had called His twelve disciples to [Him], He gave them power [over] unclean spirits, to cast them out, and to heal all kinds of sickness and all kinds of disease." And 10:5, "These twelve Jesus sent out and commanded them ..."
115 Aristobulus may be mentioned in the New Testament in the Epistle to the Romans 16:10, "... Greet those who are of the [household] of Aristobulus." However, the Aristobulus mentioned by Hippolytus may mean Aristobulus IV, son of Herod the Great, and Prince of Judea from 31 BC to 7 BC. Yet, Orthodox tradition believes he was the brother of the Apostle Barnabas, a companion of St. Paul on his journeys, while Catholic tradition identifies him with Zebedee, the father of James and John as per the New Testament.
116 Baring-Gould, Sabine, *A Book of Cornwall.*
117 Dobson, C.C., *Did Our Lord Visit Britain as They Say in Cornwall and Somerset?*
118 Lewis, Glynn S., *Did Jesus Come to Britain? An Investigation into the Traditions That Christ Visited Cornwall and Somerset.*

At any rate, when Hippolytus Romanus, Hieromartyr Dorotheus[119] (c. 255 AD–362 AD), and St. Dimitri of Rostov[120] (17th century AD), all failed to mention Yawsēp̄ of Ramah in their lists of Apostles, St. John Chrysostom[121] (c. 347 AD–407 AD) succeeded in mentioning him as one of the Seventy Apostles, perhaps the first to convey that information, followed by Mâr Solomon (13th century AD), who offered a list of seventy Disciples as well, and proposed the name of Joseph the Senator in the first selection of Apostles, after the traditional twelve we already know, along with Aristobulus in the last selection of Disciples, as substitutes of some who were rejected because of their denial of Jesus' divinity. Yet, the Bishop of Basra did not link either Joseph the Senator or Aristobulus to Britain. Instead, he wrote[122] that Joseph taught in Galilee and Decapolis and was buried in his town of Ramah, whereas Aristobulus taught in Isauria (Asia Minor) where he died and was buried.

In addition to Tertullian, Hippolytus, and later in time, Mâr Solomon, came Eusebius of Caesarea[123] (c. 260/263–339/340 AD), whom we have mentioned a few times earlier, to confirm once more that the Disciples of Christ had actually introduced the Gospel to Britain and most certainly before his time. Eusebius wrote[124]:

... But to preach to all the Name of Jesus, to teach about His marvellous deeds in country and town, that some of them should take possession of the Roman Empire, and the Queen of Cities itself, and others the Persian, others the Armenian, that others should go to the Parthian race, and yet others to the Scythian, that some already should have reached the very ends of the world, should have reached the land of the Indians, and some have crossed the Ocean and reached the Isles of Britain ...

---

119 St. Dorotheus, a knowledgeable priest of Antioch, Bishop of Tyre, and teacher of the Church historian Eusebius of Caesarea. He is traditionally credited with an *Acts of the Seventy Apostles*, which some scholars suggest it was the same work as the lost Gospel of the Seventy.

120 St. Demetrius of Rostov, a great Russian hierarch, preacher, author, and ascetic, is said to have compiled the great collection of the *Lives of the Saints* and proposed a Canon that has been widely accepted by the Orthodox Church.

121 St. John Chrysostom, Patriarch of Constantinople.

122 Solomon, Mâr, *The Book of the Bee.*

123 Eusebius of Caesarea stood in fact as one of the earliest and broadest of the Roman Church historians, an exegete and polemicist.

124 Eusebius, *Demonstratio Evangelica*, Book 3, Chapter 5.

After them, should we follow the chronology of time, appeared Saint Hilary of Poitiers[125] (c. 300 AD–368/376 AD), who seemed to have also mentioned the arrivals of the Apostles to Britain bringing the Gospel with them and building churches. Almost a hundred years later, an additional and important passage comes to us to affirm even stronger the undoubtedly established connection that firmly ties Joseph to Britain and the complete story of the Holy Grail. It was written by Maelgwyn of Llandaff, sometime around 450 AD, and it says:

> ... *Joseph ab Arimathea nobilis decurio in insula Avallonia cum xi. Sociis suis somnum cepit perpetuum et jacet in meridiano angulo lineae bifurcate Oratorii Adorandae Virginis. Habit enim secum duovascula argentea alba cruore et sudore magni prophetae Jesu perimpleta.*
>
> ... Joseph of Arimathea, the noble decurion, received his everlasting rest with his eleven associates in the Isle of Avalon. He lies in the southern angle of the bifurcated line of the Oratorium of the Adorable Virgin. He has with him the two white vessels of silver which were filled with the blood and the sweat of the great prophet Jesus.

There is no doubt about Joseph of Rameh being one of the central (twelve and seventy) Apostles who preached the words of Jesus in the surrounding regions, yet the doubts of whether Joseph arrived, preached, and taught[126] in Britain or not, has

---

125 Pagan by birth, St. Hilary received a good education and knowledge of Greek thanks to his distinctive parents, and later studied the Old and New Testaments, something that made him convert form Neo-Platonism into Christianity; he was then baptized. His knowledge made him a Doctor of the Church and his faith led him to become the Bishop of Poitiers.

126 The classical history of Christianity suggests that Christian missionaries arrived in Britain sometime in the 6th century AD. However, the tradition in Britain proposes another view, which is related directly to Joseph of Ramah and his arrival to the Land of Tin as early as 37 AD or as late as 63 AD where he established seminaries and prepared missionaries. We would certainly suggest the years 35 AD to 37 AD, and if this is true, then it would be noticed that the second Christian Church would then be in Britain and not in Rome because the first was actually in Galilee and Phoenicia. The Church in Rome could have been founded sometime during the reign of Claudius (c. 41AD–54 AD), when he ordered all the Jews to leave Rome (Acts 18:2). By this time, congregations of Gentile Christians must have flourished, for early Christianity rapidly grew apart from Judaism (because it was not related to Judaism) in the first two centuries and installed itself as a mainly Gentile religion in the Roman Empire. No wonder why historical records show that Queen Elizabeth I mentioned Joseph's missionary in England when she sent a reply to the Roman Catholic bishops in 1559 telling them that the Church

been eliminated once again by the Frankish Benedictine monk, Rabanus Maurus[127] (c. 780 AD–856 AD). Rhabanus states in his manuscript, *Life of Mary Magdalene*[128], that Joseph of Arimathea was *sent* to Britain and didn't travel all by himself but was accompanied by some followers[129] of Jesus, first to France, most probably in Marseilles, where Mary Magdalene stayed to preach[130], while he, Joseph, continued his journey, as far as Cornwall in Britain, and finished his life as a minister of religion in Glastonbury.

What is strikingly important in the manuscript is the description of the voyage and the route Joseph and his companions took to Britain, and which is definitely a Phoenician trade route to Britain, as described by the known Greek historian, Diodorus Siculus, author of many historical works between 60 BC and 30 BC. Rhabanus wrote:

---

of England (the original Christian Church) pre-dated the Roman Church in England.

127 Also known as Rhabanus, he was a distinguished theologian and Archbishop of Mainz (Germany).

128 The earliest authentic manuscript of the Maurus text is kept in the Bodleian Library of Oxford University in London.

129 According to Rabanus, the twelve followers who escorted Joseph were: Mary and Martha (the two Bethany sisters), Lazarus (whom Jesus raised from the dead), St. Eutropius, St. Salome (disciple of Jesus), St. Cleon, St. Saturnius, St. Mary Magdalen (the favorite female disciple of Jesus), Marcella (the maid of the Bethany sisters), St. Maxium or Maximin, St. Martial, and St. Trophimus or Restitutus.

130 Although the French tradition—supported by British tales—relates the arrival of Mary Magdalene in Marseilles, in the Viennoise province of the Gauls, in 35 AD, where she stayed and preached the Gospel, converting the whole of Provence, for being the first of all the Apostles to bear witness to the Glorious Resurrection of Jesus Christ, the Catholic Roman Church officially denies that. The classical Church tradition suggests instead that Mary arrived and preached in Rome before both Peter (who arrived in c. 44 AD), and Paul (who wrote an epistle to the Romans in c. 55 AD), and that she began preaching in Rome sometime in the thirties AD until the sixties AD, before moving to Ephesus, the ancient Greek city, on the west coast of Asia Minor, in nowadays Turkey (*Efes* in Turkish) where she died in c. 72 AD. Yet, there is evidence of the existence of Mary Magadene's remaining parts of her body (skull and leg) in a cave on a hill by the city of Marseilles, known as La Sainte-Baume (the Holy Cave), where it is said she lived alone for thirty years before she died, probably c. 72 AD; whereas her left hand is kept, since 1766 AD, in the Monastery of Simonos Petra (meaning in Greek, "Simon's Rock"), belonging to the Eastern Christian Orthodox religious community, in the monastic state of Mount Athos in Greece.

... Leaving the shores of Asia and favoured by an east wind, they went round about, down the Tyrrhenian Sea[131], between Europe[132] and Africa[133], leaving the city of Rome and all the land to the right. Then happily turning their course to the right, they came near to the city of Marseilles[134], in the Viennoise province of the Gauls[135], where the river Rhône is received by the sea. There, having called upon God, the great King of all the world, they parted; each company going to the province where the Holy Spirit directed them; presently preaching everywhere ...

---

131 It is traditionally believed that the Tyrrhenian Sea, which is part of the Mediterranean Sea off the western coast of Italy with main ports like that of Rome and others, was named after Prince Tyrrhenus who was the leader of the Etruscans, known as being emigrants from Lydia. However, L.A. Waddell, in his book, *The Phoenician Origin of Britons, Scots, and Anglo-Saxons*, page 159, believes that the settlement of the Trojans on the shores of the Tyrrhenian Sea, outside the Pillars of Hercules, was undoubtedly Gades, traditionally visited by Hercules and containing one of his most famous Phoenician Temples (probably that of Melkhart, the Phoenician God, copied as Hercules by the Greeks). It was established as a colony by Phoenicians of Tyre, hence the name, Tyrrh-enian Sea. The Tyrrh-eni or Tyrians had very likely founded it as a halfway house to the tin mines of Cornwall.

132 The name of the European Continent, *Europe*, derives undoubtedly from *Europa*, the daughter of Agenor, King of Tyre, whom Herodotus, the famous Greek historian, estimates lived sometime before the year 2000 BC. Legends says that her brother Kadmus went searching for her in Greece after she was kidnapped by Zeus, the Most High God of the Grecian world. During his many years of search, Kadmus introduced the Phoenician Alphabet (the Spoken Phonetic Alphabet invented by Thor, the Geblite) to the Greeks, and founded many cities; the most famous about them were Thebes and the Acropolis, which was originally named Kadmeia in his honor.

133 The land of the black-skinned people, *Africa*, was known to the Phoenicians ever since they set sails across the Mediterranean Sea. Long before the time of Hamelkon (Himilkon), the famous Phoenician sailor, and his travels to Africa, Elissa, the Tyrian Princess, known as Dido by the Romans, had sailed towards the black continent, built the city of Carthage on the coast of Tunisia, and became its Queen, sometime around the year 814 BC. Carthage, or *Kart-Hadasht*, was known in Phoenicia as the *new city* in order to distinguish it from an older Phoenician outpost, namely, Utica.

134 The establishment of the Port of Marseilles in France was for long credited to the Phocaeans, a people of Asia Minor, of the Ionic Civilization, and the Port Massilia was called as such from the 6th century BC. However, we believe that the Phoenicians founded it nearly at that time and called it *Marsa-Êl*, which means the *Docking of the Phoenician Ships of Êl!* This is absolutely true since it was one of their many trading posts and ports where their ships docked. Marsa-Êl stood as a station on their route towards Britain.

135 The date of the arrival to the Vienoise province of the Gauls (France) is estimated to be around the year 35 AD.

In fact, the list of writers who throughout the ancient history of Britain mentioned the arrival of Joseph to Britain is long. The well-known British Historian, William of Malmesbury (12th century AD) wrote[136] that Philip the Apostle sent twelve Christian disciples to Britain, one of whom was Joseph of Arimathea who seemed to have been a dear friend to the Apostle. There, the historian claims, they founded the Glastonbury Abbey, associated specifically with Joseph later on in British literature and culture. Another important account of the voyage made by Joseph of Arimathea, Lazarus, Mary Magdalene, Martha, Marcella, and a few others, comes in a clear passage from the Italian Cardinal Caesar Baronius[137] (c. 1538 AD–1607 AD) in what was to be considered as events happening under the year 35 AD of Jesus Christ. This is what he wrote[138] in Latin:

Hac ipsa dispersione Ananias discipulus profectus Damascum, collegit Ecclesiam. Insuper colligere possumus, hoc quoque tempore Lazarum, Mariam Magdalenam, Martham, et Marcellam pedissequam, in quos Judaei majori odio exardescebant, non tantum Hierosolymis pulsos esse, sed una cum Maximino discipulo, navi absque remigio impositos, in certum periculum mari fuisse creditos; quos divina providentia Massiliam tradunt appulisse, comitemque ferunt ejusdem discriminis Josephum ab Arimathaea nobilem decurionem, quem tradunt ex Gallia in Britanniam navigasse, illicque post praedicatum Evangelium diem clausisse extremum.

English Translation of the British Library in London:

In this dispersion, Ananias, having set out from Damascus gathered together a company of believers. At the same time, as one can ascertain, Lazarus, Mary Magdalene, Martha and Marcella whom the Jews regarded with great hatred, were not exactly driven away from Jerusalem but, together with the disciple Maximinus, were placed in a boat without oars and were believed to have perished in dangerous seas. By Divine providence they are said to have been driven to Marseilles. Taking with them a friend, Joseph of Arimathea, a noble

---

136 William of Malmesbury, *Chronicle of the English Kings.*
137 Caesar Baronius, the Vatican Librarian (Curator of the Vatican Library) and one of the well known ecclesiastical historian and a Cardinal.
138 Baronius, Caesar, *Annales Ecclesiatici*, Volume 1, Paragraph 5 of Jesu Christi Annus 35.

decurion, they are said to have travelled from Gaul to Britain and there he proclaimed the gospel till his last day ...

Again, the story of Joseph of Rameh does not actually end here. We know for sure he was a wealthy Phoenician merchant of tin, the great uncle of Jesus, who after the Death and Resurrection of Christ led a group of Christian disciples all the way to France and Britain where they parted to preach the world about the Word of God. Yet, there is an additional important factor to cite as per now; it is the Holy Grail. It seems that according to the semi-legend, Joseph was given the responsibility to keep the Holy Grail protected at all cost. This part of Joseph's secret life, as a secret disciple of Jesus, as per John, was fundamentally developed upon stories from the *Acts of Pilate*[139], elaborated by the French poet of the late 12th century and early 13th century AD, Robert de Boron (Bouron or Beron), author of the two famous poems, *Joseph d'Arimathe* and *Merlin*. In both Boron's *Joseph d'Arimathe*, and the *Acts of Pilate*, Joseph is pictured as having been jailed (by the Jewish elders), but it appears that the power of the Grail is what kept him safe during his confinement. Upon his release (certainly, by Pilate), he began forming his group and preparing for the trip towards France and Britain, taking the Holy Grail with him to his last destination. In Britain, Yāwsēp̄ stood as the first Christian holy man; he died there around the year 82 AD[140], where—according to Cressy, the Benedictine Monk and historian—a Latin inscription on his tombstones says, "After I had buried the Christ, I came to the Isles of the West; I taught; I entered into my rest."

---

139 According to the *Catholic Encyclopedia*, the Latin *Acta Pilati*, also called the *Gospel of Pilate*, is a falsely official document attributed to Pontius Pilate. In it, he reports about events occurring in Judea to Emperor Tiberius, and refers to the miracles of Jesus and his crucifixion. However, this text is often regarded as an appendix to both medieval works, the *Gospel of Nicodemus* and *The Narrative of Joseph*. It seems, however, that the gospel itself was cited in the works of many early Church historians like Irenaeus, Tertullian, Hippolytus, and Eusebius, who found themselves having total liberty to add certain details that could not be found in the Canonical tests.

140 If we presume that Joseph, the uncle of Maryām (who was 16 years old as per the Gospel of James) was in his thirties, as logical calculation would suggest, when she delivered Jesus, and died at 82 AD, he would then be more than 112 years of age, and this is almost impossible, without even adding the 6 to 4 years BC some historians and Biblical scholars have placed the birth date of Jesus. We therefore suggest that the alternative date mentioned for his arrival to Britain, 63 AD, could be in fact the date of his death, perhaps a few years before, and in that case, he would be in his early nineties or late eighties, and this is quite reasonable.

In fact, the suggestion that this mysterious man was the first minister of the Christian religion all over the Land of Tin is indeed based on solid ground addressed by many British tales recounting often similar stories that upon his arrival Joseph founded Christianity and was known to have built a monastery at Glastonbury in the county of Somerset, in southwest England, and hid the Holy Grail there. Glastonbury could well be identified with the Island of Avalon[141], mentioned in the Arthurian semi-legend. Tradition relates that the Knights of the Round Table had secretly quested for the Holy Grail: the Sacred Cup used by Jesus Christ at the Last Supper. It was the same Grail that Joseph of Arimathea—the Christian adept—had filled with the blood of Jesus, bleeding on the Cross, and had kept with him until he found a secret place to keep it safe in the Abbey he built at Glastonbury, most probably on the ruins of a Celtic temple from as early as the 4th century BC. As a result, the Celtic tradition coordinated primarily with Christian religion without any problems, and that most probably is due to the close contact Joseph had made with British Royalty; namely Kings Beli and others[142]. The Grail, as per the tradition, had passed down, from one generation to another in Joseph's family, who guarded it, being the true Guardians of the Grail, until the rise of King Arthur and the coming of Parsifal (Percival or Perceval) and the accounts of his adventures, mentioned by authors like the 12th century French poet, Chrétien de Troyes[143] (*Perceval, le Conte du Graal*), the German knight and poet, Wolfram von Eschenbach (*Parzival*), the English writer, Sir Thomas Malory (*Le Morte d'Arthur*), and surely, the now lost piece of poetry of *Perceval* of Robert de Boron. Our vivid memory will always trigger names such as King Arthur,

---

141 *Les vaus d'Avaron* of Robert de Boron, in French, are the valleys of Avaron in the west, also known as the Vale of Avalon.

142 It is suggested that Joseph, who was a rich merchant, having a fleet of ships, and trading tin from the mines of Cornwall in Britain to Phoenicia and perhaps to other places for the Roman Empire, made acquaintance with all the British kings, Beli, Lud, Llyr and Arviragus, who offered him a huge tract of land to settle down with his companions.

143 There is a suggestion that Chrétien de Troyes (Christian of Troyes) may have named himself as such perhaps in opposition to Rashi of Troyes, known as Solomon Ben Isaac, one of the most famous Jewish sages of France, and founder of a rabbinical Kabalistic school based on the Talmud. This could be true since Chrétien de Troyes focused on the quest for the Grail and the Knights of the Round Table, the true "Guardians of the Grail," in contrast to Rashi, the secret founder of the Templars, sometime before the year 1095 AD, and which was formed and led officially between 1114 AD and 1118 AD by Hughes, the Count of Champagne and eight other French from Troyes.

Lancelot, Merlin, Parsifal, and a few others, every time the Knights of the Round Table and their quest for the Holy Grail are mentioned. Their semi-legend has remained one of the most famous fables in recorded history. First mentioned, as early as the 6th century AD, the story has evolved progressively into its permanent popular form sometime between the 12th and 15th century AD.

His Brothers and Sisters

This issue, in particular, is delicately treated herein due to the fact that some respected Biblical scholars have suggested that Jesus actually had brothers and sisters. Most probably, the indication first came from the reading of the first Canonical text of Matthew (1:24-25), "Then Joseph, being aroused from sleep, did as the angel of the Lord commanded him and took to him his wife, and did not know her till she had brought forth her firstborn Son. And he called His name JESUS." The use of the term, "she had brought forth her firstborn son," implies that she, Maryām, had actually delivered other children (boys and girls) after Jesus, and a similar term also appears in Luke[144]. Yet, some scholars believe that such use of the term "firstborn" does not imply what it came before, or, that Jesus came before other children, therefore, Jesus was in fact the only begotten son of Maryām, and the term must have been originally written as follows, "she had brought forth a Son."

At any rate, should we consider the proposition that Jesus actually had brothers and sisters, the first candidates to be suspected as such are four of his main Disciples mentioned in both Gospels of Matthew and Mark. In Matthew (13:55-56), we read, "Is not this the carpenter's son? is not his mother called Mary? and his brethren, James, and Joses, and Simon, and Judas? And his sisters, are they not all with us? Whence then hath this [man] all these things?"

Although Matthew called Jesus the carpenter's son, Mark, on the other hand, describes him as the Carpenter himself, but we have dealt with this issue before in this chapter. Our concern here lies in the pretty obvious similarity between both Matthew and Mark regarding Jesus' supposed brothers and sisters, for we read from Mark (6:3), "Is not this the carpenter, the son of Mary, the

---

144 Luke 2:7, "And she brought forth her firstborn Son, and wrapped Him in swaddling cloths, and laid Him in a manger, because there was no room for them in the inn."

brother of James, and Joses, and of Juda, and Simon? and are not his sisters here with us? And they were offended at him."

Neither Apostle mentioned Jesus' sisters by names. We wonder: Why? If indeed Jesus, their inspiring spiritual leader, had sisters among them they would have at least mentioned their names the same way they cited the names of Mary Magdalene, Martha, Salome, etc., as the Lord's Disciples. The word "sisters" here is totally vague and would not in any way or form prove that Jesus had flesh and blood sisters; it would rather suggest that its use in the New Testament is only based on the concept of "sisters in faith and belief," and nothing more than that.

The dilemma stood strong in a way, however, concerning his brothers, but not for long, for the answer is already here in front of our eyes. It is in the Gospel according to Matthew, Mark, and Luke that we find the key that solves this mystery. We read in Matthew (27:56), "... among whom were Mary Magdalene, Mary the mother of James and Joses, and the mother of Zebedee's sons." The similarity concerning Mary, the mother of James and Joses, appears in Mark (15:40-41)[145], "There were also women looking on from afar, among whom were Mary Magdalene, Mary the mother of James the Less and of Joses, and Salome, who also followed Him and ministered to Him when He was in Galilee, and many other women who came up with Him to Jerusalem." It is also shown in Luke (24:10), "It was Mary Magdalene, Joanna, Mary [the mother] of James, and the other [women] with them, who told these things to the apostles."

Let us analyze the structure of the first two quotations. When we read in Matthew, "is not his mother called Mary?" or in Mark, "the son of Mary," we feel an immediate confirmation in the style of writing that Yāwshu and Maryām are connected as son and mother. Whereas when we read in Matthew, "and his brethren, James, and Joses, and Simon, and Judas?" or in Mark, "the brother of James, and Joses, and of Juda, and Simon," we don't feel that his so-called "brothers" are in a direct lineage to him through his mother, especially since nowhere in the two quotations do we find a solid confirmation that Mary is indeed the mother of James, Joses, Juda, and Simon.

Now, let us compare these first two quotations with the second three quotations of Matthew, Mark, and Luke. How coincidental it is to find that the first order of the two quotations mention Mary, the mother of Jesus, and his connection to his *alleged* brothers,

---

145 Another resembling citation from Mark 16:1, "Now when the Sabbath was past, Mary Magdalene, Mary [the mother] of James, and Salome bought spices, that they might come and anoint Him."

cited in the following order, James, Joses, Juda and Simon; whereas the second order of the three quotations suggest a woman, a different woman, also by the name of Mary (another Maryām), as being the mother of James the Less and Joses. How can we not pay attention to the arrangement of names in all five quotations: James and then Joses? It sounds bizarre and suspicious, and maybe, after all, this Mary is in fact, the mother of James, Joses, Juda, and Simon.

This may lead us to wonder: Who was that mysterious woman also named Mary? We have seen before that Maryām is the original Aramaic form for Mary, and it was a very common name for females in the land of Canaan-Phoenicia, a land filled with people reputed to have a great connection with the sea, hence, the composed name of "Mort-Yām" or "Mart-Yam" (Maryām), meaning, "Lady of the Sea." Conclusively though, for women to have this name in particular, should not be regarded as a mystery but a fact within the culture of the people of ancient Lebanon.

Our search in the New Testament for that distinct Mary has been indeed fruitful, for in fact, she is clearly shown as none other but Maryām's (the Virgin Lady's) sister, and this is evident in John (19:25), "Now there stood by the cross of Jesus His mother, and His mother's sister, Mary the [wife] of Clopas[146], and Mary Magdalene."

If what came from John is a true historical fact, as it sounds to be, then we can definitely determine that Mary, the mother of James, Joses, (Juda, and Simon), is indeed Jesus' aunt. (Note: We could have mentioned that relation in the previous section of Jesus' great aunts and great uncles, but the connection made here suits well the flow of thoughts we've been meticulously following in the writing of this book.) Hence, James, Joses, Juda, and Simon, are not to be considered Jesus' brothers, but rather, his cousins, who followed him as his closest Disciples (later, Apostles) ever since he began preaching in Galilee and the neighboring regions.

However, there are a couple quotations in John that appear a bit suspicious regarding this particular issue, which gives the impression that John made a certain distinction between the

---

146 Sometimes Mary the wife of Clopas (Klôpas or Cleophas) is described as the wife of Alphaeus (Alphaios or Alphee). Although the two names seem to have been intended to indicate the same person, they are in fact not identical on an etymological basis. The name *Alphaeus* is a Greek reproduction of the Aramaic name *Alphaï*, whereas *Cleophas* is a Greek shortened form of *Kleopatros*. Clopas has been identified as the younger brother of Joseph the betrothed to the Virgin Lady Maryām, and that makes him the uncle (from the father's side) of Yāwshu (Yeshu).

brothers of Jesus and his Disciples. We read in John (2:12)[147], "After this He went down to Capernaum, He, His mother, His brothers, and His disciples; and they did not stay there many days." Thorough investigation into this prompting matter found a brief critical situation of—kind of adopting—Renan's point of view that, and I quote, "The expression 'brother of the Lord' evidently constituted, in the primitive Church, a kind of order similar to that of the apostles."[148] In disagreement with Renan on the idea that Jesus had actual real brothers (unknown by names) who first opposed him, did not believe in him[149], and became like their mother—only important in Christianity after his death[150], we, however, incline to believe that the term "brothers" used here by John, may in truth mean that they are his Apostles who could have constituted a higher degree, not on the socio-intellectual basis but rather on the missionary work, which could have differed from that of the Disciples in the "inner circle" of Jesus.

At any rate, to call someone a brother does not mean he is a flesh and blood brother. It is still a way of talking here in Lebanon and most likely in many other neighboring countries—an old Hamitic and later Semitic way of calling someone by the Aramaic term *Akh* or the current Lebanese term, *Khayi*, which means "brother" or "my brother," respectively. Therefore, calling someone a brother could be for one of the three following reasons: a friend, mainly a close friend, and could designate a relative, such a cousin; someone associated with the one who is calling him in a religious group or a social community; a brother in blood.

And this is precisely what was meant when citing the brothers and sisters of Jesus in the Church New Testament. In fact, the riddle is found in the words of Jesus himself, for we read in Mark (3:31-35):

Then His brothers and His mother came, and standing outside they sent to Him, calling Him. And a multitude was sitting

147 We will also find another reference to his brothers as if different from his disciples in John 7:3, "His brothers therefore said to Him, Depart from here and go into Judea, that Your disciples also may see the works that You are doing."
148 Renan, Ernest, *Vie de Jésus*, page 126 (fn.20). Renan backs up his theory while inviting his readers to have a look at Galatians 1:19, "But I saw none of the other apostles except James, the Lord's brother." And at the following verse, 1Corinthians 9:5, "Have we not power to lead about a sister, a wife, as well as other apostles, and [as] the brethren of the Lord, and Cephas?"
149 John 7:5, "For even His brothers did not believe in Him."
150 Renan, Ernest, *Vie de Jésus*, page 126. Renan backs it up with Acts 1:14, "These all continued with one accord in prayer and supplication, with the women and Mary the mother of Jesus, and with His brothers."

around Him; and they said to Him, Look, Your mother and Your brothers are outside seeking You. But He answered them, saying, Who is My mother, or My brothers? And He looked around in a circle at those who sat about Him, and said, Here are My mother and My brothers! For whoever does the will of God is My brother and My sister and mother.

It is absolutely clear also to find out what he really meant in Luke[151]; yet, it is more specific in Matthew[152] that what Jesus meant by "Mother, Brothers and Sisters" were in fact his Apostles, in the first order, and Disciples, in the second.

His Cousins

Treating with the issue of cousins, as for now, we can be sure about his four first cousins or simply cousins, sons of Mary, James (known also by Jacob), who after the Crucifixion and Resurrection of Jesus, attained some socio-religious status of great significance in the formation years of the new religion, Christianity, and became in fact the first Bishop of Jerusalem. James had three brothers: Joses (also written as Joseph), Juda (also known as Jude), and Simon, the third Bishop of Jerusalem after his father, Alphaï (or Klôpas) who seemed to have been the second Bishop of the Holy City.

Along with these four, came the well known cousin, John the Baptist. If Élishbeth was the great aunt of Jesus as we have seen before, John the Baptist would then be his great cousin or first cousin once removed, and if indeed she was his mother's cousin as cited in Luke and James, then John would be his second cousin.

John, who died ferociously before Jesus, having his head cut off by Herod, undoubtedly played one of the most important roles at the beginning of Christianity[153]. It was the Nazarene Yāwhanan,

---

151 Luke 8:19-21, "... But He answered and said to them, My mother and My brothers are these who hear the word of God and do it."

152 Matthew 12:46-50, "While He was still talking to the multitudes, behold, His mother and brothers stood outside, seeking to speak with Him. Then one said to Him, Look, Your mother and Your brothers are standing outside, seeking to speak with You. But He answered and said to the one who told Him, Who is My mother and who are My brothers? And He stretched out His hand toward His disciples and said, Here are My mother and My brothers! For whoever does the will of My Father in heaven is My brother and sister and mother."

153 Luke 7:26-27, "But what did you go out to see? A prophet? Yes, I say to you, and more than a prophet. This is [he] of whom it is written: Behold, I send My messenger before Your face, Who will prepare Your way before You."

who baptized Yāwshu (Iesous) by the River Jordan[154], and that very precise moment was indeed the starting point of Jesus' public ministry as the Meshiha and Healer of the sins of the world, for he had been for some time under secret preparation by the Ashayas (Asayas), the Galilean-Phoenician religious group that has been waiting for the incarnation of the Most High God, Ēl inside a pure body of a child born from a virgin, Immanu-Ēl.

To be more illustrative, so as to say, regarding the "family of Jesus," please check Table 1 in the Appendix.

---

154 H.P. Blavatsky, in her famous theosophical work, *Isis Unveiled*, Volume II, page 550 (fn.6), refers to the Jordan being called Zacchar, and curiously wonders how the father of John the Baptist, the Prophet of Jordan (Zacchar) has been called Zacchar-ias.

Part II

The Christian Son of Man

His Birthplace, Historicity, and His Disciples

Chapter 4

The Geographical Region: Mt. Carmel & Bet-Lahem of Galilee

It is traditionally believed that Jesus' ministry did not only cover Judea, but also Samaria, Galilee, and Phoenicia. In fact, it started from Galilee-Phoenicia to cover Judea and Samaria. We have found many Church New Testament references relating Jesus to the Lebanese villages of Sidon and Tyre. It seems he much too often retreated to these two Lebanese villages after preaching in Jerusalem, as if he used to find shelter in ancient Lebanon and Galilee, away from the persecutor Jews. However, after many years of research, we found what could be the truth itself. His retreat was indeed backwards, to his homeland.

In some of the New Testament versions like the New International Version (NIV) and English Standard Version (ESV), we read from Matthew (15:21), "And Jesus went out from there and withdrew to the district of Tyre and Sidon." Was it by mere coincidence that we all just read the word "withdrew"? In all the dictionaries of the world, the meaning of "withdrew to" explains one thing—a retreat to a territory one belongs to (and where one always feels safe, particularly, from the enemy's attacks). This incident is said to have happened in Galilee where Jesus had to confront Pharisees and Scribes coming from Jerusalem. We, however, believe this encounter truly happened somewhere in Jerusalem.

Following the same logic here, another significant issue appears in Matthew (10:5-6), when we clearly read the following, "Jesus sent these twelve out, and commanded them, saying, don't go among the Gentiles, and don't enter into any city of the Samaritans. Rather, go to the lost sheep of the house of Israel." As a matter of fact, the words of Yāwshu herein reveal two important issues:

First, it shows that the land where Jesus and his disciples ministered was divided into three areas. There was the land of the Gentiles, known as Galilee of the Nations, geographically and culturally attached to Phoenicia[155]; the other was Samaria, where the Samaritans lived; and the third was called "the house of Israel," known as Judea, where the Jews lived.

Second, it shows that the people of Galilee, Phoenicia, and Samaria did not actually need preaching, because the Galilean-Phoenicians believed Yāwshu (*Iesous*) to be the Phoenician-Galilean Meshiha (Christ) they expected and had been waiting for. It appeared also that the Samaritans believed in his words and the words of his Disciples and had received their baptisms, as mentioned in Acts[156]. Even Simon Magus, the most famous non-Christian Gnostic of Samaria, was baptized by Philip, also cited in Acts[157]. Only the people living in Judea did not believe in him, thus they were the ones that needed preaching.

The geographical area of Galilee of the Nations seemed to be included within the territory of Phoenicia at the time of Jesus, and is separated from both Samaria and Judea as clearly shown in Map 1 in the Appendix at the end of the book. The map undoubtedly identifies the four places and differentiates them in two colors: the yellow is for Judea and Samaria; the red-yellow is for Galilee and Phoenicia.

This geographical fact has been asserted by Reverend Martin the Jesuit in his book, *History of Lebanon*, the Arabic translation (second edition). He wrote[158] that the Mountains of Galilee may appear as if they were not part of Lebanon, where in reality they were a continuation of its natural mountainous chain and that the upper Galilee region had not been conquered and occupied by the Hebrews as a place to inhabit[159], and hence it was called by the Old and the New Testament "Galilee of the Nations" or "of the Gentiles."[160] "Therefore, it is rightful for us," the Jesuit Father

---

155 The cultural attachment of Galilee to Phoenicia, and especially to Sidon and Tyre, was greatly felt on the socio-religious basis, as we shall shortly see.
156 Acts 8:5-8, "Then Philip went down to the city of Samaria and preached Christ to them. And the multitudes with one accord heeded the things spoken by Philip, hearing and seeing the miracles which he did. For unclean spirits, crying with a loud voice, came out of many who were possessed; and many who were paralyzed and lame were healed. And there was great joy in that city."
157 Acts 8:13, "Then Simon himself also believed; and when he was baptized he continued with Philip, and was amazed, seeing the miracles and signs which were done."
158 The Jesuit, Martin Rev., *History of Lebanon*—تاريخ لبنان , page 13.
159 We will definitely explain why the Jews had not been in Galilee ever since the conquest of the Maccabees ended, and later on at the time of Jesus, in the next chapter.
160 Isaiah 9:1; 1Macabees 5:15; Matthew 4:15.

continues, "to place Galilee inside the geographical territory of Lebanon."

It is easy for ancient and new geographers to confirm without any doubt that the western borders of ancient Lebanon have always been the Mediterranean Basin, which at a certain point of history was nothing but a Phoenician lake. They also feel safe believing and determining that the eastern borders were the eastern mountain chain; yet, recorded history shows that Canaano-Phoenicians also existed in the inland of what is now known as Syria, reaching as far as Damascus. Some maps, like the cover map, affirm this fact. This is one of the moving borders of the land of ancient Lebanon (Canaan-Phoenicia), changed by time and invasions, as is the case for both the southern and the northern borders as well.

This is precisely what has been suggested and proven by one of the leading Lebanese archeologists and historians, Dr. Youssef Hourany. Author of many books on the history of the Phoenicians, which confirmed his credibility as a specialist in the field, Hourany explained in his valuable book[161], written sometime around the year 1972, in Arabic, that Lebanon's natural geographical borders have not always been the same but were affected by historical changes. These independent continuous changes in historical feedback lead us to clearly observe that Lebanon's southern borders have stretched out, from time to time, to reach Mt. Carmel and even beyond to modern day Israel (south coastal part of the Land of Canaan), whereas its northern borders extended to touch the fields of Kilikya[162] in modern day Turkey (south coastal region of Asia Minor).

Hourany believes that the ever-changing geographical borders of Lebanon are, in fact, due to external factors. These factors imposed a certain momentum on the behavior and emotions of his vivid society, which found shelter in the inside core of Lebanon— every time the neighboring and other greedy intruders raided the borders—and extended while spreading out once again in time of peace when feeling secured. The observations of Dr. Hourany are undoubtedly based on facts and historical records, and we shall surely note that these external factors are specifically bound to

---

161 Hourany, Youssef, *Lebanon in the Value of its History / Phoenician Era—* لبنان في قيم تاريخه / العهد الفينيقي , page 26.

162 The fields of Kilikya seem to have extended along the Mediterranean coast, facing the Island of Cyprus. Eastward from Pamphylia to the Amanus Mountains, they are separated from Syria; whereas northward, they end on the rugged Taurus Mountains that separate them from the high central plateau of Anatolia.

economic and political variants that compose the long and rich history of Lebanon.

Yet, what we opt to particularly ascertain in this study is that the southern borders of Lebanon were in wide expansion, going through the beautiful region of Galilee and forth towards Mt. Carmel (and beyond), during the time of Jesus. We believe it was because of those historical and geographical facts that we found the term, "of the Gentiles," attached to Galilee, in the Church New Testament.

Looking again at Map 1 confirms what we have been saying and gives quite a good and clear idea of how the geographical region was precisely at the time of Jesus. What concerns us the most in this argument is in fact the Galilean-Phoenician region, which stretches from Mt. Carmel rising in the south; the plains of Galilee including the Sea of Tiberias (Bahr Tubariyeh) stretching towards the Mountains of Lebanon to the east; the Mediterranean Sea flowing westward; and finally, Ugarit, standing in the north and constituting an essential part of the land (not shown in the map, herein).

Yet, this particular map shows a lot of interesting places that formed a missionary playground for Jesus' ministry and that of his Disciples. These places were often mentioned in the New Testament as actually major key places for his socio-religious movement, for example, the villages of Capernaum, Bethsaida, Nazareth, and others. Of course, his movement was not a rebellious motion against his own people living in the Galilean-Phoenician area and who dearly believed in him ever since he started his mission, but a rebellion against the God of the Old Testament lurking in wait in the neighboring Judea, and precisely in Jerusalem.

An interesting quote comes to mind from Ernest Renan, the well-known 19th century French historian, writer, and one of the very few experts of his time of the Middle East ancient languages and civilizations. Renan states in his famous book[163]:

But the God he found there (in the desert on his journey to Jerusalem[164], as it appears) was not his God, but rather the God of Job, severe and terrible, accountable to no one. Sometimes, it was Satan who came to tempt him. He returned, then, into his beloved Galilee, and found again his Heavenly Father (the God Ēl, definitely) in the midst of the green hills

---

163 Renan, Ernest, *Vie de Jesus*, page 156.
164 We will definitely explain the importance of Jerusalem to Jesus in Part III and why he had to visit it; of course, it was not because he was Jewish.

and the clear fountains—and among the crowds of women and children, who, with joyous soul and the song of angels in their hearts, awaited the salvation of Israel[165].

Mt. Carmel

Starting with Mt. Carmel will certainly pave the way to officially recognize the ethnicity of the Christian Master and understand well his mission of Redemption. Etymologically, the origin of the name "Carmel" given to this great mountain standing between Samaria-Judea and Galilee-Phoenicia, is undoubtedly a Canaano-Phoenician term composed of two words: "Karm" or "Krm" and "Ēl", thus, *Krm-Ēl* or *Karm-Ēl* (Carm-Ēl), and signifies the "Generous Vine of Ēl", meaning, the "Spiritual offering of Ēl."

In the historical records of the Phoenician religion, we notice that Phoenician priests had long erected two temples at the top of Mt. Carmel: one dedicated to Ashirai (Anat), the Mother Goddess, and the other to Ēl and Adonis (Baal), hence the name, *Krm-Ēl.* Both temples were destroyed later on during one of the many invasions of the Egyptian Pharaoh Thutmose III (c.1505 BC–1450 BC), who in his annals, referred to this particular place as the "Sacred Island," and which we have well noted in the previous chapter before thoroughly explaining the very significance of this Holy Mountain. Yet, we shall add that at the time of Jesus, the geographical area of Mt. Carmel and Galilee (exactly as the map shows us) was part of Phoenicia, thus, its territorial boundaries belonged to both cities of Tyre (Sūr) and Sidon (Saydoun) and could be primarily connected to Saydoun, a name directly related to the sea and the art of fishing. Most Galileans were fisherman, undoubtedly. This area in fact remained a Phoenician-Lebanese territory until the end of the Ottoman era. However, in 1920 AD it became part of Palestine, and later, in 1948, of Israel.

Why? What could be the reason?

Why had this particular area changed just recently and been moved from being an ancient Canaano-Phoenician territory to become a part of the newly created state of Israel? This is a very important question to ask. I often wondered why, but the answer resides clearly in the labyrinths of politics, of course! And politics in that concern was actually a business contract between

---

165 Whether Renan meant it or not, the word "Israel" he used here, would definitely mean the "Isra-el of the non-Jews," which we shall thoroughly explain as we proceed further in this book.

Christians and Jews in an attempt to reinforce the Judeo-Christian belief, or shall I say, the organized system of religion that tarnished the truth of that ancient Phoenician Territory, the Holy Mountain and Holy Land, making it thus Jewish, only to cope with the idea of legitimizing a place to the Biblical Hebrews in the Middle East. This transformation in history has been aided with the falsification of the historical documents and geographical maps for simply politico-religious purposes that help the *modus operandi* of the Judeo-Christian agenda. This manipulation of the truth is proved on a daily basis by the meticulous historical and archeological findings that completely put an end to the existence of the Israel we read about in the Bible. Besides, the information and proof gathered herein will also reveal the Christian-Jewish plot of not only altering the reality of geographical and historical places, but also of individuals—the most important of them all being Jesus Christ.

It is complete irony for sure since we found it exposed in the New Testament itself when we read from John (7:40-53) the following paragraph:

> Many of the people therefore, when they heard this saying, said, of a truth this is the prophet. Others said, 'This is the Christ.' But some said shall Christ come out of Galilee? Hath not the Scripture said that Christ cometh of the seed of David, and out of the town of Bethlehem, where David was? So there was a division among the people because of him. And some of them would have arrested him; but no one laid hands on him. Nicodemus (he who came to him by night, being one of them) said to them, 'Does our law judge a man, unless it first hears from him personally and knows what he does?' They answered him, 'Are you also from Galilee? Search and see that no prophet has arisen out of Galilee.'

This quote says it all. It openly suggests that some people present there believed Yāwshu (*Iesous*) to be the prophet or the Meshiha they had been waiting for, and certainly these believers were not at all Jewish, because the answer of the Jews came afterwards doubting that Christ could come out from Galilee— Galilee of the Nations. The Galilee of the non-Jews. Hence, to them, and according to the scriptures they adopted, the Mashiah or Moshiah, "the anointed one," as spelled in Hebrew tongue and spoken about in their writings, should come of the Seed of David, a Jew, and out of the town of Bethlehem, where it is believed that David originated, as per the Hebrew Bible, the only ancient document that speaks of him and of his son, Solomon. So, there was a division among the people present there because of Yāwshu.

The above quote also reveals two important things on both the cultural and theological levels that cope much too perfectly with the geographical evidence we have previously presented. It first proves that Galilee was not part of Judea; and second, that no Jewish prophet arose out of Galilee. This fact stands in complete concordance with the main concept behind the writing of this book that clearly states the truth that Jesus was not in any way possible a Jewish prophet, but rather, Galilean-Phoenician.

In fact, it was only after the destruction of the Jewish Temple by Titus in 70 AD that Jews took Galilee as a place to live. And only because they were expelled from Jerusalem into neighboring regions, among them Galilee, where they gradually started to wipe away any Phoenician traces they came in contact with, such as the grotto of Bet-Lahem (Beit Lahm) or Bethlehem, located on the Northeastern base of Mt. Carmel, and which meant the "House of Bread." The Canaano-Phoenician word "Bet-Lahem" is a composed name of two words: "Bet," "Beit," or "Beth[166]," meaning, "house," "place," or "temple," and "Lahm," "Lahem," or "Lehem," having different yet similar meanings, like, "bread," "food," "plantation," and "fertility." Hence, "House of Bread" is the most correct and common explanation for the name "Bet-Lahem," but it could also mean the "Temple of the god of plantation and fertility."

Adon (Adonis[167]), that young and beautiful god of Gebel (Byblos), who incarnated the cycle of nature and represented the spring—the resurrection of every atom in the kingdom of life—was also worshipped in this Bethlehem. In his book, *The Golden Bough*, originally published in 1922, Sir James (George) Frazer wrote that Adonis represented the spirit of the corn and that he might well have dwelt and later worshiped in Bethlehem[168].

A worldwide recognized expert in myth and religion, Frazer argues in his valuable book that Jerome[169] was certainly mistaken in "probably" thinking that the grotto (or the grove) of Adonis had

---

166 It is the second letter of the Phoenician Alphabet, the oldest form of the Phonetic Alphabet in the world.
167 *Adonis* is the Greek spelling of the Canaanite-Phoenician Lord, Adon, known as *Adonai* by the Hebrews, and being one of the names used to refer to the God YHWH in their religious books.
168 Frazer, Sir James, *The Golden Bough*, page 346.
169 St. Jerome, a Roman Christian priest, theologian, and historian of the 4th century BC, who became a Doctor of the Church due to his contribution to the Christian religious beliefs and doctrine.

been prepared by the heathen[170] after the Birth of Jesus Christ for the sole reason to defile the sacred place of the Savior's birth. Jerome's accusation of the believers of Adonis, the Phoenicians, as being heathens who profaned the place where Jesus was born, most likely comes from his connection to the jealous Jews and Jewish-Christians of Antioch, where the death of Adonis was annually observed with great respect as noted during the entrance of the Roman Emperor Julian (c. 331/332 AD–363 AD) into the city[171]. But Jerome was speaking of Bethlehem of Judea, which has nothing to do with the Birth of Christ, as we shall see. At any rate, we surely believe that Frazer is absolutely right in his argument since Adon well preceded Christ in terrestrial time; yet, Christ is portrayed as a clear and most faithful image of Adon himself, since both represented the "bread of life"[172], and both died and resurrected[173].

Bet-Lahem

It seems that both Jerome[174] and Frazer who quoted him, were talking about the traditionally claimed birthplace of the Lord— Bethlehem of Judea—which the Church's father tells us was shaded by a grove dedicated to the old Syrian[175] Lord, Adonis, and that where the divine infant cried the lover of Venus[176] was bewailed. Although both were absolutely correct in mirroring the weeping of the infant Christ with the lamentation for Adonis, they were definitely mistaken regarding the exact location where the

---

170 The word "heathen" or "pagan" is wrongly and unrightfully used by Christians in their judgment, or rather condemnation of ancient civilizations, especially the Egyptians and Phoenicians, who represented their gods in statues they honored in their temples. Yet, Christianity has adopted this ancient particular form itself to honor God, Mary, and Jesus, etc.

171 Frazer, Sir James, *The Golden Bough*, page 346.

172 To the Canaanite/Phoenicians, Adon was believed to be the "god of vegetation and fertility," and he is the "spirit of the corn," as argued by Frazer, page 341-346. Accordingly, whether unconsciously or not, Christians believe that Jesus Christ is the Bread of Life, for it is noted in John 6:35-48, "I am the bread of life."

173 The story of Adon, born in Gebel (Byblos), relates that he was attacked and killed by a wild boar, said to have been sent vicariously by his enemy. His resurrection is pictured in the short-lived scarlet anemone, which sprang from his blood being sprinkled on the ground. Jesus Christ was judged by his Jewish enemies, crucified by the Romans, and gloriously resurrected after his blood was shed to erase the sins of the world.

174 Jerome, *Epistles*, No. 49.

175 The term "Syrian" is wrongly used here; Jerome should have meant instead the word "Phoenician."

176 Venus is the Greek version of the Phoenician goddess, Astarte.

two events took place, and whereabout the Canaano-Phoenician Lord of Rebirth and Vegetation and the Phoenician-Galilean Lord of Resurrection and Salvation dwelt. Yet, Frazer believed that if Adonis was really the Spirit of the Corn, then Bethlehem, "House of Bread." would be the more suitable spot for his dwelling place. But the traditional Bethlehem was not built at the time of Adonis, nor was it yet built at the time of Jesus, as we shall see soon enough.

In addition to them, a known Greek monk by the name of Gerasimos of Kefalonia (c. 1506 AD–1579 AD), who later was ordained a saint, combined Adonis with the Christ. He narrated that there was in Bethlehem a sacred grove (garden) dedicated to Adonis (God the Son) where believers used to wail in memory of his death inside the same cave (grotto) in which was born later on the Nazorean (Jesus the Nazarene)[177]. Again, the connection is correct between the two divine Sons, but the location could not be in any way or form the Bethlehem of Judea.

Although we know for sure that Jerusalem, also known as *Ur-Shalim*, meaning, "the city of Shalim, the son of Ēl," has been for ages a Canaano-Phoenician city ruled, most probably founded, by the Jebusites, an ancient tribe of the Amorites (c. 2400 BC–1100 BC), who in turn were a Canaanite tribe, and developed later on by Milki-Sedek, the Priest of the Most High God, we were unable to find any reference to any form whatsoever of ceremonial rituals related to Adon in the place called Bethlehem of Judea. However, history shows, and we affirm that the only connection between Adon and Jesus, in the Judean Bethlehem, had in fact happened after the suppression of the Jewish Bar Kochba (Cocheba) military uprising (c. 132 AD–135 AD) against the Roman power. In fact, it seems that the Roman Emperor, Hadrian or Hadrianus (c. 76 AD–138 AD), whose reign lasted almost twenty-one years from 117 AD until 138 AD and precisely after the Jewish revolt in Judea had been repressed in 135 AD, had actually built a temple for the god Adonis over the traditional Grotto of the Nativity[178], probably as a sign of his victory, and perhaps as a message, whether conscious or unconscious, sent to the world, that Jesus and Adonis are in fact one and the same, certainly on the religious level. It is most likely at this point in history that we can actually trace, besides Byblus (Gebel), the worship of Adonis, in Jerusalem.[179]

---

177 Yammine, Youssef Rev., *The Messiah was Born in Lebanon not in Judea—* المسيح ولد في لبنان لا في اليهودية, page 86.
178 This historical fact was not referred to in the texts of the New Testament for hidden reasons, of course, revealed now for sure. It was, however, mentioned by Justin Martyr about 155 AD.
179 Rawlinson, George, *History of Phoenicia*, iBooks, page 255.

That being said, the only historical, geographical, religious, and ritualistic location that would fit both Canaano-Phoenician Lords, Adonis and Immanuel, on cultural and ethnic levels, is undoubtedly Bet-Lahem of Galilee, situated at the base of Mt. Carmel. Hence, it becomes clear to the reader that the Galilean Bet-Lahem and Mt. Carmel were two inseparable places in the religious feats of the Phoenicians.

Etymologically speaking, we have seen earlier that the word Carmel from Carm-Ēl derives from *Krm-Ēl*, meaning the "Generous Vine of Ēl" or the "Spiritual offering of Ēl," and as we have seen just now, the word Bethlehem, or Bet-Lahem, means "House of Bread." These two obvious meanings of the two important names we just studied, were not coincidentally, but rather most confidently given to places having the same geographical locations—Mt. Carmel and Bethlehem, meaning together, "the Vine and Bread." Thus, they fit so perfectly with the theological concept of the most sacred ritual of all times within the religious doctrine of the Phoenicians. It is indeed the ritual of Wine and Bread, first practiced by Milki-Sedek—"my King is Righteous"—the High Priest of Ēl, and later on by Jesus Christ at the Last Supper holding high in his hands a loaf of bread and the famous sacred cup—known today as the Holy Grail.

No wonder we find that fact clearly revealed in the Church New Testament in St. Paul's Letter to the Hebrews (5:6, 10; 6:20; 7:11, 15-17, 21). Here, St. Paul spoke firmly about the clear declaration of Christ on the "House of Prayer," and described him, not a priest after the Law of carnal commandment of Aaron, that's for sure, but instead, a High Priest of God after the power of an endless life. "Thou art a priest forever after the order of Milki-Sedek," says Paul, defining by that one spiritual priesthood. We now look at the geographical truth lingering in front of our examining eyes. After tackling the significant history of one of the most religious and ritualistic places on Earth in the previous chapter, *Mt. Krm-Ēl*, let us discover the other important place that was connected to it. Bet(h)-Lahem or Bethlehem is a name and a sacred place that has lingered for centuries in the minds and memories not only of Christians but also of the adherents of basically all earth religions. On the four maps we have displayed for the readers on the last few pages of this book, our eyes would undoubtedly come across two Bethlehems: one in Judea, and the other in Galilee.

We have hitherto explained the importance of Galilee in the ministry of Jesus Christ and we shall see more of that as we attempt to focus on the two Bethlehems, encircled in red as presented in Map 1, Map 2 (Nr.108), and Map 3. We have seriously examined the etymological meaning of the Bet-Lahem (House of Bread) of Galilee and how it fits perfectly with Mt. Carmel (Generous Vine of Ēl), not only on the geographical frame that nature mysteriously shaped, but also on a religious basis. In fact, Bet-Lahem is a Galilean village situated a few miles west of Nazareth. And again, geography doesn't lie!

Today, as the human consciousness grows for better knowledge and understanding to lessen the errors we have made before, there is a growing number of academics on the international front, and I mean, theologians, scholars, historians, and archaeologists, who first believed and then suggested that the birthplace of Jesus was not Bethlehem of Judea, but rather, Bet-Lahem of Galilee. It seems they have finally identified it after gathering an immense body of evidence. However, as it seems to me, and it is not a surprising behavior of the human mind: a lot of people might not yet be ready to accept this old-new historical fact. These skeptics could well be defined as Christians, in their Catholic majority and their Orthodox and Protestant minorities. Along with them come surely the Jews, who would certainly not accept it for many reasons. In fact, the Judeo-Christian culture as a whole would ferociously stand against it. Yet, we stand here, firmly, with open eyes, mind, and heart on the Truth, and declare it with no compromise whatsoever.

The contemporary American scholar and Protestant priest, Bruce Chilton, stated that the Bethlehem of Galilee has most certainly held a close connection with Christianity since the Birth of Jesus; that both Joseph and Mary were from Bethlehem and Nazareth; and that it is possible that Mary was born in Sephoris of Galilee. Chilton also suggested that Matthew did not entirely fabricate the story of the Nativity but simply opted or chose to switch the two Bethlehems.

Well, it seems that the analysis of Chilton in that concern is correct. The decision of Matthew was not at all coincidental, nor it was an error made by him that he didn't notice. In truth, Matthew, known to have addressed his gospel to the Jews, had intended to create a story favorable to them, perhaps in a desperate attempt to convert them to the new Christian faith, a trend we shall see followed by the Early Church in Chapter 10.

As a matter of fact, the Bethlehem of Judea, near Jerusalem, has always been mentioned in the Jewish religious documents, the Torah, as the hometown of King David, the father of the well-known King Solomon. Reading that information in their scriptures and perceiving their belief—that the Messiah would come from the House of David—Matthew changed the locations only to convince them that Jesus had been born a Jew—in the Judean Bethlehem —and thus, creating a link, surely an imaginary one, between Jesus and King David.

From the archaeological point of view, however, scientists have not found a single shred of conclusive proof that Bethlehem of Judea was the exact birthplace of Jesus. Archaeological excavations done in the area have shown that there isn't any form of tangible evidence that they can take into consideration. In addition, not a single trace of habitation from the time of Jesus Christ has been found standing or lying dormant under the ground in the Judean Bethlehem. Alternatively, there has appeared much proof describing a well-established community in the Galilean Bethlehem.

In fact, studies are conclusive that the Bethlehem of Judea was established around the year 200 AD, maybe a few years before[180], as a place of pilgrimage for Gentile Romans and other communities of pagan beliefs, better to say followers of eastern religious tradition, honoring Adonis in his temple built by Emperor Hadrianus, but not for Jews who were expelled from Jerusalem after the destruction of the temple by Titus in 70 AD, and not for the Judeo-Christians (Christians of Jewish Origin) who lived in concealment for the fear of the Romans. In fact, it was at a later period, not before the 4th century AD, that Bethlehem of Judea was legally founded—sometime around the year 325 AD and under the reign of Constantine the Great, the Roman Emperor who built the Church of the Holy Sepulcher, also widely known by the Basilica of the Holy Sepulcher—in this location, and precisely over the traditional Grotto of the Nativity, in place of Hadrian's Adonis Temple where the Mysteries of the Phoenician God-Spirit of Rebirth was established. "Who knows," the great H.P. Blavatsky, founder of the Theosophical Society, stated[181], "but this was the *petra* or rock-temple on which the Church was built? The boar of Adonis was placed above the gate of Jerusalem which looked toward Bethlehem."

It seems, though—as per the *Chronography* of St. Theophanes —that at the end of the Council of Nicæa (c. 325 AD), and following the orders of Constantine, Macarius, Bishop of Jerusalem back then, from 312 AD to shortly before 335 AD (Council of Tyre), began some extensive work of excavation in search for the holy sites of the Passion, the True Cross, and the

---

180 Since that is true, then claiming that King David has been born there is totally erroneous and misleading, without mentioning the fact that such a king did not exist in true historical accounts.
181 H.P. Blavatsky, *Isis Unveiled*, Volume II, page 139.

Resurrection. Having succeeded in his mission, Macarius sent a letter to the emperor informing him of the wonderful finds he made of the hallowed monument of the Resurrection. The discovery Macarius made must have happened during Helena's (the emperor's mother's) visit to the Holy Land, Jerusalem in particular, in 324 AD, who accompanied him one year later in her successful search for the True Cross. On hearing that, Constantine wrote back to Macarius ordering him to erect the Church of the Resurrection[182] on the site—revered as the Golgotha (the Hill of Calvary), where Jesus was crucified, and where it is said he was buried (the Sepulchre)—in support of the claim decreed by the Church Authority and approved by his mother Helena.

One thing, however, remained unfound: a place they could legitimize as sacred for their empire. Bethlehem of Judea was appropriate at that moment, not only for religious reasons, but also for political ones, especially at the time the empire decided to make Christianity its official religion. There is no doubt that Jesus was crucified at the place they identified as the Golgotha, yet, once again, truth be told, the place where the Church *alleged* Jesus was born had been a public cemetery for ages. Hence, there would be no historical logic to what the Church claimed, for it couldn't have been Jesus Christ or any other ordinary person to be delivered inside a cemetery.

No matter how far they would go in denying it, they would not be able to bury it, for Holy Truth often prevails and the Divine Light always appears at the end of the darkened tunnel. There is nothing more miraculous than the stones that laid the foundation of the Roman Church of the Resurrection of Christ bearing witness to the mysteries of Adon. The enemy of Adon stood above the gate of Jerusalem, lingering in wait, his open eyes towards the Hill of Calvary, enjoying the view of the Passion of Christ, yet, Resurrection was near ...

At any rate, in addition to Reverend Chilton's suggestion, another person of similar expertise and knowledge came onto the scene more than twenty years before him. German theologian, Harmut Stegemann, also proposed back in the sixties that Jesus was born in Galilee, not in Judea, however, not in Bethlehem (of Galilee), but rather in Capernaum by the lake of Genezareth. Once again, the region of the "non-Jews Galilee" reverberates well and

---

182 The construction of Constantine's Church began sometime around the year 325/326 AD and was completed in between the years 335/338 AD. It was built as two interconnected churches over two different holy sites: the alleged place of Burial and the place of Crucifixion/Resurrection.

deep in our ears and minds as we follow the line of evidence coming from different authors of distant backgrounds around the world. Although we know the importance of Capernaum in the life of Jesus, it doesn't stand as his birthplace, yet, saying that Jesus was born in Galilee is enough at the moment. This very fact would add more legitimacy to the historical truth we enthusiastically propose behind the world's most enigmatic person, Jesus Christ, Yāwshu (*Iesous*), or in the tongue of Matthew, Immanuel.

Let's add up. Shall we?

Jacques Duquesne, the coetaneous French journalist and writer was even more specific concerning in which Bethlehem Jesus was born. In his book, *Jésus*, Duquesne alluded to the exact place of the Nativity of Jesus Christ as Bethlehem of Galilee, and not the Judean Bethlehem. He wrote[183], "We sometime wonder if the Bethlehem of the nativity is not another locality having the same name and situated at 10 kilometers of Nazareth, hence in Galilee."

It became clear to us as years passed by that there is no conclusive fact on the locality of the Nativity mentioned in the New Testament. Religious scholars, in addition to historians, archaeologists, geographical experts, and a wide variety of international thinkers and writers truly wonder if what came from the mouth of Matthew first, and Luke after him, about the Judean Bethlehem, could be but an error or a deliberate mistake (intended by Matthew), so as to say, as we have seen before.

Chilton could have well elaborated his suggestion and analysis about this particular issue on previous knowledge or rather solid thoughts, which Renan endorsed while penning his well-read book, *Vie de Jésus*. Renan shares his opinion with the eager readers and seekers of Truth[184], and I quote from the beginning of Chapter 2:

Jesus was born at Nazareth, a small town of Galilee, which before his time had no celebrity. All his life, he was designated by the name of the *Nazarene*, and it is only by a rather embarrassed and round-about way, that, in the legends respecting him, he is made to be born at Bethlehem. We shall see later the motive for this supposition, and how it was the necessary consequence of the Messianic character attributed to Jesus.

---

183 Duquesne, Jacques, *Jésus*, page 54.
184 Renan, Ernest, *Vie de Jésus*, page 122-123.

To Renan, as it clearly appears in his writings, Jesus was to have been born at Bethlehem of Judea. It is certainly plugged in the Church New Testament for none other than Messianic reasons related to Jewish tradition and beliefs that the Messiah, being Jesus, should be exactly on the image of David, the Jewish King, being born in the Bethlehem of Judea where David was born. We have talked about this alleged or fabricated connection between Jesus and David many times before. It doesn't fit at all.

At any rate, although Renan powerfully denies that Jesus was born in Bethlehem of Judea for reasons he obviously stated in his book, he strongly confirms that Jesus was born at Nazareth in Galilee. Once again, this is more support coming yet from another trusted author that would legitimize the historical truth of the Galilean region of the Nativity that we strongly endorse in this book. The only difference though is the exact spot of the Nativity, which he missed. We believe—due to the unsupportive archeological documents proving the existence of Nazareth as a town or city at the time of Jesus—that Jesus was in fact born, as we have previously revealed, in the Galilean village of Bet-Lahem, situated a few miles west of Nazareth. Again, we shall remind readers of the fact that it is most appropriate nowadays to describe Christ as Jesus the Nazarene, and not as Jesus of Nazareth.

Another important study that intersects with the line we have been drawing so far, and relates that Jesus the Nazarene was actually born in the Galilean Bet-Lahem, comes from the Lebanese reverend and doctor, Youssef Yammine. In his wonderful book, written in Arabic and published in 2009-2010, Father Yammine proves without doubt that the birthplace of Jesus Christ, the Meshiha, the Anointed One, as spoken in Aramaic, was indeed at Bet-Lahem of Galilee. He wrote[185]:

This study is in fact an impossible mission on all levels and in each and every phase along its accomplishment, from the very first point of conceiving it till termination. Isn't an impossible mission should you try to correct a belief that has been in the mind of people for ages, especially Christians, a belief that the Meshiha was born in the Judean Bethlehem, known today, and situated almost 10 kilometers away south of Jerusalem? Yet, this study proves that this belief—from historical and geographical points of views—is completely wrong because it was founded on shaky and unobjectionable basis. The

---

185 Yammine, Youssef Rev., *The Messiah was Born in Lebanon Not in Judea—* المسيح ولد في لبنان لا في اليهودية , page 24-25.

Meshiha was instead born in another Bet-Lahem, in Galilee, inside a nearby grotto situated on the Northern-Eastern slopes of Mt. Carmel, in the land of Phoenicia-Lebanon. This Bet-Lahem was a Canaanite city for centuries long, mentioned in almost all the histories and geographies of the world, and is still seen today.

Our position is that what Father Yammine penned in his book is absolutely correct. An impossible mission indeed, yet, what is the *truth*, its purpose, or even its meaning, if they had been masterminded, planned and lobbied, to quell it hidden from the ears, eyes, hearts and minds of the good people around the world?

Besides the geographical maps that show the Bet-Lahem of Galilee presented in his book, Father Yammine meticulously explains that this Bet-Lahem is the same one cited in the Old Testament itself, and not the Judean Bethlehem that came into existence much later on in time. Of course, the Lebanese priest, a great believer of the Father God Ēl (not Yahweh, of course), the Virgin Lady Maryām, and Christ, had no intention at all to discredit or put under the microscope the foundation and wonderful divine message of Christianity on the level of faith. His work was strictly based on both historical and religious levels. I certainly share with him his straightforward opinion that Jesus Christ was of Canaano-Phoenician descent and his birthplace was definitely the Bet-Lahem of Galilee.

While contrary to Bet-Lahem of Galilee mentioned in the letters of Tell Amarna that there is no citation of the Judean Bethlehem in historical records outside the Biblical tradition, Father Yammine exposes the truth of the authentic Galilean Bet-Lahem being herself called Ephrath, or Ephratha[186], and mentioned in the books of Genesis, Joshua, Ruth, 1 Samuel, 1 Chronicles, Micah, etc... .

Yet, before we proceed into examining the citations in the Old Testament, let us first understand what Ephrath or Ephratha means. It is a Canaano-Phoenician (Aramaic) term that means "the fertile and the fruitful[187]." No wonder Ephratha has been linked to the Galilean Bet-Lahem, which also has "fertility" as one of its meanings, as we have seen before. In fact, the whole region of Galilee including Mt. Carmel (Vine: Wine) and Bet-Lahem (House of Bread) has always been determined as one of the most fruitful and fertile lands in the region due to its rich natural

---

186 Ibid, page 88-96.
187 Duquesne, Jaques, *Jésus*, page 47, Bethlehem means "house of bread," but also called Ephrata, "rich in fruits."

diversity of vegetation. We can easily compare it to Bethlehem of Judea and its surrounding region, including Jerusalem, which has less fertility, almost negligible.

No one has probably described the mystical region of Galilee with all its spiritual splendor and natural beauty that somehow ties Heaven and Earth together, better than Ernest Renan. He wrote[188]:

> A beautiful external nature tended to produce a much less austere spirit—a spirit less sharply monotheistic, if I may use the expression, which imprinted a charming and idyllic character on all the dreams of Galilee. The saddest country in the world is perhaps the region round about Jerusalem. Galilee, on the contrary, was a very green, shady, smiling district, the true home of the Song of Songs, and the songs of the well-beloved. During the two months of March and April, the country forms a carpet of flowers of an incomparable variety of colors. The animals are small, and extremely gentle —delicate and lively turtle-doves, blue-birds so light that they rest on a blade of grass without bending it, crested larks which venture almost under the feet of the traveller, little river tortoises with mild and lively eyes, storks with grave and modest mien, which, laying aside all timidity, allow man to come quite near them, and seem almost to invite his approach. In no country in the world do the mountains spread themselves out with more harmony, or inspire higher thoughts. Jesus seems to have had a peculiar love for them. The most important acts of his divine career took place upon the mountains. It was there that he was the most inspired; it was there that he held secret communion with the ancient prophets; and it was there that his disciples witnessed his transfiguration.

Then he added[189]:

> The Galileans were considered energetic, brave, and laborious. If we except Tiberias, built by Antipas in honor of Tiberius (about the year 15), in the Roman style, Galilee had no large towns. The country was, nevertheless, well peopled, covered with small towns and large villages, and cultivated in all parts with skill. From the ruins which remain of its ancient splendor, we can trace an agricultural people, no way gifted in

---

188 Renan, Ernest, *Vie de Jésus*, page 152-153.
189 Ibid., page 154.

art, caring little for luxury, indifferent to the beauties of form and exclusively idealistic. The country abounded in fresh streams and in fruits; the large farms were shaded with vines and fig-trees; the gardens were filled with trees bearing apples, walnuts, and pomegranates. The wine was excellent ...

Many pilgrims and peregrinators to the Holy Lands of the Middle East and Africa that have preceded Renan and many that came after him have indeed noticed a great resemblance between the art of agriculture and farming found in Galilee and the one they found in the region of Tyre and Sidon in southern Lebanon. We have indeed proven the connection before. Many others have compared the delightful plantations they found in Galilee with the fertility of the Egyptian land around the Nile. We have also established the relation a few times earlier. Now, speaking of the fruitful and fertile, Bet-Lahem or Ephratha, let's have a look at it in the following verses.

The Books

In the book of Genesis, we read the following two verses:

So Rachel died and was buried on the way to Ephrath (that [is], Bethlehem). (35:19)
But as for me, when I came from Padan, Rachel died beside me in the land of Canaan on the way, when [there was] but a little distance to go to Ephrath; and I buried her there on the way to Ephrath (that is, Bethlehem). (48:7)

When reading the complete text these two above verses were taken from, we conclude that they were mentioned in a context that does not fit at all the geographical location of the Judean Bethlehem, but on the contrary, they do perfectly match with the Bet-Lahem of Galilee.

In the book of Joshua (19:15-16), we read:

... Included were Kattath, Nahallal, Shimron, Idalah, and Bethlehem: twelve cities with their villages. This [was] the inheritance of the children of Zebulun according to their families, these cities with their villages.

This verse identifies precisely Bethlehem as the Bet-Lahem of Galilee, since the geographical location of the villages that had been distributed to be part of the land given as a possession to the tribe of Zebulun[190], were clearly seen as hamlets located in the region of Galilee and not in Judea.

In the book of Ruth (1:2), we read the following:

The name of the man [was] Elimelech, the name of his wife [was] Naomi, and the names of his two sons [were] Mahlon and Chilion—Ephrathites of Bethlehem, Judah. And they went to the country of Moab and remained there.

We believe the Book of Ruth was influenced or directly manipulated by Persian scribes during their interconnection with the newly born Hebrew people they intended to introduce in the course of history as an ancient ethnic group. The Persians had already existed as a growing influential empire. This verse clearly or perhaps intentionally confuses "Ephrata" or "Bet-Lahem of Galilee" with the region of Judah, where they were to settle and hence give them, the Hebrews, historical credibility.

In Part III, we shall certainly explain more about the strong and clandestine yet obvious connection, established between the Persian Empire under Cyrus II, and the Hebrews or the *Aebirou-al-naher*, "those who crossed the river," in constant waves during their early years of historical formation. They were first led by an enigmatic man called Zoro-Babel. This crossing seemed to have occurred when they had just planned to build a temple in Jerusalem!

In the book of 1Samuel (17:12), we read the verse as such:

Now David [was] the son of that Ephrathite of Bethlehem Judah, whose name [was] Jesse, and who had eight sons. And the man was old, advanced [in years], in the days of Saul.

This verse has no historical or geographical truth. First, because David is a mythical person; he did not exist in real history. Second, another confusion between the two Bethlehems occurs. Yet, should we consider this verse as having some factual points regarding David, we can easily deduce that the mythical David was born in Ephratha or Bet-Lahem. Now, Bethlehem of Judah was not at all connected to Ephratha in any way or form,

---

190 This distribution has been penned by Jewish Scribes in their attempts to legitimize their conquest of lands as per divine promises. Biblically, this area was known as the land of the tribe of Zebulun.

thus David would then have been born in Bet-Lahem of Galilee, and the word Judah cited in the verse would be but an addition of later copiers and propagandists of the Judeo-Christian agenda. Perhaps then, what came in John[191] would enable us to link the birthplace of Christ to that of David, the son of Jesse, the Ephrathite of Bethlehem of Galilee and *not* of Judea. If that is so, then David would have been a Phoenician king, probably of a different name (not Jewish). But this is not our concern for the moment. This, however, fits perfectly with what we are steadfastly proposing here in this book. The historical Jesus Christ was born in the Galilean Bet-Lahem. Yet, David, King David, remains a mythical person.

In the book of 1Chronicles (4:4), we thus read:

... and Penuel [was] the father of Gedor, and Ezer [was the] father of Hushah. These [were] the sons of Hur, the firstborn of Ephrathah the father of Bethlehem.

This verse is strange, for it does not confuse the geographical locations with each other as shown in the two previous verses of Ruth and 1 Samuel, but it rather creates a complete mix up of locations with names of persons or pronouns: both Ephrathah and Bethlehem are shown here as people and not places. This verse is one of the many verses that do give concrete examples of complete works of forgery and manipulation done on the Old Testament's texts, and not only at the arrangement point of the mentioned texts but also during the long process of copying and re-copying, which was conducted by Judeo-Christians Biblical scholars.

In the book of Micah (5:2), we quote the following verse:

But you, Bethlehem Ephrathah, [Though] you are little among the thousands of Judah, [Yet] out of you shall come forth to Me The One to be Ruler in Israel, Whose goings forth [are] from of old, From everlasting.

This verse is clear in identifying Bethlehem as Bet-Lahem of Galilee, known also as Ephratha, yet, it wrongly determines its location as one little village among thousands in Judah. Again, the Bethlehem of Judea was never given the name Ephratha, and this historical error by itself makes us wonder: Why the mix up

---

191 John 7:42, "Has not the Scripture said that the Christ comes from the seed of David and from the town of Bethlehem, where David was?"

the two Bethlehems? One of the main reasons that caused this evident confusion, or had been probably made as such to confuse the readers even more, to eventually make them forget the Galilean Bet-Lahem, is the fact that there was a place near Jerusalem, not in Judea, that had an identical meaning as Ephratha. This term is known as "Ephraim," which also means "the fruitful" in Hebrew tongue and was given to one of the twelve tribes of Israel as per the Old Testament. However, the main problem that appears to discredit the Judeo-Christian claims is revealed by means of geography as well, for the land given to the tribe of Ephraim as per the Bible, is located to the north of Jerusalem, whereas the traditional Bethlehem is located south of Jerusalem, in Judea.

At any rate, the Micah verse has been mirrored by the Church New Testament Gospel of Matthew (2:6), as such, "But you, Bethlehem, [in] the land of Judah, Are not the least among the rulers of Judah; For out of you shall come a Ruler Who will shepherd My people Israel."

Or, was it the opposite? Church interpolation into Micah's text? Again, as we have seen and explained a few times before, Matthew seems so confident in himself and aware of what he was doing in his attempts to mix the two Bethlehems. In his verse, the term, "Ephratha," that was tied to Bethlehem in that of Micah has been totally erased. Although we know that despite Matthew's plan of switching the two Bethlehems—a plan that has been exposed—he always managed to send secret messages in his Gospel, and perhaps by removing Ephratha here, he in fact wanted his readers to see what he did and the reason he did it.

Let's take a deep breath now and continue in just a bit with this extraordinary journey into our revolutionary exposé of the true origins of Christianity. Some have been long and carefully hidden, others, skillfully manipulated by the underground secret lobby of the Christian-Jewish Biblical scholars who belong to a later period in time. Thus, scriptural events have been created and cannot be traced as actual historical facts taking place some thousands of years ago. First, they have meticulously modeled Ancient Biblical Israel to appear in the Old Testament as such, something that the Methodology of the History of Biblical Israel coupled with serious modern Biblical archaeology are unable to, nor they would at any time, confirm its veracity. Second, relating the origin of Christianity to Judaism has been yet another dangerous plot that will certainly fall, too, as you turn the pages of this book.

Chapter 5

The Historical Evidence of "Jesus the Galilean"

Now that we have seriously tackled and profoundly examined the geographical area in which Jesus Christ ministered during his lifetime in the previous chapter, we will try as much as possible in this present chapter to reveal the multitude of historical evidence that undoubtedly relates him to non-Jewish historical, social, and genetic roots, and connects him directly to Phoenician-Galilean origin.

I will pinpoint in the following few paragraphs important revelations made by historians and theologians across the world, communicating to us the fact that Jesus was born in the non-Judean Bethlehem and would actually have (from some of them) a different historical background than what has been claimed traditionally by the official Church.

Yet, before we venture into the new discoveries, let us just pause for a thought, to remember the celebrated Wedding of Kana (Qana), mentioned in the Church New Testament, to which Jesus, his mother, and disciples, were invited. It was most probably a wedding ceremony of one of their relatives, and it was there where Yāwshu (*Iesous*) proclaimed his divinity. He effectively turned water into wine, accomplishing by his supernatural feat, a request made by his mother, the Virgin Lady Maryām. Once again, if we look at Map 1, we will certainly find the village of Kana, encircled in blue, very close to the ancient city of Tyre (Sūr), in the heart of Phoenicia.

As a matter of truth, the concept that Yāwsēp̄, Maryām, and Yāwshu were from the region of Galilee is not at all new, or confined to theories written by modern historians. Indeed, the theory, or rather say, this *fact*, has been presented before objective and professional modern scholars, who found it while looking into important proof that had been neglected by the Judeo-Christian community of propagandists—proof that should be highly considered.

Where was Jesus Christ born? Who was he in reality? Was he simply a Jewish prophet? Was he Jewish-Galilean or Phoenician-Galilean? These are the most essential questions that we should reach a solid answer to after analyzing the nine proofs, cited below. It is most certain that more new objective and serious evidence is surfacing nowadays, tending towards the region of Galilee, not Judea, being not only Jesus' birthplace, but also the locality where the Divine Spirit of the Father Ēl blew in him the power and authority for a special mission to undertake in his life —saving the world from its sins by Death and Resurrection, like the Phoenix, like Adon.

The novel approach concerning the true identity of Jesus Christ that some respected scholars are dealing with now (or similar approaches others may have dealt with in the past/ may be dealing with in secret in the present) is by itself quite an interesting accomplishment, not only on the archaeological and historical levels but also on the theological, cultural, and genetic levels as well. There is no doubt anymore in the minds of the brave and the intelligent that not only was Jesus Galilean, but so were his mother, father, and most of his Disciples, except for probably two. We will elaborate more on that issue in the next chapter; as for now, let us engage in a quick yet comprehensive analysis on the following nine important proofs, among many ...

Important Proofs

Proof 1: Sometime around the 8th century AD, a theologian by the name of Saint John of Damascus—known to have been very devout to the Virgin Lady Mary—wrote that Mary was born at Sephoris in Galilee, a few kilometers from Nazareth, and very close to Bethlehem (Bet-Lahem) of Galilee.

Proof 2: One of the most credible notations comes from the contemporary American scholar and Protestant priest, Bruce Chilton, who seems to have based his studies about Mary being born at Sephoris in Galilee on the work of Saint John of Damascus who lived more than a thousand years before him. Chilton stated that Bethlehem of Galilee certainly had a close relationship with Christianity since the Birth of Jesus. He also expressed that both Joseph and Mary were from Bethlehem and Nazareth and that it is possible that Mary was born in Sephoris of Galilee. Chilton also suggested that Matthew had not entirely invented the story of the Nativity, but simply chose to switch the two Bethlehems.

Analysis of Proofs 1 and 2: Maryām and Yāwsēp̄ (Mary and Joseph), the parents of Yāwshu (Yeshu), are both from the region of Galilee, not Judea. This becomes an evident fact, but the question we may then ask is from which Galilean village they originated. There are in fact three proposed locations: Sephoris, Nazareth, and Kafar Kanna. We, however, believe that Maryām was indeed from the Lebanese Village of Kana, and we shall tackle once again this issue in the Analysis of Proof 4. As for now, she is Galilean, and by logical historical terms and geographical laws existing at the time of Jesus it would be impossible, rather illogical for her, especially during conception, to make a trip outside Galilee. She have had to travel for about a week, covering approximately a distance of 90 miles (140 km) from Nazareth of Galilee, across Samaria, to eventually deliver her son in some location in Judea, called Bethlehem, were that the actual location of his Birth. However, a young pregnant woman in her ninth month, as mentioned in Luke (2:1-7), would not be able to make this long awkward trip without losing her baby since the only available methods of transportation known back then would either be walking on foot, mounting an animal, or riding a chariot. The important question that strongly imposes itself on our minds would then be: Why did Matthew decide to shift the two Bethlehems, as Chilton suggested? It would not be out of error, of course, but rather a deliberate act by him who seemed to have quoted Micah from the Old Testament, as we have shown in the previous chapter. The Matthew-Micah resemblance could be a Judeo-Christian Bible alteration of a later period, used as a notion that Jesus was the expected Messiah of the Jewish people. Micah (5:2) is said to have predicted that out of Bethlehem (of Judea) would "come a ruler who will be the shepherd of my people Israel." Matthew's (2:6) verse is said be tied with that of Micah. This sounds too plotted to be regarded coincidental or divinely prepared by YHWH.

It is known that Matthew wrote his testimony several decades after the death of Jesus, and confusing the two Bethlehems could not be fathomed without realizing that, as we have seen, his gospel was mainly addressed to the Jews, with the special intention to create a story favorable to them, perhaps in a desperate attempt to convert them into the new Christian faith. Thus, in order to fasten the *invented* link between Jesus and David, and perceiving that the Jewish Messiah should come from the House of David, Matthew changed the locations only to convince them that Jesus had also been born a Jew, in the Judean Bethlehem, which has been traditionally mentioned as the hometown of King David, father of King Solomon. Yet, this Bethlehem falls down in history for both the mythical David and the historical Jesus.

Some Christians have found it convenient to abide by the wishes of Matthew, although, while linking Jesus to the Judean Bethlehem, he wrote something quite strange in his evangelical story that Christians seem to have not paid attention to. In Matthew (1:23), we read, "Behold, the virgin shall be with child, and shall bring forth a son. They shall call his name Immanuel, which means God with us." Jesus was then *Immanuel*, "Ēl with us." Ēl is the Phoenician Most High God, as we have thoroughly explained. In Matthew's—conscious or unconscious, deliberate or non-deliberate decree, Jesus is the son, the Divine holder of the Spirit of the Father, Ēl.

Again we read from Matthew (2:22-23), "... having been warned in a dream, he (Joseph, Jesus' father) withdrew into the region of Galilee, and came and lived in a city called Nazareth; that it might be fulfilled which was spoken through the prophets: He will be called a Nazarene." Another striking revelation from Matthew. But why did Matthew say that Jesus would be called a Nazarene as a fulfillment to the prophecy spoken by the prophets? Which prophets? The answer to this important question is found in Part III, but let us for the time being conclude that the majority of respectful academics state that the story of Matthew about the Nativity of Jesus in Judah is distant from historical fact. In truth, Jesus was called "Jesus of Nazareth," but in correct words he was a *Nazarene*. Being one, he must have been born in Nazareth, or around it, where he spent most of his life. It was certainly in the region of Galilee. Remember the words: "Nazareth! Can anything good come from Nazareth?" or "This is the Christ. But some said, shall Christ come out of Galilee?" Since Nazareth was built in a later period, sometime before the 2nd century AD, it then could not be Jesus' place of birth. Yet, if we examine the maps at the end of the book, we find that the Bet-Lahem of Galilee is a village located only a few miles west of what would become Nazareth. Geography doesn't lie! And neither does history, for the real Bethlehem was in fact in Galilee, not in Judea. Jesus was Galilean. Historically speaking, Galilee was essentially populated by Canaano-Phoenicians (Aramaens), Syrians, Romans, Greeks, and a few others of different nations. Jews were not living in this area at the time of Jesus, and if there were any by any chance, they would have formed an extremely small and closed group. In fact, the clear name given to Galilee by the Jews back then undoubtedly answers the very basic question central to this book. They called it: "Galilee of the Nations," or "Galilee of the Gentiles," as stated in Matthew (4:15). That description came from the certainty that Galilee was inhabited only by Gentiles, and therefore, non-Jews!

Although Reverend Chilton believes that Jesus' parents were Galileans and that there was a strong connection between the Galilean Bethlehem and Christ, blaming Matthew for switching it with the Judean Bethlehem, he seems to have always considered Jesus a Jew, particularly a Jewish rabbi[192], as presented in his work, *Rabbi Jesus* (2002).

I always wondered why Chilton and others would still consider Jesus a Jew after suggesting the above. It is well known that Galilee has been considered "Galilee of the non-Jews" in the New Testament itself. In fact, it was only after the destruction of the Jewish Temple by Titus, in 70 AD, that Jews took Galilee as a place to live, only because they were expelled from Jerusalem into neighboring regions and among them, Galilee, where they gradually started to wipe away any Phoenician traces they came in contact with, such as the grotto of Bet(h)-Lahem (Beit Lahm) or Bethlehem, located on the Northeastern base of Mt. Carmel, and which meant in the Phoenician language: the "House of Bread." Adonis, that young and beautiful god of Gebel who incarnated the cycle of nature and represented the spring—the resurrection of every atom in the kingdom of life—was also worshipped in this Bethlehem. In his book, the *Golden Bough*, Sir James Frazer, wrote that Adonis represented the spirit of the corn and that he might well have dwelt and later worshiped in this Bethlehem[193]. There is plenty of evidence that strongly suggests the non-Jewishness of Jesus. Even his name Immanuel (God Ēl with us) expresses that ...

In fact, Jesus' teaching of a universal God, Ēl, Father to all, whom he mentioned during his crucifixion, will not in any way cope with the Jewish image of the God YHWH being a national and tribal god worshiped by the Jews back then. I still wonder why Jesus spoke to the Jews in that strong way in John 8. At any rate, Ernest Renan wrote in his famous book, *Vie de Jésus,* that Mary, the mother of Jesus, was most probably from the small

---

192 We will definitely explain why Jesus could not have been a Jewish rabbi in Chapter 8.

193 In fact, Frazer was referring to the Judean Bethlehem, as we have seen before. He should have known instead that the Galilean Bet-Lahem was the one related to Adon (son of Ēl), and after him, to Immanuel (incarnation of Ēl).

Galilean village of Cana[194], and that Jesus was Galilean, and not from the House of David.

Although Jesus and his family are being portrayed for some time as Galileans, the general trend among scholars is still identifying them as Jews. I have a different view of course . . . We both, the majority of scholars and I, surely have different and opposite points of view concerning the true identity of Jesus. Not only that, but the majority of Christian believers seem to share the scholars' belief that Jesus was a Jew, probably on the basis of the Church New Tetsament. But the main question addressed to scholars and believers that comes to mind is why Galileans were considered Jews at the time of Jesus knowing that Galilee was called "Galilee of the non-Jews" in the New Testament? To scholars, the answer is simple. Their belief, as is clearly shown in their works, mainly comes from the conviction that Galilee's Jewish population rose after the conquest of the Maccabees during the 2nd century BC, and which thus determine that Jesus' family would then belong to that population.[195]

This belief is shared by many Biblical scholars like the American Dr. James Strange, archaeologist from the University of South Florida, and both John Dominic Crossan, professor emeritus of religious studies at DePaul University, Chicago, and Jonathan L. Reed, leading authority on first-century Palestinian archeology who is now the lead archeologist at Sepphoris, in Galilee. Crossan and Reed joined Biblical studies to archaeology in their work, *Excavating Jesus*, where they stated[196]:

... Palestine [became] a buffer zone between the Ptolemaic dynasty in Egypt and the Seleucid dynasty in Syria. After these dynasties were weakened by a succession of wars with each other, a power vacuum was created in the second century B.C.E. This period witnessed considerable movement of peoples, including the movement of Jews into Galilee.

Yet, what strikes me the most is that Dr. Strange, both Professor Crossan and Dr. Reed, and many others, perhaps misread Maccabees and/or probably ignored the fact that the

---

194 Although Renan doesn't say that Mary is from Kana (Qana), the Lebanese Village; he was referring to another: Cana of Galilee. However, I will explain soon why Renan has been mistaken about it, and why he should have known instead which one of the two formed the authentic cradle of Maryām.

195 This is an issue we have tackled before and we have attributed Jesus' family to Canaano-Phoenician Aramaic origin, not Jewish.

196 Crossan, John Dominic & Reed, Jonathan L., *Excavating Jesus*, page 32.

Jews—if they were any in reality as per the book of Ashaya or Isaiah (9:1), a work that was written before the time of the Maccabees, and demonstrated by our Phoenician historical records—had in fact left Galilee after the Galilean conquest of the Maccabees[197] sometime around the middle of the 2nd century BC. This is evident in the Book of 1 Maccabees (5:1-23), and it is what we actually need to show here in this study. It narrates that (italics mine):

When the Gentiles all around heard that the altar had been rebuilt and the sanctuary dedicated as it was before, they became very angry, and they determined to destroy the descendants of Jacob who lived among them. So they began to kill and destroy among the people. But Judas made war on the descendants of Esau in Idumea, at Akrabattene, because they kept lying in wait for Israel. He dealt them a heavy blow and humbled them and despoiled them. He also remembered the wickedness of the sons of Baean, who were a trap and a snare to the people and ambushed them on the highways. They were shut up by him in their towers; and he encamped against them, vowed their complete destruction, and burned with fire their towers and all who were in them. Then he crossed over to attack the Ammonites, where he found a strong band and many people, with Timothy as their leader. He engaged in many battles with them, and they were crushed before him; he struck them down. He also took Jazer and its villages; then he returned to Judea. Now the Gentiles in Gilead gathered together against the Israelites who lived in their territory, and planned to destroy them. But they fled to the stronghold of Dathema, and sent to Judas and his brothers a letter that said, The Gentiles around us have gathered together to destroy us. They are preparing to come and capture the stronghold to which we have fled, and Timothy is leading their forces. Now then, come and rescue us from their hands, for many of us have fallen, and all our kindred who were in the land of Tob have been killed; the enemy have captured their wives and children and goods, and have destroyed about a thousand persons there. While the letter was still being read, other messengers, with their garments torn, came from Galilee and

---

197 The Maccabees are shown in the Books of Maccabees as a reputed Jewish family who is said to have defended Jewish Rights and Tradition in the 2nd century BC. The most famous among them was Judas, the Maccabeus, one of the sons of Mattathias (a priest), who proved to be a great leader of his people and a capable warrior who fought and won battles against Roman generals and many other nations of the Gentiles.

made a similar report; they said that the people of Ptolemais and *Tyre and Sidon, and all Galilee of the Gentiles*[198], had gathered together against them to annihilate us. When Judas and the people heard these messages, a great assembly was called to determine what they should do for their kindred who were in distress and were being attacked by enemies. Then Judas said to his brother Simon, Choose your men and go and rescue your kindred in Galilee; Jonathan my brother and I will go to Gilead. But he left Joseph, son of Zechariah, and Azariah, a leader of the people, with the rest of the forces, in Judea to guard it; and he gave them this command, Take charge of this people, but do not engage in battle with the Gentiles until we return. Then three thousand men were assigned to Simon to go to Galilee, and eight thousand to Judas for Gilead. So Simon went to Galilee and fought many battles against the Gentiles, and the Gentiles were crushed before him. He pursued them to the gate of Ptolemais; as many as three thousand of the Gentiles fell, and he despoiled them. *Then he took the Jews of Galilee and Arbatta, with their wives and children, and all they possessed, and led them to Judea with great rejoicing.*

It leaves no doubt though after reading the last emphasized sentences that Simon the Maccabee, after winning over the Gentiles, as the narration evokes, took the Jews out of Galilee (men, wives, children, possessions, etc.) and led them back to Judea where they rejoiced in reaching home. There is an important point here that we should highlight. This very fact of transporting the Jewish population from Galilee of the Gentiles to Judea of the Jews is in direct opposition to the cultural and ethnic factors modeling the character of Jesus the Galilean, who always felt at the risk of assassination from the Jews in Judea, and forever feeling safe back home in Galilee, Tyre, and Sidon, with the company of the Gentiles, especially, the Phoenician-Galileans.

---

198 Jesus used to often retreat to his homeland (Phoenicia-Galilee) after preaching in Jerusalem, as cited in Matthew 15:21, "Jesus went out from there (most likely Jerusalem, not Galilee), and withdrew into the region of Tyre and Sidon." Unquestionably then, the Gentile Phoenician-Galileans of Galilee, Tyre, and Sidon, had constituted the first group of believers in Jesus Christ, whom they had previously worshiped through Él and his son Adon (worshipped in the Galilean Bet-Lahem: House of Bread). Indeed, Jesus had expressed happiness in retreating to the place where he had first felt accepted.

The feeling of threat was not only felt by Jesus, who did not actually fear the Jews in Judea and appeared confident to face them come what may, but was also felt by his close disciples who seemed to have been very worried that he might get killed over there. It is plainly shown in John while narrating the visit Jesus made to Lazarus of Bethany when he was sick[199]. After staying two more days in Bethany, in the company of Lazarus and his two sisters, Mary and Martha, Jesus made up his mind to move. His sudden decision to leave Galilee for Judea at a critical time in his ministry shocked his Galilean disciples. They immediately objected to his trip and advised him against it because the Jews might harm him or even seek to kill him. Another piece of evidence to support our proposition: had there been Jews in Galilee, they would have represented the same danger at home, an issue not raised since there were none!

At any rate, it appears that the majority of Biblical scholars and historians believe the Books of the Maccabees[200] to be at least historically acceptable and authentic, though only to a certain extent. They somehow narrate the unfurling events and their conquests as they might have probably occurred, of course, from their own perspective of portraying themselves as holy warriors and winners, accomplishing God's will—their national God, YHWH.

The Books of the Maccabees stand as the final known records of the Jews in the Old Testament, and thus, if we should take the account narrated above as true history, we would come to the logical straightforward conclusion that ever since the conquest of Galilee, the Jews were ultimately transferred to Judea "for safety reasons" by their own leaders sometime around the year 160 BC, and never returned to the Galilee of the Gentiles until late after the destruction of the temple in 70 AD. Therefore, their sudden re-emergence or novel appearance in the region of Galilee at the time of Jesus, as the Church New Testament suggests and would like us to believe, is in truth very questionable on the historical level, extremely debatable on the archaeological level, and highly mythical on both religious and political levels.

When we further investigate the authenticity of the Books of the Maccabees, we find interesting analysis given by Thomas L.

199 John 11:6-8, "So, when He heard that he was sick, He stayed two more days in the place where He was. Then after this He said to [the] disciples, Let us go to Judea again. [The] disciples said to Him, Rabbi, lately the Jews sought to stone You, and are You going there again?"
200 1Maccabees and 2Maccabees were considered Apocrypha, but were integrated into the text of the Old Testament along with other books of the Maccabees that were not incorporated.

Thompson in his beautiful enriching book, *The Mythic Past*. He suggests that the Books of Maccabees did not exist in Hebrew at all but were originally written in Greek and could be (specifically 2 Maccabees) just a fictional account of known traditions—perhaps orally, since they imply that there could be no stable collection of written tradition that had survived the Maccabean wars—and might be read as supporting the Maccabees' view of the Jewish Tradition and of their role in protecting the traditional way of life in Hellenized Palestine. Thompson continues his analysis by saying that Judas Maccabee's efforts to preserve the Jewish Tradition might be only a collection or a reference to what is now seen as a fragmented past, and that the Bible (Old Testament) should not be dated before sometime in the 1st century BC, since the Book of Maccabees we mentioned above offers a serious argument about the final formation of the Hebrew Bible that could well have been written after the completion of that book[201].

In addition, Thompson believes that reading the Bible as a book of history is not easy as hoped and expected, but it becomes even more frustrating as we come closer to the time the texts were originally written. Books such as Ezra and Nehemiah, 1 and 2 Maccabees, 1 Esdras in the Apocrypha, the Dead Sea Scrolls' "Damascus Covenant," and, Josephus' *Antiquities of the Jews*, possessed a great freedom in their narration, hence, the stories they told of the past, whenever they had a potential one to tell, recycled them as if they were true historical accounts, and many were certainly created in the hope of weaving a continuous narrative[202].

At any rate, what concerns us here in this study is not whether the Old Testament narrative is historically authentic or not; we may leave this issue as a subject for a future book. In fact, what concerns us here and now is that the region of Galilee was empty of Jewish habitation at the time of Jesus. The Book 1 of Maccabees (5:1-23) we just read, which mentions the preparation for an attack against Galilee, showed that Simon Maccabee, sent by his brother, Judas, won the war over the Gentiles. However, what makes us wonder is why, after a successful conquest, Simon chose not to stay or at least leave the Jews, *now secured*, in the defeated land of the Gentiles? On the contrary, he opted to lead them out of Galilee and back into Judea with great rejoicing. There is no logic behind what he did as a leader-warrior because in the art or strategy of war, taking an enemy land, securing it, and then immediately leaving it, is altogether not a reasonable,

---

201 Thompson L., Thomas, *The Mythic Past*, page 293-294.
202 Ibid., page 216.

coherent military action. Unless of course, the narration is not historically authentic and the Jews whom Simon was said to have rescued in Galilee were not actually living there in the first place.

To end this historical observation, to us, what is truly meant by the above text, is the direct implication that since the Jews left Galilee for Judea during the Maccabees' time, sometime around 164 BC–160 BC, and they never returned back, hence, they were not in Galilee at the time of Jesus. This conclusive proof is supported by Matthew himself in the New Testament when he referred to Galilee as being of the Gentiles[203]. In fact, the Rabbinical writings of the *Mishnah*[204] section of the Talmud that date back to around 200 AD, appears to assert that the Jews—after the fall of Jerusalem at the hand of the Roman General, Titus, around 70 AD—reestablished their cultural and religious life at a city called Jamnia before *moving* (not returning) later, probably around 118 AD, to Galilee.

To think, or rather believe that there were truly Jewish temples and synagogues in some parts of both the upper and lower Galilean regions of the Gentiles, like Capernaum, Bethsaida, Nazareth, and Bethlehem (Bet-Lahem) at the time of Jesus, is one of the biggest historical/archaeological mistakes to have been committed by Biblical scholars. The Christian-Jewish propagandists among them appear to have often hoped and seemed to have always worked, truly hard, to impregnate history and religion with their hidden political goals. Such an approach certainly endangers the pursuit of Truth in what concerns the pure reality of the birth of Christianity. To them, of course, "Jesus the Jew" is much more welcomed and applauded than "Jesus the Phoenician." To these propagandists, the Truth is not at all higher than their political and economical agenda. To them, those who dare say and believe otherwise are but enemies of the history they invented and the present they are creating, accordingly.

Proof 3: Another contemporary person who examined the case was the German theologian and professor, Harmut Stegemann. His work was for the most part founded on Christianity, with great interest in both the New Testament and the Dead Sea Scrolls, in which he specialized. Stegemann, who became one of the world's leading scholarly experts on Biblical archaeology and

---

203 Matthew 4:15.
204 The *Mishnah* does not concur with either text, the New Testament or those of Josephus, about many things concerning the Jewish religious system and Tradition in connection with the authority given to the Sadducees, Pharisees, and Scribes.

the Qumran Community, proposed back in the sixties that Jesus was not born in Bethlehem (of Judea), but rather in Galilee, in Capernaum by the lake of Genezareth.

Analysis of Proof 3: Although it is true that Jesus chose Capernaum as one of the most essential towns during his public ministry in the region of Galilee, probably his headquarters, as we have seen earlier, enacting many miracles there, especially of healing nature, he definitely could not have favored it over any other Galilean town or village that he loved, like Bethsaida, Nazareth, etc. His entry to Capernaum was mentioned by both Matthew[205] and Luke[206], though the timing of his arrival to Capernaum may slightly differ between the texts.

However, to believe that *Kfar-Naa-Um*, by the Sea of Tiberias, was the birthplace of Jesus Christ is totally wrong, even as a hypothesis. Stegemann might have built his conclusion on the great importance of this town in the life of Jesus. He may also have taken too literally the words of the two Synoptics attributed to both Matthew[207] and Mark[208]. The first instance was when Matthew referred to Capernaum as Jesus' own city, and in the second, when Mark alluded to Jesus' house in Capernaum; or perhaps he may have reached such a conviction after relating the issue of Jesus and his teachings at the synagogue of Capernaum! Yet, herein, at this very moment of praise, everything falls apart, not only for Stegemann, but also for all others around the world who believed in the truthfulness of the Canonical texts concerning Jewish synagogues.

Why everything is falling apart? One may ask. The answer is very clear: there is no historical or archaeological proof whatsoever regarding this particular matter, simply because, truthfully and once for all, there were no Jewish temples or synagogues at all, either in the village of Capernaum or in Nazareth, and not even anywhere else in Galilee at the time of Jesus.

---

205 Matthew 4:13, "And leaving Nazareth, He came and dwelt in Capernaum, which is by the sea, in the regions of Zebulun and Naphtali."

206 Luke 7:1, "Now when He concluded all His sayings in the hearing of the people, He entered Capernaum."

207 Matthew, 9:1, "So He got into a boat, crossed over, and came to His own city."

208 Mark 2:1, "And again He entered Capernaum after [some] days, and it was heard that He was in the house." And Mark 9:33, "Then He came to Capernaum. And when He was in the house He asked them, "What was it you disputed among yourselves on the road?"

Before we exhibit the archaeological evidence that denies the existence of synagogues in Capernaum in just a bit, we would like first to have a look at Nazareth at the time of Jesus. In *Excavating Jesus*, John Dominic Crossan and Jonathan L. Reed, wrote[209]:

> ... first-century Nazareth was anything other than a modest village void of public architecture ... . Excavations underneath later Christian structures uncovered no synagogue, but also no fortification, no palace, no basilica, no bathhouse, no paved street, nothing. Instead, olive presses, wine presses, water cisterns, grain silos, and grinding stones scattered around caves tell of a population that lived in hovels and simple peasant houses.

The archaeological discovery made there in Nazareth definitely supports our theory of the inhabitants of this place, as we shall see along this chapter. At any rate, the Canonical texts, those of Mark[210], Luke[211] and John[212], which have cited the entrance of Jesus into the synagogues to teach and read, are but the efforts of many—now exposed—to link Jesus to the legendary Jewish King of Messianic nature, David. This attempt is similar to the one we previously saw in Matthew (2:1, 6). The story of Jesus' Birth in the Bethlehem of Judea, with all that enchanting scenario that framed the event—the manger, the three kings and/or astrologists[213] who followed a twinkling celestial sign, the Star that had led them to the grotto where they came to witness this divine event, along with the complete idea of a fulfillment of a Hebrew Biblical prophecy[214]—was a later addition, some say of almost a hundred years, most likely, during the construction of the gospels either by the attributed authors or by their copiers. Such a prophecy has not been found anywhere in the Old Testament and

209 Crossan, John Dominic & Reed, Jonathan L., *Excavating Jesus*, page 31-32.
210 Mark 1:21, "Then they went into Capernaum, and immediately on the Sabbath He entered the synagogue and taught."
211 Luke 4:14-16, "Then Jesus returned in the power of the Spirit to Galilee, and news of Him went out through all the surrounding region. And He taught in their synagogues, being glorified by all. So He came to Nazareth, where He had been brought up. And as His custom was, He went into the synagogue on the Sabbath day, and stood up to read." And Luke 7:5, "for he loves our nation, and has built us a synagogue."
212 John 6:59, "These things He said in the synagogue as He taught in Capernaum."
213 Some say they were Persian magi, but we very much doubt it for reasons we shall see later on.
214 Matthew 2:23.

could not be related to Bethlehem of Judea for many reasons, some of which we have already seen and others we will see later on. Truth be said, this prophecy actually belongs to another group of people: the Nazarenes of Phoenician-Galilean origin.

The systematic falsification of the New Testament texts occurred because the new Galilean and Gentile Christian religion was attacked and rejected[215] by the already established Jewish religion in Jerusalem. Hence, relating Christianity to Judaism seemed to be the only way for the new faith to enter Jerusalem and gain adherents or converts among Jews. The logic behind Matthew and the other authors of the New Testament (or their copiers) is understandable to a certain extent, but not at all forgiven in the name of historical truth. We shall see more about that in Chapter 10.

And therefore, to expose even further the manipulation that has been circulating for ages, and precisely in regards to Jesus teaching in the synagogues, whether in Capernaum or in any other location in Galilee, archaeology, the most revealing of all sciences of ancient history, seems to offer the best support of our assertion of the Truth. In his book[216], archeologist Jonathan L. Reed explains:

> That a synagogue building, perhaps similar to the nearby first-century synagogue of Gamla, once stood in Capernaum cannot really be confirmed by the Gospel references to a synagogue, since the term refers primarily to a gathering and only secondarily to a structure in the earlier periods of Palestine.

In fact, archaeological excavations to date have uncovered some kind of a structure in ancient Capernaum that has been dated to the 4th century AD. This structure is termed as the white stone synagogue, however, a local dark-black basalt foundation of an earlier structure has been unearthed at the site, and archaeologists, mainly Judeo-Christians, suggest that it belongs to the synagogue mentioned in the New Testament in Jesus' time.

Yet, with no firm or rather finite knowledge of the exact time this synagogue was built, we would determine its probable or alleged existence to be in the 1st century AD, and if archaeology

---

215 It was the Pharisees, the religious sacerdotal body of the Jews, along with soldiers and officers from the chief priests, who came to arrest Jesus when he was on Mount Olives, as in John 18:1-6. They worked hard enough immediately after, through Pilate, the Roman governor, to have Jesus judged and crucified, as mentioned in Matthew 27:1-26; Mark 15:1-15; Luke 23:1-25 and John 19:1-16.

216 Reed, Jonathan L., *Archeology and the Galilean Jesus*, page 154-155.

does confirm it, to be not before the time Jerusalem was destroyed by Titus in around 70 AD and the migration of the Jewish people to the Gentile Galilean region.[217] That Capernaum and some other Galilean villages, like Nazareth, bear the traits of typical Jewish villages in Roman Palestine is largely confirmed in the 4th century AD, but totally negligible at the time of Jesus. They could have been consistent with Jewish style of building before the Macabbees' time and their successful revolt led by Simon, which would have concluded in the transfer or deportation of the Jewish population from the entire region of Galilee to Judea in c. 164 BC–160 BC, as we have earlier seen in the Book 1 of Maccabees (5:23). Yet, the events that describe the existence of Jews in Galilee and their war against the Galilean Gentiles, as cited in the text, are debatable.

Reed seems to have suggested in his reputed book[218] that, "The archeological evidence indicates that Capernaum was a Jewish village, a point apparent in the literary evidence." He then adds a few sentences later, "The archaeology confirms this, first, by uncovering the site's foundation as a village in the Late Hellenistic Period, which coincides with the widespread Jewish settlement of Galilee and parts of the Golan."

To end the confusion: although there is no concrete proof of a Jewish temple, a place of worship of any kind, or a precise synagogue in Capernaum before the 4th century AD, Reed's unusual suggestion, if I could say, may sound a bit relieving to the Jewish-Christian community of Biblical scholars. We, on the other hand, find his proposition both illogical and weak for two reasons. First, we believe there would be a cultural and religious need for a temple by a people living in a certain area, something that was not found in a supposedly Jewish Galilee, and thus contradicting the Biblical and literary evidence. Second, there is no archaeological evidence for the complete era of the Late Hellenistic Period that stretches from 160 BC to 30 BC. If the Jewish population had left Galilee with Simon the Maccabee some four years before the Late Hellenistic Period had started, then the archaeological evidence Reed spoke about would only present the remaining parts of their deserted houses, storage facilities, courtyards, etc. And if the Late Hellenistic Period ended in 30 BC, then it has no relation to Jesus' time. At any rate, we strongly

---

217 In the compilation book of nine essays, *Evolution of the Synagogue: Problems and Progress*, published in 1999, scholar and editor, Howard Clark Kee, argues that synagogues arose in the aftermath of the destruction of the Temple of Jerusalem, in 70 AD.
218 Reed, Jonathan L., *Archeology and the Galilean Jesus*, page 161.

believe that there was no Jewish population in all of Galilee between the years 164/160 BC and 70 + AD, and if there were any, for the sole reason of rolling the dice on the table for luck, they would not have formed a substantial minority as some wish, but quite the opposite: a minor minority.

Proof 4: One of the most famous authors in the history of the Levant and who has enlightened us with an even more striking revelation than the previous three regarding the true identity of Jesus Christ, was indeed Ernest Renan, the well-known French historian, and a peregrinator to the Holy Land. He clearly wrote in his famous book, *Vie de Jésus*—published at the end of the 19th century—that Mary, the Mother of Jesus, was most probably from the Galilean Cana[219], known also as *Kafar Kanna*, a small village on the road to Nazareth, and that Jesus was Galilean and not from the Family (or House) of David[220].

Analysis of Proof 4: Although Ernest Renan states the above, he, like many other historians and theologians failed to look at Jesus in a different way or from a different perspective, as is the usual case with the traditional approach made by the Christian-Jewish civilization in their consideration of Jesus as a Jew. Not only that, his statement that Mary, the Mother of Jesus, was probably from the Galilean Cana could also be wrong for a couple of reasons. We are determined to say that being a Galilean is a direct insinuation that Maryām was not Jewish, and archaeological finds prove that she could not be from Cana or Kafar Kanna in Galilee, a few kilometers away from Nazareth, but rather from the small Lebanese Village of Kana or Qana, close to Tyre. Yet, both villages having the same name were indeed part of Phoenicia back at the time of Jesus, as shown in the maps.

The Lebanese archaeologist and historian, Dr. Youssef Hourany, explained well in his book[221] that the Kana of Galilee cited in the Church New Testament is indeed the Lebanese Kana located in southern Lebanon, a place very well known to Jesus,

219 Renan, Ernest, *Vie de Jésus*, page 157. The Galilean Cana, or *Kana el-Djelil* as it is known today, could be acceptable to a certain extent as the place from which Mary originated, only because it is in Galilee. We, however, believe it is not the right place and that Renan had probably switched the Lebanese Kana with the Galilean Cana (Kafar Kanna), perhaps in the manner of Matthew, or most likely had mistaken it for the small village of Kana in Lebanon.

220 *Ibid.*, page 122-123 (fn.4), 273-274.

221 Hourany, Youssef, *Lebanon in the Value of its History / Phoenician Era*— لبنان في قيم تاريخه / العهد الفينيقي , page 232.

who used to stroll in the region of Tyre and Sidon. The wilderness where he and his disciples seemed to have always preferred to camp matches the surroundings of Kana, which appeared to be the perfect place for such activities. Dr. Hourany and all the others who have tackled this issue refer to Kana as the same one mentioned in both John[222] and Joshua[223], being a location in Phoenicia.

Along with the reputed Lebanese historian comes another person of equally high caliber, Dr. Youssef Yammine, a Lebanese priest who explained without a shred of doubt that the famous event regarding the wedding ceremony and the miracle of turning water into wine, mentioned in the New Testament took place in the small village of Kana (Kfar Kanna) of Galilee actually happened in Kana of Lebanon[224].

Furthermore, Martiniano Pellegrino Roncaglia—the Italian professor, historian, and writer—succeeded in proving that fact as well in his two explanatory books: *Cana*, released in 1995, and *In the Footsteps of Jesus, the Messiah, in Phoenicia/Lebanon*, released in the year 2004. Both books confirmed that Jesus had performed his first miracle of turning the water into wine, there, in Kana, and not in Kafar Kanna, which was a different tiny place on the road to Nazareth.

A verity proved nowadays by so many historians and archaeologists, like Mr. George Nasr, the Lebanese researcher, scriptwriter, and director, who showed in his television documentary[225] that almost twelve kilometers southeast of Tyre, the famous wedding of Kana mentioned in the New Testament remains still engraved on a rock, picturing people, disciples, the bride, and the faces of both Jesus and John the Baptist! It was at that particular wedding that Mary, the Mother of Jesus, had asked him for the miracle of turning water into red wine.

Another Lebanese archaeologist of high caliber, Dr. Antoine Khoury Hareb, also proves in his well-researched and illustrated book[226] that the reputed wedding cited in the New Testament actually happened in the small Lebanese village of Kana.

---

222 John 2:1, "On the third day there was a wedding in Cana of Galilee, and the mother of Jesus was there."
223 Joshua 19:27-28, "It turned toward the sunrise to Beth Dagon; and it reached to Zebulun and to the Valley of Jiphthah El, then northward beyond Beth Emek and Neiel, bypassing Cabul [which was] on the left, including Ebron, Rehob, Hammon, and Kanah, as far as Greater Sidon."
224 Yammine, Youssef Rev., *The Galilean Kana in Lebanon—قانا الجليل في لبنان* , page 42-52.
225 Nasr, George, *If Lebanon Told its Story*, produced for the Lebanese Ministry of Tourism, 1997.

Kana seems to have presented itself in history as an important place in the life of Jesus for two reasons. First, it is believed to be the birthplace of Maryām, as we shall see one more time in Proof 7. Second, it was the chosen place for Yāwshu to manifest his divinity by performing his first public miracle. We agree with others who posit that it is fitting that Jesus should have chosen to enact his divine powers at the birthplace of his mother and at her request.

On the etymological level, *Kana* or *Qana* is undoubtedly a Canaano-Phoenician-Aramaic word that could have three different meanings: "own/possess," "place/house," "red/red color[227]." Of course, knowing the linguistic roots of the term is indeed interesting for us to identify the origin of the place, yet it is also very important to know that an event as famous as the Wedding of Cana, with both theological and historical significance, was not mentioned in the Synoptics, for we only find it in John (2:1-13):

On the third day there was a wedding in Cana of Galilee, and the mother of Jesus was there. Now both Jesus and His disciples were invited to the wedding. And when they ran out of wine, the mother of Jesus said to Him, 'They have no wine.' Jesus said to her, 'Woman, what does your concern have to do with Me? My hour has not yet come.' His mother said to the servants, 'Whatever He says to you, do [it].' Now there were set there six waterpots of stone[228], according to the manner of purification of the Jews[229], containing twenty or thirty gallons apiece. Jesus said to them, 'Fill the waterpots with water.' And they filled them up to the brim. And He said to them, 'Draw [some] out now, and take [it] to the master of the feast.' And they took [it]. When the master of the feast had tasted the water that was made wine, and did not know where it came from (but the servants who had drawn the water knew), the

---

226 Khoury Hareb, Antoine, *The Christian Roots in Lebanon—*جذور المسيحية في لبنان, page 40-49.

227 Yammine, Youssef Rev., *The Galilean Kana in Lebanon—*قانا الجليل في لبنان, page 12.

228 The Catholic Encyclopedia exhibit a tradition that goes back to the 8th century AD, which identifies Cana of the wedding with the town of Kafar Kanna, situated some 7 km to the northeast of Nazareth. Yet, the setting of the waterpots of stone used in the miracle of turning water into wine, and all the ambiance of a wedding ceremony, were not at all found in Kfar (Kafar) Kanna or Kefr Kenna of Galilee, but rather in Kana or Qana of Lebanon. Please see the Maps & Pictures in the Appendix for more visual clarity.

229 Purification by water was not a Jewish tradition. It was instead a Canaano-Phoenician custom and was used by the Galileans and the Asayas. Hence, the ritual of baptism performed by John the Baptist.

master of the feast called the bridegroom. And he said to him, 'Every man at the beginning sets out the good wine, and when the [guests] have well drunk, then the inferior. You have kept the good wine until now!' This beginning of signs Jesus did in Cana of Galilee, and manifested His glory; and His disciples believed in Him. After this He went down to Capernaum[230], He, His mother, His brothers, and His disciples; and they did not stay there many days. Now the Passover of the Jews was at hand, and Jesus went up to Jerusalem[231].

No matter how hard and severe the criticism of some Judeo-Christian Biblical scholars on the facts proposed herein, and no matter how harsh they would appear in their many probable and foreseeable attempts to tarnish this very fact, they would not succeed at all in their plans, for it is very clear to the sane seeker of Truth, that the greatest deeds of Yāwshu (Jesus) appear to have occurred in his homeland, in the land of Phoenicia-Galilee.

At any rate, Ernest Renan, who believes that Jesus was Galilean, suggests that, and I quote from his book[232]:

The journey of the family of Jesus to Bethlehem (of Judea) is not historical. Jesus was not of the Family of David, and if he had been (a supposition refused by many), we should still not imagine that his parents should have been forced, for an operation purely registrative and financial, to come to enroll themselves in the place whence their ancestors had proceeded a thousand years before.

This is quite evident, yet Aviram Oshri approaches the issue from another angle that we shall mention as soon as we come to tackle his point.

What is striking in Ernest Renan (and many others like him) is the fact that he strongly rejects the concept of Jesus being of the House of David, yet, still considers him a Jew for reasons not known, or maybe by an unconscious brainwashed default ("Jesus must be Jewish"). A reputed man such as Renan surely

---

230 If they were in Kefr Kenna or Kafar Kanna, then they would be going *up* to Capernaum. Instead, they went *down*, which means they were in Kana of Lebanon, as the maps show.

231 Here the Apostle John states that the Passover of the Jews was to be celebrated in Jerusalem. Why not celebrate it in the temples or in the synagogues of Galilee if they were Jews over there? The fact is evident that there were no temples, no synagogues, and no Jews in Galilee at the time of Jesus.

232 Renan, Ernest, *Vie de Jésus*, page 122-123 (fn.4)

contradicts himself when revealing later in his book[233], "It is doubtful, however, if he (Jesus) understood the Hebrew writings in their original tongue." Why then did an *alleged Jew* not know any Hebrew, either in reading or in writing, although we know that he was educated and used to write, as per John[234]? It seems logical to me and to the reasonable mind to believe that Yāwshu's education was purely Canaano-Phoenician-Aramaic, not Hebrew, since all his biographers, including the accepted gospels[235], mention this Nazarene/Galilean as being well versed in Aramaic. He actually spoke Aramaic. Could anyone imagine a German not speaking German, or a Briton not speaking English? How then could we imagine a Jew not speaking Hebrew, especially at the time of Jesus when most people didn't have the chance to travel outside their country or give birth to their child in foreign countries? At a time when people didn't have the opportunity to send their children outside their territory to get some foreign education? Immigration was not an attitude back then. A Jew would have known Hebrew, as one plus one equals two, so what then if he was an educated Jew? The answer is very simple: he was not an educated Jew. On the contrary, he was an educated Aramean, of course, not as in reference to the ancient biblical Aram/Syria, but to the ancient Biblical Phoenicia/Galilee.

Proof 5: The reputed French author, Edouard Schuré, known for his profound engagement in serious esoteric research into the secret history of religions, wrote in his most read book, *Les Grands Initiés*—first published in 1926 and still considered a classical work of esoteric thinking—that Jesus was probably born in Nazareth, and that it was in that lost corner of Galilee where he was raised as son of Maryām, a Galilean of a noble family, and affiliated to the Essenes[236].

---

233 Ibid., page 130.

234 John 8:6, "This they said, testing Him, that they might have [something] of which to accuse Him. But Jesus stooped down and wrote on the ground with [His] finger, as though He did not hear."

235 Matthew 27:46 and Mark 15:34, on Jesus crying out loud, saying, "Ēli, Ēli, (Ēloi, Ēloi), lama sabachthani?" wrongly translated as, "My God, My God, why have You forsaken Me?" We have seen in the Introduction that the correct Aramaic sentence Jesus used on the Cross might have been "Ēli, Ēli, lemana shabakthani!" meaning, "My God, my God, for this I was spared!" or "Ēli, Ēloi, lamash (lemana) baktani (bachthani)!" meaning, "My God, my God, how much have you praised (glorified) me!"

236 Schuré, Édouard, *Les Grands Initiés*, page 428.

Analysis of Proof 5: Schuré added (in the footnote related to the subject above) that it would be extremely impossible for Jesus to have been born in Bethlehem (of Judea), and that this tradition in particular is an addition of a later cycle of legends attributed to the Holy Family and the Birth of Christ. Interesting indeed, yet Schuré still considered Jesus a Jew—the mainstream conception of Jesus—mirroring some of the prophets of the Old Testament, precisely Samson[237] and Samuel[238], who were declared Nazarites (or Nazarenes) from their mothers' wombs.

Again, since we believe that the Biblical narration, especially the Old Testament, lacks any form of credible proof on all levels, mainly archeologically, we would consider Schuré's suggestion about Jesus reflecting Jewish prophets to be purely fictitious, irrelevant, and only based on the imagination and hopes of the Judeo-Christian culture. Historical reality does not support this alleged claim either.

What concerns us now is the proposition made by Schuré about Jesus being born in Nazareth. Most probably, Schuré based his claim on the texts he read in the New Testament, and precisely the Gospels of both Matthew and Luke, yet, there are many references to Nazareth as the place of origin of the Holy Family. In Matthew (2:23), we read (italics mine):

And he (Joseph) *came and dwelt in a city called Nazareth*, that it might be fulfilled which was spoken by the prophets, He (Jesus) shall be called a Nazarene.

Another one from Matthew (4:13) clearly suggests that Jesus was actually living in Nazareth before leaving to Capernaum to start on his mission, as we have evidently seen before. It says (italics mine):

And *leaving Nazareth*, He came and dwelt in Capernaum, which is by the sea, in the regions of Zebulun and Naphtali ...

The following verse is from Luke (italics mine):

---

237 Judges 13:5, "For behold, you shall conceive and bear a son. And no razor shall come upon his head, for the child shall be a Nazirite to God from the womb; and he shall begin to deliver Israel out of the hand of the Philistines."

238 1Samuel 1:11, "Then she made a vow and said, Oh Lord of hosts, if you will indeed look on the affliction of your maidservant and remember me, and not forget your maidservant, but will give your maidservant a male child, then I will give him to the Lord all the days of his life, and no razor shall come upon his head."

Then He went down with them and *came to Nazareth*, and was subject to them, but His mother kept all these things in her heart. (Luke 2:51)

Another verse from Luke appears as a continuation of the previous one (italics mine):

So He came to *Nazareth, where He had been brought up.* And as His custom was, He went into the synagogue on the Sabbath day, and stood up to read. (Luke 4:16)

The Church New Testament suggests that it was such a critical and difficult time for the Holy Family, fleeing to Egypt, away from Herod's intention to get rid of newborn children two years and under, believing that Jesus was the King of the Jews to be born in Bethlehem of Judea. After the news of Herod's death, the family seemed to have returned back to Nazareth, as Matthew suggests. However, the main question that remains to be asked is: Why not return to Bethlehem of Judea if they were actually from there? There was no danger lingering in the dark anymore. Herod the Great, who sought to kill the infant, was already dead. (But we have dealt with this issue before in Chapter 3.)

We can certainly add the American journalist, Lee Strobel, to the list of names in favor of Nazareth. Strobel explained that his intensive research led him to decide that the Jesus Christ we think of is Jesus of Nazareth, who most likely was born and raised in Nazareth[239]. Many other scholars and researchers around the world believe Nazareth was the birthplace of Jesus. Ernest Renan was one of them[240]. In fact, they are not completely wrong. They are halfway to the truth. It was not in Nazareth itself where the Meshiha was born, but in the closer surrounding region, in a tiny place called Bet-Lahem, located few kilometers west of Nazareth.

A little reminder of what we have seen before: Nazareth, as a village or town, was not already established, in the real sense of the word, at the time of Jesus Christ. Authors John Dominic Crossan and Jonathan L. Reed believe that first-century small *Jewish* Nazareth had a population of no more than 200 to 400 inhabitants[241]. Professor James Strange shares the same conviction that Nazareth was only a very small place, perhaps around sixty acres, at the beginning of the 1st century AD, with a

---

239 Strobel, Lee, *The Case for Christ*, page 102-104
240 Renan, Ernest, *Vie de Jésus*, page 122.
241 Crossan, John Dominic & Reed, Jonathan L., *Excavating Jesus*, page 32.

population of probably no more than 480 people.[242] We don't actually know how Dr. Strange calculated the number of people inhabiting Nazareth at the time or where he received this number. In an email correspondence with him, he informed me: "Most of my conclusions about population were based on the amount of arable land and the area occupied by the ancient village." Strange later added that Nazareth was not cited in ancient Jewish sources earlier than the 3rd century AD, which reflects its lack of prominence in both Galilee and Judea.

Many other archaeologists and historians around the globe share Strange's view, still, they argue that the absence of any textual references to Nazareth, as a defined locality in the Old Testament, the Talmud, the writings of the Apostle Paul, and even in the reputed works of the Roman-Jewish historian Flavius Josephus, would consequently suggest that a town by the name of "Nazareth" did not exist at the time of Jesus. This could be absolutely true. Nazareth was not established before at least the 2nd century AD[243], some say sometime around the 3rd century AD or even as late as the beginning of the 4th century AD. Therefore, any connection to it as being the birthplace of Jesus would be a major error committed by the community of Biblical scholars, thousands of years after the gospels were penned, who have basically misunderstood or misinterpreted the term "Nazarene" used by Matthew and attributed to Jesus.

We strongly believe that the word "Nazareth" is mainly a derivation from the Canaanite/Phoenician/Aramaic term "Nazar," which we explained the meaning of in Chapter 1. The terms "Nazars," "Nazarenes," or "Nazoreans," were given to a special chosen group of people that belonged to the Galilean sect of the Ashayas (or Asayas); a vital topic we have thoroughly tackled before. It is important to note though that this group of people had most likely chosen an *unnamed or unknown* locality in Galilee as their place of habitation and later gave the name "Nazarene," which was attributed to them, to this locality, hence the name, "Nazareth." This entices us to believe that the population inhabiting Nazareth at the time of Yāwshu was very small indeed, certainly less than 480 people. Not all Ashayas were Nazarenes, or, those "specially consecrated to God, Ēl." Since the village most likely hosted a very small number of selected people (similar to later Christian monks or perhaps hermits), it could be described as a kind of primitive or isolated village. The archeological

---

242 Strobel, Lee, *The Case for Christ*, page 103.
243 Mordillat, Gerard, Prieur Jerome, *Corpus Christi*, Volume 4, *Roi des Juifs*, page 30.

discoveries made in Nazareth and mentioned in *Excavating Jesus*, as we have seen before, support this way of life.

Proof 6: Another Frenchman by the name of Jacques Duquesne, a well-known journalist and writer, was even more specific regarding the birthplace of Jesus. He simply penned in his valuable book, *Jésus*—published in 1994—that Jesus Christ was Galilean[244], not of the Bloodline of David[245], and most probably born in Bethlehem of Galilee, not in the Judean Bethlehem[246].

Analysis of Proof 6: I sincerely find no need to analyze the above proof, for it is evident in the mind of Jacques Duquesne that the *Jésus* he wrote about was totally different from the New Testament account of Jesus, and of course, only on the historical level. The French author could not dare to elaborate more on the true bloodline of Jesus, which he had actually found incompatible with the blood type (genealogy) of the mythical Jewish king, David. Like his compatriot, Renan, before him, it seems that was the limit Duquesne would dare to go in his literary historical work, or perhaps they both missed the whole point like many others before and after them. If Duquesne had enough courage in his heart or at least, had he thought out of the box during his research, he would have finally found Jesus' bloodline perfectly matching the blood of the Phoenicians.

Proof 7: One of the leading researchers and theologians in Lebanon, and the author of many books including an encyclopedia on the history of Atom, is the contemporary Christian Maronite priest, Dr. Youssef Yammine. He undoubtedly demonstrates that Jesus was in fact born in the "Bet-Lahem of Galilee"—precisely, in a grotto located at the northeastern foot of Mt. Carmel[247]. He depended in his work on historical and theological evidence and backed his revelation with numerous explicative maps. In his books, he proves without any shred of a doubt that Maryām (Mary), the Mother of Yāwshu (Jesus), did indeed originate from Kana (Qana) of Lebanon[248]. Father Yammine is one of the few theologians all across the thinking world who

---

244 Duquesne, Jacques, *Jésus*, page 21.
245 Ibid., page 38.
246 Ibid., page 54.
247 Yammine, Youssef Rev., *The Messiah was Born in Lebanon Not in Judea*— المسيح ولد في لبنان لا في اليهودية , page 296-308.
248 Yammine, Youssef Rev., *The Galilean Kana in Lebanon*—قانا الجليل في لبنان , page 65-66.

dares to declare his firm belief, leaving no place for hesitation in the mind of his readers, that Jesus was not a Jew. To him, Yāwshu was undoubtedly Canaanite/Phoenician.

Analysis of Proof 7: Yes, we certainly find ourselves compelled by extreme logic and evidence to add our voice to his and share with him our support for this obvious fact. Jesus was born in Bet-Lahem of Galilee and not in Bethlehem of Judea. Yes, Jesus was Phoenician-Galilean, not Jewish. In fact, what has been written and explained in this book ties tightly with Father Yammine's work on the true authentic Christian history that has been manipulated by the Jewish-Christian Biblical community throughout the ages.

However, even the recent Pope Benedict XVI, with all due respect to his position as head of the Catholic Church, does not attest to the Truth. He seems to have rejected in his latest book[249] the notion proposed by an increasing number of scholars, that Jesus was born in Nazareth, or very close to it, in Bet-Lahem. The Pope believes, as the Church New Testament traditionally suggests, that Jesus was in fact born in Bethlehem of Judea, although he made the effort to correct a couple of mistakes mentioned in the scriptures, like the date of Jesus' birth, which he believes happened a few years before the traditional date, an issue we have dealt with in the introduction; also that there were no oxen or other animals in the Nativity scene. It is true that Jesus was not born in Nazareth itself, as we have previously explained, but not in the Bethlehem of Judea, either. Unfortunately, the Pope overlooked the Galilean Bet-Lahem.

That Maryām (Mary) was actually from any Judaic town, is not at all supported by archaeological findings or historical evidence. That she was Phoenician-Galilean by birth is greatly proven not only by scientific proof but also by the gospels' many references. That she probably originated from one of the following Galilean towns— Nazareth (as the majority claim), or the neighboring Sephoris (as both St. John of Damascus and Bruce Chilton propose)—could not be proven for lack of historical evidence, as we have seen before. That she was originally from the Galilean Cana, Kfar (Kafar) Kanna, or Kefr Kenna (as Ernest Renan suggests), is also without credibility due to archaeological deficiency. Finally, that Maryām is actually from the Lebanese village of Kana or Qana is strongly demonstrated by Father Yammine and the few other academics we have just cited, all

---

249 Ratzinger, Joseph (Pope Benedict XVI), *Jesus of Nazareth: The Infancy Narratives.*

backed up immensely by archaeological findings, as we have previously revealed in the Analysis of Proof 4, and as we shall see later on in the pictures displayed in the Appendix.

Proof 8: Lebanese Dr. Antoine Khoury Hareb, a contemporary reputed historian and archaeologist, has categorically stated in his esteemed work that Galilee was indeed the homeland of Jesus the Galilean. It undoubtedly played the most important role in the foundation of early Christianity and that is based on the solid relationship between the Meshiha (God and Man) and Galilee (Land and People)[250].

Analysis of Proof 8: Again, we find that the latest archaeological and historical discoveries made by this great Lebanese scholar match very well with what we have concluded in this book. Jesus was Galilean, and his relation to Canaano-Phoenician genes is therefore established beyond doubt by the historical, cultural, and geographical position of the Galilee of the Nations in the heart of Canaan-Phoenicia. Having declared this once again with great supporting evidence, we need not go any further in explaining this fact, fear of redundancy.

Proof 9: New evidence comes this time from the recent work of Aviram Oshri, a senior archaeologist working for the Israeli Antiquities Authority (IAA). He believes that there is surprisingly no archaeological evidence that ties Bethlehem in Judea to the period in which Jesus would have been born. His findings[251], reported to *National Geographic* are extremely important, and we would like to convey them now for the reader to mull over. The Israeli archaeologist seems to have wondered a bit, saying, "If the historical Jesus were truly born in Bethlehem, it was most likely the Bethlehem of Galilee, not that in Judea." He then adds, "The archaeological evidence certainly seems to favor the former, a busy center (of Jewish life) a few miles from the home of Joseph and Mary, as opposed to an unpopulated spot almost a hundred miles from home."

In the Bet-Lahem of Galilee, Oshri and his team unearthed what could be a few remains of a Christian monastery of a later period than the time of Jesus, along with a large Byzantine Church. These findings[252] made him wonder why such huge Christian monuments for worship were to be ever built in the

---

250 Khoury Hareb, Antoine, *The Christian Roots in Lebanon*—جذور المسيحية في لبنان, page 20.
251 Marisa Larson, "Bethlehem," *National Geographic*, 2008-JUN-17.

heart of a Jewish area. Yet, his judgment is as striking as his archaeological discoveries. Oshri concluded that it is because early Christians certainly revered the Galilean Bet-Lahem as the place where Jesus was born. "There is no doubt in my mind," Oshri continued, "that these are some impressive and important evidence (sic) of a strong Christian community established in Bethlehem [of Galilee] a short time after Jesus' death."

Analysis of Proof 9: It is magnificently significant to read once again the words of Oshri and ponder them before digesting them. Jesus could not have been born in Bethlehem of Judea for lack of archaeological evidence, which is in fact evident in the Bet-Lahem of Galilee from the time of Jesus' birth. The Israeli archaeologist supports the argument of this book.

Yet, Oshri, should not have wondered at all why there was a lively Christian presence in an alleged Jewish area, for in fact, this Christian presence is natural at the time of Yāwshu (Jesus), not only in Bet-Lahem, but in all the surrounding towns and villages of Galilee, which formed an interconnected element with Phoenicia and precisely with both cities of Tyre and Sidon, where Jesus used to always visit, feeling at home and safe[253]. The abnormality in this case is thus not the Christian presence—say "pagan Christian"—in the *Gelil-Haggoyim* or Galilee of the Gentiles, but the presence of a Jewish society in the "Galilee of the non-Jews," as referred to in both, the Old Testament[254] and the New Testament[255]. Two books that the Church joined together into one book, the *Holy Bible*, in the 4th century AD, became a source of inspiration—with all its errors—to historical books and geographical maps. Yet, archaeology, if without bias, would certainly unearth the facts from beneath the ground's surface.

At any rate, the presence of Christians in Galilee not only started to appear after the time Jesus died, but all the way before and during his life, in the form of Gentile groups, mainly known by the Phoenician-Galileans presented as the Ashayas and their famous ascetic branch, the Nazarenes or *Nazoreans*—the term used to identify early Christians.

We have so far exposed all the necessary important proof we have thus found that support this very fact. Let us now move forward and meet the Galilean Disciples of Jesus!

---

252 The structures discovered in the Bet-Lahem of Galilee are undoubtedly Christian, and some of the relics found on the site are mainly composed of bronze crosses, oil lamps with crosses, and baptismal receptacles.
253 Mark 7:24; Luke 6:17; Matthew 15:21.
254 Isaiah 9:1, 1Macabees 5:15.
255 Matthew 4:15.

Chapter 6

The Galilean Disciples of Jesus

Why have we been manipulated to believe that a Galilean is a Jew? Why have we discarded the fact that Galilee was considered *Gelil Haggoyim*, which is translated into "Circle of the Gentiles," "Galilee of the Nations," or "Galilee of the non-Jews"? The truth, we shall see, is supported by history, geography, and archaeology.

Although not to be trusted on some of his accounts of history, particularly Jewish history, as Thomas L. Thompson has suggested in his widely read historical work[256], the Roman-Jewish historian, Flavius Josephus, wrote in his reputed book, the following geographical and topographic description of Galilee:

> Now Phoenicia and Syria encompass about the Galilees, which are two, and called the Upper Galilee and the Lower. They are bounded toward the sun-setting, with the borders of the territory belonging to Ptolemais, and by Carmel; which mountain had formerly belonged to the Galileans, but now belonged to the Tyrians ...[257]

It is very interesting to acknowledge at this point the precise description made back then by Josephus, some fifty years after the death of Christ. His geographical account appeared to be a credible work indeed since it copes well with all the maps we have at hand. It definitely mirrors the cultural development of the Galilean territory that we have described earlier, along with Mt. Carmel, which at Josephus' time belonged to the Tyrians.

It is not by luck then or by mistake that Yāwshu is said to have "retreated" to Tyre and Sidon in the second year of his ministry, as we have seen before. It is not by illusion that a few years after his death, as early as 41 AD, the gospel was preached in Phoenicia[258] almost ten years before it was spread around the

---

256 Thompson L. Thomas, *The Mythic Past*, page 216.

257 Josephus, Flavius, *The Wars of the Jews; or the History of the Destruction of Jerusalem*, Book III, Chapter 3:1.

258 Rawlinson, George, *History of Phoenicia*, iBooks, page 437. It is written in Acts 11:19, "Now those who were scattered after the persecution that arose over Stephen traveled as far as Phoenicia ..."

world as a result of the Council of Jerusalem, held sometime between 49 and 52 AD, as we shall explain. It is not by chance that Herod Agrippa, the grandson of Herod the Great, received an embassy from them (early Christians) of Tyre and Sidon at Cæsarea in 44 AD, and by whom he was highly offended[259]. It is not by coincidence what Rawlinson observed[260]:

> ... about A.D. 57, we have evidence that the great religious and social movement of the age had swept the Phoenician cities within its vortex, and that, in some of them at any rate, Christian communities had been formed, which were not ashamed openly to profess the new religion.

Certainly, they were not ashamed to preach the religion of their son, Yāwshu. At any rate, the other significant revelation from Josephus comes in the following note:

> These two Galilees (Upper and Lower Galilee), of so great largeness, and encompassed with so many nations of foreigners, have been always able to make a strong resistance on all occasions of war ...[261]

Again, we have additional confirmation from the Roman-Jewish historian that the Galileans composed a mixture of so many nations and foreigners, hence the reference made by the New Testament, which displayed the region of Galilee as that of the Nations, the non-Jews. We have previously, on two occasions, presented the many nations of Galilee as Canaano-Phoenicians (Aramaens), Syrians, Romans, Greeks, with maybe a few others. This would logically mean that the identity of a Galilean whoever he/she was, was not at all Jewish. We have thoroughly shown why we believe, in respect to the Galilean Family of Jesus, that they were mainly Phoenicians, therefore, we have adopted the term "Phoenician-Galilean," or vice versa. In fact, we don't generalize the inhabitants of Galilee as forming a particular ethnicity, and thus, when we use the term Phoenician-Galilean, we don't differentiate between the two, and we mean by that the

---

259 Acts 12: 20, "Now Herod had been very angry with the people of Tyre and Sidon; but they came to him with one accord, and having made Blastus the king's personal aide their friend, they asked for peace, because their country was supplied with food by the king's [country]."
260 Rawlinson, George, *History of Phoenicia*, iBooks, page 436-437.
261 Josephus, Flavius, *The Wars of the Jews; or the history of the destruction of Jerusalem*, Book III, Chapter 3:2.

Galileans were of Phoenician lineage. From this lineage, came Yāwshu.

Moreover, not only the Holy Family, represented by Yāwsēp̄ (Joseph), Maryām (Mary) and Yāwshu (Jesus) were Galilean-Phoenicians from Galilee, as we have learned before, but also all the Disciples were from that Phoenician region, as well, except for two that we will expose in a bit. We have explained earlier the importance of the region of Galilee in the Ministry of Jesus Christ, and we shall see more of that as we attempt to identify the birthplaces of the Disciples of Jesus.

That being said, let us now discover the true identities of Jesus' Disciples. Among the 12 known Disciples officially cited in the New Testament, we found two of them as having non-Galilean roots, and they could have been Jews in origin, if not for certain they were.

The Non-Galilean Disciples of Jesus

The first has been portrayed as "Judas the Iscariot," the man who betrayed him, from the *Îš-Qrîyôth* (man of Kerioth) city of Judea, located almost eight kilometers southwest of Jerusalem.

The Gospel of John (13:31-32) refers to Judas as being present during the Last Supper, "So, when he had gone out ..." It refers to Judas Iscariot leaving the room fast after being spotted in his plan to betray Jesus and deliver him to the Guardians of the Jewish Temple to crucify him. John (18:3-5) continues:

Then Judas, having received a detachment [of troops], and officers from the chief priests and Pharisees, came there with lanterns, torches, and weapons. Jesus therefore, knowing all things that would come upon Him, went forward and said to them, 'Whom are you seeking?' They answered Him, 'Jesus of Nazareth.' Jesus said to them, 'I am [He].' And Judas, who betrayed Him, also stood with them.

A reminder of the capture of Jesus at Mount Olives and the Jewish cabal raised against him appears also in Acts (10:36-39):

The word which [God] sent to the children of Israel, preaching peace through Jesus Christ—He is Lord of all—that word you know, which was proclaimed throughout all Judea, and began from Galilee after the baptism which John preached: how God anointed Jesus of Nazareth with the Holy Spirit and with power, who went about doing good and healing all who were oppressed by the devil, for God was with Him. And we are witnesses of all things which He did both in the land of the Jews and in Jerusalem, whom they slew and hanged on a tree.

The second has been portrayed as "Nathanael," the man who refused Yāwshu as a prophet when he heard about him as Jesus of Nazareth. Yāwshu, on the other hand, instantly recognized him as an Israelite indeed, "in whom there is no deceit."

Again it is in John (1:45-51) where we read that Philip found Nathanael and told him about Jesus of Nazareth, the son of Joseph, but Nathanael said to him:

'Can any good thing come out of Nazareth? Philip said to him, 'Come and see.' When Jesus saw Nathanael coming to him, he said, 'Behold, an Israelite indeed, in whom there is no deceit!' Nathanael said to him, 'How do you know me?' Jesus answered him, 'Before Philip called you, when you were under the fig tree, I saw you.' Nathanael answered him, 'Rabbi, you are the Son of God! You are King of Israel!' Jesus answered him, 'Because I told you, I saw you underneath the fig tree, do you believe? You will see greater things than these! Most certainly, I tell you, hereafter you will see heaven opened, and the angels of God ascending and descending on the Son of Man.'

We undoubtedly understand from this paragraph that when Jesus saw Nathanael under the tree, he immediately knew he was not a Galilean, but rather a Jew; an "Israelite indeed, in whom there is no deceit." When Nathanael asked Jesus if he was the King of Israel, Jesus did not answer him. He did not say he was, for indeed he was not from the House of David, as we have learned earlier. In fact, more light has been shed on that transcendent issue all through the book.

At any rate, the question that lingered in my mind for some time is why Yāwshu took Judas and Nathanael as disciples although he knew they were not Galileans. The Church New Testament shows that he didn't actually choose them by himself. It was the Rabbis of the Jewish Temple who sent Judas to Galilee on a mission to spy on Jesus, as we will see in the words below. That being said, we believe they were both secretly activated to come to him, and it appeared as well that he knew very well who they were: both were agents for the Rabbis' Secret Service! This may sound a little fantastic, but the actual facts on the ground support this claim. Yes, the Rabbis had secret agents, and this is evident in Luke (20:19-20), as we come to the following verse (italics mine):

'The chief priests and the scribes sought to lay hands on him that very hour, but they feared the people—for they knew he had spoken this parable against them. They watched him, and *sent out spies*, who pretended to be righteous, that they might trap him in something he said, so as to deliver him up to the power and authority of the governor.'

Surely, the plan was to deliver him to the Roman governor, for the Jews had no political authority themselves in either Galilee or Judea. The fact that they were not living in Galilee, and therefore sending out spies to Galilee in order to trap him because he spoke against them, could only be more proof that Jesus was not a Jew. Certainly it is so, because spies are usually dispatched from one country to another, especially in times of conflict, be it political or cultural. They would have no need to *send out* spies against the people of their own country. This is supported by Jacques Duquesne, the French journalist and writer we quoted earlier. Duquesne does not mention Nathanael as non-Galilean; however, he plainly suggests that Judas was the only Judean within the group: he was an agent of the Temple.[262]

Now let us discover the true Galilean identity of the remaining ten officially recognized Disciples of Jesus as per the New Testament. Our search that led us to identify them as Galileans has proved them also to be of Phoenician origin.

The Galilean Disciples of Jesus

Before delving into the true identity of the Disciples of Jesus and proceeding further in uncovering the tarnished truth, let us just note that it is not at all correct to believe that Jesus had only twelve male Disciples as the Church New Testament suggests. What about Bartholomaios then: Should history prove he has been wrongly identified with Nathaniel? We shall see that in a moment. What about his great uncle, Joseph of Arimathea or Yāwsēp̄ of Rameh (Ramah) cited earlier? What about his female disciples, among them, the most known, Mary Magdalene?

We clarified in Chapter 3 that Hippolytus Romanus (c. 170 AD–236 AD); St. Dorotheus (c. 255 AD–362 AD); Eusebius of Caesarea (c. 260/263 AD–339/340 AD); St. John Chrysostom (c. 347 AD–407 AD); Mâr Solomon (13th century AD); St. Dimitri of

---

262 Duquesne, Jacques, *Jésus*, page 240.

Rostov (17th century AD), along with a few other figures that played significant roles in writing about the theology and history of Christianity, seemed to have put the names to the unknown seventy disciples unnamed by Luke[263], and whom Christ sent forth to spread his word of Love and Peace. The seventy (or seventy-two, in some other manuscripts) disciples or Apostles are not alluded to by the other writers of the New Testament, who only recognize the traditional known Twelve Disciples as chosen by Jesus in both Matthew[264] and Mark[265].

At any rate, let us not lose our attention now on the number proposed and focus on the ten remaining Disciples that we have found to be Galileans, *ipso facto*, Phoenicians. In John (1:39-44), we see Jesus walking by the River Jordan, in Galilee (not in Judea), where he was always ministering, gathering his disciples around him. In Galilee, Jesus found Philip and said to him, "Follow me." Philip was from Bethsaida, the city of Andrew and Peter.

Etymologically speaking, "Bethsaida" or *Bet(h)-Saida* means "House of Saida." It is strongly related to the city of Saida (*Sidon*), also pronounced as "Saydoun[266]," one of the greatest and oldest Phoenician ports. Saida, or its original name, *Saydoun*, is a Canaano-Phoenician word that means, "fishing," thus *Bet(h)-Saida* would eventually mean, "House of Fishing." Note that almost all the Disciples of Yāwshu (the Ten), except perhaps for Matthew, were known to be *fishermen*. It seems the New Testament, which mentioned *Saida* (Sidon) along with *Sūr* (Tyre)[267]

---

263 Luke 10:1, "After these things the Lord appointed seventy others also, and sent them two by two before His face into every city and place where He Himself was about to go."

264 Matthew 10:1, "And when He had called His twelve disciples to [Him], He gave them power [over] unclean spirits, to cast them out, and to heal all kinds of sickness and all kinds of disease." And 10:5, "These twelve Jesus sent out and commanded them ..."

265 Mark 6:7, "And He called the twelve to [Himself], and began to send them out two [by] two, and gave them power over unclean spirits."

266 Tradition conveys that the name of this coastal Phoenician city was related to Saydoun, known as the elder son of Canaan; the father of the Canaano-Phoenician race. A powerful figure of his time and a charismatic leader with a magnificent vision, Saydoun built the city in his name, nearly three thousand years BC. This Phoenician city reached its peak around the 12th and 10th century BC, playing a spiritual, scientific, and economic key role in Mediterranean culture. Such major impact has prevailed through time until now. This port-city carried the name that correlated to the act of fishing, as well; fishing having been one of the most vital food sources for the inhabitants of that area. In fact, the majority of the Saydonians acquired a solid reputation as successful fishermen.

267 In his book, *The Phoenician Origin of Britons, Scots, & Anglo-Saxons*, page 323 (fn.4), author L.A. Waddell wrote, "Tyre and Sidon had early Christian

as a safe haven to Jesus, also cited *Bethsaida* as one of the most important places for him, where he revealed his divine powers by performing some of his most significant miracles of all times, like Walking on the Sea of Galilee[268], Feeding of the Multitudes[269] and Healing the Blind Man[270].

Should we fetch the Appendix at the end of the book and look attentively at Map 4 and Map 2 (Nr.65), we would certainly find that Bethsaida is situated a few kilometers—perhaps around two kilometers—on the northern shore of the Sea of Tiberias, known also as the Sea of Galilee.

It is interesting to know after more than two thousand years now that three out of ten of Jesus' disciples, Philip, Andrew, and Peter (Simon Peter), were indeed from the Phoenician-Galilean city of Bethsaida. The search would not end here of course, for more revelation continues to unfurl in front of our eyes as we decode the origin of the remaining seven Galilean Disciples.

In Matthew (4:17-24), we see once again Yāwshu walking by the Sea of Galilee, gathering yet another two disciples. Other than Simon (Simon Peter) and his brother, Andrew, who were both fishermen from *Bet(h)-saida*, he found James, the son of Zebedee, and John his brother, two other fishermen who followed him. James the Elder and his brother John, were portrayed as being native of both Bethsaida and its neighboring town, Capernaum. It seems these two were partners with Simon Peter[271].

This is absolutely supportive to what the Church New Testament is revealing. The fact that I'm a dedicated Lebanese Christian notwithstanding, I have certainly, many times before, missed those interesting historical details, until just recently. So far, we count five out of ten Disciples of Jesus exposing themselves as being Galileans, mainly Phoenician-Galileans. All five were fishermen, and became also "fishers-of-men," from Phoenicia-Galilee. Who were then the other five?

One of them was Simon the Canaanite, wrongly portrayed as Simon the Zealot for the sole purpose of giving his name a Hebrew meaning. The name was noted in both Matthew (10:1-4) and Mark (3:18). In fact, St. Jerome could not have mistaken the word "Canaanite" for anything else. This very fact only signifies one

---

congregations (Acts 21:3-7), and the Bishops of the Christian synod of Tyre (335 AD) were Arians." By Arians, he surely meant Phoenicians.

268 Matthew 14:25; Mark 6:48; John 6:19.

269 Matthew 14:19; Mark 6:37-44; John 6:10-13.

270 Mark 8:22-25.

271 Luke 5:10, "... and so also [were] James and John, the sons of Zebedee, who were partners with Simon. And Jesus said to Simon, Do not be afraid. From now on you will catch men."

thing and it is that Simon was either from Cana or from any other town or village within the Canaano-Phoenician territory.

Now, six Galilean Disciples of Jesus reveal themselves to be from the Phoenician-Galilee of the Gentiles—Galilee of the non-Jews. To make things even more clear, let us now find out who the other four Disciples were: Matthew the tax collector, unlike the other Apostles who were all fishermen; James (the Younger); Jude, known also as Thaddeus; and Thomas, also known as Didymus. Almost all references reveal that these four were also from Galilee. It is not strictly known which Galilean town gave birth to Thomas or who his family was, but it is very probable that the other three, Matthew, James the Younger, and Jude were brothers from the Galilean town of Capernaum.

On the etymological level, Capernaum is *Kfar-Naa-Um*, a Canaano-Phoenician-Aramaic word that means, "the place or village full of consolation and comfort," or, "where consolation and comfort is fully practiced by the consoler or comforter"—*Naa-Um*. Both Map 4 and Map 2 (Nr.67) also locate *Kfar-Naa-Um* a few kilometers—very close to Bethsaida—on the northern shore of the Sea of Tiberias or the Sea of Galilee. We have already seen why Jesus chose it as one of his main headquarters in Galilee. Besides, it was the home of almost half of his Disciples, as was the town of Bethsaida.

So far, out of 12, the traditional New Testament number of the Disciples of Jesus, two of them were found to be non-Galileans—Judas the Iscariot and Nathanael—and were undoubtedly Jews of Judea that had infiltrated Yāwshu's circle as secret agents of the Temple. The remaining ten have all been found to be Galileans, definitely of Phoenician origin, and are described in the following form:

Philip, Andrew, and Peter (Simon Peter) – from the Phoenician-Galilean town of Bethsaida

James the Elder and his brother John – from the Phoenician-Galilean towns of Bethsaida and Capernaum

Simon the Canaanite – from either the Phoenician village of Kana (Qana) or from any other town or village of Canaan-Phoenicia

Thomas – of an unknown Galilean town or village

Matthew, James the Younger and Jude – from the Galilean town of Capernaum

Bartholomaios – from the Lebanese village of Kana (Qana) as we shall see that in a bit

Exceeding now the traditional Twelve Disciples of Jesus, we add another four who turned out to be his Phoenician-Galilean cousins, wrongly claimed to be his brothers. They followed him closely ever since he began his ministry in Galilee and are mentioned in Chapter 3. Let us remind the eager reader of their names. They are James (known also as Jacob), who after the Crucifixion and Glorious Resurrection of Yāwshu attained an important socio-religious status and played a significant role in the formation years of the new Christian religion: he became the first Bishop of Jerusalem. And Joses (derived from the Aramaic name "Yāwse" or "Yāse"; It is etymologically linked to Yāwsēp̄, Yosef, or Joseph), Juda (or Jude), and Simon (or Symeon) the third Bishop of Jerusalem (some say he was the second bishop) after his father Cleopas (Clopas, second bishop), who succeeded his son James over the Christian religious throne of Ur-Shalim.

Another important name that could well be added to the inner circle of Yāwshu's Disciples is certainly Bartholomaios. The New Testament shows that Nathaniel is known also as Bartholomew. This theory by itself is not based on enough evidence. Judeo-Christian Biblical scholars try to reason the name Bartholomew in Hebrew as *Bar*: "son," and *Talmai*: "of Talmai." In fact, his real name, properly pronounced as Bartholomaios in the Greek version of the Church New Testament, seems to be an Aryan name, not Hebrew. This finely judged analysis comes from L.A. Waddell's book[272]. Waddell believes that the name Bartholomaios contains the element "Barat" or "Brit-on" conjoined also with the Aryan affix –*oloma*, which is a recognized variant of -*olon*.

I may not have explained this in my novel, *The Phoenician Code*, because I didn't find it appropriate to go into those details in a thriller, but here, in this academic work, it is an entirely different case. (I sincerely apologize to my readers around the world, particularly in the case where I have mixed up the two names of Nathaniel and Bartholomew as one person, should that have caused any confusion.)

What Waddell suggested at the break of the 19th century AD is powerful, since the word "Barat" or "Briton" originated from the Sea and Earth Phoenician Guardian Goddess of Good Fortune— *Barati*. No wonder the Capital of Lebanon still carries the name "Beirut," *Brut*. The Aryan name of Bartholomaios as per Waddell could only be a Phoenician name in truth, since Waddell repeatedly aims to link the Aryans with the Phoenicians.

---

272 Waddell, L.A., *The Phoenician Origin of Britons, Scots, & Anglo-Saxons*, page 82 and (fn.5)

There is no doubt in my mind now that this Bartholomaios, whom we have earlier quoted from his gospel concerning the Great Annunciation of Maryām and the Divinity of Jesus, is not at all Nathanael who—according to John (1:45-51)—strongly suspected that a good thing might come out of Nazareth, Galilee, due to the fact that Galilee was regarded by the Jews as Galilee of the Nations or of the Gentiles, hence, nothing of good nature should come out of this place in the eyes of the Jews, as if goodness was an attribute that belonged to the House of David, the house of the Chosen People!

Let us continue past the idea of the acclaimed chosen people and focus immediately on the additional evidence at hand, bearing in mind that the above quotation presented by John, and the insistence of Philip to the Jew Nathaniel to "come and see ... Jesus of Nazareth, the son of Joseph ..." definitely carries significance in terms of the identity of Yāwshu and his birthplace in the region of Galilee.

Traditionally, Bartholomaios is believed to have lived in Cana of Galilee, though, we confirm he lived in the Lebanese village of *Kana* (Qana)—a Phoenician-Galilean-Gentile for sure. According to St. Jerome and a number of other scholars, he was the only one of the so-called Twelve Disciples who came from royal blood or was of noble birth. It is most probable that the Wedding Feast of Kana, where Jesus enacted his first miracle of turning water into wine, was Bartholomaios' own wedding. If that is true, then Bartholomaios of Qana could well be a relative of the Virgin Lady Maryām, who was present at the wedding. While their relation is yet to be confirmed, it could probably be explained by the close connection and private discussion—concerning the Great Annunciation—he had with the Mother of the Lord in his gospel (which we addressed in Chapter 2). The revelation of this Divine and Ultimate Secret by Lady Maryām to Bartholomaios could then legitimize their familial relation.

The suggestion that *Kana* was the place of origin of Lady Maryām was indicated before by Renan, Father Yammine, and many others. Yet, the difference between the two mentioned authors lies in the fact of determining which Cana was the right one. We have earlier explained that it could not be Kafar Kanna, cited by Renan[273] and others, for many different major reasons such as the archaeological evidence for the wedding scene that did not exist at all in Kefr Kenna. Instead, we have demonstrated that the right location is indeed Kana or *Qana* of Lebanon,

---

273 Renan, Ernest, *Vie de Jésus*, page 157 (fn.3)

eloquently proved by Dr. Father Youssef Yammine[274]; professor and historian, Martiniano Pellegrino Roncaglia[275]; archaeologist/ historian, Dr. Youssef Hourany[276]; and many other highly reliable scholars like the historian and archaeologist, Dr. Antoine Khoury Hareb[277].

Now, the logical indication to the fact that Maryām was originally from Kana was detected in the New Testament, and precisely in John (italics mine):

On the third day there was a wedding in Cana of Galilee, and *the mother of Jesus was there.* Now both Jesus and His disciples were invited to the wedding. (John 2:1-2)

This interesting verse from the Gospel of John undoubtedly proves that Maryām was already present in Qana, not only because of the wedding ceremony of her *supposed* relative, Bartholomaois, but being actually there as a resident, hence, a native of Kana. This is proven by Father Youssef Yammine (Proof 7, previous chapter), and also by Renan, who certainly got mixed up between the two Canas as we have previously explained. He stated[278], "It seems that, becoming by the death of her husband, a stranger at Nazareth, she withdrew to Cana, from which she may have come originally."

Moreover, should we continue analyzing the words of John cited in that particular verse, we find that Jesus and his Disciples were not originally in Kana before the wedding, but soon arrived there as guests to attend the wedding ceremony of his Disciple and *supposed* relative, Bartholomaois. This is also attested by the Apostle John (4:46), "So Jesus came again to Cana of Galilee where He had made the water wine. And there was a certain nobleman whose son was sick at Capernaum." Again, this verse clearly indicates that the wedding ceremony cited to have taken place in Cana of Galilee and which was related to the miracle of turning water into wine undoubtedly happened in the Qana of Lebanon, as we have been demonstrating. Please see the pictures of the people at the wedding engraved on rocks in the Appendix and dating back to 1st century AD.

274 Yammine, Youssef Rev., *The Galilean Kana in Lebanon—*قانا الجليل في لبنان , page 65-66.
275 Roncaglia, Martiniano Pellegrino, *Cana.*
276 Hourany, Youssef, *Cana of Galilee in South Lebanon—*قانا الجليل في جنوب لبنان , page 10-11.
277 Khoury Hareb, Antoine, *The Christian Roots in Lebanon—*جذور المسيحية في لبنان , page 40-49.
278 Renan, Ernest, *Vie de Jésus*, page 157.

That explained, let us go back to Bartholomaois of Qana once more before moving on. It becomes obvious now that he could not be Nathanael of Judea. The latter appeared only in the Gospel of John, precisely in the scene where he uttered his famous phrase, "Can any good thing come out of Nazareth?" Only once is he included as a Disciple in the list of Disciples proposed by John[279], where he was defined as of Cana in Galilee, whereas Bartholomaois' name clearly appears with every single list of Disciples proposed by the Church New Testament, as in Matthew[280], Mark[281], Luke[282], and Acts[283], in direct connection with Simon the Canaanite and Philip, who like Andrew (Andrewus) and Bartholomaios (Partolon), bore Gentile-Phoenician names, not Hebrew.[284]

It could be noted that the Biblical scholars most probably got mixed up and confused the name of Nathanael of Cana in Galilee with Bartholomaois of Qana, who appeared in all the other Synoptic lists and in Acts. They erroneously identified the two as one person. At any rate, Bartholomaois appeared to be the author of a Gospel of Bartholomew, deemed heretical later on by the Church. But why? This important question is directed to the officials of the Church to answer. We consider the gospel to be highly important, as we have quoted from it in Chapter 2.

At any rate, we are inclined to believe, as we have firmly stated before in Chapter 3, that the term "brothers" used in the New Testament mistakenly gives the impression that Jesus and the disciples were brothers in the biological sense of the word. The word has been used by the Apostle John (2:12; 7:3; 7:5), by Paul in Galatians (1:19), 1Corinthians (9:5), and also by Luke in the Acts

---

279 John 21:1-2, "After these things Jesus showed Himself again to the disciples at the Sea of Tiberias, and in this way He showed [Himself]: Simon Peter, Thomas called the Twin, Nathanael of Cana in Galilee, the [sons] of Zebedee, and two others of His disciples were together."
280 Matthew 10:3-4, "Philip and Bartholomew; Thomas and Matthew the tax collector; James the [son] of Alphaeus, and Lebbaeus, whose surname was Thaddaeus; Simon the Cananite, and Judas Iscariot, who also betrayed Him."
281 Mark 3:18, "Andrew, Philip, Bartholomew, Matthew, Thomas, James the [son] of Alphaeus, Thaddaeus, Simon the Cananite;"
282 Luke 6:14, "Simon, whom He also named Peter, and Andrew his brother; James and John; Philip and Bartholomew;"
283 Acts 1:13, "And when they had entered, they went up into the upper room where they were staying: Peter, James, John, and Andrew; Philip and Thomas; Bartholomew and Matthew; James [the son] of Alphaeus and Simon the Zealot; and Judas [the son] of James."
284 Waddell L.A., *The Phoenician Origin of Britons, Scots, & Anglo-Saxons*, page 83.

(1:14). However, we oppose those mistakes, as well as Renan's idea and many others before and after him, that Jesus had blood brothers (unknown by names). Instead, we believe that these men were his Apostles, who played an important missionary role of higher degree in the nearby region of Phoenicia-Galilee and across the world. The great mission they had been entrusted to undertake would constitute by itself a logical conjuncture to differentiate them just a little bit from the Disciples, in the "inner circle" of Yāwshu. It was highly probable for this sole reason that they were called "brothers."

It has been suggested that the number of Apostles, besides the twelve traditional Disciples of Jesus, reached about seventy or seventy-two, as mentioned, unnamed, only in Luke. Their names, however, could be found listed by a few early Christian theologians and historians that we have cited before. Historical records show there are indeed four famous complete lists of the seventy Apostles of Christ. It is most likely that Hippolytus Romanus penned the first list of them, followed by a second, authored by St. Dorotheus, Bishop of Tyre. A third list has been proposed by Mâr Solomon, and the fourth, by St. Dimitri of Rostov. This is the complete first list presented by Hippolytus[285]:

1. James[286] the Lord's brother, Bishop of Jerusalem.
2. Cleopas, Bishop of Jerusalem.
3. Matthias, who supplied the vacant place in the number of the Twelve Apostles.
4. Thaddeus, who conveyed the epistle to Augarus.
5. Ananias, who baptized Paul, and was Bishop of Damascus.
6. Stephen[287], the first martyr.
7. Philip, who baptized the eunuch.
8. Prochorus, Bishop of Nicomedia, who also was the first that departed, believing together with his daughters.
9. Nicanor died when Stephen was martyred.
10. Timon, Bishop of Bostra.
11. Parmenas, Bishop of Soli.
12. Nicolaus, Bishop of Samaria.
13. Barnabas, Bishop of Milan.
14. Mark the Evangelist, Bishop of Alexandria.*
15. Luke the Evangelist.*

---

285 Hippolytus, *On the Seventy Disciples.*
286 We have proved that James was Jesus's cousin.
287 Acts 7:58-60.

*These two belonged to the Seventy Disciples who were scattered by the offense of the word which Christ spoke, "Except a man eat my flesh, and drink my blood, he is not worthy of me." But the one being induced to return to the Lord by Peter's instrumentality, and the other by Paul's, they were honored to preach that gospel on account of which they also suffered martyrdom, the one being burned, and the other being crucified on an olive tree.

16. Silas, Bishop of Corinth.
17. Silvanus, Bishop of Thessalonica.
18. Crisces (Crescens), Bishop of Carchedon in Gaul.
19. Epænetus, Bishop of Carthage.
20. Andronicus, Bishop of Pannonia.
21. Amplias, Bishop of Odyssus.
22. Urban, Bishop of Macedonia.
23. Stachys, Bishop of Byzantium.
24. Barnabas, Bishop of Heraclea.
25. Phygellus, Bishop of Ephesus. He was of the party also of Simon.
26. Hermogenes. He, too, was of the same mind with the former.
27. Demas, who also became a priest of idols.
28. Apelles, Bishop of Smyrna.
29. Aristobulus, Bishop of Britain.
30. Narcissus, Bishop of Athens.
31. Herodion, Bishop of Tarsus.
32. Agabus the Prophet.
33. Rufus, Bishop of Thebes.
34. Asyncritus, Bishop of Hyrcania.
35. Phlegon, Bishop of Marathon.
36. Hermes, Bishop of Dalmatia.
37. Patrobulus, Bishop of Puteoli.
38. Hermas, Bishop of Philippi.
39. Linus, Bishop of Rome.
40. Caius, Bishop of Ephesus.
41. Philologus, Bishop of Sinope.
42. Olympus
43. and Rhodion were martyred in Rome.
44. Lucius, Bishop of Laodicea in Syria.
45. Jason, Bishop of Tarsus.
46. Sosipater, Bishop of Iconium.
47. Tertius, Bishop of Iconium.
48. Erastus, Bishop of Panellas.

49. Quartus, Bishop of Berytus.
50. Apollo[288], Bishop of Cæsarea.
51. Cephas.
52. Sosthenes[289], Bishop of Colophonia.
53. Tychicus, Bishop of Colophonia.
54. Epaphroditus, Bishop of Andriace.
55. Cæsar, Bishop of Dyrrachium.
56. Mark, cousin to Barnabas, Bishop of Apollonia.
57. Justus, Bishop of Eleutheropolis.
58. Artemas, Bishop of Lystra.
59. Clement, Bishop of Sardinia.
60. Onesiphorus, Bishop of Corone.
61. Tychicus, Bishop of Chalcedon.
62. Carpus, Bishop of Berytus in Thrace.
63. Evodus, Bishop of Antioch.
64. Aristarchus, Bishop of Apamea.
65. Mark, who is also John, Bishop of Bibloupolis.
66. Zenas, Bishop of Diospolis.
67. Philemon, Bishop of Gaza.
68. Aristarchus
69. and Pudes.
70. Trophimus, who was martyred along with Paul.

Having finished the listing of the Seventy Apostles of Christ, we found that there are a few names that most probably were listed twice in one particular list, and names that are omitted from other lists to be replaced instead with some other names that are not already written in the original text. For this important reason, and others, like the claim that says the Apostles were seventy-two not seventy, and to discourage confusion, we drew Table 2 of seventy-two Apostles that we urge you to review in the Appendix. We believe it would clarify the issue more efficiently. There are indeed 33 similar names that were listed in the four lists altogether; 27 identical names in three lists; and 12 similar names in two lists. There are additional unique names that are not inscribed in the table, but are found in list three alone as follows: Jude (brother of James, cousin to Yāwshu); Manaeus (?);

---

288 A reference to him can be found in Acts 18:24, where he is cited as *a* "Jew, born at Alexandria, an eloquent man," who came to Ephesus. We very much doubt his identity as a Jew. His *Gentile* name does not support this position.
289 Sosthenes is mentioned in Acts 18:17 as "the ruler of the synagogue" at Corinth. We very much doubt this. His *Gentile* name does not support this position.

Nicodemus (the archon); Nathaniel (the chief scribe); Mnason (who received Paul); Manaël (the foster-brother of Herod); Alexander; Simon the Cyrenian (father of Lucius); Eurion or Orion (the splay-footed); Thôrus (?); Thorîsus (?); Zabdon; Zakron; Milichus; Kîrîtôn (Crito); Abrazon (?); Popillius (Publius); Stephen (not the Corinthian); Aggai (the disciple of Addai); Mâr Mâri, and five others (two by the name of Simon, and three by the name of Jude). The other unlike names found in list four alone are as follows: Archippus (Bishop of Colossae); Quadratus (Bishop of Athens); Aquila (Bishop of Heraclea); Fortunatus; Achaicus, and Dionysius the Areopagite (Bishop of Athens).

It is considerably important to realize in all the four lists we have studied that the names of almost all the Apostles we have been introduced to had no Jewish origin; instead, they hold Gentile appellations. There is no doubt about that. The question that rises again would be then why Christianity, if it was a continuation of Jewish religion and prophesies, began its actual expansion across the ancient world with so-called pagan missionaries, Gentiles, or people from the nations? The answer to this question is simple. Christianity is in fact a Phoenician/"pagan" religion.

We are much concerned in the personality of Yāwsēp̄ of Ramah (Joseph of Arimathea), the man we believe he was more than a Disciple or Apostle—a man who played one of the most important roles in the early formation of Christianity. We have talked plenty about him in Chapter 3, thus there is no need to repeat his biography herein. Yet, in the first list of Hippolytus, the second of Dorotheus, and the fourth of St. Dimitri of Rostov, Aristobulus was shown as Bishop of Britannia. We believe, however, that he was not the first but probably the second, after Yāwsēp̄ of Ramah, who was not cited in the three lists. However, in Chapter 49 of Mâr Solomon's book, *The Book of the Bee*, we found inscribed the names of all the 12 Disciples and the 70 Apostles of Yāwshu[290], where both Aristobulus and Yāwsēp̄ were indeed mentioned, but neither was connected to Britain, as we have seen in Chapter 3.

Unfortunately, none of the four lists we have presented mention any female disciple, Apostle, or even a follower of Yāwshu, but the Church New Testament and the Gospel of

---

290 Mâr Solomon ends his list by stating, "It is said that each one of the twelve and of the seventy wrote a Gospel; but in order that there might be no contention and that the number of 'Acts' might not be multiplied, the Apostles adopted a plan and chose two of the seventy, Luke and Mark, and two of the twelve, Matthew and John."

Bartholomaois, in particular, reveal other than Maryām, his Mother, some of the names that have been strongly connected to him, his life, and ministry. Let us have a look at them.

The Female Disciples of Jesus

There is no doubt anymore about the fact that Jesus had female adherents to his Circle, in the form of followers, like Mary of Bethany, and in the form of disciples and/or Apostles like Mary Magdalene—the most famous among them. The New Testament is clear about that, for we read in Matthew (italics mine):

> And many women who followed Jesus from Galilee, ministering to Him, were there looking on from afar, among whom were *Mary Magdalene, Mary the mother of James and Joses*, and the *mother of Zebedee's sons*. (Matthew 27:55-56)

A similar declaration of additional importance is found in Mark (italics mine):

> There were also women looking on from afar, among whom were Mary Magdalene, Mary the mother of James the Less and of Joses, and *Salome,* who also followed Him and ministered to Him when He was in Galilee, and many other women who came up with Him to Jerusalem. (Mark 15:40-41)

Again, Mark (16:1) mentions the three women in the following verse, "Now when the Sabbath was past, Mary Magdalene, Mary [the mother] of James, and Salome bought spices, that they might come and anoint Him."

Luke the Evangelist also had a say in this issue, and adds another name to the four names just cited. In Luke (24:10), we read (italics mine):

> It was Mary Magdalene, *Joanna*, Mary [the mother] of James, and the other [women] with them, who told these things to the apostles.

Having just quoted from the gospels, we undoubtedly come to realize that the Church New Testament does in fact reveal the names of five female disciples or Apostles, and leaves us dramatically wonder about the names of many others when we read in Matthew, "many women"; in Mark, "many other women"; and, in Luke, "the other women."

In the *Book of the Resurrection of Christ*[291] by the Apostle Bartholomaois, we find four additional names and one unidentified person. Here is what is said (italics mine):

> Early in the morning of the Lord's day the women went to the tomb. They were Mary Magdalene, Mary the mother of James whom Jesus delivered out of the hand of Satan, Salome who tempted him, *Mary* who ministered to him and *Martha* her sister, Joanna (al. Susanna) the wife of Chuza who had renounced the marriage bed, *Berenice* who was healed of an issue of blood in Capernaum, *Lia (Leah)* the widow whose son he raised at Nain, and the *woman* to whom he said, 'Thy sins which are many are forgiven thee.'

Another female disciple is found in a passage written by the Italian Cardinal Caesar Baronius (c. 1538 AD–1607 AD). We know him as the Curator of the Vatican Library and one of the well-known ecclesiastical historians. In his *Annales Ecclesiatici*[292], the Cardinal wrote (italics mine):

> In this dispersion, Ananias, having set out from Damascus gathered together a company of believers. At the same time, as one can ascertain, Lazarus, Mary Magdalene, Martha and *Marcella* whom the Jews regarded with great hatred, were not exactly driven away from Jerusalem but, together with the disciple Maximinus, were placed in a boat without oars and were believed to have perished in dangerous seas. By Divine providence they are said to have been driven to Marseilles. Taking with them a friend, Joseph of Arimathea, a noble decurion, they are said to have travelled from Gaul to Britain and there he proclaimed the gospel till his last day ...

Should we count again, we may find the number of Yāwhu's female disciples, Apostles, and followers, reaching 11, but we are solidly sure there were many other women around him, like perhaps the Samaritan woman we found in John[293]. But for now, let us try to find out who those 11 were, starting with the most famous among them:

---

291 Other than his gospel that we have cited before, this turns out to be another work attributed to him.

292 Baronius, Caesar, *Annales Ecclesiatici*, Volume 1, Paragraph 5 (Jesu Christi Annus 35).

293 John 4:39, "And many of the Samaritans of that city believed in Him because of the word of the woman who testified, 'He told me all that I [ever] did.'" Also John 4:42.

Mary Magdalene: Should we look at Map 1, we find a location encircled in yellow called *El-Mejdel*, a Phoenician-Galilean town a few kilometers away from the Sea of Galilee. This place is undoubtedly Magdala, as per Map 2 (Nr.68), the birthplace of Maryām El-Majdalia, or Mary Magdalene. It is indeed in Galilee and fits well in the picture where the scene of Jesus' movement took place more than two thousand years ago. She certainly played an important role, mainly spiritual, within the Inner Circle of Yāwshu.

Mary, the mother of James and Joses: Our search in the New Testament to identify this Mary (originally spelled as Maryām) has been indeed fruitful, for in fact, we have found that she was none other but Maryām's (the Virgin Lady's) sister, and this is evident in John (19:25): "Now there stood by the cross of Jesus His mother, and His mother's sister, Mary the [wife] of Clopas, and Mary Magdalene." Having said this, we conclude one more time that she was Yāwshu's aunt, as explained in Chapter 3. She was wife to Clopas or Cleopas, also known as Alphaeus or Alphaï, the younger brother of Joseph, Yāwshu's foster father.

The mother of Zebedee's sons: This unnamed woman is Phoenician-Galilean as well. She was the mother of James the Elder and John[294], the two fishermen who were described as partners with Simon Peter, who became the Disciples of Jesus with him ever since the beginning. They are portrayed as being native of both Bethsaida and Capernaum.

Salome: Other than in Mark, this woman that could have been originally called, Shalime, is also found in Chapters 19 and 20 of the Protoevangelium of James, during the Birth of Jesus in a cave at the bottom of the mountain, most certainly, Mt. Carmel, as we have seen in Chapter 3. She first entered into the scene in 19:18, "And the midwife departed from the cave and met Salome and said to her, 'Salome, Salome, I have to describe this new miracle for you. A virgin has given birth, although her body does not allow it.'" We have previously explained that Salome or *Šalime* was one of the women that belonged to the Phoenician-Galilean-Asayas who had their headquarters based on the top of Mt. Carmel and in Galilee.

Mary and Martha her sister: It looks like Mary and Martha were sisters from the Jewish town of Bethany as per John[295]. Of

---

294 Mark 10:35, "Then James and John, the sons of Zebedee, came to Him, saying, Teacher, we want You to do for us whatever we ask."
295 John 11:1, "Now a certain [man] was sick, Lazarus of Bethany, the town of Mary and her sister Martha."

course, Yāwshu, who was filled with Universal Love, seemed to have loved[296] them as well as their sick brother Lazarus who died and was then resurrected by Jesus as described in John (11:39-44)[297]. This family of Jewish origin, like very few of them, believed in him and followed him ever since.

Joanna (or Susanna): We know nothing of her other than what came in the Church New Testament and in the *Book of the Resurrection of Christ* by Bartholomaois.

Berenice and Lia (or Leah): We know nothing of them other than having their names cited by the Apostle Bartholomaois.

The sinner woman[298]: Many have confused her with Mary Magdalene, but in truth, they were completely two different persons.

Marcella: We know nothing of her other than what came in the *Annales* of Cardinal Baronius.

Having finished now an overall exposé of the Phoenician-Galilean Disciples and/or Apostles of Yāwshu, let us take a break now before continuing this journey of discovery. In the following upcoming pages, we will get to know more about the cultural and religious entourage of Jesus, his faith, theology, and the universal message he carried to us from his Abba Ēl. To clarify the picture even more, we would definitely begin with the Canaano-Phoenician, Enoch, also known as Enoch-Taautus, the Prophet, High Priest, seer of visions, and "father of the spiritual laws." We will pass by Milki-Sedek (Melchisedeck), the righteous King and High Priest of the ancient city of Ur-Shalim (Jerusalem), and continue with few others that have well marked the profound philosophy and eternal wisdom of the Great White Fraternity.

---

296 John 11:5, "Now Jesus loved Martha and her sister and Lazarus."

297 It is interesting though to mention the following dialogue between Jesus and his Father (Abba) on this occasion. Thus, we read from John 11:41-42, "Then they took away the stone [from the place] where the dead man was lying. And Jesus lifted up [His] eyes and said, 'Father, I thank You that You have heard Me. And I know that You always hear Me, but because of the people who are standing by I said [this], that they may believe that You sent Me.'"

298 Luke 7:37-39, "And, behold, a woman in the city, which was a sinner, when she knew that Jesus sat at meat in the Pharisee's house, brought an alabaster box of ointment, and stood at his feet behind him weeping, and began to wash his feet with tears, and did wipe them with the hairs of her head, and kissed his feet, and anointed them with the ointment. Now when the Pharisee which had bidden him saw it, he spake within himself, saying, This man, if he were a prophet, would have known who and what manner of woman this is that toucheth him: for she is a sinner."

Part III

The Christian Son of Man, Son of God

His Cultural/Religious Entourage, Un-Jewishness, Father, & Temple

Chapter 7

The Cultural and Religious Entourage at the Time of Jesus

Should we search for the word "Gentile" in the *Oxford Essential Dictionary of Difficult Words*, we would certainly find the following meaning: "a person who is not Jewish," as in, "Christianity spread from Jewish into Gentile cultures." We conclude that the meaning of the word is correct, yet, the example provided by the dictionary is not entirely true, for, in reality, it should read: "Christianity spread from Gentile into Gentile world." But the Judeo-Christian Biblical writers support Christianity as coming from Jewish roots for lots of reasons, many of which we have already seen.

We have previously explained the Gentile origins of Christianity on all the important historical, geographical, genetic, and cultural levels. Remember that when we say Gentile origins, we mean Canaano-Phoenician origins. And, thus, to make our exposé even more powerful, we are going to discuss the theological and religious background of the Phoenician origin of Christianity and compare it with Judaism.

Since the Canaano-Phoenicians were connected to the Egyptians in many different ways, especially on theological and religious levels, for example, the implementation of monotheism in the ancient world, a smart religious concept adopted later (not invented) by Judaism, Christianity could in fact be an evolution, or rather, an extension to such an ancient Hamitic[299] or Afro-Asiatic[300] discipline.

Should we look more than two thousand years back in time—at the time of Jesus—we would find that the major civilizations that could have influenced the character of Yāwshu are: the Canaanite/Phoenician and Egyptians, the Babylonians, the Persians, the Hebrews, the Romans, and the Greeks. Our search automatically eliminates both the Romans and Greeks, although,

---

299 Canaan is described in the Old Testament as the son of Ham, and Egypt is described as the Land of Ham.
300 Afro-Asiatic or Semito-Hamitic is the term defined in Thompson L. Thomas' *The Mythic Past*, page 111.

they were among the few nations that inhabited some parts of the Gentile regions of Galilee where Jesus ministered most of the time. We know for sure that the connection between Christianity and the Romans was mainly related to the Christmas festivity date appointed to the Birth of Jesus and which could have been an adaptation of a Roman religious date, as we have seen in the Introduction. There is no connection with the Greeks either, as Renan put it[301], "Neither directly nor indirectly, then, did any element of Greek Doctrine reach Jesus." Moreover, if Jesus was affected to a certain extent by any Greek doctrine, say essentially, Stoicism and Pythagoreanism, it would no more be determined as Greek influence, but rather, Canaano-Phoenician, since both Zeno[302] and Pythagoras[303] were of Phoenician origin.

That being said, the most favorite candidates that could have played vital roles in the formation of the theological and religious mind of Jesus could be hence divided into two major groups. The first and the most ancient are the Canaanite/Phoenician and Egyptians; the second group connected the Babylonians to the Persians, who created the Hebrews. Should we elaborate further regarding this issue, we would find out that there were indeed two main intellectual, social, theological, and religious orders in the ancient world that are in existence even today through their progenies. In fact, both are significantly old and go back thousands of years. The most authentic and ancient, however, is the Great White Fraternity that originated with Enoch-Taautus himself, "founder of the First Religion." The second order could be described as the Babylonian Brotherhood that originated in Babylon through the Persians during their military expeditions in the region at the time of Cyrus II. Let's have a brief summary on both Orders:

The Great White Fraternity

It began as a Canaanite/Phoenician-Egyptian monotheistic fraternity that believed, with anchored faith, in the resurrection of the self to its higher level and into the immortality of the spirit. Monotheism lay at the foundational core of the theological concept of the Great White Fraternity. In Phoenicia, the High Priest—

---

301   Renan, Ernest, *Vie de Jésus*, page 133.
302 Stoicism was a philosophical school of thought established in Athens in early 3rd century BC by Zeno of Citium (in Cyprus) of Phoenician origin. We may consider a work on Zeno in the future.
303 Please refer to *Pythagoras the Mathemagician*, 2010, published by Sunbury Press Inc.

Milki-Sedek, "the righteous King," himself a direct adept of Enoch-Thor—preached the belief in the Universal God Al-Ēlyon, the Most High. King Ahiram of Gebel and King Hiram of Tyre profoundly believed in the God Ēl, and pledged to Enoch-Thor. In Egypt, Pharaoh Akhenaton preached the belief of Aton as the Universal God. His predecessor, Thutmose III, one of the most erudite Pharaohs, keenly adopted the concept of the Universal God during his many expeditions and military campaigns he led through Asia[304]. There, he established a great empire that expanded even beyond the Euphrates and acquired a high interest in the Asiatic gods with a special focal point in monotheism—already established in Phoenicia. Both Ēl and Aton represented the first Light of Creation, symbolized by the Sun. It is not known when Phoenicians started to believe in the One High God Ēl, but their belief is definitely as old as the rising of that civilization itself.

As a matter of fact, it was on Mt. Carmel[305] where Thutmose III encountered some Phoenician Enochian Priests, direct adepts of Enoch, the seer of Mt. Hermon. After watching them worship the One Most High God Ēl, he was incited by the great idea of monotheism, as he weighed it against the over seven hundred city-gods worshipped in Egypt. In a spark of genius, he speculated the possibility and benefits of combining all major Egyptian gods into One Supreme Being. In consequence to this revelation he built a new religious centre—a school of initiation—on some of the ruins of the Temple of Ashirai (Asherah)[306]. This school that supported the concept of monotheism immediately found ground in Egypt in the form of a Mystery School as a Phoenician-Egyptian monotheistic fraternity, known a bit later as the Great White Fraternity. This special relationship between Canaan-Phoenicia and Egypt persisted for a long time, and therefore, both Memphis and Gebel subsisted as twin religious cities. A bit over a hundred years later, monotheism emerged in Egypt in the form of a religious reform against the system imposed by Ramses II, with

---

304 A name given to the Land of Canaan. It is probably because of that, Thompson L. Thomas, called the Canaanites "Afro-Asiatic" in his most reputed book, *The Mythic Past.*

305 Among the many locations he occupied in Phoenicia, Mt. Carmel presented the most suitable place for *Initiation.* In his annals, Thutmose III referred to it as the "Sacred Island." The name "Carmel," as discussed earlier in Chapter 3, derives from the Phoenician word, *Krm-el,* the "Generous Vine of Ēl," meaning, the "Spiritual offering of Ēl."

306 Phoenician priests built two great Temples at the top of Mt. Carmel; one dedicated to the Most High God Ēl (Baal), and the other to Ashirai (Anat), the Mother Goddess—partly destroyed during one of the many invasions of Thutmose III.

Pharaoh Amenhotep IV (c. 1370 BC–1350 BC)—the great religious reformer known as Akhenaton. It surfaced in his religious city: Akhetaton, "Horizon of Aton." His father, Amenhotep III, was the son of Thutmose IV, who took for spouse the Phoenician queen Tia, a believer in the One God Ēl. Thutmose IV was the son of Amenhotep II, the offspring of the famous Pharaoh Thutmose III (c. 1505 BC–1450 BC) or Thut-Mosis, "Initiate of Thut," or Thot-Taautus. In the footsteps of his father, Amenhotep III married a Phoenician queen, Tiy, also a believer of the One God Ēl. In conclusion, the monotheistic relationship between both Canaan-Phoenicia[307] and Egypt[308] was also a strong religious family tie! Hence, during the rule of Akhenaton, the Egyptians' belief led to the laying of the very last foundation stone of the Great White Fraternity. As Memphis stood for the religious twin city of Gebel, so did Akhetaton to Mt. Carmel.

The Babylonian Brotherhood

It is traditionally believed that Abraham, the genetic father of the Hebrew people, originated from the city of Ur of the Chaldeans in Babylon. This piece of information is found in the Old Testament itself in both the Book of Genesis[309] and the work of the Scribe Nehemiah[310]. Now, according to the Biblical story, Abraham was called Abram first, but when he was chosen by the Hebrew God to keep the Covenant[311] and enter the Land of Canaan[312], Yahweh changed his name into Abraham[313]. It seemed though that the Hebrew God changed the name of the man's wife[314] too,

---

307 Enoch-Thor, Milki-Sedek, Kings Ahiram, and Hiram ...
308 Thot-Taautus; Pharaohs Thut-Mosis III, Amenhotep II, Thutmose IV, Amenhotep III, Amenhotep IV ...
309 Genesis 11:31, "And Terah took his son Abram and his grandson Lot, the son of Haran, and his daughter-in-law Sarai, his son Abram's wife, and they went out with them from Ur of the Chaldeans to go to the land of Canaan; and they came to Haran and dwelt there."
310 Nehemiah 9:7, "You [are] the LORD God, Who chose Abram, And brought him out of Ur of the Chaldeans, And gave him the name Abraham;"
311 Genesis 17:9, "And God said to Abraham: 'As for you, you shall keep My covenant, you and your descendants after you throughout their generations.'"
312 Genesis 12:1, "Now the LORD had said to Abram: 'Get out of your country, From your family And from your father's house, To a land that I will show you.'"
313 Genesis 17:5, "No longer shall your name be called Abram, but your name shall be Abraham; for I have made you a father of many nations."
314 Genesis 17:15, "Then God said to Abraham, 'As for Sarai your wife, you shall not call her name Sarai, but Sarah [shall be] her name.'"

probably for the same reason of giving them new names and new identities in a new land—the Promised Land. Whatever the case or hidden meaning, if there was one behind that story, Abraham or Abram remains a Babylonian. Yet, was he the Aramean wanderer mentioned in the Old Testament? Are they the same person? In fact, historical records show that the Chaldeans, although a Semitic group of people, were distinguished from the Aramean stock of humanity.[315]

At any rate, the striking similarity in both the Book of Genesis and that of Nehemiah is very important in regards to the promise made by the Hebrew God to Abraham and his descendants. We read in Genesis (12:1-7; 17:1-8):

> Now the LORD had said to Abram: Get out of your country, From your family And from your father's house, To a land that I will show you. I will make you a great nation; I will bless you And make your name great; And you shall be a blessing. I will bless those who bless you, And I will curse him who curses you; And in you all the families of the earth shall be blessed. So Abram departed as the LORD had spoken to him, and Lot went with him. And Abram [was] seventy-five years old when he departed from Haran. Then Abram took Sarai his wife and Lot his brother's son, and all their possessions that they had gathered, and the people whom they had acquired in Haran, and they departed to go to the land of Canaan. So they came to the land of Canaan. Abram passed through the land to the place of Shechem, as far as the terebinth tree of Moreh. And the Canaanites [were] then in the land. Then the LORD appeared to Abram and said, To your descendants I will give this land. And there he built an altar to the LORD, who had appeared to him.

We read in Nehemiah (9:7-8):

> You [are] the LORD God, Who chose Abram, And brought him out of Ur of the Chaldeans, And gave him the name Abraham; You found his heart faithful before You, And made a covenant with him To give the land of the Canaanites, The Hittites, the Amorites, The Perizzites, the Jebusites, And the Girgashites— To give [it] to his descendants. You have performed Your words, For You [are] righteous.

---

315 Wikipedia, *Chaldea*.

Should we read carefully, we would find the original place from which Abraham departed and the destination he had in mind, as the Old Testament shows, inspired and directed by the Hebrew God. There is undoubtedly a conquering mentality in the text, or if I may say, as always has been the case for all conquerors, a stealing mentality. The Hebrew God chose a group of people to rob the adjacent lands and occupy the Promised Land—Canaan.

And the Book of Genesis (15:18) continues elaborating on that particular point saying that while Abraham was in the Land of Canaan, the Hebrew God appeared to him:

On the same day the LORD made a covenant with Abram, saying: To your descendants I have given this land, from the river of Egypt to the great river, the River
Euphrates ...

The selection of the occupied territories herein cited, decided to be given to Abraham by his God, is actually mentioned in many other different places in the Old Testament[316], and were in reality the same territories occupied by the Persians at the time of Cyrus II in that part of the ancient world.

It would be a serious error to believe that Abraham actually existed around two thousand years BC as the Old Testament wants us to think. Not only that, but it becomes evident to most free-minded academics that the preceding claims of the Old Testament are pretty obsolete. It is not at all a historical document for Christians to base their religious lives on, especially when they consider that Jesus is not connected to Abraham or David on the genetic level as we have seen before. It is a flaw indeed for the New Testament to keep that binding with the Hebrew Bible. Great uncertainties have been fairly uttered not only regarding the authenticity of the Patriarchs mentioned in the Book of Genesis, but also, very intelligently questioning the historicity of the kings David and Solomon, as well as personages like Moses, Joshua, and the Judges, too.

In reality, the city of Ur is mentioned several times in the Old Testament as Ur of the Chaldeans and as the birthplace of the First Hebrew Patriarch, Abraham. The 2000 years BC proposed as the date of his birth would thus be nothing but pure invention and he could only be a false historical figure. Why? The claim that Abraham, his wife, children, and descendants, are said to have "crossed the river" to the Promised Land of Canaan to settle and take it as their new land, surely not a homeland, could not have

---

316 Deuteronomy 1:7; 11:24; Joshua 1:4; 2Kings 24:7.

happened in 2000 years BC because credible historical facts state that the Chaldeans settled in Iraq sometime around 800 BC—maybe a bit before, but not that long before—and were actually based in Babylon sometime between the 7th and 6th century BC. Therefore, in simple calculation, there is a difference of about a minimum of 1200 years. And in concordance with the latter period, the famous edict—issued by the Persian Emperor, Cyrus II (known as the Great), in the 6th century BC—is a valid historical fact; an edict in which he gave the promise to a few chosen Babylonian families and people of a new *home*land in the Land of Canaan. Hence, the Old Testament's famous promise of the Hebrew God to his people was, in fact, that of Cyrus. No matter what else we might think of, the city of Ur stands as the primary point of foundation for the Hebrews, only at the time of Cyrus II, and it is then and there that things started happening for them.

This is a proven fact, for we find a notable connotation for this action, in the Old Testament. We thus read in Ezra (italics mine):

The Lord stirred up the spirit of Cyrus King of Persia, that he made a proclamation throughout all his kingdom, and put it also in writing ... Thus saith Cyrus King of Persia, the Lord God of heaven hath given me all the kingdoms of the earth; and he hath *charged me to build him a house at Jerusalem, which is in Judah.* (Ezra 1:1-2)

And in Isaiah (italics mine):

Thus saith the Lord to his *anointed*, to Cyrus, whose right hand I have holden, to subdue nations before me. (Isaiah 45:1)

The above two quotations were written as if in homage to Cyrus and his power to take ultimate possession of all the kingdoms of the earth and subdue all nations. They are extremely important and similar in many ways—especially in terms of the psychological frame of a military doctrine and a conquering mind —to what was previously mentioned in Genesis and Nehemiah concerning the so-called "Promised Land" the Hebrew God offered to Abraham and the power he gave him to conquer additional territories, mainly from the River Euphrates to the river of Egypt, and subdue their nations.

This may appear bizarre and shocking to the majority of readers, especially to Christian scholars who probably haven't paid attention to it, as was the case with me before it dawned on me, just recently. There is not a single word of homage or respect to any Gentile gods, priests, kings, kingdoms, or even to any group of people belonging to any nation—the *goyim*—by the Hebrews in the Old Testament. It would be thus too much of a coincidence to find that the Hebrews, at the time, who had much too often considered themselves the only Chosen People, had indeed written that their Lord God stirred up the spirit of a Goy, say a Persian, to build him a temple in Jerusalem, and even more, anointed him to become a kind of a Messiah, a savior! Why? One may wonder ...

Persians were not Goyim in the eyes of the Hebrews for the simple fact that it was the Persians who created the Hebrews. It may not at all be neglected that the two scribes of the Old Testament, Nehemiah and Ezra (or Esdras), were in fact Persians and eminent members of the Babylonian Brotherhood. The real and actual, not mythical and falsified, history of the Jewish people starts with them. (We shall clearly see examples and evidence from the Old Testament in a bit.) Additionally, the connection is not only based on the historical level, but surely expands to the religious level as well. Renan states[317], "The prophetic tone of many of the teachings of Iran had much analogy with certain compositions of Hosea and Isaiah." He then adds[318], "The whole book of Esther breathes a great attachment to this dynasty." Renan undoubtedly indicated that this dynasty were the Achemenidae[319], under which he then declared, "Israel reposed."

Please bear in mind that this book is not meant to narrate the real and complete genesis of the Hebrew people, as much as we know such a work would require a whole volume, but we need to mention certain facts concerning them that truly help enlighten the way ahead of us in our search for the real Jesus, the Phoenician.

Instead, here is a briefing of the Hebrew genesis ...

At the time of the Persian Empire's expansion, the adjacent city of Babylon fell into the hands of the Persian King Cyrus II, around the year 539 BC, and became a province of the Great Persian Empire. The Persians, like the Babylonians and Assyrians before them, exercised a systematic relocation program—for the subjugated populace—from one occupied land to another. This particular program was greatly endorsed by an all-encompassing

---

317 Renan, Ernest, *Vie de Jésus*, page 143.

318 Ibid., page 143 & (fn.7)

319 The Achaemenid Persian Empire (c. 550 BC–330 BC), from the Old Persian word, *Parsā*, name of the ruling dynasty, *Haxāmanišiya*, also known as the First Persian (Iranian) Empire in Western Asia, founded by Cyrus the Great (c. 559 BC–529 BC) who overthrew the Median confederation. It ended with Darius III (c. 336BC–330 BC) in around 330 BC.

political and religious propaganda. In that concern, Thompson so eloquently explains in his work[320]:

They (in reference to the resettlement policies) had a very complicated impact on the development of ethnic and national identities within the empire. They also played a decisive role in the growth of ideas about monotheism and about saving 'messiahs.' The metaphors of the restoration of Israel's God in Jerusalem, the rebuilding of the temple and the return of a repentant remnant from 'exile'—all these images find their origin in such policies. All of these concepts play a vital role in the creation of a 'new Israel,' a new 'people of God' centered in Jerusalem.

Thus, understanding the basics of the resettlement policy herein practiced by the Persians, we come to conclude that after several years of controlling Babylon, Cyrus II and some Chaldean priests might have established the Babylonian Brotherhood, almost one year after the fall of Babylon. In fact, Cyrus issued his famous edict in 538 BC that consisted of ordering the transfer of a group—composed of Chaldean priests and families, belonging to the Brotherhood—from Babylon to the Promised Land. We have thus observed that this transfer was not a resettling plan, but instead, a settling program.

So, the promise made by Cyrus II had a hidden agenda of some sort. It was a historical declaration, all in the hope that it would strengthen their authorities, which stated that the power of the Persian Empire should not be comprised by any geographical boundary. The Persians reached the southern part of the land of Canaan-Phoenicia, including Jerusalem, and controlled it some few years later after being in command of Babylon. Later—in 525 BC, under Cambyses II, the son and successor of Cyrus II—the Persians attacked Egypt and destroyed all its religious monuments. In time, the Persians controlled most of western Asia.

The man who seems to have been the first to lead the people—known as the *Aebirou-al-naher* or the Hebrews who "crossed the river" in constant waves from Babylon towards the Land of Canaan—was called Zoro-Babel, an eminent member of the Babylonian Brotherhood. That began with him (or with his uncle, as we shall see in a bit) under the patronage of Cyrus II the Great, and this occurred when they had just thought of building a temple in Jerusalem, as we have seen before, when the Lord

---

320 Thompson, Thomas L., *The Mythic Past*, page 190-191.

stirred up the spirit of Cyrus and charged him to build him a house in Judah. Again, Renan had a say about that matter when he declared[321], as openly as he knew at the time (italics mine), "The victory of Cyrus seemed at one time to realize all that had been hoped. The grave disciples of the Avesta and the adorers of Jehovah believed themselves *brothers*."

Having said that, we then would like to note that Zoro-Babel (or Zerubbabel) was not the Hebrew leader who brought the *alleged* ancient Jews out of their exile and into Jerusalem, and was not the Prince of Judea of Davidic lineage, as the Scribes of the Old Testament wanted the whole world to believe. Truth be said, the name Zoro-Babel is a Babylonian or Assyro-Babylonian name, written as such, *Zeru Bābel*, and it surely means, "Seed or Son of Babel (Babylon)." He was a Babylonian by birth before the Hebrews (or the Jews) were in existence as an ethnic group, and this is supported by the work of many professional historians and archeologists like Thomas L. Thompson, who explained in his book[322]:

Related terms show up in Sumerian, Assyro-Babylonian and Egyptian texts in the forms of *Hapiru* and *Apiru*. These terms refer to individuals and groups who were not accepted within the accepted political structures of patronage alliances and loyalties that governed society. These 'Hebrews' were both literally and figuratively 'outlaws,' not terribly unlike such legendary characters in story as the David of I-II Samuel or the Abraham of Genesis 12 and 14, where they are called 'Hebrews.'

Further explanation concerning this issue comes from Israel Finkelstein and Neil Asher Silberman, authors of *The Bible Unearthed*. They clearly wrote[323]:

In the past, scholars have suggested that the word *Apiru* (and its alternative forms, *Hapiru* and *Habiru*) had a direct linguistic connection to the word *Ibri*, or Hebrew, and that therefore the Apiru in the Egyptian sources were the early Israelites. Today we know that this association is not so simple. The widespread use of the term over many centuries and throughout the entire Near East suggests that it had a

---

321 Renan, Ernest, *Vie de Jésus*, page 143.
322 Thompson, Thomas L., *The Mythic Past*, page 79.
323 Finkelstein Israel, Silberman Neil Asher, *The Bible Unearthed*, page 103.

socioeconomic meaning rather than signifying a specific ethnic group.

Thompson had earlier suggested[324], "The lack of a reliable historical context for the Bible (he meant the Old Testament) has been a great hindrance to modern Biblical studies." This is so true because Biblical scholars were looking for historical and archeological proof as per the narration of the Old Testament itself, and have utterly neglected the Persian case that we are disclosing here. Thus, with no historical or archaeological verification offered regarding the kingdom of Biblical Israel and the temple, the issue is not therefore a resettlement program for a rebuilding of a temple and the restoration of ancient Israel, but rather a settlement plan and the creation of the State of Israel accompanied with a building of a temple. In fact, the majority of respected Biblical historians, such as Thomas L. Thompson, Philip Davies, Niels Peter Lemche, Israel Finkelstein, Neil Asher Silberman, Keith Whitlam, etc., share, to a certain extent, a similar exciting explanation. They tend to believe that, for some ideological and political reason, the whole Biblical narration of the history of Ancient Israel could in fact be nothing more than the intricate operation of a skillful clandestine group of priests living in Jerusalem at some *post-exilic* time. We would add that this secret group of priests was actually the Babylonian Brotherhood.

Let us not linger too much on this breathtaking truth now, yet, I urge readers to give it a profound thought later on. We shall for the moment embark on understanding the national culture and religious differences that obviously existed between the Great White Fraternity, represented now and directly by the Canaanite/Phoenicians, who were basically the indigenous people of the Land of Canaan, and the Babylonian Brotherhood, played now by the Hebrew/Jews, who *conquered* the Promised Land and *created* the Biblical Israel.

Hebrew/Jewish National Culture

What did they believe in? The question is simple to answer. It is their national God YHWH. But before we venture into their religion, let us first investigate the historicity of the state or the country this religion was based in. The Old Testament mentions it as Israel.

What does the word Israel mean? It is an Aramaic name composed of two words: "Israt" or "Ashirat," and "Ēl." It clearly

---

324 Thompson, Thomas L., *The Mythic Past*, page 4.

means the "Religious Family (Tribe) of the God Ēl." The word Israel in this context does not make sense to the Hebrews, for the main reason that they are believers in the God Yahweh. The word Israel in the Biblical Hebrew/Jewish context would typically refer to the tale in the Old Testament (Genesis 32:22-32) about Jacob. Although the *Aebirou-al-naher* are shown to have conquered the Land of Canaan and defeated their greatest enemy, the Canaanites, as per the narration of the Old Testament; the figure of Jacob as the founder of the state of Israel, who is said to have struggled with the God Ēl, does not match at all the action the *Aebirou-al-naher* did to the Canaanites and their God the Most High, Ēl-Ēlyon. The Old Testament clearly reflects the fact that they didn't actually struggle with Ēl, but rather strove against Him and against his people. Jacob would then appear to have defeated Ēl, changing his name into Israel, and becoming the Hebrew founder of the state of Israel. Consequently, it would be more logical and truthful for the Hebrews to name their religious state "Israyhwh," for they were indeed Isra-Iao or Ashirat-Yahweh —the children and family of Yahweh, not of Ēl.

Not only that, but there is too big a gap in time to support such a story. This personality is not as old as the Old Testament wishes us to believe. In fact, Jacob did not exist, like Abraham, the so-called mythical genetic father of the Hebrews, who originally came from the city of Ur in southern Mesopotamia and settled along with his family in the town of Haran in the upper area of the River Euphrates before heading towards Canaan. The only personality that would fit the character of Abraham, say, in actual history, could be Sheshbazzar[325] or Shenazzar[326], the uncle of Zerubbabel, who is said to have led or set forth to lead the first group under Cyrus II. Moreover, the only character that would fit the character of Jacob would be Zorobabel, who came abruptly into the story, replacing Shenazzar. It seems that Zorobabel actually led the Jews to Canaan, having been appointed by Darius I as governor over the district of the Province of Judah. It is suggested by scholars, however, that both Sheshbazzar and Zorobabel were the same person.[327]

---

325 Ezra 1:8, "and Cyrus king of Persia brought them out by the hand of Mithredath the treasurer, and counted them out to Sheshbazzar the prince of Judah."
326 1Chronicles 3:18-19, "[and] Malchiram, Pedaiah, Shenazzar, Jecamiah, Hoshama, and Nedabiah. The sons of Pedaiah [were] Zerubbabel and Shimei. The sons of Zerubbabel [were] Meshullam, Hananiah, Shelomith their sister,"
327 Both had been named Governors of the Province of Judah under the Persians and both are credited with setting up the foundation stone of the Temple. Sheshbazzar in Ezra 5:16 and Zerubbabel in Ezra 5:2.

In fact, the ultimate role and goal of the *Aebirou-al-naher* was to assure the control of the Babylonian Brotherhood in all of the Land of Canaan, supported by the Persian propagandists. It was clever propaganda indeed destined to create a new political situation in the conquered region founded on a new form of religion, since religion has always been considered a powerful tool to subdue nations. The Persians, who created the Babylonian Brotherhood, most likely invented Judaism. Yet, the Hebrews, with their imaginary genetic father Abraham and Israel with its imaginary founder Jacob, needed yet another personality that would stand as their essential religious figure. Thus, they came up with of Moses. It would not be a surprise or a coincidence to all of us now to know that the image of Moses was originally made on the image of another Babylonian of a previous period, Sargon the Great—the ancient King of Akkad and founder of the Akkadian dynasty—who reigned between the years c. 2335 BC–2279 BC. Assuredly, the fall of Babylon and the whole of Mesopotamia into the hand of the Persians would allow them, the Persian propagandist group, infinite access to all Babylonian historical records and legends.

One of the greatest birth stories that survived the ages and became an essential part of Babylonian literature and legends was that of Sargon. The similarity between his birth and that of Moses is undeniable. That being said, we would like to share the words of Sargon concerning his birth as it appeared in the Babylonian records[328]:

> I am Sargon, the mighty king, king of Agade (Akkad) ... My mother, the high priestess, conceived me; in secret she bore me. She set me in a basket of rushes; with bitumen, she sealed my lid. She cast me into the river, which rose not over me ...

The story of the birth of Moses is narrated in Exodus (2:1-3) as follows:

> And a man of the house of Levi went and took [as wife] a daughter of Levi. So the woman conceived and bore a son. And when she saw that he [was] a beautiful [child], she hid him three months. But when she could no longer hide him, she took an ark of bulrushes for him, daubed it with asphalt and pitch, put the child in it, and laid [it] in the reeds by the river's bank.

---

328 Thompson, Thomas L., *The Mythic Past*, page 13.

Not only that, the Hebrews or *Aebirou-al-naher* were all Babylonian priests and families transferred from ancient Iraq to the Land of Canaan at the time of the Achaemenid, but also their key genetic, political, and religious leaders, known respectively as Abraham, Jacob and Moses, were all Babylonians, as we have just proved.

The Old Testament's image of Moses standing his ground as a rebel against the great Pharaoh Ramses II of Egypt, and a liberator of his people, was in fact nothing but a replica of the actual story of an Egyptian Priest of Heliopolis by the name of Osarsiph or Hosarsiph[329]. Many, however, believe he was the cousin of Mernephtah, the son and successor of Pharaoh Ramses II. He was the son of the Royal Princess, sister of the Pharaoh[330]. Quite naturally, and for the simplest logical reason of all times, Egyptian historical records do not mention any kind of Hebrew/Jewish rebellious actions against the ruling Egyptian dynasty at the time Moses was injected into history. However, it would not be difficult for the Persian scribes, Esdras and Nehemiah, to create a Biblical story about a man they called Moses, and paint him as a hero freeing his people based on one or many Egyptian figures, since the Persian occupation of the Land of Ham, Egypt, was definitely a successful conquest. All Egyptian annals about important figures and events could have fallen in their hands.

We have recently seen that the group(s) of people called Apiru, *Hapiru* or *Habiru*, found in Egyptian sources, and whose name is believed by scholars to have a direct linguistic link to the word *Ibri* or *Hebrew*, were not the early Israelites as was long thought by Judeo-Christian Biblical scholars. The Hebrews/Israelites/Jews were not there at all, for they didn't yet exist on the timeline of real history. At any rate, the Apiru rebellious actions were driven by difficult socioeconomic situations and did not indicate a defined ethnic group.

It was proven earlier that monotheism was not the invention of the Hebrews; neither was it a declaration of the Zoroastrian

---

329 Hosarsiph or Osarsiph appeared almost 200 years after the time of Akhenaton, the Egyptian Sun worshipper, and preacher of the monotheistic God—Aton. Egyptian history tells that Pharaoh Ramses II continued suppressing the monotheistic religious idea, brought about openly by Akhenaton in Egypt. However, Osarsiph, a learned priest and loyal secret follower of Akhenaton, rebelled against the Pharaoh and his son— Mernephtah—all in hopes of restoring the cult of Akhenaton—the belief in one God.

330 Schuré Edouard, *Les Grands Initiés*, Page 174.

religion that inspired the Persian Empire. In fact, monotheism indeed arrived in Egypt through Canaan/Phoenicia. Thus, the monotheistic religious concept attributed to the invented mythical personality of Moses and the political propaganda the Persians had fabricated in support to this group of people, the *Aebirou-al-naher*, whom they gradually and successfully transferred from Babylon to the Promised Land, would not stand any longer in truth. Once and for all, truth be said, monotheism should be instead accredited secretly to Thutmose III or Thut-Mosis[331], the *Initiate of Thut*, and then openly, to Akhenaton. Yet, well before them, monotheism was practiced by Milki-Sedek and a few other Canaano-Phoenician initiates and priests of the Most High God, Él-Alyon.

It was very logical for the Persians to think that while they had already invented Abraham (Sheshbazzar or Shenazzar) as the Babylonian genetic father of the Hebrews and offered him the Land of Canaan to possess; Jacob (Zoro-Babel or Zerubbabel) as the founder of the state of Israel to be positioned in that Land; and Moses (Sargon/Hosarsiph/Thutmosis) as the religious prophet and leader for that state, like every other nation living on the face of Earth, there must be a place for them to practice the religion and worship the god or the deity they believe in. Having realized that, the Lord stirred up the spirit of the *Anointed* Cyrus, King of Persia, gave him all the kingdoms of the earth, and charged him to build him a temple at Jerusalem in Judea.

We have all read this before in both Ezra (Esdras) and Isaiah. I have no intention of annoying my readers by repeating this issue herein once again, but it is very important for all of us to realize the importance of such a historical, political, and religious proclamation made by the King of Persia in the Old Testament. Having absorbed well that concealed fact, let's have a quick look now at the Hebrew religion and major sects. We will, however, examine their God and the temple they built in Jerusalem, in Chapter 9.

Hebrew/Jewish Religion

The Hebrew/Jewish religion is known as "Judaism" and derived from the Hebrew word, *Yehudah*, Judah. It represents the faith and the way of life of the Jewish people based on the Hebrew Bible (also known as the *Tanakh*[332], the Masoretic Text) or what is

---

331 Could *Moses* be an alteration of the Egyptian name Thut-*Mosis*?
332 The Hebrew-composed word, "TaNaKh" represents the primary letters of the three traditional subdivisions found in the makeup of the Old

obviously called, the Old Testament by Judeo-Christians. It mainly focuses on the special relationship established between a certain god called YHWH (Yahweh or Jehovah) and the Covenant he made with the religious Children of Israel (should be Israyhwh), the Jews, through the laws and commandments revealed to the (*mythical*) Moses on Mt. Sinai in both written and oral methods known as the Torah, where the brilliant concept of monotheism has been claimed as "theirs."

At any rate, Judaism is not only confined to the Old Testament's literary narration but is also found in later texts such as the Talmud. Judaism was found to be practiced by three essential religious movements at the time of Jesus. In fact, this is exactly the area of research that concerns us. These three main groups were always in conflict and opposition with each other and are recognized as the Sadducees, the Pharisees, and the Essens. We will talk about them briefly herein.

The Sadducees

There are in fact two different theories on the origin of the Sadducees. The first one proposes that they actually belong to the House of Zadok, drawing their name from "Tzadok" (related to the Canaanite/Aramaic root or Hebrew term *sādaq*, which means "to be right and just"), who was the first *Kohen Gadol* (High Priest[333]) to preside over the First Temple, or what is known as the Temple of Solomon. This theory by itself does not hold up for the simple reason that there is no actual physical archeological evidence of the existence of such a temple—as we will see in a bit and in more detail in Chapter 9—nor is it backed by historical writings outside the Old Testament. The second theory, which is acceptable by the historical logic we have been suggesting here in this book, argues that the Sadducees (with their founder Tzadok or Zadok) originated together with a closely related group known as the

---

Testament's text. They are divided as such: The *Torah* (or the Teaching, also known as the Five Books of Moses), the *Nevi'im* (or the work of the Prophets, also known as the narrative books of Joshua, Judges, Samuel, Kings, Isaiah, Jeremiah, Ezekiel, and the Twelve Minor Prophets: Hosea, Joel, Amos, Obadiah, Jonah, Micah, Nahum, Habakkuk, Zephaniah, Haggai, Zechariah, Malachi), and the *Ketuvim* (the Writings or Scriptures such as I and II Chronicles, Ezra, Nehemiah, Psalms, Proverbs, Job, the Song of Songs, Book of Ruth, the Book of Lamentations, Ecclesiastes, Book of Esther, Book of Daniel).

333 According to the Hebrew/Jewish tradition, the high priests are linked directly to Hebrew/Jewish priestly families that trace their origin back to Aaron, the brother of Moses, and who is known to have been the first high priest.

Boethusians (with their founder Boethus) during what is known as the Second Temple Period—a period that began around the years 530 BC or 516 BC (either under Cambyses II—son and successor of Cyrus the Great—who ruled from 530 BC until 522 BC—or under Darius I, Darius the Great—who ruled from 522 BC until 486 BC). According to classical Jewish Biblical history, it is the period of time that began with the construction of what is called the Second Temple in Jerusalem[334] and ended with its destruction along with Jerusalem by Titus in 70 AD during the first Jewish-Roman war. Yet, both Tzadok and Boethus seem to have been official students of the Jewish scholar Antigonus of Sokho, who flourished sometime around the first half of the 3rd century BC. If that is so, and we might completely agree on the timing since it copes well with our direct suggestion that the Hebrews were created by Cyrus the Great (c. 539 BC) and sent in different waves to some parts of the occupied Land of Canaan, hence Jerusalem, then the Sadducees could have actually begun sometime around 300 BC and 250 BC.

At any rate, the reputed Roman-Jewish historian, Flavius Josephus (c. 37 AD–100 AD), who was credited to have preserved some of the stories of the Jewish people, being the only source outside the Old Testament, mentioned them in his book[335] as such, "While the Sadducees are able to persuade none but the rich, and have not the populace obsequious to them ..." This by itself shows that the sect could have represented only the upper socio-economic class within Jewish society—an aristocratic, wealthy, and traditional group of elites. Yet, they seem to have fulfilled various political, social, and religious roles.

Their political roles seem to have consisted of supervising many of the formal affairs of the ancient state of Israel, from the domestic administration of the government to representing it on the international level like regulating the relationship with the Romans. They convened in the Sanhedrin (known as the

---

334 We opt to believe that this was in fact the First Hebrew/Jewish/Israeli Temple ever built. The project of building a temple in Jerusalem, as per the Old Testament, was initiated by the Persian King, Cyrus the Great and seems to have been approved by his son Cambyses II, and financed by the third King of the Persian Achaemenid Empire, Darius I the Great. It is said that it was completed under the leadership of the last three of the twelve minor prophets: Haggai, Zechariah and Malachi. Yet, we believe that the construction was not actually started around 516 BC under Darius I, but some hundred years later during the reign of Darius II, the seventh King of the Achaemenid Empire, who ruled from c. 423 BC to c. 405 BC.
335 Flavius, Josephus, *The Antiquities of the Jews*, Book 13, Chapter 10, Paragraph 6.

Assembly, Council, or High Court), where they would participate in making decisions about many different issues, such as intervening in national protests. In addition, the Sadducees collected taxes from Jews living in Jerusalem and from those in the Diaspora, and also equipped the army with necessary weapons and led them in battle.

Their religious roles seem to have included the maintenance of the temple at the heart of Jerusalem, thus their high social-economic status was supported by their priestly prestige, as entrusted to them in the Torah, after having claimed themselves descendants of the House of Zadok, the first family of High Priests of the *alleged* Temple of Solomon. Thus, preserving this priestly line was surely a necessity to own complete authority of the temple. At any rate, the priests of the temple, which often represented the highest class in Hebrew/Jewish society, were not all from the Sadducees—the Religious Sacerdotal body of the Jews —for in fact, many were Pharisees, and a few others were not adherent to any known group within the society. Their main role was performing sacrifices at the temple, which was in fact the initial way of worship in Ancient Israel. They considered the Torah ("the Teaching," or the written law of Moses) as the one and only source of divine authority, and their main beliefs consisted of the following concepts: man has the free will to choose between good or evil; the soul is not immortal, hence no afterlife; and there is no resurrection of the dead.

The Pharisees

Similar to the Sadducees, who seemed to have correctly begun during what is known as the Second Temple Period, the Pharisees appear to have been in existence during that period as well, and played almost the same roles as those of the Sadducees but on all different social, political, and religious levels. Classical Biblical accounts suggest that the Pharisees began under the Hasmonean Dynasty[336] sometime around 160 BC and 140 BC. If this is true, that puts them after the Sadducees in chronological order.

Etymologically speaking, it is said that the name "Pharisees" comes from the Hebrew and Aramaic term, *pĕrûshîm*, which is the verbal plural form of the word *pārûsh* or pārûshi, and which means, "set apart," or "one who is separated."

---

336 The Hasmonean Dynasty was founded under the leadership of Simon the Maccabee some twenty-three years later after the Maccabean Revolt (c. 164 BC) started by his brother Judas, as we have seen earlier in the book.

We certainly approve on the period of time the Pharisees came into existence—after 516—in Hebrew/Jewish history, but we may differ on when exactly they actually began and what could be the correct origin of their name. It appears to us that the Pharisees actually began as a secret group of Babylonian priests within the groups of Babylonian priests and families that were transferred from Babylon to the Land of Canaan. These clandestine priests formed what we call the Babylonian Brotherhood and were among the many different waves of the *Aebirou-al-naher*, who settled mainly in Jerusalem and were known later on as Hebrews in the broadest sense of the word. The Pharisees were first assigned to lead the people out of Babylon into Jerusalem and build the temple Cyrus II had pledged to house the deity in. Their mission was designed to accommodate the Persians' socio-religious and political ambitions. My analysis of that situation sparked a belief that Zerubbabel was the actual leader of the Pharisees, hence, we see him accredited with the title, "Prince of Judea," where the temple was erected.

In that concern, H.P. Blavatsky was clear enough to state in her book[337]:

It was Darius Hystaspes (Darius I, the Great) who was the first to establish a Persian colony in Judaea; Zoro-Babel was perhaps the leader. The name *Zoro-babel* means 'the seed or son of Babylon'—as Zoro-aster (Zoroaster), is the seed, son, or prince of Ishtar. The new colonists were doubtless *Judaei*.

She next added:

When the Asmonean (Hasmonean) period began, the chief supporters of the Law were called Asideans or Kasdim[338] (Chaldeans), and afterward Pharisees or Pharsi (Pârsîs). This indicates that Persian colonies were established in Judaea and ruled the country; while all the people that are mentioned in the books of *Genesis* and *Joshua* lived there as a commonalty.

Another important passage came to us from Albert Pike, the Sovereign Grand Commander of the Supreme Council 33° of the Scottish Rite, and author of *Morals and Dogma of the Ancient and Accepted Scottish Rite of Freemasonry*, an interesting work that was meant only for the brothers within the Craft, but then became public. Pike declared that the dominant religious system

---

337 Blavatsky, H.P., *Isis Unveiled*, Volume II, page 441.
338 They are the Hasidim, or Hasideans (Hasidæans or Assideans).

among the Hebrews/Jews was indeed that of the Pharisees (or Pharoschim). He wrote[339]:

> Whether their name (the Pharisees) was derived from that of the Parsees, or followers of Zoroaster, or from some other source, it is certain that they had borrowed much of their doctrine from the Persians. Like them they claimed to have the exclusive and mysterious knowledge, unknown to the mass. Like them they taught that a constant war was waged between the empire of Good and that of Evil. Like them they attributed the sin and fall of man to the demons and their chief; and like them they admitted a special protection of the righteous by inferior beings, agents of Jehovah. All their doctrines on these subjects were at bottom those of the Holy Books.

Blavatsky adds[340]:

> The Jews, coming from the Persian country, brought with them the doctrine of *two principles*. They could not bring the *Avesta*, for it was not written. But they—we mean the *Asideans* (Chasîdîm) and *Pharsi*—invested Ormazd with the secret name of YHWH, and Ahriman with the name of the gods of the land, Satan of the Hittites, and *Diabolos*, or rather *Diobolos*, of the Greeks.

Academics or Judeo-Christian Biblical scholars may criticize the above quotes, saying that both H.P. Blavatsky, the famous founder of theosophy, and the Masonic reformer, Albert Pike, could not be considered credible sources on the Pharisees or Jewish religion for that matter. However, their interesting revelations have been affirmed by the renowned historian, Renan, as we have seen before, and by every other single piece of evidence we have been exposing and examining with the readers so far. And thus, Renan, who said that Old Testament books like those of Hosea, Isaiah, and Esther had many analogies with the prophetic tone of many of the teachings of Iran, and that the adorers of Jehovah and the disciples of the Avesta believed themselves brothers—indeed they were—adds[341] another significant assertion, saying:

---

339 Pike, Albert, *Morals and Dogma of the Ancient and Accepted Scottish Rite of Freemasonry*, page 259.
340 Blavatsky, H.P., *Isis Unveiled*, Volume II, page 501.
341 Renan, Ernest, *Vie de Jésus*, page 146.

It was the Pharisee, the believer in the resurrection, who was the innovator. But in religion it is always the zealous sect which innovates, which progresses, and which has influence. Besides this, the resurrection, an idea totally different from that of the immortality of the soul, proceeded very naturally from the anterior doctrines and from the position of the people. Perhaps Persia also furnished some of its elements.

In fact, I confidently state that the Religious Rabbinical body of the Jews, known as the Pharisees, have taken their name from the word "Pharsi," *Pârsîs* or *Parsees*—the Persians. They took not only their name, but their costume, their beliefs in magic and sorcery, in the influences of the stars on humans, in the immortality of the souls and their transmigration, in resurrection, in angels and demons, and in the concept of dualism that controls the physical world. All these elements and more that actually formed the Hebrew/Jewish Religion seem to have been based principally on the ancient Persian religion, on that of Zarathustra —the main religious doctrine practiced by Cyrus II and the Achaemenid Empire—and on Babylonian doctrines, as well.

It is said that their religious views were lenient and heterogeneous; their teachings were non-creedal and non-dogmatic. It is because of that, and additionally the Sadducees who only believe in the Written Laws of Moses (the Torah), that the Pharisees believe that there exists another Torah, a corpus of Oral Laws transmitted by God to Moses orally on Mt. Sinai and then passed down from him to his successors over generations of prophets and pious men. This Oral Torah is not similar to a fixed text in the memory of the ages and the sages of the Mishnah and the Talmud, but rather an ongoing process of analysis, argument, and debates among rabbis and in which YHWH is actively involved through continuous revelations. Like the Sadducees, they believed that people have free will, but add that God also has precognition of human fate. Their socio-political system may have experienced some changes along the line as they had the ability to amend or introduce any specific laws according to their needs and the situation at hand.

Flavius Josephus, himself a Pharisee, noted[342], while distinguishing his sect from that of the Sadducees, "... but the Pharisees have the multitude on their side." Not only that, but it seems that the Pharisees were a bit more tolerant than the Sadducees, who showed some cruelty and were a bit more

---

342 Flavius, Josephus, *The Antiquities of the Jews*, Book 13, Chapter 10, Paragraph 6.

intellectual and diplomatic than the others, who were proud and arrogant. Perhaps the difference in the characteristic of the two Hebrew/Jewish sects comes from their dissimilar belief systems. While the Pharisees were open to an afterlife and a literal resurrection of the dead, the Sadducees were nihilists. Indeed they were, as they vanished completely after the destruction of Herod's temple in 70 AD, leaving the room for the Pharisees, who survived what befell them and emerged as the dominant form of Judaism.

The Essenes

Like the other two Hebrew/Jewish sects, the Sadducees and Pharisees, along with our carefully arranged interpretation regarding their true meaning and the time they actually began, which surely differs from the Biblical main stream classical and historical narration, the Essenes would also be examined herein with the same scrutiny.

Hence, before we venture back into their origin, beliefs, and secrets, let us first try to understand what their name means. In truth, it appears that a main problem faces us as we try to identify the name this group has called themselves. We find that the word "Essenes" has a few uncertain different meanings because it has been applied to the Jewish sect itself and to other identical groups of different ethnicity ever since they appeared in the course of history.

We shall review the three original sources that have mentioned them in just a bit, but let us first see how these sources have chosen to address them. While Josephus called them *Essen(s)* or *Essaioi(s)*, Pliny named them *Esseni*, and Philo termed them *Essaioi* or *Ossaioi*. Whether the name has Aramaic origin, Hebrew, or Greek spelling, etymologists seemed to have not reached a final decision as to what the meaning could be, however, suggestions have been made for "holy ones" and "pious ones." Another proposed meaning to the term is "healers."

Now, let's move further ahead in our search. Flavius Josephus, who essentially tackled the Jewish *History and War*, mentioned the Essenes in his three esteemed works[343] as being part of the three Jewish sects that dominated Judaism for a while. He wrote[344]:

---

343 Flavius, Josephus is attributed as the author of: *The Jewish War, The Antiquities of the Jews*, and *The Life of Flavius Josephus*.
344 Flavius, Josephus, *The Antiquities of the Jews*, Book 13, Chapter 5, Paragraph 9.

At this time there were three sects among the Jews, who had different opinions concerning human actions; the one was called the sect of the Pharisees, another the sect of the Sadducees, and the other the sect of the Essens.

Having said that, and should we believe his words, the Essens would then be a sect that existed during the period of the Second Temple Judaism, very much like the Sadducees and Pharisees. Hence, after the deportation from Babylon, the date suggested for their emergence would be sometime between the end of the 2nd century BC to early 1st century BC. Some Biblical scholars relate them to Zadok, as well, the High Priest of the alleged Temple of Solomon, and that puts them along with the Sadducees as descendants from the Zadokite family of priests. Others claim they are the descendants of the Hasidim (Asideans), the chief supporters of the law during the Hasmonean period, known later as the Pharisees (Pharsi). We, however, tend to link them more to the Sadducees.

Although we have explained many times before that the Temple of Solomon never existed in real history, and that the Sadducees could not be related to the *mythical* High Priest Zadok, but rather to another later personality by the same name[345], the claim that the Essens are also descendants of Zadok probably came from the Dead Sea Scrolls. The scrolls are the famous religious documents discovered in caves by the Dead Sea sometime between 1946 and 1956, which have been attributed to the Essens living there, although there is no proof to support their authorship.

J.M. Allegro, probably one of the very primary scholars who has examined the scrolls, wrote the following note in his appreciated book[346]:

The Sect's own leader was called the *Teacher of Righteousness*, although his actual name, real or assumed, may well have been Zadok. Themselves they called the *Sons of Zadok*, which probably had as much reference to Ezekiel xl. 46 as to the name of their leader.

The Teacher of Righteousness, we believe, could not be identified with the *mythical* figure of Zadok, and they, the Essens,

---

345 Please refer to the section on the Sadducees.
346 Allegro, J.M., *The Dead Sea Scrolls*, page 95.

could not be the Sons of Zadok, as cited in Ezekiel[347], nor could they be related to Milki-Sedek (Melchizedek), the Canaanite/Phoenician King and High Priest of Ur-Shalim (Jerusalem), mentioned in Genesis[348], Psalms, and the Letter to the Hebrews. If their actual historical existence happened to have started sometime in the 2nd century BC, they could then be in direct relation to the Sadducees and their founder Tzadok or Zadok, around the first half of the 3rd century BC. If that is true, the Essens, being much fewer in number, could well have developed into an Orthodox Hebrew/Jewish sect, adopting a different lifestyle after having separated themselves from mainly the cast of Priests of the Sadducees and secondary the cast of Rabbis of the Pharisees, the two major groups that constituted the main stream of Judaism.

Another important reference, probably older than Josephus, comes to us from the Roman writer, Pliny the Elder, who died around 79 AD. He wrote in his *History of Nature*[349]:

> The Race of the Esseni. Along the West Coast retire the Esseni: a Nation living alone, and beyond all others throughout the World wonderful: without any Women, casting off the whole of Venus, without Money: keeping company only with Date-trees ... . Thus for thousands of Ages (beyond belief to say), the Race is eternal in which no one is Born: so prolific to them is the Repentance of Life of other Men. Beneath them stood the Town Engadda, for Fertility (of Soil) and Groves of Date-trees the next City of Hier-osolyma, now a Place for the Dead. Beyond it is Massada, a Castle upon a Rock, and not far from Asphaltites.

In short, Pliny suggests that the Esseni spent their lives single, without money, and had existed for thousands of years in an area that was located in the Qumran desert, notably in Ein Gedi (En-Gedi), situated west of the Dead Sea (Lake Asphaltitus), near the ancient fortification of Masada in the southern district of Israel. However, it seems that Pliny made a topographical error, or was it the typographical error of the copyist who confused Jericho for Jerusalem, since both begin in Latin with *Hier*. It is absolutely true that Jericho, not Jerusalem, known for palm trees or Dart-

---

347 Ezekiel 40:46, "The chamber which faces north [is] for the priests who have charge of the altar; these [are] the sons of Zadok, from the sons of Levi, who come near the LORD to minister to Him."
348 Genesis 14:18, "Then Melchizedek king of Salem brought out bread and wine; he [was] the priest of God Most High."
349 Pliny, the Elder, *History of Nature*, Book 5, Chapter 17.

trees, is mentioned by Pliny. Thus, it would be worthy to note that the Esseni might have lived also in Jericho intersected by the water of a river flowing from the Dead Sea, an important element for the purification rituals of the Essens. Jerusalem is too far inland and dry. That the Esseni—say, the Hebrew/Jewish Orthodox sect—existed for thousands of years, as Pliny wrote, is surely a doubtful matter, unless he was referring to another ascetic group with a different cultural background and ethnicity living in the area and having a quasi-similar name. But, we will come to that in a bit.

Earlier than Pliny the Elder, the Hellenistic Jewish philosopher, Philo of Alexandria (c. 20 BC–50 AD), also called Philo Judaeus, who lived in Alexandria, Egypt, during the Roman Empire, declared that the Essaioi (Ossaioi) lived in another area as well. He wrote[350]:

> Moreover Palestine and Syria too are not barren of exemplary wisdom and virtue, which countries no slight portion of that most populous nation of the Jews inhabits. There is a portion of those people called Essaioi in number something more than four thousand in my opinion, who derive their name from their piety, though not according to any accurate form of the Grecian dialect, because they are above all men devoted to the service of God, not sacrificing living animals, but studying rather to preserve their own minds in a state of holiness and purity.

By that reading, we come to learn that a person—a Jew, even though Greek—could not have mistaken Israel for Palestine and Syria, or maybe out of jealousy of the Gentiles' wisdom, considered the Essaioi to have been Jews inhabiting the most parts of Palestine and Syria, unless the notion that pious people are found living there, say, in the Land of Canaan, would suggest the existence of other similar groups as well.

Now the main trend that enveloped the way of life of the Essens is common knowledge to all those who first wrote about them, like Josephus[351], Pliny, or Philo, and for all those who searched for their traces later on. They are described as having lived separated from major cities, in towns and villages near rivers, lakes, or seas, gathered in closed groups of basically adult

---

350 Philo, of Alexandria, *Quod Omnis Probus Liber Sit (Every Good Man is Free)*, XII: 75.
351 Flavius, Josephus, *The War of the Jews*, Book 2, Chapter 7, Paragraph 2-13.

males practicing some sort of communal life, dedicating their lives to asceticism and poverty (without the need of any personal property), with daily immersion in the water of rivers (or lakes) as part of their purification rituals. They abstained from the pleasures of the flesh, living a celibate life, considering women promiscuous, thus incapable of fidelity, though Josephus stated that there is another group of the Essens that allowed marriage, mainly for the propagation of the species.

Furthermore, it appears that the sect of the Essens was apolitical, organized in the form of a monastic order with Superior Officials to whom the members showed utter respect and obedience. Under the surveillance of priests wearing all white garments, they met for ceremonial prayer at dawn in wait for the rising sun. They engaged thereafter in pastoral works, agricultural activities, and handicrafts prior to their midday meals blessed by the priests, and then continued their work until evening before gathering again for silent diners. They strictly observed the Sabbath, the Torah, and the Levitical laws, but had a different interpretation of the Jewish Bible as a whole and had sacred and secret writings of their own. They believed in the immortality of the soul, very much like the Pharisees, but in contrast to them, for they deemed the existence of an unalterable destiny—a belief that suggests that they denied personal free will. While avoiding the temple worship in Jerusalem, they pledged piety towards their God, preserved the sect's secrets, and transmitted the sacred teachings to other fellow Essens in *Initiation* after the oath had been taken, and when a brother had showed loyalty to his brethren, to the order's secret teachings, and after he had completed his probationary period. It is said that when one blasphemed the name of Moses or committed another crime like divulging the secrets of the Order to outsiders, he would then be punished by death or expelled from the sect, respectively.

Their belief in continuous war between good and evil may suggest some Persian dualistic influence, however, one can understand more about it when one recognizes that this war of Apocalyptic nature was in fact launched by the Angel of Darkness, who leads the Children or Sons of Darkness, who were the evil people outside the Essen world, against the Prince of Light(s), who leads the Children or Sons of Light, themselves, as discovered in the Dead Sea Scrolls[352]. In addition, there seems to be a more

---

352 Allegro, J.M., *The Dead Sea Scrolls*, page 121 (on Sons of Light & Sons of Darkness) and Page 124 (on Prince of Lights & Angel of Darkness)

philosophical approach to their religious doctrine, which Josephus revealed in his book[353]:

> For their doctrine is this: That bodies are corruptible, and that the matter they are made of is not permanent; but that the souls are immortal, and continue forever; and that they come out of the most subtle air, and are united to their bodies as to prisons, into which they are drawn by a certain natural enticement; but that when they are set free from the bonds of the flesh, they then, as released from a long bondage, rejoice and mount upward. And this is like the opinions of the Greeks
> ...

Having some sort of Gentile influence, precisely Greek, on the religious doctrine of the Essens, here suggested by Josephus is so important for us to know for now, regardless of the Pythagorean elements that have existed in their ways of life. Thus, before we end this section on the Essens, we would like to convey to our readers the very fact that there appear to be many *connected and separated* religious groups of that particular era that shared similar beliefs in ways of Mysticism and Asceticism, along with alike Messianic and Eschatological approaches. These groups could be divided as follows: the Essens of the Qumran Community and the Nabateans by either sides of the Dead Sea; the Ashaya-Nazarenes and the Galileans in and around Mt. Carmel and Galilee; and a few others flourishing elsewhere, like the Therapeutae of the Egyptian desert. These different secret groups, which lived within a close geographical area that stretches from Nabatea-Jordan and Judea-Palestine around the Dead Sea to Galilee-Phoenicia around the Sea of Galilee, could well have been conjointly referred to by scholars as the Essenes. We shall tackle this important subject in the next chapter as well as in the last chapter when we discover the religion and theology of Jesus. In that matter, the vital question that has been often asked, mainly secretly, but rarely answered for political reasons, is the following: Could Jesus have been a non-Jew? Of course he could. He was Phoenician in every possible way.

Canaanite/Phoenician National Culture

As we all know, the Canaanite/Phoenician Civilization is one of the greatest civilizations the ancient world has ever known, and

---

353 Flavius, Josephus, *The War of the Jews*, Book 2, Chapter 7, Paragraph 11.

to fully cover would require from us a whole volume, perhaps volumes. However, due to the fact that this book is about Jesus, we will then only expose a brief history about them, their origin, culture, and their astonishing religious system that undoubtedly inspired the founder of Christianity.

Starting with Herodotus, he pictures the Phoenicians, as per the stories of the Persians, in the following words[354]:

These (the Phoenicians), they (the Persians) say, came from that which is called the Erythraian Sea (which translates as Red Sea and includes the Indian Ocean and the Persian Gulf) to this of ours (refers to the Mediterranean); and having settled in the land where they continue even now to dwell, set themselves at once to make long voyages by sea. And conveying merchandise of Egypt and of Assyria they arrived at other places and also at Argos ...

His description is not at all true, since the Phoenicians were not of the Aryan stock of humanity; although, authors like L.A. Waddell consider them as such[355]. In fact, the Canaanite/Phoenicians may well have voyaged to the Persian Gulf and way beyond, reaching the Indian Ocean, which may have given the notion that they originated from there, at the time they were set to come back on ships towards the Land of Canaan on the Mediterranean coast. Besides, the Persian version of the origin of the Phoenicians may well have been part of their political propaganda to discredit the Phoenicians of their original land—the Land of Canaan—they were about to conquer and use to house the Hebrews instead! At any rate, the Phoenician interaction with the Aryans, especially Indians and ancient Germans, may have concluded in a cultural and linguistic exchange. Other authors across the world describe the Phoenicians to have originated from the Arabic Peninsula, giving them by that a Semite root of humanity; this is also wrong. We shall explain.

Old historical and geographical books, including the Old Testament—which is not by the way a book of history in any real sense of the word—describe the Phoenicians as "Hamites." They were the native people of ancient Greater Lebanon, the Land of Canaan. Although he may have noted in his *History of Phoenicia* that the Phoenicians had primitive seats upon the shore of the

---

354 Herodotus, *The Histories*, Book 1, Chapter 1, page 3.
355 Waddell, L.A., *The Phoenician Origin of Britons, Scots, & Anglo-Saxons*, page vi.

Persian Gulf, British author George Rawlinson later wrote[356], "Pigmy and misshapen gods belong to that fetishism which has always had charms for the Hamitic nations; and it may be suspected that the Phoenicians adopted the Cabeiri from their Canaanite predecessors, who were of the race of Ham."

The Phoenicians did in fact migrate from Africa, probably Ethiopia[357], through Egypt and then towards the land they named Canaan perhaps after their founder[358], or after the Hamitic/Afro-Asiatic meaning of the word *Kana'a*: "to settle or to inhabit[359] or, to bow or kneel[360] in front of God the Most High." Another explanation of the term that we find unfit is the Semitic root *kn'* which means "low," as in "lowlands," in contrast with Aram, meaning "highlands."[361] Another suggestion is that the name derives from the Hurrian term, *Kinahhu*, which refers to the purple color, thus Canaan-Phoenicia would be synonyms to the Land of Purple.[362] The Hurrian term is perhaps of a much later period, when both Tyrians and Saydonians, began the manufacturing of the Purple Dye.

In the old books, supported by the anthropological facts on the ground, the Canaano-Phoenicians settled along the coastal cities and some major parts of the inlands, Lebanon in particular, as the heart of the Land of Canaan; then some western parts of Syria as far as the old city of Ugarit in the North; followed by Palestine, northwestern Jordan, Israel, and even the Al-Arish area in Egypt in the south. Whereas to the east, stretched vast plains and majestic mountains stood overlooking the Great Mediterranean Sea flowing in the west. Thus, the Phoenicians and Canaanites are the same people. Canaanites were the Phoenicians living up in the highest mountains. Phoenicians were Canaanites living along the coastal cities.

Whereas the Aryan theory of the origin of the Phoenicians has lost ground over time, the Semite theory is still in practice. With all due respect to the scientific minds of modern day, this could only be true on linguistic grounds since the Semitic language became spread in the whole region due to Assyrian influence. This

---

356 Rawlinson, George, *History of Phoenicia*, iBooks, page 257.
357 Blavatsky, H.P., *Isis Unveiled*, Volume 1, page 566.
358 Genesis 9:18, "Now the sons of Noah who went out of the ark were Shem, Ham, and Japheth. And Ham [was] the father of Canaan." And also Genesis 10:6, "The sons of Ham [were] Cush, Mizraim, Put, and Canaan."
359 Yammine, Youssef Rev., The Galilean Kana in Lebanon—قانا الجليل في لبنان, page 12.
360 The Jesuit, Martin Rev., *History of Lebanon*—تاريخ لبنان, page 62 (fn. 4).
361 Ibid., page 62.
362 Wikipedia, *Canaan*.

wide diffusion of Semitism might have compelled the Phoenicians to change their language from Hamitic to Semitic[363], perhaps only for the laymen, not for the Priests, who we think may have kept their original language, adopting from time to time a mixture of both. It is always the same error even with today's ethnographers, who would add the Canaanites/Phoenicians to the Semitic groups of the ancient days, like the Babylonians, Assyrians, Hebrews, Arabs, etc. But, in fact, the Phoenicians belonged to the Hamitic/Afro-Asiatic groups of people—like the Egyptians, who preferred to stay in Africa—and they included many tribes such as the Ammonites, Amorites (*Amurru*), Jebusites (*Ib-u-ś*), Hyksôs[364], and later, the Arameans. We shall see these tribes in more detail in the upcoming pages.

Great men and women have come out of this stock of humanity and they have covered almost every known area of life, like religion[365], invention[366], geography[367] & navigation[368], legislation & law, architecture & building, politics, history, astronomy & arithmetic[369], science, medicine, mathematics, philosophy, etc. Should we list some of them, at least the most important, we can begin with Enoch-Thor-Taautus of Gebel (religious figure, more than 3,000 BC); Kadmus of Sūr (Important figure who spread the Alphabet in Greece and founded many cities there, like Thebes, c. 2000 BC); Europa of Sūr (she was the Sister of Kadmus, c. 2000 BC); Amurru-Abi or Hammurabi (Amorite king and legislator, c. 1792 BC to 1750 BC); Milki-Sedek of Urušalim or Melchizedek (religious figure, most probably Late Bronze Age); King Ahiram of Gebel (political figure, Late Bronze

---

363 Blavatsky, H.P. *Isis Unveiled*, Volume 1, page 568.

364 Manetho, the Egyptian historian, called the Phoenicians, *Ph'Anakes*. They are the children of Phenok, Henoch, Enoch, or Anak. They are the Anakim (Giants) of Canaan, the Hyksôs.

365 Despite their Pantheon, the Phoenicians conceptualized a monotheistic belief in a Supreme God, as we shall see in a bit.

366 The Phoenicians excelled in so many inventions, like the Phonetic Alphabet, ships, the Purple-Dye, etc.

367 Strabo, *Geography*, Book 3, Chapter 2:14, "I repeat that the Phoenicians were the discoverers [of these countries], for they possessed the better part of Iberia and Libya before the time of Homer, and continued masters of those places until their empire was overthrown by the Romans." This statement by Strabo gives enough evidence that the Phoenicians were the first people of the ancient world who located geographical places.

368 Strabo, *Geography*, Book 16, Chapter 2:23, "... by the skill of the people in the art of navigation, in which the Phoenicians in general have always excelled all nations ..."

369 Strabo, *Geography*, Book 16, Chapter 2:24, "It is thought that geometry was introduced into Greece from Egypt, and astronomy and arithmetic from Phoenicia."

Age); Eshmun of Saydoun (physician who was later worshiped as god of healing, early Iron Age); King Hiram of Sūr (political figure, 10th century BC); Hiram-Abi of Sūr (architect, 10th century BC); Adoni-Sedek of Urušalim or Adonizedek (religious figure, 10th century BC); Sanchoniaton of Birot (Beirut) or Sunchoniathon (historian and priest, 10th century BC); Mochus[370] of Saydoun (scientist, 8th/7th century BC); Thales of Miletus-Sūr (scientist and astronomer, 7th/6th century BC); Pherecydes of Syros-Saydoun (scientist and man of religion, 7th/6th century BC); King Hanno of Carthage or kartha-hedesh, which means "the New town" (political figure, voyager, 7th/6th century BC); Hamilkon of Sūr, Hamilcar or Himilkon (sailor and author of history and geography, 7th/6th century BC); Pythagoras of Saydoun (religious figure, philosopher, scientist, and founder of Pythagoreanism, 6th century BC); Haniba'al of Carthage (political and military figure, 5th century BC); Elissa of Carthage (political figure, 5th century BC); Zenon the Stoic (philosopher, 3rd century BC); Iamblichus of Chalcis-Anjar (philosopher, 2nd century BC); Yāwshu the Galilean (religious figure, Son of God, founder of Christianity, 1st century AD); Philo of Gebel (historian and author, 1st century AD); Marinus of Sūr (geographer, 1st century AD); Ulpian of Sūr (lawyer, mid 3rd century AD); Papinian of Birot (lawyer, mid 3rd century AD); Porphyry[371] of Sūr (philosopher, 234 AD–304/5 AD); Pamphilus of Birot (librarians and Bishop of Ceasaria, 3rd century AD).

Canaanite/Phoenician Religion

Ancient records have shown that the Canaanite/Phoenicians had a long and rich history of religious concepts along with their great social and cultural achievements. Their most important religious ritual of all time was that of Bread and Wine, performed

---

370 Mochus gave the name "Tom" to the particle of matter that can be decomposed. It was later copied by the Greek scientist Democritus who called it "Atom," referring by that to the particle of matter that cannot be decomposed. With the advance of science, however, Mochus was proved right. In his *Geometry*, Book 16, Chapter 2:24, Strabo wrote, "If we are to believe Poseidonius, the ancient opinion about atoms originated with Mochus, a native of Sidon ..."

371 According to Rawlinson, Porphyry's original name was Malchus, a name derived from Melek or Malik, which means "king." Rawlinson adds, "To disguise his Asiatic origin, and ingratiate himself with the literary class of the day, who were chiefly Greeks or Grecised Romans, he took the Hellenic and far more sonorous appellation of Porphyrius, which he regarded as a sort of synonym, since purple was the royal colour." *History of Phoenicia*, iBooks, page 438.

first by Milki-Sedek and later by Yāwshu. Both were of the same ancient Order of Priesthood, the Great White Fraternity, which we have already introduced. There is something unique, rather genius in the Hamitic/Afro-Asiatic mind regarding religion and their perception of the Divine.

Phoenicians in fact inspired a whole pantheon of gods, chiefly based on the powers and processes of nature which they did not fathom yet regarded in high esteem. These gods were all ruled by One Supreme God of the Kosmos (Cosmos) or the Universe, Ēl, the Most High, although, mythologically speaking, Ēl appeared to be one God among many other gods. He practically stood alone as the chief of the remaining gods, being the main object of worship and the great ruler and protector of the Phoenicians[372]. That being said, the Canaanite/Phoenicians proved to have exercised a strong religious sentiment of monotheism in the first place[373], however, their later polytheist feelings are depicted in the gods they divided into three main categories:

First, we have the female Divine principle, represented by *Ashirai* (Asherah), the Mother-Goddess of the Phoenicians, who was in fact the Virgin Lady *Anat* (Anath, Anaitis) herself—the Queen of Heaven. Her daughter was called *Astarte*[374] (Ashtarte) and had a position of the Ba'alat (Baalith, Baaltis), meaning "lady of" any place she was venerated in. For example, Astarte is the Ba'alat of Gebel. In short, Ashirai, Anat, and Astarte, are similar; they symbolize Love, Motherhood, Heavenly Compassion, Life's Giving, and Source of Women's Fecundity.

Second, comes the *Ēlohim*, or "Sons of Ēl," represented by *Yāw* (or Yam), the god of waters, rivers, seas and oceans; *Šalim* (Shalim), the god of dusk and peace; *Ba'al*, the rider of the clouds, the god of thunder, the god of the Canaano-Phoenician cities, also as *Ba'al-Šamin*[375], the Lord of Heaven, and *Ba'al-Hammon*[376], the god of fertility and renewer of all energies; lastly comes *Adon*, originally a sun-god *par excellence*, then rendered as the god of resurrection.

Third, a list of the remaining gods, each in importance to his/her stature: *Sydyk* (Sedek or Suduc), the god of righteousness

---

372 Rawlinson, George, *History of Phoenicia*, iBooks, page 247.
373 Ibid., page 245.
374 She is the Egyptian Isis. Her Greek copy is mainly Aphrodite and her Roman is Venus, but sometimes, she is Hera, Juno, and Diana for the Romans, and Athene, Artemis, Selene, Rhea, or Cybele for the Greeks. She is Beltis and Ishtar in Babylonia, and recognized as Ashtoreth in the Old Testament.
375 His Greek copy is Zeus and his Roman is Jupiter.
376 He is identical to the Egyptian Ammon.

and justice; *Ešmun*[377] (Eshmun), son of Sydyk, the god of medicine and healing; *Dagon*, the god of agriculture, discoverer of wheat, and inventor of the plough; *Milikartha*[378] (Melek-Kartha, Melqart), the lord (king of the city) and god of Eden (the first Garden of Vegetation on earth); *Mot* (Moth), the god of Death; *Hadad*, a sun-god; *Shamash*, a sun-god; *Shapash*, a sun-goddess; *Shahar*, the god of dawn; *Resheph*[379], the god of earth; *Yārikh*, a moon-god; *Tanit* (Tanith or Tanata), the goddess of Carthage; and the *Cabeiri* (seven Great Ones), were the gods of navigation, patrons of sailors and ships, etc.

Once again, we confirm that despite this long list of various gods, the Canaanite/Phoenicians thought of one Father of everything presiding over them. Their theological approach gives us the certainty that they were monotheistic. In additional confirmation to that matter, Rawlinson wrote[380]:

> The names by which they designated him were El, 'great'; Ram or Rimmon, 'high'; Baal, 'Lord'; Melek or Molech, 'King'; Eliun, 'Supreme'; Adonai, 'My Lord'; Bel-samin, 'Lord of Heaven,' and the like.

He then added:

> How far the Phoenicians actually realized all that their names properly imply, whether they went so far as to divest God wholly of a material nature, whether they viewed Him as the Creator, as well as the Lord, of the world, are problems which it is impossible, with the means at present at our disposal, to solve. But they certainly viewed Him as 'the Lord of Heaven,', and, if so, no doubt also as the Lord of earth; they believed Him to be 'supreme' or 'the Most High'; and they realized his personal relation to each one of his worshippers, who were privileged severally to address Him as Adonai—'my Lord.' It may be presumed that at this early stage of the religion there was no idolatry; when One God alone is acknowledged and recognized ...

---

377 His Greek copy was Asklēpiós, Aesculapius, or Asclepius. Some say he was a physician of divine powers that allowed him to be worshiped as god of healing.

378 Heracles is the Greek copy.

379 Resheph was an Egyptian-Phoenician god having his Temple—Temple of the Obelisks—erected in Gebel.

380 Rawlinson, George, *History of Phoenicia*, iBooks, page 245-246.

While religion played an essential role in their social life, the Phoenicians formed a nation of believers where Temples were planted in each and every city, becoming centres of attraction to all. Both kings and populace of the various Canaanite/Phoenician mountainous villages and coastal cities maintained the honor of the gods at all costs, exhibited a great feeling of piety through the decoration of their temples with important offerings, and bore religious names in homage to the god or goddess they venerated. In fact, they worshipped their gods and goddesses, like most other ancient people on the planet, and their rituals consisted of prayers, hymns of praise, processions, votive offerings, and sacrifices. Each temple had its festival time, mainly annually, sometimes seasonally, according to the function of the god or goddess specifically venerated there. Examples of such are the festivities practiced at the Temple of Adon (Adonis), that young and beautiful god of Gebel (Byblos), which always took place in the spring because Adon incarnated the cycle of nature and represented the spring—the resurrection of every atom in the kingdom of life.

Besides the festivities that were practiced on an annual and seasonal basis, there were ceremonies almost every day, most likely on Mondays, Wednesdays, Thursdays, Fridays, and Sundays. The priests (perhaps also priestesses) of each temple, clothed in white garments of cotton, probably of linen[381], and wearing a stiff cap or mitre upon their heads—guided by a High Priest[382], cloaked in a purple robe all over his body[383] with a golden conoid tiara ornament his head[384], accomplished their religious duties inside the temples, where the faithful assisted to offer prayers or sacrifices. The ordinary sacrifices offered, singly

---

381 This note proves that the white linen garment worn by Galilean Essenes, hence by Yāwshu, was a Phoenician priestly habit, shared by the Egyptians, and later, the Pythagoreans. It is not by coincidence that Christian priests wear white when baptizing a new child for his/her new life. In the same context, it would be thus totally erroneous to consider that the white garment used by the Pope originated in Jewish customs.

382 It is noted that the High Priest stayed in his office only for a year before another was chosen to succeed him.

383 Although it is traditionally said that the purple robe worn by Popes and Cardinals was copied from the Roman Senate, we cannot deny the fact that purple, or royal purple, came from the Phoenicians. While the Romans wore purple during their political meetings, Christians wore purple during their religious affairs, and this matches greatly with the religious custom practiced by Phoenician High Priests.

384 What about the golden tiara over the Pope's head? Isn't that evident?

and upon altars were animals such as oxen, cows, goats, sheep, and lambs; except for swine who were regarded as unclean.[385]

As for human sacrifices, the nobler and the more honorable the better—children in particular, the eldest sons or the most pure of them, offered by their parents to Moloch as in Carthage—they were consumed by fire in order to pacify the wrath of the deity! However, all that we have of that terrifying practice has been proven, historically and archaeologically, to be nothing but a deliberate propaganda fabricated by jealous people such as the Romans in the course of the Punic wars against the Great Hannibal, and the Hebrews, as cited in the Old Testament (2Kings 21:1-11), against the Canaanite/Phoenicians (Amorites) who were shown to be one of the biggest enemies of Biblical Israel.

We will certainly not linger on that nonsense another instant, for we believe, like any other reasonable mind, that the Canaanite/Phoenicians with their sophisticated and innovative religious system and spiritual aspiration were not at all barbaric. Instead, they were a people of great faith in Ēl, God the Most High, and their salvation as a nation happened through the sacrifice of his Son presented as Adon, who himself was but a preamble of the sacrifice of Christ for Humanity as a whole. Yet, they both conquered death and gloriously resurrected.

At any rate, wherever the Canaanite/Phoenicians sailed, their splendid ships held images of the gods and goddesses in the form of statues, mainly those of the *Cabeiri*, the gods of navigation, patrons of sailors and ships, that of *Yam*, the god of waters, rivers, seas and oceans, that of *Astarte*, the Lady of the Sea, and that of *Barati*, the Guardian Goddess of the Sea. Wherever they landed, they introduced their religion and worship to the indigenous people, erecting a temple or temples in honor to the gods and goddesses, perhaps in each and every settlement and almost everywhere throughout their worldwide territories from the Mediterranean Sea towards the Americas, passing by both Africa and Europa, the same gods and goddesses that were worshipped in the Land of Canaan/Phoenicia for ages.

It is not known exactly when Canaanite/Phoenicians started to believe in the One High God Ēl, but should we track the religion in Phoenicia, we would certainly go back long in time to Enoch or Anak, the Canaano-Phoenician seer and prophet of Mt. Hermon in ancient Loubnan (Lebanon). Tradition says that angels descended on top of Mt. Hermon and taught him a great universal, spiritual, and occult doctrine that Enoch accepted and called the *Kabala*, meaning "accepting" in the Phoenician-Hamitic language. Enoch

---

385 Rawlinson, George, *History of Phoenicia*, iBooks, page 261-262.

is Henoch or Phenoch, the Phoenix that symbolized the secret cycle and *Initiation*. He was the first Teacher-Initiator and possessor of the true mirific name. He linked Humanity through an eternal concordance with the Father.

Later, Enoch walked down the mountain, carrying the Tradition with him to Gebel, which could be articulated as *Geb-Ēl* in the Hamitic tongue, meaning, "the Sacred Land of Ēl." There, in Gebel, Enoch, who became known as Thor, established his doctrine, and built a temple to God, the Most High. Originally, he'd built it in the image of the open semi-temple he'd previously erected with the help of his first adepts at Mt. Hermon—the Mountain of Acceptance and Meetings. This semi-temple could have been composed of a flat horizontal rock lying at the top of a wide vertical rock, thus forming an altar, probably the first, framed by two pillars on both sides. Enoch, the High Priest, performed upon the altar the most sacred ritual of all time, that of Wine and Bread. The right red pillar stood for the vine, while the left golden pillar meant to symbolize the wheat. Milki-Sedek, a direct adept of the Enochian priests, practiced the same rite later on at the Temple of Šalim in Jerusalem—Wheat and Vine, Bread and Wine, Beth-Lahem and Mt. Carmel! The link would not escape the wit of the thinker. Jesus Christ performed this same rite at the Last Supper!

From the ancient port of Gebel, Enoch-Thor and some of his early adepts sailed to the Land of Ham and introduced the Tradition to the Egyptian priests in Memphis and Giza, where the great Pyramids were built. He became known as Thot-Taautus in the Egyptian religion. The pyramid denoted nothing more than a grandiose symbol of the Temple of God, dedicated by the Egyptians to their divine messenger: Thot-Taautus. Then, the Tradition journeyed around the world, and Enoch-Thor/Thot-Taautus became known as Mithra to the Hindus and Persians, Enki/Ea in Mesopotamia, Nebo in Babylonian mythology, Quetzalcóatl to the Mexican Aztecs, Thor in the Scandinavian tradition, Hermes[386]-Kadmos in Greece, and Mercury in Rome. He was Adam-Kadmon for the Kabalists. He later became known as Edris for the Arabs and Muslims, and recently, Enoch for the Druzes. Sometimes, the Father of the Spiritual Laws—considered as the divine messenger who accepted the word of God—was also regarded as the god of wisdom and science.

Later on, the Chaldean savants and magi used the Kabala, based on the esoteric meanings of the Alphabet, incorporating one

---

386 Please note that the name Hermes, given to him by the Greeks at a later stage, might be a derivative of Hermon.

of the most ancient languages on Earth to invoke the spirits, either in the written form of talisman or in the oral form of incantation. That was surely a deviation from its original source. Throughout history, many religious sects and secret societies, whether in the East or the West, adopted the Kabala in their ceremonies of Initiation, certainly under the influence of the Chaldeans, and its later version, that of the Hebrews.

However, very few indeed underwent *Initiation* into the secrets of the authentic Kabala practiced in both Phoenicia and Egypt. In fact, Enoch, who became a Metatron, standing before Ēl the Most High on Mt. Hermon—where Yāwshu was glorified through his transfiguration—was the Founder of the First Religion and with whom the authentic Tradition of the Great White Fraternity actually originated. A Canaanite/Phoenician-Egyptian fraternity that believed with anchored faith in the resurrection of the self to its higher level and the immortality of the spirit had monotheism at the foundational core of its theological concept. In Canaan/Phoenicia, the High Priest Milki-Sedek preached the belief in the Universal God Ēl-Ēlyon, the Most High. In Egypt, monotheism entered as a Mystery School with the *Initiate of Thut* to eventually surface as a religious reform with Akhenaton who preached the Universal God, Aton. Both Al and Aton represented the first Light of Creation, symbolized by the Sun, where the Egyptian *Ankh* was but a replica of the Sacred Tau, the Phoenician cross, which undoubtedly stood as the first prototype of the Christian cross.

And thus, Christianity is in fact an evolution, or rather, an extension of the ancient Hamitic/Afro-Asiatic discipline (Phoenician and Egyptian), not Semitic (Hebrew or alike). In the same context, Blavatsky explained[387]:

> Out of all the sacred writings of all the branch nations, sprung from the primitive stock of mankind, Christianity must choose for its guidance the national records and scriptures of a people perhaps the least spiritual of the human family—the Semitic.

What a historical mistake!

---

387 Blavatsky, H.P., *Isis unveiled*, Volume 2, page 434.

Chapter 8

The Hypothetical "Jesus the Jew" Fails to Prove Himself Once Again

Should we go slowly backwards in this book, we would realize that we have so far covered most of Jesus' life. We have started with Chapter 1 analyzing the names attributed to the Galilean Christian Savior and have reached a conclusion that all names had Aramaic/Canaano-Phoenician origin. We see this by beginning first with the famous name, Immanuel, which means "El with us," and continuing with the second name, Jesus, which means "Healer" when pronounced in Greek in the form of Iessus or Iesous and/or as Yāwshu or Ye'shu when uttered in Phoenician and correctly interpreted as "May YĀW Saves," not "May Yahweh saves," as traditionally believed and hoped by the Judeo-Christian community. We then highlighted the third name, Nazarene, meaning, "Chosen and Dedicated to God," and ended with the fourth name, Messiah, or better say, Meshiha in Phoenician, meaning "Anointed One" and translated into "Christos" by the Greeks.

After having successfully demonstrated that the names given to Jesus were all Canaano-Phoenician appellations, we moved to Chapter 2, where we investigated the Great Annunciation of Maryām that happened inside a Temple. We have concluded that since women were not regarded religiously important enough in Judaism to enter the Temple and receive communion from God or his Archangel, then the event would not have happened to a Jewish woman. Instead, this phenomenon by itself could only be labeled as a purely Canaanite/Phoenician and Egyptian practice, where women were not only considered important on both religious and social levels but had also reached the position of priestesses and goddesses. This approach fits well the Mother of God.

Having done that with the most accuracy possible, we turned to Chapter 3, where we introduced the family of Yāwshu. All family members lived in the Galilean region of Canaan-Phoenicia and all had Canaano-Phoenician names, like Yāwsēp , Joseph, the adoptive father of Jesus, and which means "May YĀW add";

191

the name Maryām (Mort or Mart-Yām), carried by Mary, his mother, which means "Lady of the Sea"; his grandfather Yāwqîm or Yāw-yāqîm, meaning "he whom YĀW has set up firm"; and his grandmother, Anna, a name coming from the Goddess Anat; along with the other remaining members of the family, such as his uncle Yāwsēp of Rameh, his aunt, and his cousins.

In Part II, we demonstrated that Jesus was not born in Bethlehem of Judea but rather in the Galilean *Bet(h)-Lahem*, meaning "House of Bread," a grotto located at the bottom of Mt. Carmel, one of the holiest mountains of the Canaanite/Phoenicians; the original name *Krm-el* means "Generous vine of Ēl" and "Spiritual offerings of Ēl." We have submitted authentic maps that undoubtedly show this Bethlehem in Phoenicia to support the astounding historical/geographical argument, demonstrating the origin of Jesus Christ and his Phoenician-Galilean royal bloodline, not Jewish, as traditionally believed. Referring to precise details in the New Testament and other Christian sources, we have attested to the Galilean origin of his female and male Disciples, except for two, who appeared to have been Jewish.

After we have explored the cultural and religious entourage at his time, in the previous chapter, comes now another interesting chapter. We shall see that Yāwshu has no relation whatsoever with any sects within Judaism nor with Judaism itself as a whole. Thus, the God he lovingly called "Father" could not be the fierce Jewish God YHWH in any way possible. In fact, his heart was deeply beating on a different divine rhythm, his mind was vibrating on another holy sphere, and his spirit was floating beyond earthly boundaries. The hypothetical "Jesus the Jew" fails to prove himself once again herein and as we turn the pages further along.

Jesus, a Sadducee? NO

For centuries before the Dead Sea Scrolls were discovered and gained great reputation among scholars and the Christian world, many Biblical researchers tried hard enough to identify which of the three main Jewish sects Jesus would have been connected to. But, as a matter of fact, no one linked him to the Sadducees, the caste of priests within Judaism. Why not?

We have previously seen that the Sadducees, who were thought to have drawn their name from Tzadok, the first *Kohen Gadol* (High Priest) to preside over the rituals in the *alleged* First

Temple of Solomon[388], could have indeed originated from a much later founder also by the name of Tzadok or Zadok, as we have revealed before. Being an official student of Jewish scholarship, Antigonus of Sokho (first half of the 3rd century BC), Tzadok would then have founded the Sadducees sometime between 300 BC and 250 BC. We very much approve on that date since it copes very well with the suggestion that the Hebrews were created by Cyrus the Great (c. 539 BC) and deported in different waves to some parts of the occupied Land of Canaan, chiefly Jerusalem.

The information imparted to us by the Roman-Jewish historian, Flavius Josephus, in his *Antiquities of the Jews*, relates that the Sadducees were directly affiliated to the rich and elite within the Jewish society. In fact, their engagement in the political affairs concerning the State of Israel and its relation with the Romans; their association with the Sanhedrin; their collection of taxes; their equipping the army for war—all these elements do not stand in favor of connecting Jesus and his divine elevated peaceful mind to them. Besides, their main beliefs, consisting on the three following concepts: man has the free will to choose between good or evil; the soul is not immortal nor is there an afterlife; there is no resurrection of the dead—these also demonstrate absence of coherence with the religious and spiritual teachings of Jesus and with his principal act of resurrection that added to his divinity. In addition, their religious role based on the Temple at the heart of Jerusalem and their relation to the *alleged* House of Zadok, the first family of Hebrew High Priests that goes back to Aaron[389], does not endorse at all a connection with Yāwshu as proven in the New Testament's epistle to the Hebrews (6:20)[390], "where the forerunner has entered for us, [even] Jesus, having become High Priest forever according to the order of Melchizedek."

That being said, it would be thus fathomed why Yāwshu called the Sadducees a "brood of vipers" in the New Testament. We are firmly determined to think and believe that he could not have been one of them, a Sadducee, a priest connected to the Hebrew Aaronic priesthood, but rather a priest forever according to the

---

388 We believe that during the composition of the Old Testament, either during the Persian Period, the Hellenistic, or even after, the scribes inserted the Sadducees back in history just to show them as old as the Canaanite/Phoenicians to justify their mythical past existence in the Land of Canaan for the future generation to come.

389 He is the older brother of Moses (Exodus 4:14; 6:20) and prototype of the Jewish High Priest (Exodus 28:1; 29) of the *alleged* Tabernacle of Meeting, which later evolved into the Temple of Solomon as per the Old Testament.

390 Also Hebrews 5:6, 10; 7:15, 17, 21.

order of the Canaanite/Phoenician Milki-Sedek, the High Priest of the Most High God Ēl[391]. Thus, Sydyk, Sedek, or Suduc, the Canaano-Phoenician god we have mentioned in the previous chapter, could not have been anything but an epithet of the God Ēl.

Jesus, a Pharisee? NO

When it has failed to identify him a Sadducee since the beginning, scholars instead associated him with the Pharisees, the cast of Jewish rabbis. In fact, we have seen him called a few times as such, a "rabbi," in the New Testament. Yet, the New Testament was clear enough to show how Jesus despised the Pharisees as much as he refused the Sadducees every time they came to hear what he had to say during his very few trips he made to Jerusalem. An example of such is found in Matthew (3:7), "But when he saw many of the Pharisees and Sadducees coming to his baptism, he said to them, Brood of vipers! Who warned you to flee from the wrath to come?"

Moreover, the contempt Jesus showed for them grew in intensity in chapter 23, written by Matthew. It is important to read it to the last phrase. An example extracted from this chapter is the following condemnation:

> But woe unto you, scribes and Pharisees, hypocrites! For ye shut up the Kingdom of Heaven against men: for ye neither go in yourselves, neither suffer ye them that are entering to go in. (Matthew 23:13)

Another one of striking importance has been written as such:

> Woe unto you, scribes and Pharisees, hypocrites! For ye compass sea and land to make one proselyte, and when he is made, ye make him two-fold more the child of hell than yourselves. Woe unto you, ye blind guides, which say, Whosoever shall swear by the temple, it is nothing; but whosoever shall swear by the gold of the temple, he is a debtor! (Matthew 23:15-16)

---

391 Hebrews 7:11, "Therefore, if perfection were through the Levitical priesthood (for under it the people received the law), what further need [was there] that another priest should rise according to the order of Melchizedek, and not be called according to the order of Aaron?"

For the historical record, a *proselyte* means "any convert to any other religion"; however, it is always the term used for a Gentile converted to the Jewish faith. As thus understood, we believe that this is yet another piece of evidence that shows Jesus was not a Jewish rabbi or a priest as we have seen in the prior section, and that he was always in conflict with the Jewish faith.

That has been said and more; Jesus could not be labeled a Pharisee, hence, not a Rabbi. In fact, the term *Rabban* and *Rabbi* seem to have been first mentioned in the Mishnah some 200 years AD, which would suggest that its occurrence in the New Testament in its Greek transliteration of the 4th century AD, was only referring to Pharisees and Scribes, and then, in a total incorrect way of speech, addressing Jesus as a Pharisee. At any rate, the usage of the term *Rabbi* that was given to Jesus differs in number from one version of the New Testament to another. Although it is found in the Canonical texts of Matthew (26:25, 49), Mark (9:5; 11:21; 14:45) and John (1:49; 3:2; 4:31; 6:25; 9:2; 11:8), except for Luke who simply used the word "Teacher," the meaning of it resonates clearly in our ears as explained by John. We thus read in John (1:38), "Then Jesus turned, and seeing them following, said to them, What do you seek? They said to Him, 'Rabbi' (which is to say, when translated, Teacher), where are You staying?"

Yes, and most certainly, the word "Rabbi" used in Hebrew in addressing the Pharisees and Scribes is in fact a derivation from the original Aramaic term that could be used in depicting something as Great, Revered, Divine, and Holy, and would also be used to describe someone being a Great Revered Divine Teacher or Master. An example of such a Master is of course the *Nazarene*, the "Devoted to God"; he is the Meshiha, the Anointed One; he is Immanuel, "God with us." All these terms fit exactly the personality of Jesus the Phoenician. They do not fit at all the personality of Jesus the Jewish Pharisee or Rabbi.

An important passage that backs up what we are saying even more comes to us from John (11:7-8). It says, "Then after this He said to [the] disciples, Let us go to Judea again. [The] disciples said to Him, Rabbi, lately the Jews sought to stone You, and are You going there again?"

Indeed, the term Rabbi used here in reference to Jesus who asked his Galilean Disciples to go with him to Judea where the Jews lived, does not indicate that Jesus was a Jewish Rabbi, or a Pharisee for that matter, since the Disciples answered back warning him that the Jews just recently sought to stone him when he was there. If he was indeed a Jewish Rabbi or a Pharisee, they would have warned him instead that the Sadducees—who were somehow in conflict with the Pharisees—sought to stone him. The notion is clear that it was the Jews in Judaea who stood as his enemy—the enemy of Jesus the Phoenician-Galilean Rabbi or Divine Teacher, for many different reasons. One of them, majorly important, would be his definite quaking of both their religious and social systems all over. He presented a threat to Judaism as a whole. This certainty was felt by Renan, who suggested that Jesus was put to death because he spoke of something else and said more than what they used to say in Synagogues.[392]

According to the Jewish Pharisaic laws and customs, a Rabbi should have a female partner, a wife he would commit to in the act of marriage, a requirement not fulfilled by Jesus, additional evidence that he was not a Jewish Rabbi as some have suggested. It has been approved by historical records, the New Testament, and the Christian Church all over the world that Jesus actually lived a celibate life. No doubt about it, for he was a Nazar—an elected Son of God.

As a follow up to that logic, author and research professor of New Testament Studies, Ph.D. Darrell L. Bock was clear enough to explain the position held by Jesus *vis-à-vis* the Jewish religion. In his book, *Breaking the Da Vinci Code*, published in 2004, Bock wrote[393]:

> Jesus was not technically a rabbi, and He did not portray Himself as one. The apostles called Him rabbi in Matthew and Mark because He was their teacher, not because He held an official Jewish role. In fact, when Luke described Jesus' role, he used the term *teacher* rather than *rabbi* ... As far as the Jewish leaders were concerned, Jesus had no recognized official role within Judaism.

In short, Yāwshu openly exposed them, and the attitude he showed in the New Testament was a spiritual and socio-human revolution against the God of the Old Testament. That would be the reason for the Crucifixion that led to his Glorious Resurrection—the real aim of the Divinity of Jesus. In that sense, Martin Luther wrote[394], "Therefore the Promises of God belong to the New Testament. Indeed, they are the New Testament."

Indeed, the Church New Testament reveals a lot in that regard, as it pinpoints very well the differences that existed

---

392 Renan, Ernest, *Vie de Jésus*, page 46.
393 Bock Darrell L., *Breaking the Da Vinci Code*, page 37.
394 Luther, Martin, *Christian Liberty*, page 26.

between the religious and theological system brought up by Jesus and the one proposed by the Jews. In fact, the accusation he uttered against the Pharisees and Scribes, as we have just seen in Matthew, by making a proselyte—a convert to Judaism—two-fold more the child of hell than themselves, is powerfully supported by another accusation also found in the New Testament, yet this time from John (8:19-47):

Jesus told them, You know neither me, nor my Father. If you knew me, you would know my Father ... Therefore Jesus said to them, If God were your father, you would love me, for I came out and have come from God. For I haven't come of myself, but he sent me. Why don't you understand my speech? Because you can't hear my words. You are of your father, the devil, and you want to do the desires of your father. He was a murderer from the beginning, and doesn't stand in the truth, because there is no truth in him. When he speaks a lie, he speaks on his own; for he is a liar, and its father. But because I tell the truth, you don't believe me. Which of you convicts me of sin? If I tell the truth, why do you not believe me? He who is of God hears the words of God. For this cause you don't hear, because you are not of God.

In truth, there is no way we can defy or deny what has been written herein, not the least, on the theological level. It clearly shows two different ministries, and they could not fit together. This is a straightforward testimony that the Father of Jesus is not the Jewish God, YHWH. Of course, Jesus knew that the Devil was not an entity, but rather, the Tempter; and his words, from that perspective, are not to be taken literally. The Devil is an errant force of nature, working from the second dimension, the base level of consciousness, which is formed by a chain of malicious wills that create evil actions, like murders. Blind powers coerce this lowest level, set in movement by error and sin. Jesus told them the truth, but they did not believe him. Therefore, and according to Jesus, had they been impelled by God; they could have definitely heard the words of God. Yet, they did not, for they were guided, not by God, but by these blind forces. He often said to them, "Woe unto you, ye blind guides ..."

Since the clear, divine vision had been manifested in words and spoken by Jesus, the Word Incarnate, and led us along the way to reach the conclusion that YHWH, the Jewish God, could not be his Father who art in Heaven, then the question *Who was Yahweh?* surges strongly in our minds. However, before we venture into that new dimension in the following chapter, let us throw an investigative look now at the possibility of Jesus being a Zealot, or a member of the Qumran Community.

Jesus, a Zealot? NO

Scholars have also tried to associate him with the Zealots, an anti-Roman revolutionary group founded in the 1st century BC by a certain Judas of Galilee (also called Judas of Gamala) in collaboration with someone by the name of Zadok the Pharisee. It seems that Ernest Renan was one of the historians who tried to link Jesus with Judas. He wrote[395], "A movement which had much more influence upon Jesus was that of Judas the Gaulonite, or Galilean."

As a political movement, it is said that the Zealots encouraged the people of Judaea to exercise armed rebellious actions against the Romans in order to expel them from the Holy Land. It reached its peak during the Great Jewish Revolt sometime between 66 AD and 70 AD—a time when Judaea lost the war and Jerusalem was destroyed. Josephus wrote[396]:

> Yet was there one Judas, a Gaulonite, of a city whose name was Gamala, who, taking with him Sadduc, a Pharisee, became zealous to draw them to a revolt, who both said that this taxation was no better than an introduction to slavery, and exhorted the nation to assert their liberty; as if they could procure them happiness and security for what they possessed, and an assured enjoyment of a still greater good, which was that of the honor and glory they would thereby acquire for magnanimity.

It could have been the idea of rebellion that happened to exist in the mind of Judas and the concept of reform that inhabited Jesus' mind that made Renan link the two men, and only on a certain supposition that they could have met in Galilee. We very much reject this baseless logic for a meeting between the two in the non-Jewish Galilee that is said to have created a fertile ground for a Jewish revolt movement. Besides, there are many different reasons; one of them is that Yāwshu was not at all interested in politics or any political movement whatsoever. He rejected politics the same way he refuted the Pharisees, the Sadducees, or any

---

395 Renan, Ernest, *Vie de Jésus*, page 149.
396 Flavius Josephus, *The Antiquities of the Jews*, Book 18, Chapter 1, Paragraph 1.

other Jewish religious, political, or social movement for that matter. Renan knew that very well, yet his mind, a little bit mixed up with unclear historical analysis of what could have happened almost two thousand years ago, projected a confused statement[397]:

> Perhaps Jesus saw this Judas, whose idea of the Jewish revolution was so different from his own; at all events, he knew his school, and it was probably to avoid his error that he pronounced the axiom upon the penny of Cæsar. Jesus, more wise, and far removed from all sedition, profited by the fault of his predecessor, and dreamed of another kingdom and another deliverance.

It would be quite naive to really believe that the total rejection of money or gold by Jesus as we have seen before in Matthew[398] had anything to do with a certain Judas and his school of murder and terror, if I may say. What Jesus believed in is a universal religion of Love and Peace and his seldom contact and conversation with the Jews—any Jews—was solely based on the idea of reforming their religion and making it better. He did not need a certain Judas to influence him, for he was already shaped by the Phoenician-Galileans, as we have explained all along this book.

The Zealots were described as the fourth sect in Judaism by Josephus, yet, classifying them as such would not be a valid fact since they mostly agreed with everything presented by the Pharisees. They seemed, however, to have been attached to freedom, regarding it as much better than life itself, and believed that YHWH was their only God and Ruler. They were described as assassins and could be related to the *Sicarii*, a group of contract-killers using the *sicae*, small daggers, hidden inside their black robes, hence the name, Sicarri, the "dagger-men." Although Josephus seemed to have differentiated between the two groups—Zealots and Sicarri—he did not explain what the differences were. In fact, they could be termed as the militia of the Pharisees—the Rabbis—taking their orders immediately from them and sometimes, on very rare occasions and in certain situations, they would act by themselves when they saw necessary. Their margin of action on their own could have created the notion or hypothesis that they formed a fourth sect within Judaism.

---

397 Renan, Ernest, *Vie de Jésus*, page 151.
398 Matthew 22:17; Matthew 22:21, "They said to Him, Caesar's. And He said to them, Render therefore to Caesar the things that are Caesar's, and to God the things that are God's."

Jesus, an Essen, member of the Qumran Community? NO

Yāwshu proved he had no relation whatsoever with mainstream Judaism and its sects. He was not a Sadducee, nor a Pharisee, nor a member of their military group, the Zealots. However, could he succeed in proving his identity as an Essen, a member of the Qumran Community? We shall discuss that now ...

As a quick reminder from the previous chapter, we have learned that there appear to be many *connected and separated* religious groups of that particular era that seem to have shared similar beliefs practiced in different ways concerning mysticism and asceticism, along with Messianic and Eschatological approaches. Much like the Therapeutae of Egypt and a few others flourishing somewhere else, these diverse secret groups like the Essens of the Qumran Community and the Nabateans of Nabatea-Jordan and Judea-Palestine by either sides of the Dead Sea, and the Ashaya-Nazarenes and the Galileans of Galilee-Phoenicia by the Sea of Galilee, could have been conjointly referred to by the term "Essenes."

The Essens of the Qumran Community seem to have appeared from around the 2nd century BC until the 1st century AD, where they vanished along with the Sadducees after the destruction of Jerusalem temple in 70 AD. Only the Pharisees survived as the dominant facet of Judaism. However, before their demise as a consequence to the first Jewish-Roman war, the Essens, like the Sadducees, were said to have been related to Tzadok or Zadok, and that puts them as direct descendants from the Zadokite High Priests of the *alleged* Temple of Solomon and the preceding Aaron lineage of priesthood of the Tabernacle of Meeting.

We have previously explained that neither the Sadducees nor the Essens of the Qumran Community could in any way be related to the Tabernacle of Meeting, or to its developed version, the Temple of Solomon and its High Priest Zadok, for the simple reason that this structure and this line of priesthood never existed in real history at the time Biblical tradition wants us to believe. The main personality the two movements could have been related to may have been the other later person by the same name Tzadok or Zadok, appearing around the first half of the 3rd century BC. This would most probably place the foundation of the Sadducees around 300 BC–250 BC and the Essens, shortly after, most likely issuing gradually from them and appearing in few numbers in the 2nd century BC as an Orthodox Hebrew/Jewish sect. They isolated themselves in the Qumran Desert, especially in Ein Gedi, located west of the Dead Sea, and experienced a different socio-religious discipline than the other two major sects of mainstream Judaism.

Having said that, the claim made by Biblical scholars concerning that mythical ancestry could not have been proposed if they hadn't actually found the famous Dead Sea Scrolls and attributed them to the Essens living there, although, there is no proof that supports their authorship. At any rate, the scrolls give the name of "Teacher of Righteousness" to the sect's own leader, and call them "Sons of Zadok," which may hint that his true or presumed name may well have been as such since it is translated as "Just or Righteous."

Accordingly, the Teacher of Righteousness they had in mind as Orthodox Jews could not be identified with the mythical figure of Zadok, nor could they be the "Sons of Zadok," as cited in Ezekiel[399], but rather, sons of the later Zadok, as we have plentifully explained. This gives us the feeling that the Jewish book of Ezekiel, whose Babylonian/Hebrew name, *Ye-hezqe'l*, means "YHWH strengthens," was probably composed after the creation of the sect, in or after the 2nd century BC, not in the 6th century BC, as traditionally thought, unless the Book of Ezekiel was in fact an original Canaanite/Phoenician book that has been manipulated to appear to be a Hebrew/Jewish work during the writing and revising of the Old Testament text that lasted well even after the birth of Christ. If that is so, the Canaanite/Phoenician/Aramaic Ezekiel, whose name, *Hazak-Ēl*, which means "Strength of Ēl," could be in fact referring to the Gentile Galilean Essenes or Asayas as Sons of Zadok or Sons of Sydyk, and that would open a door for us to relate them—not to the Essens of the Qumran Community—directly to Milki-Sedek (Melchizedek), the Canaanite/Phoenician king and High Priest of Ur-Shalim, Jerusalem.

Although the following intriguing paragraph coming from the Dead Sea Scrolls relates one of the most important Canaanite/Phoenician religious rituals—that of Wine and Bread, emerging from the inner realm of the Order of Priesthood established by Milki-Sedek and accomplished by Yāwshu—to the Teacher of Righteousness or the Qumran Messiah, it does not, in fact, cite the High Priest Milki-Sedek, but rather, the Hebrew priest Aaron, the brother of Moses. This by itself is a major twist, a total contrast to the religious figure of Christ mentioned in the

---

399 Ezekiel 40:46, "The chamber which faces north [is] for the priests who have charge of the altar; these [are] the sons of Zadok, from the sons of Levi, who come near the LORD to minister to Him."

New Testament's letter to the Hebrews (7:11). The *Manual* exhibit could be termed as the Messianic Banquet of the Qumran Community. It read[400] (italics mine):

[This is (the order of) the ses]sion of men of repute, [who are called] to meet for the Council of the Community. When [God] begets the Messiah with them, there shall come [the Priest], head of all the congregation of Israel, and all the priests, e[lders of the children of] *Aaron*, [invited] to the Meeting as men of repute. And they shall sit be[fore him, each] according to his rank, corresponding to his st[ation] in the camps and marches. And all the heads of the el[ders of the Congregation] shall sit before them, each man according to his rank. And [when] they are gathered at the communion ta[ble, or to drink] the new wi[ne], and the communion table is laid out, and the new wine [mixed] for drinking, [let no man stretch forth] his hand on the first of the bread or the [wine] before the Priest; for [he will bl]ess the first of the bread and win[e, and will stretch forth] his hand on the bread first. And after[wards], the Messiah will str[etch forth] his hands upon the bread, [and then] all the Congregation of the Community [will give bles]sings, each [according to] his rank. And after this prescription shall they act for every ass[embly where] at least ten men are assembled.

This paragraph undoubtedly proves the definite divergence between the Essens of the Qumran Community and both Milki-Sedek and Yāwshu in terms of the Priesthood concerned. It directly links them to the alleged Jewish Priesthood of Aaron of the Tabernacle of Meeting, the predecessor of Zadok the High Priest of the Temple of Solomon. Historically speaking, not mythologically, these Essens are traced back to the true founder of the Sadducees, Tzadok, of the first half of the 3rd century BC. Their later emergence sometime at the end of the 2nd century BC —early 1st century BC as an offshoot of the Sadducees—is proven in the text cited in the scrolls at the time of the rising of the powerful Hasmonean dynasty in the 2nd century BC[401].

During that time, the two already established Jewish sects, the Sadducees and Pharisees, functioned mainly as religious-

---

400 Allegro J.M., *The Dead Sea Scrolls*, page 115.
401 The Hasmonean or Asmonean Dynasty was officially founded by Simon the Maccabee in c. 141 BC and ended at the time Herod the Great became king in c. 37 BC, an event that made out of Israel a Roman client-state, marking the end of the Hasmonean Dynasty.

political parties. The Pharisees, however, seem to have opposed the many wars the Hasmoneans launched on the neighboring regions and their ambitious goals of expanding the rising empire they were working for. The forced conversion of the adjacent people of Idumea (Edom) created a political rupture between the two, and it grew even wider after the Hasmonean King of Judea, Alexander Jannaeus, who ruled from 103 BC to 76 BC, refused their demand to choose between being a king or High Priest. Jannaeus (also Jannai or Yannai) decided to be both, openly sided with the Sadducees, and adopted the rituals they often practiced in the temple. As a result of his actions, a riot was ignited and was a major factor that led to an eight year Judean civil war that ended with total subjugation of the Pharisees.

In that context, we found J.M. Allegro explaining[402]:

Taking the fullest advantage of the weakness of their Seleucid[403] foes, the Hasmonean House greatly expanded the territory of their Jewish Kingdom, and then took to themselves the title of King as well as High Priest. This was another step in the rising consternation of the orthodox priests and their followers, and matters reached a head one day during the Feast of Tabernacles, when they beheld the most hated of all these warrior priest-kings, Alexander Jannaeus, offering the scared sacrifice at the temple altar.

It seems that the Hasmoneans, by the person of Alexander Jannaeus—considered primarily by the Pharisees and secondarily by the Sadducees as having no right to his high office as a priest and king since he was the son of a slave woman, not of pure noble descent—gained the Sadducees to his side by adopting their religious ways, as he fought back against the Pharisees, causing a bloodshed. As a result of all that, Allegro added[404]:

We should not be far wrong if we saw the hand of the Qumran Teacher behind these events, for one of the scrolls looks forward to the time when 'bastards and sons of strangers' should never again set foot in the restored temple of the New Jerusalem. In any case, it seems most probable that, at this

---

402 Allegro J.M., *The Dead Sea Scrolls*, page 98.
403 The Seleucids were of Greek-Macedonian origin. They created an empire that was ruled by the Seleucid Dynasty founded by Seleucus I Nicator in c. 312 BC following the divisions that occurred to the Hellenistic Empire created by Alexander the Great who died in c. 323 BC.
404 Allegro J.M., *The Dead Sea Scrolls*, page 98.

time, the Teacher gathered together some of the faithful priests[405] of the Holy City and fled to the deserts of Qumran.[406] There they began their exile from mankind, which would end only when God saw fit to vindicate His faithful and bring in His Kingdom.

It is there in the Qumran deserts where the Essens found refuge and built for themselves a type of monastery and temporary sanctuary where rituals and sacrifices were performed by the hands of their Teacher of Righteousness, their Messiah, regarded then as the true High Priest of Israel. It is there where they began their total orthodoxy, directly against the authority of the Hasmonean king and High Priest of Jerusalem and its temple, Jannaeus, and indirectly, against the Sadducees and Pharisees, who are said to have been summoned by him before he died and asked them for a reconciliation that allowed them to function again there as the two main political parties.

The Essens settled in the deserts of Qumran, separated from major Judean cities, living in towns and villages, near natural streams of water. Yāwshu and his movement, on the other hand, had more than one main headquarters, like Capernaum and Bethsaida, located near a natural stream of water (the Sea of Galilee). Others scattered all around the Galilean-Phoenician land, like the small not-then-a-town Nazareth, Tyre, Sidon, and a few other interesting places that actually played a major role during his ministry and that of his disciples—places that were often mentioned in the New Testament as key places for the Christian movement.

The Essens gathered in closed groups of mainly adult males, practicing some sort of communal life, dedicating their lives to asceticism, abstaining from the pleasures of the flesh, living a celibate life, and considering women promiscuous and thus incapable of fidelity, probably following the instruction of their

---

405 These "faithful priests" were most probably of the Sadducees who refused to compromise with his plot at calming them down by adopting their rites in the temple.

406 Some scholars have suggested that the appearance of the Essens may have occurred a few years before, either in the time of John Hyrcanus, Simon the Maccabee's third son, who ruled from 135/4 to 104 BC, or during the reign of Jonathan (Yonoson/ Yonatan) the middle brother between Judah and Simon the Maccabee, sometime around 160 and 142 BC. This theory suggests that the Qumran Community may have actually existed as part of a larger "Brotherhood of the Essens" that had actually began to flourish in Palestine and Judea before they moved to Qumran to settle there separated from the other Jewish sects and parties, including the Essens who remained in the cities and towns.

Teacher of Righteousness. Yāwshu and his movement, on the other hand, were not made of adult males seeking refuge away from women but considered "the woman" essential in the religious formation and evolution of the human race.

While the Essens had strictly observed the Sabbath, the Torah, and the Levitical Laws, although having a different interpretation of the Jewish Bible as a whole, and had sacred and secret writings of their own, Yāwshu and his disciples on the other hand, never observed the Sabbath and didn't have affinities to the Jewish teachings and laws as we have seen—they were two different ministries. Their inobservance of the Sabbath comes from Luke (6:1-2):

Now it happened on the second Sabbath after the first that he was going through the grain fields. His disciples plucked the heads of grain, and ate, rubbing them in their hands. But some of the Pharisees said to them: Why do you do that which is not lawful to do on the Sabbath day?

Indeed. If Yāwshu and his Disciples had been Jews adhering to any of the known Jewish sects, including the Essens of Qumran themselves, or if they were just laymen, they would have respected the Law of the Sabbath and abstained from work, which brings us to the logical conclusion that they were not, in fact, Jews of any kind.

While the Essens believed in an unalterable destiny, probably denying personal free will, Yāwshu, on the other hand, believed that man is absolutely free, for it is written in Galatians 5:1, "Stand fast therefore in the liberty by which Christ has made us free, and do not be entangled again with a yoke of bondage." This same spirit of free will divine connection with humanity has been uttered in John 8:35-36, "And a slave does not abide in the house forever, [but] a son abides forever. Therefore if the Son makes you free, you shall be free indeed." Also in John 15:9-10, "As the Father loved Me, I also have loved you; abide in My love. If you keep My commandments, you will abide in My love, just as I have kept My Father's commandments and abide in His love."

Although the Essens shared some similarities with Yāwshu, like the belief in the immortality of the soul[407]; pledging piety towards God[408]; wearing all white clothes[409]; meeting for ceremonial prayer at dawn in wait for the rising sun; preserving

---

407 The Canaanite/Phoenician religion, the Egyptians, Thales, Pherecydes, Pythagoras, the Greek philosophers, the Pharisees, and many other religions and sacred groups believed in the Immortality of the soul.

the sect's secrets and transmitting its sacred teachings to other fellow Essens in Initiation after the oath had been taken[410] by a brother who showed great loyalty to his brethren and to the order's secret teachings, and had completed his probational period[411]—all these do not at all prove that Yāwshu was particularly one of them, since the similarities are also shared by other established religions and other secret and sacred groups around the world (as noted in the footnotes of this paragraph).

The Essens shared some exclusive similarities with Yāwshu, like when they avoided the temple worship in Jerusalem and referred to themselves by the "Sons of Light," an expression similar to the one used by Yāwshu when he said, "I'm the light of the world,"[412] and when they called themselves "Those who choose the way", a term identical to the one used by Yāwshu in John (14:6), "I am the way, the truth, and the life. No one comes to the Father except through Me."[413]

Even though the daily immersion in the water of rivers (lakes or seas)—as part of the purification rituals or as part of the rite of baptism by water—was practiced by the Essens, historical records reveal that such baptism and purification rituals had been also practiced by the group of Yāwshu and his great cousin Yāwhanan the Baptist[414] and ages before by a very few religions like the Canaanite/Phoenician, the Egyptian, the Zoroastrian, along with some other secret and sacred groups.

In spite of the fact that a similar belief in a continuous battle between good and evil (light and darkness) in the very nature of man, and which prompts the coming of a Messiah, a kind of a

---

408 It appears that the majority of the High Priests (and priests) of the ancient religions and the majority of the Hierophants of mostly all secret and sacred groups pledged piety towards their supreme deity.

409 The "white linen garment" was the everyday dress code of the Pythagorean Fraternity.

410 Matthew 7:6, "Do not give what is holy to the dogs; nor cast your pearls before swine, lest they trample them under their feet, and turn and tear you in pieces."

411 This is exactly a discipline similar to the one practiced by the Pythagoreans in their "white city". Please refer to *Pythagoras the Mathemagician*, 2010, published by Sunbury Press Inc.

412 John 8:12, "Then Jesus spoke to them again, saying, I am the light of the world. He who follows Me shall not walk in darkness, but have the light of life." And also in John 9:5, "As long as I am in the world, I am the light of the world."

413 This expression uttered by Christ had surely inspired the early Christian Church to choose a dictum to themselves as "Those of the way" or "The way of God".

414 Matthew 3:13-17; Luke 3:16; John 1:25-30.

savior for mankind that has been shared between the Essens and Yāwshu along with similar ascetic groups as we have seen before, nothing basic really links the Jewish Orthodox sect of the Essens of the Qumran Community and Yāwshu in the perception of how salvation could happen.

The Essens, who considered themselves as the "Children or Sons of Light," are described in the scrolls discovered in the First and Fourth Cave as the Jews of Levitic, Judahite, and Benjamite ancestry, giving the order to a well formed army of soldiers made of troops, cavalry, officers, and commanders, all led by the Head Priest for a battle in an apocalyptic war against the "Children or Sons of Darkness," described as the forces of Edom (Idumea), Moab, Ammon, Philista, and the "Kittim." Before the attack of this religious war began, the whole army of the People of God shouted out loud to strike terror and fear in the very heart of the enemy while the names of Israel and Aaron and the twelve tribes of Israel were included in the slogans written on the banners that the army held in its hands.[415]

So, while the Essens envisioned a final bloody war with a material enemy that would end up with their great victory against what they called the Sons of Darkness, Yāwshu the Meshiha, on the other hand, had neither material nor spiritual enemies to fight against in wars of blood, but rather, sinners and wrongdoers that needed to be finally judged before the God of Love, whom he called Father. An example of such a judgment is when he once declared during one of his Messianic banquets, yet to come, as we see in Luke (22:18, 29-30):

> For I say unto you, I will not drink of the fruit of the vine, until the kingdom of God shall come ... . And I appoint unto you a kingdom, as my Father hath appointed unto me; That ye may eat and drink at my table in my kingdom, and sit on thrones judging the twelve tribes of Israel.

In addition, while the Essens regarded their Teacher of Righteousness as the "High Priest of Israel," Yāwshu the Priest Forever, according to the order of Milki-Sedek, refused to be called "King of the Jews," as it came in John (18:33-36):

> Then Pilate entered the Praetorium again, called Jesus, and said to Him, Are You the King of the Jews? Jesus answered him, Are you speaking for yourself about this, or did others tell you this concerning Me? Pilate answered, Am I a Jew? Your

---

415 Allegro J.M., *The Dead Sea Scrolls*, page 121-122.

own nation and the chief priests have delivered You to me. What have You done? Jesus answered, My kingdom is not of this world. If My kingdom were of this world, My servants would fight, so that I should not be delivered to the Jews; but now My kingdom is not from here.

Truth be told, Yāwshu refused to be called King of the Jews, and never claimed it actually, simply because he was not, nor did he ever want to be; he would not claim truth in a lie. He plainly declared that his Kingdom was not from this world, and added something very important, proclaiming that if it were of this world, he would then ask his servants to defend him and fight so that he would not be delivered to the *Jews*. Notice this: he did not say, "I would not be delivered to my own nation." In fact, this is a two-fold answer to Pilate, with one meaning, spiritual; the other, material. His material answer would suggest that he meant to inform Pilate that he was Galilean, not Jewish. His spiritual answer would mean that his Kingdom is the Kingdom of God—of Love—to which he is the beloved Son, who never chooses evil ways—like war—to save himself from his enemies; except that Yāwshu has no enemies, as God has no enemies.

After hearing the reply to his first question, Pilate seems to have rephrased, to Jesus' great delight, by simply calling him a king and not King of the Jews, as we read in John (18:37):

Pilate therefore said to Him, Are You a king then? Jesus answered, You say [rightly] that I am a king. For this cause I was born, and for this cause I have come into the world, that I should bear witness to the truth. Everyone who is of the truth hears My voice.

Having examined the similarities and differences between the Essens of Qumran and Yāwshu, we conclusively believe he was not one of them, as also thought by many scholars and historians, and figured out by J.M. Allegro, who wrote[416], "There is no evidence that he (Jesus) was ever a member of this body (The Qumran Community), and, indeed, since his life was mostly spent in Nazareth, such a close connexion is highly improbable."

Indeed, for Yāwshu rather belonged to a more ancient religious fraternity or community living in the region of Phoenicia-Galilee, known as the Ashayas or Asayas, whom we have mentioned several times before and will eventually connect to Him in the last chapter of this book.

---

416 Allegro, J.M., *The Dead Sea Scrolls*, page 160.

Chapter 9

Which God and What Temple?

After all that we have so far covered and proved, it will be of no more use to repeat that Jesus was not a Jew in any context or in any way possible; neither a Sadducee, nor a Pharisee or a Zealot, and not even an Essen of the Qumran Orthodox Jewish Community. The question that automatically comes to mind now is: Was Jesus, or Yāwshu, really a Galilean-Phoenician as we have been proposing in this book? YES. If that is so, then who was his Father who art in Heaven? Which Temple did he address as being the Temple of his Father? These are the two basic questions to which answers will open to us a new approach to understand the true religion and theology of Jesus the Phoenician.

The Canaanite/Phoenician God YĀW and the Hebrew/Jewish God YHWH

It has been noted by scholars, as per the Hebrew Bible, that the name attributed to the Jewish God in its most traditional form, YHWH or Yahweh, was not used by the Hebrew people before the time of Moses. Undoubtedly, it appears that the Biblical (Old Testament) records show that the names, Ēl, Ēl Ēlyon (God Most High), Ēl Shaddai (God Most Powerful), or/and Ēlohei Shamayim (God of Heaven), were the basic names given to the God the Hebrews venerated, either when led by Abraham, their so-called genetic father, or by Jacob, their so-called founder of the Biblical State of Israel. It was then not until Moses, their so-called religious leader, that the name of God changed from Ēl to YHWH.

The Old Testament seems to have noted the time and the event that led to this shift in the Hebrew perception of the nomenclature of God. It was during the time, it says, that Moses fled Egypt and its powerful Pharaoh all through the Desert of Sinai and towards the Promised Land of Canaan. It was there, in the Egyptian Desert, says the book of Exodus, where he met Jethro, his father-in-law, a Kenite (or Cainite) priest of Midian who initiated him in a cave at Horeb, the mountain of God, introducing him to the new God—by the probable names of: *Yah,*

Yahu, Yahve, Yâho, Yaw, Iaw, Iaô, Yo or *Yeho*—who then appeared to him from the midst of a burning bush, unveiling the meaning of his mystery name. He said, "I am who I am,"[417] and sent Moses back to Egypt on a mission to rescue the Israelites from captivity.

Should we consider the narration of the Hebrew Bible a fact—which we actually reject as true historical account—we would definitely reason out the situation that Abraham and Jacob believed in Ēl, while Moses, in Yahweh[418]. Yet, we know that the Midianites were known as wise men, or Sons of Snakes (Serpents, hence the brazen Serpent of Moses), as well as being known as Canaanites and Hamites like the Egyptians[419]. Such a revelation would make the priest, Jethro, the son of Raguel and the father-in-law of Moses, either a Canaanite/Phoenician or Canaanite-Egyptian, hence a Hamite, not a Semite.

The probable relation between the Hebrews/Israelites and the Canaanites has been thought about and investigated for so long a time; it was because some scholars who took the Old Testament for granted as a historical book that they connected the two people. It was believed by some that the early population of the Israelites (Hebrews or Jews) were indeed Canaanites or Phoenicians. This connection had been explained by the identical deities worshiped by both people as presented in the Old Testament, from the Most High God Al, Ēl, Ēl-Ēlyon, Ēl Shaddai to his son Adon or Baal, and finally Yāw as Yahweh. Thus, it would be understandable to think, as Thompson puts it in his book[420] that "El Elyon has made Yahweh God for Israel." If that was the case, then it would be logical to look upon Ēl as a much higher God than Yahweh.

Archeological evidence shows that there were indeed a few references to the name of Yāw included in the form of personal human names, or being alone inscribed in the form of a divine

---

417 Exodus 3:2, "And the Angel of the LORD appeared to him in a flame of fire from the midst of a bush. So he looked, and behold, the bush was burning with fire, but the bush [was] not consumed." And Exodus 3:4, "So when the LORD saw that he turned aside to look, God called to him from the midst of the bush and said, Moses, Moses! And he said, Here I am." Also Exodus 3:13-14, "Then Moses said to God, 'Indeed, [when] I come to the children of Israel and say to them, The God of your fathers has sent me to you,' and they say to me, What [is] His name? what shall I say to them? And God said to Moses, 'I AM WHO I AM.' And He said, Thus you shall say to the children of Israel, I AM has sent me to you."
418 Exodus 6:3, "I appeared to Abraham, to Isaac, and to Jacob, as God Almighty, but [by] My name LORD I was not known to them."
419 Blavatsky, H.P., *Isis Unveiled*, Volume II, page 449.
420 Thompson, Thomas L., *The Mythic Past*, page 24.

name, in the ancient world. It is highly probable that the earliest and most famous body of texts that mention the name are the ones found in both Canaanite/Phoenician cities of Ebla, known today as Tell Mardikh, Syria (Early Bronze Age, between 3300 BC to 2100 BC) and Ugarit, known today as Ras Shamra, also in Syria (Late Bronze Age between 1550 BC to 1200 BC). In the case of human personal names, we find the element *Yaw*, or *Ya*, *Yah*, and *Yahu*, was used as a grammatical ending of the name, like Milkiya and Milkiyahu which means in Aramaic "My King is Ya," or "My King is Yahu," hence, "My King is Yāw," could well be an abbreviation of the divine name itself. However, in the case of the divine name itself, we find that the name Yāw or Yeuo is indeed the name of a deity believed to be the god of Rivers and Sea, the same as Yam, used by all the Phoenician coastal cities of Tyre, Sidon, Byblos, etc., as the god of the Sea and Water.

In fact, the Aramaic/Canaanite Yāw or Yam is regarded as one of the Ēlohim, or Sons of the Most High God Ēl, same as Shalim, the god of Dusk; Baal, the god of Thunder; and Adon the god of Resurrection, being himself identical to Yāwshu or Ye'shu ("May YĀW saves"), or again, Immanuel ("Ēl with us") as presented in the Phoenician-Galilean and Galilean-Christian form. And thus, as we have seen before in Chapters 1 and 3, it is undoubtedly logical to connect the Canaano-Phoenician god of the Sea to the Christian-Galilean-Phoenicians, known to be greatly associated with the sea and the art of fishing. The description given to the disciples of Yāwshu in the New Testament as being all fishermen is quite understandable.

It is important to note that since Yāw is mentioned as the Son of Ēl, his position as "God for Israel" as appointed by his Father would not make any historical sense if looked upon from the Biblical Jewish point of view. It would, however, mean a lot to the Canaanite/Phoenician *Isra-Ēl-is*, or the "House of the Family of Ēl." We have previously highlighted the essential difference between the two meanings given to the word "Israel," as seen by both the Canaanites/Phoenicians on one side and the Hebrews/Jews on the other side. It would be vital to explain more in a bit; however, let us resume our search for Yāw.

In the New Kingdom Egyptian texts, we may find a reference to the word Yaw, but in a different context. They didn't refer to a personal name with or without a divine element to it, nor to a divine name itself, but rather, a place, more specifically, a geographical area of southern Edom, Udumi(u), Idumaea, or Idumea on the western borders of the Arabian Peninsula. These texts were associated with a group of people called Shasu and

Shutu, known to have been nomadic-raiders or desert-dwellers. One example from the texts is a letter penned by an Egyptian scribe that mentioned them as the "Shasu of Yah," moving to watering holes inside the Egyptian territories during the time of the Egyptian Pharaoh Merneptah (or Merenptah), who reigned sometime between 1213 BC and 1203 BC. He was the son and successor of the Great Ramses II.

It became quite legitimate to think that the Biblical story of Moses, his relation to Yah that he met in the Desert of Sinai, and his conflict with the Egyptians, was inspired and appropriated by the Biblical scribes from Egyptian texts, just like the *Habiru* or *Apiru* argument, which we have seen earlier. In fact, there is no historical or archeological evidence that could support that the Edomites were the Hebrews of the Bible, and one of the simplest reasons to note is that there was not a single mention of the Hebrews as a people at the time Egyptian texts referred to the Edomites as nomadic people dwelling the desert. However, the Edomites' original land could have stretched from the adjacent Desert of Jordan to the Desert of Egypt, including the region of Mt. Seir located on the Canaanite Egyptian border, and their relation to the Nabataeans or Nabateans, as Strabo has suggested to be their origin[421], should not be taken lightly, especially on cultural and religious levels, since it is believed that the Nabateans were greatly influenced by the Canaanites/ Phoenicians/Aramaeans.

Having said that, we suggest that the Edomite religion could have consisted of similar gods worshiped by the neighboring people of Canaan/Phoenicia like the known divine trinity composed of Ēl, Baal, and Asherah, along with Kaus(h)[422] and Yāw. In his interesting book[423], American professor, Biblical scholar, and author, Mark S. Smith, suggests that the oldest Hebrew Biblical tradition places the Jewish God Yahweh as the deity of southern Edom, which may have actually originated in the regions of Edom, Teman (a desert to the south of Edom), Seir, and Sinai before being adopted in Israel and Judah.

This significant fact has also been confirmed by Thompson, who wrote[424], "The Bible frequently recognizes that Yahweh was worshiped by others than Israel. It understands him as having

---

421 Strabo, *Geography*, Book16, Chapter 2, Paragraph 34.
422 Kaus(h) or Kos(h) is also known as Qaus(h), Qos(h), or Qaws, being the national god of the Edomites, a mountain god that may be connected to Dusharrres, Dusares, or Dushara, the lord of the mountain worshiped by the Nabateans at Petra and some other places.
423 Smith, Mark S., *The Origins of Biblical Monotheism*, Page 140-145.
424 Thompson, Thomas L., *The Mythic Past*, page 176.

come from Midian, Teman and Seir." The "Israel" he meant here is none other than the Hebrew Israel that the Jews inhabited, although he referred to another Israel in his book, as we have seen before, which he called the Historical Israel, and on its people he also wrote[425]:

> They are referred to in the stories of Ezra 4 as enemies of Benjamin and Judah. Their offence: they wish to help in the building of a temple to 'the God of Israel' in Jerusalem. They are rejected in the story by Ezra's Jews and given a sectarian identity as 'Samaritans' by historians. This Israel is not the Israel that biblical scholars who write 'histories of Israel' have been interested in. It is not the Israel that we find in our biblical narratives. It is historical Israel.

Indeed, historical, archeological, and geographical logic imposes on our active mind to think of two Israels; while the first is strongly connected to the Gentile population inhabiting the wide Land of Canaan stretching from Ugarit to the Delta of the Nile, the other is only related to the Jews living in Hebrew Israel. Yet, the only extra-biblical reference to the name "Israel" comes from an Egyptian text found inscribed on a stele that clearly describes a destructive military campaign that had been undertaken in the Land of Canaan sometime at the end of the 13th century BC by the same Pharaoh Merneptah (or Merenptah) we have just recently mentioned. The stele mentions a group of people by the name of "Israel" already living in "Canaan," who received a fatal attack and to whom the Pharaoh desired to see their seeds end back then.

This interesting inscription could well fit with the dramatic part of the Biblical narration describing Moses' conflict with Pharaoh Ramses II, the father of Merneptah. Yet, reality on the historical level is totally different, for nowhere do we find a reference to Moses in the Egyptian texts. The text on the stele could only be seen in the light of an Egyptian religious reform against the polytheistic practices at the time, a reform that started secretly with Thutmose III (Thut-Mosis), the *Initiate of Thut*, then openly with Akhenaton, the Sun worshipper and preacher of the monotheistic God, Aton, and almost two hundred years later in the form of a revolution led by Hosarsiph or Osarsiph, a learned priest and loyal secret follower of Akhenaton. This revolution was set against both the suppressors of monotheism, Ramses II and his son, all under the inspiration and initiative of the people of

---

425 Ibid., page 190.

Isra-Ēl, "the House of the Family of Ēl," already living in Canaan under the wise guidance of Canaanite/Phoenician Initiates and Priests of the Most High God, Ēl-Alyon, the Father of Yāw, the God of Israel—Israel of the Canaanites/Phoenicians.

Thompson resumed his exposé on the worship of Yāw[426]:

> We also have a number of first-millennium Assyrian and Persian period texts that demonstrate just such a geographical spread of the worship of Yahweh. There is clear historical evidence that the Bible's was not the only religious tradition that recognized Yahweh as God.

He then immediately adds, referring to texts from the early first-millennium century:

> Texts from Sinai and southern Palestine refer to Yahweh as the god of Samaria[427]. They mention his wife Asherah[428]. Undoubtedly, the divine couple were the dominant deities of Palestine's highlands. In the Persian period, Yahweh is worshipped along with his wife Asherah, together with Ba'al and other deities[429] at the town of Ekron in the southern Palestinian coast and as far south as Elephantine in Egypt. Biblical texts identify Yahweh as the name of the traditional deity of the ancient state of Israel, for whom a temple was built in Jerusalem. This deity was understood as identifiable with the universal God of spirit *Elohe Shamayim*.

In fact, many other archaeological and historical findings confirm the spread of Yāw into Sinai in texts dated to the first

---

426 Ibid., page 176.

427 Samaria is the "Historical Israel" as per Thompson.

428 Asherah or Ashtoreth (Astarte) has always been cited—sometimes identified with Anat—as the wife-daughter of Ēl in Canaan-Phoenicia.

429 Asherah or Ashtoreth (Astarte) has always been mentioned as the Canaanite/Phoenician main Goddess. The many references to her also in the name of Ashtaroth or Asheroth and as an escort to the god Ba'al in the Hebrew Bible (Deuteronomy 16:21; Judges 2:13; 3:7, 6:25-30; 10:6; 1 Samuel 7:4, 12:10; 1 Kings 11:5, 33; 15:13; 18:19; 2 Kings 21:7; 23:4-7) are solid examples of the Canaanite/Phoenician worship of these deities, and certainly a cult not practiced by the Hebrews/Jews who were not in the land before the Persian Achaemenid Empire set its control in the region. In fact, the many references to Canaanite/Phoenician deities in the Old Testament undoubtedly reveal the meticulous works of forgery done by Persian scribes, like Esdras and Nehemiah, in attaching them (Ēl, Ba'al, Asherah ...) to the rising *Aebirou-al-naher* religious culture they powerfully endorsed by organized propaganda.

millennium BC and cite him as "Yah of Teman." It is most certain that this deity was copied later on by the Biblical scribes in the story they created about Moses and the god he was introduced to by Jethro, the Midianite/Hamite, as we have seen before. Although we don't think that the Biblical Moses actually existed at that time with that name, the Hebrew Bible failed to introduce the god YĀW in its Jewish form YHWH as a purely Hebraic invention, but rather an adoption of an already existing god worshiped by an old man—a Gentile—the Old Testament introduces as his father-in-law. Even that Biblical concept itself, and I mean, the act of borrowing deities, whether it was Adon (Adonis in Greek) as Adonai, or Yāw in the form of YHWH, identifying him with the God of Heaven, Elohe Shamayim, does not at all make out of them an entirely exceptional people labeled as the "Chosen People," but on the contrary; they were just below the ordinary group of people with neither divine or spiritual inspiration of their own nor an intellectual genuineness.

Certainly the spread of the cult of Yāw in the adjacent designated regions from Edom to Sinai could not be understood without considering it to be a socio-religious extension of the notion of Yāw presented in Ebla and most importantly the belief in him as the god of Rivers and Sea as pictured in Ugarit. If that is so, then Yāw—like Yam on the Phoenician Coast—would have taken the shape of the god of the Dead Sea close to Edom and the Red Sea close to Sinai. It would then be logical to analyze, as per the Old Testament narration, that the god that helped the mythical Moses to divide the water of the Red Sea in two parts on his way back to Midian away from the Egyptian forces was essentially a deity who had the power of control over the element of water, a god of water, hence Yāw, the god of Jethro, his father-in-law. Yet, the main obstacle in that narration has always been the Hebrew Moses himself, a person whose extra-biblical history and archeology is not identified as being real. A figure that had one of his characteristics was intentionally shaped on the image of Osarsiph, the Egyptian revolutionary priest, as seen before.

It is worth reminding the readers that names including words such as "Yehi" or "Yehaw" were undoubtedly in use by Canaano-Phoenician kings, like the 10th or 8th century BC King of Byblos Yehi-Milk (King Yehi), and Yehaw-Milk (King Yehaw), another Byblos King of the 5th-4th century BC. These two exact recorded historical dates show the first preceding and the second accompanying the true—not *mythical*—date the Hebrews entered the Land of Canaan in an organized complete manner.

No matter what, the issue that the Hebrew God Yahweh could be identified with the Phoenician God Yāw is very erroneous for the simplest reason that Yahweh, as pictured by the Jews, is not the god of water. Historical records show the Chaldean-Babylonians from which, according to the Hebrew Bible, Abraham emerged, as having originated from the city of Ur, believed in a god by the name of Iaô, Yâho, or Ea, Ia. The Biblical records, which appear to have no historical authenticity as to the exact correct time periods and names of characters implemented in the Old Testament narration, seem to coincide with our approach that the Biblical Abraham could have well been the historical Sheshbazzar, Shenazzar, or even Zoro-Babel or Zerubbabel, the Chaldean-Babylonian genetic father of the Hebrews, as cited before.

Both archaeological and historical records show that the Chaldean-Babylonian deity Ea was part of a triad of deities completed with Anu and Enlil. Ea has been mainly considered as the Lord of Apsu (Abzu), which means "fresh waters beneath the earth," hence god of Water (in seas, lakes) and may have also signified the purification ritual by water. It has additional different characteristics, like being the god of sorcery and incantation as well as patron god of craftsmen and artists, being a bearer of culture, an intelligent and wise god that evolved with the Akkadians into being devious and cunning. Recognized as the father of Marduk, the national god of Babylonia, Ea also stood as a form-giving god, or simply, god of Creation.

It is believed that the Akkadian-Babylonian Ea was worshipped before by the Sumerians under the name of Enki, as shown in their mythologies. However, etymologically speaking, Enki may have a confusing linguistic root, yet, the common translation would be: "Lord of the Earth." Enki has been associated with the act of fertility and regarded as god of Creation who devised men in such a way to be slaves to the gods. On the other hand, some say that Ea is Hurrian[430] in origin, while others believe it has Semitic origin mainly from the western region, or simply as we think, a Hamitic origin, in the sense of having its roots based in Aramaic-Phoenician-Egyptian (Afro-Asiatic) root: *hya* or *haya*, which means "life," manifested by the water element.

---

430 It is not known who the ancient Hurrians were, but some have identified them with the Horites mentioned in the Old Testament. The Hurrians seem to have lived first in Iraq (East of Tigris River) and Iran (mountain region of Zagros) sometime in the 3rd millennium BC before migrating west towards Turkey (Anatolia) and Syria during the 2nd millennium BC. Records show that they established the Mitanni Kingdom in the 15th century BC.

It could be because the gods Enki and Ea were counterparts, combined together in the form of Enki/Ea as "Lord(s) of the Earth and Water," that made the Chaldean-Babylonians portray him as a half-goat, half-fish creature, and from which the ancient astrological figure of the Capricorn was conceptualized.

Adding to that, it is most certain that the Chaldean-Babylonian god Ea or Ia has been spelled as "Iaô" by H. P. Blavatsky, who clearly wrote[431]:

In the old religion of the Chaldeans, the highest divinity, enthroned above the seven heavens, representing the spiritual light-principle and also conceived as demiurge was called *Iaw* who was like the Hebrew Yâho mysterious and unmentionable.

The Chaldean/Hebrew Iaô, she added[432]:

... would—etymologically considered—mean the 'Breath of Life', generated or springing forth between an upright male and an egg-shaped female principle of nature ... . In Hebrew, Iâh means life.

That being said, the Hebrew Yahweh, a demiurge, could not be regarded as the Supreme God but rather a creator of matter, and thus looked upon as a subsidiary deity to the Most High God. Therefore, the Hebrew God Yahweh could be solely identified with the God Iaô, Iâho(h), Yâho, Ea or Ia, the Chaldean god of Creation. He is Ye(a)va, Iahvh, Jove or Jahve (Yahveh), Jehovah (Yehovah), the Androgynous Supreme Divinity of the Hebrew-Israelites, being Ievo-hevah, Adâm-Hâwa (Adam & Eve) or the Kabbalistic, Yod(h)-Heva.

It is not by coincidence but by a deliberate fact or rather a clear conviction in the mind of the Jewish Chosen People that the deity they have always worshiped is YHWH. Since the beginning, they have pictured him in such a way that presents him as not being One and unique like the Pythagorean Monad (Nous), or like Êl, the Father of Jesus who resides in Heaven, but instead, a decomposable Being similar to the manifested forms human beings have taken on earth. Thus, the Old Testament that opens up with the Book of Genesis (1:1), "In the beginning God created the heavens and the earth," continues its description of the creation of the world by saying (1:27), "So God created man in His

---

431 Blavatsky, H.P., *Isis Unveiled*, Volume II, page 297.
432 Ibid., Volume II, page 299.

[own] image; in the image of God He created him; male and female He created them."

The Jewish Yahweh, in his demiurgic act of creation, may represent the Breath of Life of the material world, the Phoenician Yāw, god of water—whose Philo of Byblos gave witness to his worship in Phoenicia even in the 2nd century AD and probably all around the coastal and eastern Mediterranean region until the end of the Greco-Roman Period—and represents the element of life and purification of the living human being. This fits very well the image Jesus appeared with in the world of matter as Yāwshu, "Yāw Saves," walking on water, holding within him the Way, the Truth and the Life[433], and saving people by healing and purifying them from their earthly sins[434]. It is not by coincidence that Christianity adapted baptism by water as one of its major religious rituals—a secret initiation of accepting human beings as members within the Christian Community saved by the Meshiha Immanuēl.

At any rate, every deity needs a place where he can be worshiped, a house of prayer for the believers, and that goes as well for the God worshiped in Jerusalem. Let's have a look.

The Canaanite/Phoenician Temples of Shalim in Ur-Shalim, Ba'al-Melkart in Sūr, and the Hebrew/Jewish Temple of Yahweh in Jerusalem

It appears even now, centuries later, after the conception of the Jewish religion, that the Temple of Jerusalem remains still at the center of the Biblical Tradition. It is this temple that authenticates the Hebrew religion and the Jewish God residing inside. Yet, extra-biblical historical references of the ancient world, say, the Mesopotamians, Egyptians, and the Canaanite/Phoenicians, do not mention at all such a temple at the time the Old Testament suggests it was built, sometime between 1000 and 900 years BC. Judeo-Christian Biblical scholars who felt overwhelmed by this story named this period that covers the reigns of King David and his son Solomon—the alleged builder of the temple—the First Temple Period.

---

433 John 14:6, "Jesus said to him, I am the way, the truth, and the life. No one comes to the Father except through Me."
434 Bartholomaios 4:65, "When he had thus prayed, Jesus said unto him: Bartholomew, my Father did name me Christ, that I might come down upon earth and anoint every man that cometh unto me with the oil of life: and he did call me Jesus that I might heal every sin of them that know not ... and give unto men the truth of God."

Until now, in 2013 AD, the only reference we have of the so-called Holy Temple, spelled *Bet HaMikdash* in Hebrew, is the Old Testament itself. Both archaeological excavations and historical presentations have so far failed to prove the existence of a Jewish custom-made temple belonging to that era. It seems, however, that objective scholars may have identified a Jebusite Temple at the site of what is called the Temple Mount (also Mt. Zion[435]) years, perhaps centuries, before the date assigned to the First Temple Period.

Before we remind the excited readers who the Jebusites were, whom we have cited a few times earlier, let us just for a brief moment recall the religious aim mentioned in the Old Testament as having preceded the building of the temple. It is said that the dwelling place (the *Mishkan* in Hebrew) of the God of Israel was not originally just an ordinary altar, but a movable shrine, known as the Ark of the Covenant, placed in the Holy of Holies in the Tabernacle Tent. Ever since his meeting with "I am what I am" in the burning bush at the desert of Midian, Moses, who had been given the Ark, became by that the first spiritual leader of the Hebrews, known as the "Chosen People." Thus, the Ark of the Covenant—that special agreement between the Hebrew God and his people—traveled with them everywhere they went. It dwelt with them for forty years in the Desert of Sinai and later accompanied them into the Land of Canaan, traveling inside the Tent from one place to another.

After experiencing a long nomadic life, the Hebrews, armed with a God wiser and stronger than any other God, defeated everyone who stood against them along the way, from the Pharaoh of Egypt to the indigenous people of Canaan, occupying their land, including Jerusalem, in which they mainly lived among other neighboring villages, as well. There existed, however, a people in the region, the Old Testament narrates, always ready to fight against them: the Philistines. During those endless wars, the Philistines succeeded once in stealing the God-dwelling Ark, which was restored back to its original place in the heart of the Tent after a ferocious battle at the time of David, who having successfully unified all Israel thereafter, brought the Ark to the newly occupied city, Jerusalem (spelled in Hebrew as *Yerushalayim*), which he chose to be the Israeli national capital.

---

435 The *Encyclopædia Britannica* suggests that the etymology and meaning of the name "Zion" are obscure. It appears to be a pre-Israelite Canaanite name of the hill upon which Jerusalem was built; the name "Mountain of Zion" is common.

Having settled there now in his house built by Phoenician artificers[436], David then decided to build a temple to house the Ark in an everlasting place. He bought a threshing-floor for the site of the Temple[437] from a certain Ornan or Araunah[438] of the Jebusites, but Yahweh, the Old Testament continues, abstained for unknown reasons from giving his king official permission to build him a temple. With his son and successor, Solomon, this was destined to change. The Ark would no more be carried by nomads wandering around in a portable Tent, as had previously been the case. On the contrary, it would finally find a resting place inside a Temple to be built especially in reverence to the Holy Covenant made between YHWH and His Chosen People. That being lastly decided, Solomon began the planning, preparation, and construction of the Temple[439].

In fact, not only does the Old Testament narrate that a particular relationship was established between the Hebrews with King David and the Phoenicians with King Hiram, but that special relationship[440] continued even during the reign of King Solomon, who asked for the expertise of Phoenician architects, sculptors, and artificers coming from Tyre, and craftsmen and stone-cutters from Gebel (Byblos) for the construction of both his royal palace and the Temple[441].

---

436 2Samuel 5:11, "Then Hiram king of Tyre sent messengers to David, and cedar trees, and carpenters and masons. And they built David a house."

1Chronicles 14:1, "Now Hiram king of Tyre sent messengers to David, and cedar trees, with masons and carpenters, to build him a house."

437 1Chronicles 21:18, "Therefore, the angel of the LORD commanded Gad to say to David that David should go and erect an altar to the LORD on the threshing floor of Ornan the Jebusite."

1Chronicles 21:22, "Then David said to Ornan, Grant me the place of [this] threshing floor, that I may build an altar on it to the LORD. You shall grant it to me at the full price, that the plague may be withdrawn from the people."

438 Although *Araunah* may mean "Lord" in Hittite, we reject the supposition that he was Hittite. His other name, *Ornan*, has Amorite origin and also means "Lord." Having been mentioned in the Biblical narration as a Jebusite who sold his threshing floor to David suggests that he was an Amorite native of Jerusalem, probably a man of noble rank or high office or even a king.

439 1Kings 5; 6; 7; 8.

440 2Chronicles 2:3, "Then Solomon sent to Hiram king of Tyre, saying: As you have dealt with David my father, and sent him cedars to build himself a house to dwell in, [so deal with me]."

441 1King 5:10, "Then Hiram gave Solomon cedar and cypress logs [according to] all his desire." And 1Kings 5:18, "So Solomon's builders, Hiram's builders, and the Gebalites quarried [them]; and they prepared timber and stones to build the temple." Also 1Kings 9:11, "(Hiram the king of Tyre had supplied Solomon with cedar and cypress and gold, as much as he

If that is true history, then it would be absolutely logical to express that both the Hebrew God, as we have explained in the previous section, and the Temple consecrated to him, were not actually the work of the Hebrews, rather, a complete adaptation from religious inspiration and architectural works already established by the Canaanites/Phoenicians. That being said, it would be straight to the point to say that the Hebrews'/Jews' God and their Temple are not theirs but belong to a different culture than theirs.

With all the glory and pride that I may feel as a descendant of the Phoenicians, I would not fall to that, and because I am a Christian, I only bear witness to the Truth, and the Truth is not at all what was written in the Old Testament. The thing is that the Biblical narration, written sometime between the 5th/4th and the 1st century BC, is not in accord with historical and archeological findings. Neither King David nor his son Solomon or his Temple ever existed.

The clear description the Old Testament mentions regarding the construction of the alleged "Temple of Solomon" and the way it was civilly engineered, does not only disclose that it was built by Tyrian and Geblite craftsmen but also in the Canaanite/ Phoenician fashion. However, with no archaeological or historical findings to support this narration of the Old Testament in particular, it would be important to share some legitimate information we have gathered regarding two of the most ancient Canaanite/Phoenician Temples: Temple of Shalim in Ur-Shalim and Temple of Ba'al-Melkart in Sūr. It is widely suggested and believed that the Hebrew Bible based its story of the mythical Temple of Solomon on these two Great Temples.

Temple of Shalim in Ur-Shalim

We have briefly tackled this issue before, but what concerns us right now is the exact time such a Temple was erected in Jerusalem and to whom the credit should be given. This very question takes us back to the Jebusites. In fact, Jerusalem is a derivation from the word "Ur-Shalim," the city of Shalim, one of the Ēlohims—a son of Ēl. Shalim or *Šalim* was the "god of dusk" in the Canaano-Phoenician list of gods. Ēl, Al-Ēlyon, or Ēloi, is the father of all the gods in the Phoenician pantheon, and represented the very First Light of Creation. It has been archaeologically and

desired), [that] King Solomon then gave Hiram twenty cities in the land of Galilee." And 1Kings 9:14, "Then Hiram sent the king one hundred and twenty talents of gold."

historically observed that Jerusalem was—for ages before the coming of the Hebrews into the scene—a Canaanite/Phoenician city.

The Amorites themselves appear to have existed in a time period that stretched from phase III of the Early Bronze Age (EBA III) through the Late Bronze Age (LBA II B) and ended with the first one hundred years of the Early Iron Age. That would be from c. 2400/2100 BC–1550/1200 BC–1200/1100 BC. They formed an Eastern Canaanite group or tribe who dominated the history of Mesopotamia, Syria, and Palestine. Sometime during the early 2nd Millennium BC, they were referred to as *Amurru* in the Akkadian language, a term designating not only an ethnic group but also a language and a geo-political formation, the land of the MAR.TU, stretching beyond the Euphrates, from northern Palestine to the neighboring land of Phoenicia and the Syrian Desert—thus, the Land of Canaan. At that time, having been great in number, as they appear to have been, a large number of them seem to have migrated towards southern Mesopotamia, either triggered by the 22nd century BC drought or maybe a determined expansion in an attempt to occupy Mesopotamia or settle it. Their move resulted in the occupation of Babylon and the mid-Euphrates region. Such an expansion was probably one of the essential causes that led to the downfall of the Sumerian Third Dynasty of Ur sometime around 2112 BC and 2004 BC.[442] Amongst the Amorite Kings that had governed Babylon ever since was the famous Hammurabi, a First Dynasty 6th king of Babylon. It is said he founded it or rather transformed it into a city-state to reign over from 1792 BC to 1750 BC (or minus 64 years if considering the short chronology). He was Ammu-rāpi, "the kinsman is a healer," or in fact, Amurru-Abi, "My Father is an Amorite." One of their famous capitals was at Mari (known today as Tall al-Hariri, in Syria); the second in importance as a political center was Halab (Aleppo, in nowadays Syria), another center at Hazor in Palestine. Mesopotamia, on the other hand, was an impermanent station, for as a matter of fact, the Amorites totally disappeared from Babylonia and the mid-Euphrates region sometime between 1550 BC and 1100 BC.

We believe sometime around 2000 BC or maybe before that Jerusalem was founded as a minor city by the Amorites. Egyptian

---

442 It is most probably back then that Yāw, the Canaanite/Phoenician/Amorite god of the waters entered Babylon and Ur where it was rendered into Ea, and became known later as Iaô, Iâho(h), Yâho, or Ia, with the Babylonian-Chaldean-Hebrew priests and families. With them, it represented the dual principle of Creation through Yahweh (Yod(h)-Heva, Adām-Hāwa), the Androgynous Supreme Divinity of the Biblical Hebrew-Israelites.

sacred texts of the Middle Kingdom (c. 19th century BC) support this claim and identify it as *Rušalim*, meaning, "Ru" ("Spirit") of "Šalim" (Shalim, son of Ēl). Hence, it could not be regarded as an imaginary spiritual city as some have suggested. It was later called Jebus[443], *Ib-u-ś*, by the Jebusites (Yəḇûsî or Ib-u-śu), an ancient Canaanite/Amorite tribe, before it was given back its quasi-original name of Ur-Shalim, later on, by Milki-Sedek. The *Urušalimin* mentioned in the Amarna letters sent by a certain Abdi-Heba[444] to Pharaoh Akhenaton around 1350 BC and 1330 BC, supports this fact. Abdi-Heba wrote[445]:

Say to the king, my lord: Message of Abdi-Heba, your servant I fall at the feet of my lord 7 times and 7 times. Consider the entire affair ... . (there is more here to it before he said) Consider Urušalimin! This neither my father nor my mother gave to me. The strong hand (arm) of the king gave it to me. Consider the deed! This is the deed of Milkilu and the deed of the sons of Lab'ayu, who have given the land of the king to the 'Apiru[446]. Consider, O king, my lord! I am in the right!

Having said that, we surely conclude that *Urušalimin* would etymologically mean the "city or foundation of the god Šalim (Shalim or Shalem)," the Canaanite/Phoenician deity of the Bronze Age, presumably identified with the evening star, Venus, in Ugaritic mythology[447]. The Old Testament later referred to Jerusalem as "Salem" (*Urušalim*) rather than "Jebus" and relates it to Milki-Sedek (Melchizedeq) as being its king and Priest of the Most High God, Ēl[448]. It suggested that he lived at the time of Abraham, who, according to the Hebrew tradition was living

---

443 1Chronicles 11:4-5, "And David and all Israel went to Jerusalem, which is Jebus, where the Jebusites [were], the inhabitants of the land. But the inhabitants of Jebus said to David, You shall not come in here! Nevertheless David took the stronghold of Zion (that is, the City of David)." Jebus is also mentioned in Josiah 18:28; Judges 19:10-11.

444 His name is also written as *Abdi-(K)hebat*, most probably translated as "servant of Hebat," a Hurrian goddess. Abdi-Hebat, possibly a Hurrian chief, was appointed by the Egyptians to rule the city as a king.

445 This letter is recorded as EA287 and was found in the *Amarna Letters*. Jerusalem's king Abdi-Heba sent six letters to the Pharaoh informing him of the political situation there. They are recorded as EA285 to EA290.

446 The Apiru whom we have tackled earlier in the book were first mentioned here in these letters.

447 This presumption might be given due to the astronomical observation that Venus is the second planet from the Sun and it revolves around it. Now, the Sun being a physical reflection of the Most High God Ēl-Ēlyon, Šalim (Venus) is then the Son revolving around the Father.

sometime in the earlier part of the 2nd Millennium BC, thus, in the Middle Bronze Age period (c.2100 BC–1550 BC).[449] However, since we do not give any sort of historical credit to the Old Testament's chronological narratives before the time of Cyrus II, we would not take this time period as being the correct time when Milki-Sedek lived, knowing that this period—Middle Bronze Age—might well fit with the mentioning of Rušalim in the Egyptian sacred texts of the Middle Kingdom (c. 19th century BC). We have reasons though to believe that Milki-Sedek either lived during the Late Bronze Age (c. 1550 BC–1200 BC) in the history of the Canaanites, or sometime in the Early Iron Age, during the time of King Hiram of Sūr, the great builder, and that would be around the 10th century BC, as we shall see further on.

In fact, both possibilities have powerful endorsing elements. First, in the case of Milki-Sedek living during the Late Bronze Age —an issue I shall refer to as Case 1—we have three elements that add to that possibility. Šalim presents himself as a deity of the Bronze Age and his presumable identification with the evening star in Ugaritic clay tablets of the Late Bronze Age proves it. In addition, the obvious citation of the name Urušalim(in) in the Amarna Letters that coincides with the Late Bronze Age proves that the city had indeed existed at that time, yet, the only hindrance to that development of thought would be our lack of evidence if it was indeed dedicated to Šalim with a cult and a Temple. The third element that backs up this theory comes from the knowledge that the name of the Canaanite/Phoenician god, Saduq, has also been found in the Ugaritic tablets. This deity, Saduq, Sydyk, Sydek, Sedek, or Suduc also appeared in a theological work accredited to the 1st century AD Phoenician historian and writer Philo of Byblos (64 AD–140 AD) in an account preserved to us by the first Christian Church historian, exegete, polemicist, and bishop, Eusebius of Caesarea (260/63 AD–339/40 AD) in his Praeparatio Evangelica[450] (Preparation for the Gospel) and attributed to a most ancient Canaanite/Phoenician historian and author, Sanchuniathon. The name Suduc, potentially from the Phoenician root ṣ-d-q, cited by Philo as the father of the Cabeiri (the Kabbirim: "inventors of ship"), was given

---

448 Genesis 14:18, "Then Melchizedek king of Salem brought out bread and wine; he [was] the priest of God Most High."

449 In his The Historicity of the Patriarchal Narratives (1974), Thomas L. Thompson argued that there is no compelling evidence that suggests that the Hebrew patriarchs lived in the 2nd millennium BC since the Biblical texts reflect the 1st millennium BC conditions and concerns. Thompson based his argument on archaeological findings and ancient extra-biblical texts.

450 Eusebius, Praeparatio Evangelica, Book 1, Chapter 10.

its Greek meaning as *dikaion*, which is translated into "righteousness, justice, just, or the just one." Suduc is mentioned as brother of Misor, the father of Taautus.[451] In fact, what has been conveyed in the work of Sanchuniathon proves the familial ties between Canaan/Phoenician and Egypt (Misor).

Saduq, Suduc, or Sydyk is then one of the deities mentioned in the Canaanite/Phoenician pantheon, most probably not as son of Ēl like Shalim, Baal, and Yāw (Yam), but rather in the form of Tzedek, one of his attributes or epithet; *righteousness*. That being said, then Milki-Sedek (King of Righteousness or my King is Righteous) could well have lived in the Bronze Age, most safely to say, in the Late Bronze Age, as King of Salem and High Priest of the Most High God Ēl-Ēlyon. If that is true, then we can establish Case 1 and conclude that it was Milki-Sedek who changed the name of the city from *Ib-u-ś* (Jebus) to *Urušalim* (City of Shalim), referring it back to its original name *Rušalim* (Spirit of Shalim) and dedicating a Temple to the god of dusk. We cannot be sure though, as per today, to resolve if his reign was before or after the reign of Abdi-Hebat, the Hurrian chief of the 14th century BC.

L.A. Waddell affirms the existence of such an ancient Canaanite/Amorite/Jebusite Temple but without identifying a precise date. He wrote[452]:

The presence of Gentile Sun-priests in the temple on Mt. Moriah at Jerusalem is explained by the fact that, besides the name 'Moriah'—which is recognized as meaning 'Mount of the Morias or Amorites'—that temple, long before the occupation of Jerusalem by David and its rebuilding by Solomon was a famous Sun-temple of the Hittites or Morites.

It is important to note that the Hittites' connection to the Amorites is essentially based on the Hebrew Bible, which links them directly to Heth, one of the descendants of Ham, through his

---

451 His Canaano/Phoenician original name is Thor the Geblite: inventor of the first written Alphabet. He is also the Egyptian Thoth, and the Greek Hermes.
452 Waddell, L.A., *The Phoenician Origin of Britons, Scots, & Anglo-Saxons*, page 274. Of course when L.A.Waddell wrote in the early 20th century, there were but little archaeological excavations done to parallel with the narration of the Old Testament, which certainly differs from the truth revealed nowadays by archeological and historical realities that deny the existence of both David and Solomon. Facts that might consider the Hebrew occupation of Jerusalem to have happened after the decree written by Cyrus II, in the 6th century BC. Along with that, the relationship he shows between the Hittites and Amorites as being so genetically close could not be confirmed.

son Canaan. That would count them amongst the Canaanite tribes, just like the Amorites and Jebusites. Not only that, but the Old Testament Book of Ezekiel[453] connects the foundation of Jerusalem to the Hittites as well. In fact, the Hittite element here is erroneous of course for two main reasons; first, they were not Canaanites, thus not Amorites, and second, they hadn't reached the location where Jerusalem was founded. Historical records show that they were an ancient Anatolian people, probably originated from the area beyond the Black Sea, or of Indo-European origin, who had established an Empire at Hattusa (Hatti) in north-central Anatolia (also known as Asia Minor, modern day Turkey) sometime around the 18th century BC (Old Kingdom: c. 1700 BC–1500 BC). The empire took control of the Euphrates River down to Babylon, putting an end to the Amorite dynasty (c. 1590 BC), and expanding towards the 14th century BC (New Kingdom: c. 1400 BC–1180 BC) into the northern Canaan (northern part of Aram/Syria and very little parts of northern Phoenicia/Lebanon) along with the Upper Mesopotamia region (the uplands and great outwash plain of northwestern Iraq and northeastern Syria). It then began its gradual decline in front of the rising power of the Assyrians in the 13th century BC and came to an end immediately after in the following century (c. 1180 BC) where it was divided into several independent Neo-Hittite city states or Syro-Hittite kingdoms, some of which lasted until the 8th century BC.

It was agreed by most Biblical scholars that the temple of Solomon cited in the Old Testament was simply a natural evolution of the Temple built by Milki-Sedek and dedicated to Šalim (Shalim) or Sydyk (Sedek). However, since there are no archeological proofs and no extra-biblical historical accounts in regards to David[454] and his son Solomon, we simply reject this

453 Ezekiel 16:3, "and say, Thus says the Lord GOD to Jerusalem: Your birth and your nativity [are] from the land of Canaan; your father [was] an Amorite and your mother a Hittite." And Ezekiel 16:45.
454 The only reference to David (the king of the House of David, *bytdwd*) in relation to the King of Israel outside the Hebrew Bible has been found for the first time inscribed in Aramaic—by an unknown someone, presumably Hazael of Aram-Damascus, an important regional figure in the late 9th century BC—on a broken stele, known as the Tel Dan Stele during excavations done on site (Tel Dan: northern part of modern Israel) by Israeli archaeologist Avraham Bergman (Biran) in 1993/94. The discovery itself generated considerable debate among Biblical scholars and many articles have been written about it. Yet, very few among them, basically Judeo-Christians, believe it is authentic on the ground, that it supports the existence of the Biblical David; others conclude that it does not logically do that at all; and some, like Niels Peter Lemche believe it to be probably a

supposition and believe that the temple of Solomon (pronounced in Hebrew as *Shlomo*) is nothing but an etiological myth, a linguistic forged signature of the Temple of Shalim. We think this counterfeit was done during the Persian period and with the help of the Persians themselves, knowing that such a historical claim for the presence of the temple in the Promised Land of Canaan would give them enough religious/political power of control in the newly conquered region. This geo-political observation has also been asserted by many other prominent authors like Philip Davies[455], who dated the foundation of "Biblical Israel" to the Neo-Babylonian period[456], which had its beginning preceding the beginning of the Achaemenid Persian Period (550 BC–330 BC) by almost 75 years and intersected with it in its final years. On the other hand, Niels Peter Lemche certainly suggests a later period of time in placing the origin of the Biblical Israel—the Hellenistic (3rd–2nd century BC). He wrote[457]:

> The Israelite nation as explained by the biblical writers has little in the way of a historical background. It is a highly ideological construct created by ancient scholars of Jewish tradition in order to legitimize their own religious community and its religio-political claims on land and religious exclusivity.

Let us investigate for a minute if Milki-Sedek could have lived during the time of King Hiram of Sūr, in 10th century BC is also legitimate—an issue I shall refer to as Case 2. The Old Testament narration of building the temple in Jerusalem by Solomon the son of David, fails to prove itself on both the archaeological and historical levels, once and for all. The story of such a distinguished temple does not exist in extra-biblical sources. We do not find historical characters, Hebrew in particular, by the names of David and Solomon in any written document or account belonging to any of the world's ancient civilizations like the Egyptians or Phoenicians. If such a royal family had truly existed in time and a relationship had been established with Phoenician royalty, we would have read about them at least in the Phoenician records that mention King Hiram of Sūr. Yet, there is nothing.

---

forgery.

455 Davies, Philip, *The Origin of Biblical Israel*, page 62.

456 The Neo-Babylonian Empire or the Chaldean Empire was an empire that existed in the Mesopotamian history during a period of time that began in c. 626 BC and ended in c. 539 BC.

457 Lemche, Niels Peter, *The Israelites in History and Tradition*, page 165-166.

The composition of this Hebrew Biblical narration describing an event happening in the 10th century BC suggests that it was nothing but an altered story from a Phoenician account and that both David and his son Solomon were a deliberate insertion into the original text during the formation of the Hebrew Bible. That certainly explains why the only two Hebrew actors in the story are David and Solomon, whereas all the other actors are recognized as Canaanite/Phoenicians. The land owner was the Canaanite/ Jebusite Ornan or Araunah; the person who helped in the building of the temple was King Hiram of Sūr; the architect was Hiram Abiff[458] of Sūr; the other architects, artisans, sculptors, craftsmen and stone-cutters were all from Sūr and Gebēl. It couldn't be more obvious than that, for all the elements herein presented, along with the materials used in the building like the Cedar trees, Cypress logs, and timber, add to the veracity of a Phoenician historical account rather than a Hebrew one.

Unless of course, we consider as true the suggestion proposed by a few scholars, like E. Raymond Capt[459] and others, that the Israelis/Jews were Canaanites/Phoenicians, having been rooted in them and/or being a tribe issuing from them[460], or having a close connection with them in one way or another, either through the similarities in the language or by a direct unified historical, cultural, and geographical expansion. Such a weak hypothesis has been seriously noted by author Martin Bernal of Sephardic Jewish roots, in his controversial book, *Black Athena*, most probably for a few important and necessary reasons. The most important of them would be to give some legitimacy to the rather unauthentic and debatable Hebrew-Israeli-Jewish-Semitic "biblical history," associating it with the already well established

---

458 1Kings 7:13-14, "Now King Solomon sent and brought Huram (Hiram) from Tyre. He *was* the son of a widow from the tribe of Naphtali, and his father *was* a man of Tyre, a bronze worker; he was filled with wisdom and understanding and skill in working with all kinds of bronze work. So he came to King Solomon and did all his work." Whether a person by the name of Hiram Abiff really existed or not, it would be suggested that his name refers not to a person by that particular name but a person that could be identified as the "son of King Hiram," thus, "Hiram is my father" (Hiram Abi or Abiff in Phoenician tongue).
459 Capt, Raymond E., *The Traditions of Glastonbury*, page 23-31. The author identified the Hebrews/Israelites with Phoenicians tin traders.
460 If this is true, then Jesus would have been directly looked upon as belonging to a Judaic-Phoenician tribe, which would make this book unnecessary in one way or another.

Canaanite/Phoenician/Hamitic "religious history." Bernal wrote[461]:

> The scattered Jewish components of my ancestry would have given nightmares to assessors trying to apply the Nuremberg Laws, and although pleased to have these fractions, I had not previously given much thought to them or to Jewish culture. It was at this stage that I became intrigued—in a Romantic way —in this part of my 'roots.' I started looking into ancient Jewish history, and—being on the periphery myself—into the relationships between the Israelites and the surrounding peoples, particularly the Canaanites and Phoenicians. I had always known that the latter spoke Semitic languages, but it came as quite a shock to learn that Hebrew and Phoenician were mutually intelligible and that serious linguists treated both as *dialects* of a single Canaanite language.

We have dealt with this issue before in Chapter 1 and firmly identified that the Hebrew language is a mixture of both, an *Aramaic* dialect and an *Akkadian-Babylonian* idiom. Yet, the Aramaic itself is a direct descendant vernacular from the Canaanite/Phoenician language, which is why many modern scholars typically indicate that the word "Hebrew" in the New Testament refers to "Aramaic." Definitely, on their first arrival to Canaan-Phoenicia during the Achaemenid Persian Period, the Hebrews' already established Akkadian-Babylonian language was inoculated by the indigenous Phoenician Aramaic, although we know that Aramaic (the evolved form of Canaanite/Amorite) became the official language of Canaan-Phoenicia and Mesopotamia sometime in the middle of the 1st Millennium BC. So, in other words, what Bernal wrote does not match up with his attempt to connect both Phoenician and Hebrew cultures and histories together through similarities in language. Yet, Bernal seemed excited, or desperate, to link them historically together when he hinted[462], "Jews and Phoenicians had long, and rightly, been seen as closely related." Then, joining them racially when he added[463], "The 'Semites' they had in mind were Jews and/or Phoenicians ..."

The confusion in Bernal's mind and others alike has been answered many times before in this book where we clearly

---

461 Bernal, Martin, *Black Athena: The Afroasiatic Roots of Classical Civilization, Volume I: The Fabrication of Ancient Greece*, page xiii.
462 Ibid., page 344. Also in pages 33, 351, 415.
463 Ibid., page 350.

identified the Canaanite/Phoenician/Isra-ēl as the "Religious Family of Ēl" of Afro-Asiatic or Hamito-Semitic roots, and described the Hebrew/Jews/Israelis as the "Religious Family of YHWH" of purely Semitic roots. They were two different races of humanity with various cultures and religions that had been coexistent on the same geographical spot of Canaan ever since the Persians deported the latter, the Hebrews, towards the Promised Land.

At any rate, following the Canaanite/Phoenician cultural, historical, and religious perspective, King Hiram, who is shown as having built a Temple to Ba'al Melkart in Sūr, as we shall see in the following section, could have also helped constructing a similar Temple in Ur-Shalim. Why not? We have every reason to believe he could have done that. If that is so, then Milki-Sedek, King of *Urušalim*, could have been the one who asked King Hiram to send him the best architects and artisans from Sūr and the stone-cutters from Gebal to build the Temple in dedication to the god Šalim, making him the patron-god of the city. That being said, we can therefore establish Case 2 as well.

Whether Milki-Sedek (Melchizedek), the Just and Righteous King of *Urušalim* and its High Priest, who preached the belief in the Universal God Al-Ēlyon—being himself of a direct lineage of adepts spreading forth from Enoch-Thor—lived in the Late Bronze Age or sometime in the 10th century BC, we cannot deny the fact that he existed in the course of history as an important Canaanite/Phoenician religious figure. He has been strongly related to the city of Ur-Shalim and its great Temple—a Temple that was destroyed by the Neo-Babylonian king, Nebuchadnezzar II (c. 634 BC–562 BC) after the siege of the holy city around the years 586/587 BC. His reign lasted about forty-three years between 605 BC and 562 BC, and, according to the Hebrew Bible, conquered both Judah and Jerusalem, sending the Jews into exile to Babylon in the aftermath. In truth, however, the story of the exile to Babylon does not stand at all, either.

Temple of Ba'al-Melkart in Sūr

One of the most mysterious Canaanite/Phoenician authors and historians was probably a priest by the name of Sanchuniathon of Berytus (Sanchoniathon of Beirut). His authenticity has been for some time a subject of debate by a few historians, though not anymore. He has been considered to be the author of three lost works written originally in the Phoenician language. A little knowledge about him and his great work seems to have survived only in the form of excerpts, summarized and quoted in Greek translation by Philo of Byblos. The information we have about Philo and his translation and interpretation of Sanchoniathon's "Theology of the Phoenicians", came to us from Eusebius's work, *Praeparatio Evangelica*—a work consisting of fifteen books.

The very few fragments we have of the three works credited to Sanchoniathon and the nine works attributed to Philo on the history of the Phoenicians, most likely constitute the largest extensive historical and literary source regarding the Phoenician religion in either Greek or Latin tongues. Unfortunately, most of the Phoenician historical sources, along with maybe all of the Phoenician literature on religion, culture, and habits, were lost—written on parchments, which are now hard to find or on walls and pillars of the Temples that had been destroyed.[464]

Eusebius also quotes the Pythagorean (or neo-Platonist) writer and philosopher, Porphyry of Sūr (234 AD–304/5 AD), introducing him as "the author in our own day of the compilation against us mentions these things in the fourth book of his treatise *Against the Christians*, where he bears the following testimony to Sanchuniathon, word for word." Porphyry is said to have stated[465]:

Of the affairs of the Jews the truest history, because the most in accordance with their places and names, is that of Sanchuniathon of Berytus, who received the records from Hierombalus[466] the priest of the god Ieuo[467]; he dictated his history to Abibalus[468] king of Berytus and was approved by

---

464 It seems that the preserved fragments of Sanchoniathon's writings have been judged accurate as revealed by the mythological accounts found on the Ugaritic clay tablets.

465 Eusebius, *Praeparatio Evangelica*, Book 1, Chapter 9.

466 Hierombalus could be Hiram'ba'al or Hiram, King of Tyre, who built the temple of Ba'al Melkart in Sūr, and that would make Sanchuniathon living at the time of that great king sometime around 971 BC and 939 BC, not during the time the text of Eusebius quoting Porphyry suggests.

467 We have earlier investigated the origin of the name of the god *Ieuo or Ieuô* who is most certainly Yāw, the Phoenician god of the waters and not the Hebrew Yahweh.

468 We believe that Abibalus mentioned here as King of Berytus could be erroneous; the exact name should be Abd-Baal who was king around 1300 BC. We have records of Abibalus or Abi-Ba'al King of Tyre (not Berytus), followed by Hiram. In George Rawlinson's, *History of Phoenicia*, page 325-326, we read, "Abi-Baal (Abibalus) was succeeded on the Tyrian throne by his son, Hiram or Hirôm, a prince of great energy, of varied tastes, and of an unusually broad and liberal turn of mind."

him and by the investigators of truth in his time.[469] Now the times of these men fall even before the date of the Trojan War, and approach nearly to the time of Moses, as is shown by the successions of the kings of Phoenicia. And Sanchuniathon, who made a complete collection of ancient history from the records in the various cities and from the registers in the temples, and wrote in the Phoenician language with a love of truth[470], lived in the reign of Semiramis, the queen of the Assyrians, who is recorded to have lived before the Trojan War or in those very times. And the works of Sanchuniathon were translated into the Greek tongue by Philo of Byblos.

That being said, it would be then estimated that the Phoenician priest Hierombalus and his compatriot historian Sanchoniathon lived sometime in the 13th century BC. This hypothesis came from the information transmitted to us by Herodotus who wrote that the Trojan War occurred in the mid-13th century BC. Yet, some say it could have happened some 50 years earlier. The Biblical tradition, on the other hand, does not cite the Trojan War of course, but believes the *mythical* Moses to have lived sometime around the 14th century BC. As for Semiramis, the *legendary* beautiful queen warrior of the Assyrians, whom the Persians accredited with the founding of Babylon, seems to have lived in the mid of the 13th century BC.

Although it is interesting to observe such a hypothesis, we tend not to consider it a conclusive historical fact, thus, not giving much credit to Eusebius on this particular matter, especially after knowing that he appears to have forged the works of Porphyry; he destroyed and burned them. This could have happened after actually stealing all the literary and historical texts written by both Phoenician authors Sanchoniathon and Philo that he discovered, along with the work of Porphyry and other sacred and theological works, at the library of Ceasaria in Palestine, founded by the reputed bibliophile Pamphilus[471] of Phoenician origin. It

---

469 This event could well be regarded as the first scientific council ever to discuss a thesis on cultural matters, as expressed by Dr. Youssef Hourany. Hourany, Youssef, *The Cosmogonic Theory of the Phoenicians—نظرية التكوين الفينيقية*), page 29.

470 According to Eusebius quoting Porphyry, *Sanchuniathon* (Sanchoniat(h)on or Sancuniates) means the "Friend of the Truth" in the Phoenician language.

471 Pamphilus (~latter half of the 3rd century–309 AD) stood as one great among the Christian Biblical scholars of his time. In *Martyrs of Palestine* and *Ecclesiastical History*, Eusebius states that Pamphilus was a rich and honorable man from a family of Beirut. He sought perfection through his

was a library that had formed an important center of religious learning for the Christian community in the city. This terrible crime in the name of historical and religious truth might have actually happened after the death of Pamphilus, his wise teacher, after whose name he was nicknamed Eusebius the Pamphili[472]. In the part that follows, we will talk more about him and his other work, *Historia Ecclesiastica* (Church History), which most probably formed the basis for the Church New Testament through a careful process of selecting from the many Christian Writings already in existence.

Although a disciple of the Phoenician Pamphilus, who treated him as if he was his son, Eusebius' attacks on the Phoenicians, mainly Philo of Byblos on Sanchoniathon and Porphyry of Tyre, by discrediting their so-called "pagan" culture and counterfeiting their works, could not be any longer acceptable in the historical sense by professional academics. It was rather based on a religious-political agenda administered by the Christian Emperor who seemed to have ordered Eusebius to forge in the name of Porphyry some writings that he would then use in a political sense.[473] In fact, Constantine's religious-political dictatorship did not only target paganism, as characterized by the Christians of the Roman Empire, such as Eusebius and the like, but also the

---

generosity that surpassed all men for he is said to have given all his property to the poor and to scholars throughout his lifetime. He was ordained a priest in Ceasaria and suffered martyrdom in the seventh year of the Diocletian Persecution, after spending two years in prison where he is said to have written in collaboration with Eusebius who used to frequently visit him, an *Apology for Origen* divided into five books to which Eusebius added a sixth volume. A work that defended Origen Adamantius also known as Origen of Alexandria (184/185 AD–253/254 AD), the famous scholar and theologian of the early Christians noted as responsible for assembling usage information concerning the texts which became the New Testament, and whose work Pamphilus was greatly devoted to, although he had Pierius (nicknames Origen the Younger), a priest, an exegetical writer, preacher and head of the famous catechetical school in Alexandria, as his teacher. We are not conclusively sure that Eusebius worked with Pamphilus on such a title as a whole or throughout some parts of its contexts, but we are certain that Eusebius had access to Pamphilus great library, where he/they studied the Biblical Canon. A lot of texts previously collected by Origen had moved to Pamphilus library at Origen's death. Both the Roman Catholic Church and the Eastern Orthodox Church consider Pamphilus a Saint.

472 Hourany, Youssef, *The Cosmogonic Theory of the Phoenicians*—نظرية التكوين الفينيقية), page 16-18.

473 In fact, the "Letter of Constantine about Porphyry" sent to the bishops and nations everywhere and the "Eunapius' Fragment on Porphyry," suggest that there was an edict by the Emperor to destroy him.

Pythagoreans of the beautifully magnificent school of Pythagoras[474], who became an unwelcome minority.

At any rate, what concerns us just now is an interesting paragraph that Eusebius transmitted to us without probably knowing at all its scientific importance. Though, he might have exposed it on purpose to show the Phoenician "pagan" belief in the powers of nature, which had been considered at the time heretic practices standing as a threat to Christianity. The text shows that Sanchuniathon, translated by Philo of Byblos, related the existence of probably the first quasi-Temple to be erected in the city of Sūr, and its two pillars could have actually been the first symbols of worship ever mentioned in the history of the world. Sanchuniathon wrote through the words of Philo[475]:

Hypsuranius inhabited Tyre, and contrived huts out of reeds and rushes and papyrus: and he quarreled with his brother Ousous, who first invented a covering for the body from skins of wild beasts which he was strong enough to capture. And when furious rains and winds occurred, the trees in Tyre were rubbed against each other and caught fire, and burnt down the wood that was there. And Ousous took a tree, and, having stripped off the branches, was the first who ventured to embark on the sea; and be consecrated two pillars to fire and wind, and worshipped them, and poured libations of blood upon them from the wild beasts which he took in hunting. But when Hypsuranius and Ousous were dead, those who were left, he says, consecrated staves to them, and year by year worshipped their pillars and kept festivals in their honor.

It is very possible that after sailing the sea Ousous reached the island of Sūr[476], not far away from the city of Sūr, and erected two pillars, one for fire and the second for wind. Once done, he faced them abashed, wondering what they really meant to him. He then realized that they now stood as a representation of the two fearsome elements hidden within the powers of nature—elements he could not control. He then set his mind in worship, for he feared the natural elements the pillars represented, and believed them to be deadly measures that the gods used in their fury against people.

---

474 Porphyry wrote a book, *Vita Pythagorae*, on the life of Pythagoras, which remains still an important source about Pythagoreanism.
475 Eusebius, *Praeparatio Evangelica*, Book 1, Chapter 10.
476 In the old times, Sūr was divided into two parts, an inland and an island, before they joined into one.

It is probable that this open air demi-temple or perhaps another one similar to it laid the foundation to what became known later as the Temple of Ba'al-Melkart, built at the time of King Hiram of Sūr around 971 BC–939 BC. Logically, the Temple must have been completed before he died. The date mentioned for the building of the Phoenician Temple in Tyre coincides with the period the Old Testament mentions was allegedly the time of the construction of the Temple of Solomon in Jerusalem with the help of King Hiram of Tyre and his skilled architects and artisans coming from both cities of Sūr and Gebēl. At the time, like their brothers the Egyptians, the Afro-Asiatic Phoenicians were reputed all over the ancient world as a great nation of Sacred Builders, and great builders in Phoenicia prospered mainly in Gebel, a city as old as time itself, so to speak. Surely, if a famous Master Architect by the name of Hiram Abiff had ever existed in Phoenicia, and most probably in Tyre, he would definitely have used the skills of the Geblites in the building of a Temple for his king.

To be more punctilious, moreover, Herodotus (485 BC–425/414 BC)—one of the great Greek historians, known as the "Father of History"—confirmed, without doubt, having seen the whole Temple of Ba'al-Melkart at Sūr. He wrote[477]:

I moreover, desiring to know something certain of these matters so far as might be, made a voyage also to Tyre of Phoenicia, hearing that in that place there was a holy Temple of Heracles[478]; and I saw that it was richly furnished with many votive offerings besides, and especially there were in it two pillars, the one of pure gold and the other of an emerald stone of such size as to shine by night. Having spoken with the priests of the god, I asked them how long time it was since the Temple had been set up. I found these also to be at variance with the Hellenes, for they said that at the same time when Tyre was founded, the Temple of the god also had been set up, and that it was a period of two thousand three hundred years since their people began to dwell at Tyre.

Herodotus seemed to have learned from the Phoenician Tyrian priests that the "temple of god" he saw had been erected a long time ago, or perhaps had been actually built on the ruins of a more ancient one that dated back to the time Tyre was

---

477 Herodotus, *The Histories*, Book II, Paragraph 44, page 94.
478 Heracles is the Greek name for the sun-god Ba'al and Melkart (Melqart).

established[479]. That by itself fits very well the Sanchoniaton version of the story. He could have been, though, mistaken about one little detail—the emerald stone—or then again, maybe not, for in fact, other Phoenician records narrate that the Temple was one-of-a-kind in all of ancient Loubnan. It stood magnificently impressive. At each side of its entrance, two winsome pillars stood as guards to the main door—made of Cedar wood. One of them was made of Hajjar al Urjouwan, the Purple Stone or Ruby (not an emerald stone), and the other shone as Crystal or Pure Gold. These two Pillars could no longer symbolize fire and wind as was the case of the first Temple prototype, but rather Justice and Mercy, the two great functions of the Universal God Al-Ēlyon.

At any rate, this is a beautiful representation of the Temple of Sūr that mirrors to a certain extent the story of Solomon's Temple in the Old Testament. Yet, once again, the same question whirls in the mind of the suspicious. Could the Temple of Solomon be then just a plain exact copy of the Temple of Ba'al-Melkart? The answer is simple: NO. Unlike the Temple of Solomon, which is supported by no historical or archaeological proof and was only mentioned in the Old Testament, the Temple of Sūr was cited by Sanchoniathon (in its most ancient version), could have been used for the *Initiation* ceremony of Pythagoras, was mentioned by Herodotus, and was visited by Alexander the Great. The latter, who deemed himself to be the son of the incarnated god Heracles (Hercules), known as Melkart, had a dream to visit it. He did, but not only did he pay Heracles homage, but he convened a ritual there; something the Priests of Baal utterly refused, for only the High Priest could perform such an honorable, holy feat. Obviously, we can openly deduce and in conclusive verification after what has been thus far thoroughly exposed, that the Temple of Solomon is nothing but an imaginary copy of both the Temple of Ba'al-Melkart and that of Ur-Shalim. The Temple of Solomon as presented to us in the Old Testament is hence only a myth. Therefore, the First Temple Period is entirely and undoubtedly a fictive period in the history of the Hebrews for reasons we have plainly exhibited in this book, particularly concerning the exact time period of their origin, which had proved to be in harmony with the rising of the Persian King, Cyrus II. That being said, then when was the first real Temple of the Hebrews erected in the occupied Jerusalem?

Temple of Yahweh in Jerusalem

---

479 If it is to be calculated as 2300 years from his time then it would be noticed that Tyre was founded sometime around 2750 BC.

The *Aebirou-al-naher*—known as the Hebrew priests and families who began crossing the river from the time Cyrus II wrote his famous edict of transfer and support—were Chaldean-Babylonians, as we have seen before. They lived, prospered, and multiplied in what is now called Iraq, and precisely in the city of Ur, of Sumerian origin and later Akkadian, which means "city" in these two languages—an important city-state of ancient Sumer, chiefly, its capital. It continued to be one of the most significant places during the Chaldean period, thus, "Ur of the Chaldeans," cited in the Old Testament.

The natives[480] of the Land of Canaan-Phoenicia called these newcomers the *Aebirou-al-naher* (those who crossed the river), *Ebraniyine*, later known—under the leadership of Ezra—as the Hebrews. In their venture to settle down, the Hebrews encountered great difficulties and local resistance against their many attempts to build the Temple and control the land, as mentioned in the Old Testament in both accounts of Ezra 4 and Nehemiah 2. In fact, Hebrew/Jewish/Israeli history began with both Ezra (Esdras) and Nehemiah; both were Persian scribes.

It is relevant to quote Ezra (4:1-3):

Now when the adversaries (the indigenous people of the Land) of Judas and Benjamin (the Ebraniyine), heard that the children of captivity built the Temple unto the Lord God of Israel, they came to Zerubbabel and to the chief of the fathers, and said unto them, 'Let us build with you: for we seek your God, as ye do; and we do sacrifice unto him ... ' But Zerubbabel and Jeshua and the rest of the chiefs ... said unto them, 'ye have nothing to do with us to build a house unto our God; but we ourselves together will build unto the Lord God of Israel, as King Cyrus the king of Persia hath commanded us[481].'

---

480 At the time, the native population of the Land of Canaan/Phoenicia were mainly a component of Canaanite/Phoenician tribes like the Amorites, Jebusites, (Arameans), etc., mentioned in Judges 1:1-36 to have continued to dwell in Jerusalem (and other places in the Land of Canaan) within the territory mainly occupied by both tribes of Judah and Benjamin. Other Gentile groups like the Syrians, Samaritans, etc., seem to have existed there as well.

481 The use of such a sentence "as King Cyrus the king of Persia hath commanded us" to build a house to the Lord God of Israel is quite an interesting note to ponder.

Reading that will immediately entice us to wonder: Why would the people of the land want to share the Ebraniyine in the building of a Temple to the God of Israel? From what we have perceived so far, and if the text was correct, it could be understood from a different view: a linguistic misinterpretation. To the Ebraniyine, the word "Israel" meant "Striving against Ēl," which translates into striving against the Canaanite/Phoenician God, as we have explained in Chapter 7. To the Phoenicians, "Israēl" meant *Ashirat-Ēl* or *Israt-Ēl*, which signifies the "Religious Family of Ēl." Therefore, a Temple to the God of Israel—for the Phoenicians—meant a Temple to Ēl constructed by his loving family of priests. However, a Temple to the God of Israel—for the Hebrews—insinuated a Temple to the Babylonian God, Ea, Iaô, Iâh, Yahve, built by the people who strove against Ēl, his land, and his people. Within that context, we could once again refer to the tale in the Old Testament (Genesis 32:22-32) about Jacob (Zoro-Babel or Zerubbabel), who strove against the God Al (not struggling with Him), defeated him, changed his name into Israel, and became the Hebrew founder of the state of Israel. In fact, they could have stated, more truthfully, that they intended to build a Temple to the God of *Ashiratyahweh* or *Israyhwh*, for they were Isra-Yâho—the children and family of Yahweh.

Indeed, they could well have done so, for striving against the God Ēl was their biggest issue and concern, as written in the Old Testament and the Dead Sea Scrolls. It was, in fact, their main goal. The People of the Land—the Canaanite/Phoenicians—rejected the project of the Ebraniyine, the Biblical people of Judah and Benjamin, as soon as they realized that these foreigners were, in truth, striving against their Father-God. That being said, it would be then understood why the Hebrews/Jews actually strove against the son of Ēl, *Immanuel*, Jesus Christ, later on, as clearly stated in the New Testament.

And so, in Ezra (6:14-15), we read:

So the elders of the Jews built, and they prospered through the prophesying of Haggai the prophet and Zechariah the son of Iddo. And they built and finished [it], according to the commandment of the God of Israel, and according to the command[ment] of Cyrus, Darius, and Artaxerxes king of Persia. And this house [temple] was finished on the third day of the month of Adar (March), which was in the sixth year of the reign of Darius the king.

The text herein reflects the fact that "Darius the King" was in fact Darius II—King of Persia from 424 BC to 404 BC—the son of Artaxerxes I, who reigned between 465 BC and 424 BC. Accordingly so, they would then have completed the Temple in c. 418 BC, six years after Darius II came to power in 424 BC. That being said, the claim that it was under construction in c. 520–515 BC, under Darius I, as mentioned in the Old Testament itself, would then be totally erroneous. Besides, it would not be logical to believe that such a temple would have taken them some hundred years to build, from c. 516 BC to 418 BC.

It is, though, a bit strange to read in the Old Testament that both temples' narratives (the *alleged* first and the real second) were almost written in the same manner, using Phoenician artificers and materials in the building process[482]. This surely suggests the large amount of forgery done on the Biblical text. We frankly don't understand why the authors wanted to parallel the narration of the construction of the two temples, but we might greatly suppose that the temple built under the Persian authority was most probably erected on the ruins of the Temple of Shalim.

Following from that perspective, we believe that when Biblical scholars termed this period as the Second Temple Period in the history of the Biblical Hebrew/Jewish nation, they made one of their biggest historical mistakes. In truth, this period, the Persian Period, is the Hebrew/Jewish First Temple Period. Henceforth, we confidently suggest that this is the Temple of Solomon (*Shlomo*) and was built in 418 BC on the ruins of the Temple of Shalim built by Milki-Sedek and destroyed later by the Neo-Babylonian king, Nebuchadnezzar II, in c. 586/587 BC.

It is probably on the ruins of the ancient Canaanite/Phoenician Temple of Šalim (Shalim) that formed the courtyard of the much later Persian/Hebrew[483] Temple of Solomon (Shlomo),

---

482 Ezra 3:7, "They also gave money to the masons and the carpenters, and food, drink, and oil to the people of Sidon and Tyre to bring cedar logs from Lebanon to the sea, to Joppa, according to the permission which they had from Cyrus king of Persia." Please compare this quote with 2Samuel 5:11; 1Chronicles 14:1; 1Kings 5; 6; 7; 8; and 2Chronicles 2:3.

483 Ezra 6:1-5, "Then King Darius issued a decree, and a search was made in the archives, where the treasures were stored in Babylon. And at Achmetha, in the palace that [is] in the province of Media, a scroll was found, and in it a record [was] written thus: In the first year of King Cyrus, King Cyrus issued a decree [concerning] the house of God at Jerusalem: Let the house be rebuilt, the place where they offered sacrifices; and let the foundations of it be firmly laid, its height sixty cubits [and] its width sixty cubits, [with] three rows of heavy stones and one row of new timber. Let the expenses be paid from the king's treasury. Also let the gold and silver articles of the house of God, which Nebuchadnezzar took from the temple which [is]

that the "man in white," say Yāwshu the *Ashaya*, had firmly stepped in, after they turned it into an imperfect structure. With great fascinating authority, he shoved out the impious traders and money dealers from the Temple[484], saying[485], "It is written, My house shall be called a house of prayer, but you have made it a den of thieves."

Similarly in citing the outer court as the place where this event happened, L.A. Waddell wrote[486]:

> The small size of the Temple proper is accounted for by the fact that *the worshippers remained outside, the priests only went within. The altars were in the court in the open air. In this great or outer court the prophets generally addressed the people, as also did our Lord on many occasions; and even this court is termed 'The House of the Lord,' and is 'The Temple' in the New Testament.* It must certainly have been this outer court of 'the temple' which Christ called 'My Father's House,' from whence he drove out 'the sheep and the oxen, and he poured out the changer's money and overthrew their tables'; for neither religiously nor physically could these have been within the temple-house proper.

Although we agree with him on the location where this might have happened, we are totally in disagreement with him on the official position of Jesus Christ. It is not because these things could not have been practiced within the temple-house proper on both religious and physical levels, that Yāwshu walked in, casting out the merchandise and money traders, but because this outer-court formed an essential part of what was left from the Temple of

---

in Jerusalem and brought to Babylon, be restored and taken back to the temple which [is] in Jerusalem, [each] to its place; and deposit [them] in the house of God."

484 Matthew 21:12, "Then Jesus went into the temple of God and drove out all those who bought and sold in the temple, and overturned the tables of the money changers and the seats of those who sold doves." Also in Mark 11:15-16.

485 Matthew 21:13. Also in Mark 11:17, "Then He taught, saying to them, Is it not written, My house shall be called a house of prayer for all nations? But you have made it a 'den of thieves.'" This is also mirrored in the book of the *Ashayas* that had been purposely transformed to appear Jewish. Isaiah, 56:7, "Even them I will bring to My holy mountain, And make them joyful in My house of prayer. Their burnt offerings and their sacrifices [Will be] accepted on My altar; For My house shall be called a house of prayer for all nations."

486 Waddell, L.A., *The Phoenician Origin of Britons, Scots & Anglo-Saxons*, page 277-278.

Shalim, built by Milki-Sedek, who, after his *Order*, Christ was proclaimed a Priest Forever. Besides, Yāwshu had no formal role or any role whatsoever within the Judaic religion; he was neither a rabbi of the Pharisees, nor a priest of the Sadducees with Jewish authority to enter the temple and practice some sort of ritual, as we have explained in the previous chapter.

Part IV

Yāwshu the Ashaya

Extra-New Testament Sources, the Church New Testament, His Religion & Theology

Chapter 10

The Extra-New Testament Sources

After having practically examined all things related to the persona of "Jesus the Phoenician," beginning with the few Canaanite/Aramaic names and surnames given to Him; his holy conception in the Temple; his family and relatives; his place of birth in the Galilean Bet-Lahem; his disciples; his cultural and religious entourage; his alterity to any of the known Jewish sects of his time; and ending with our perception of the true identity of his Father in Heaven and the Temple of the Son in Ur-Shalim, there are still a few important elements to tackle in this final part of the book.

That being said, we shall learn more about both the religious and socio-political nature that played the most vital part in the development and formation of the Church New Testament. We shall also set sail backwards in space and time and meet the prophesied *Yāwshu the Ashaya* through assimilating his Canaanite/Phoenician-Galilean religious and theological system after tackling the importance of the Q Source and the Doctrine of Marcion—finally, understanding the Christian symbols and the universal message of Love and Peace that characterized his divine and human being. But first, let's have a quick look at the extra-New Testament sources that mention Jesus.

There are actually four main sources that cite an event that could be related to "Christ," "Jesus," or "Christians," outside the Canonical texts. The four sources, however, are not totally clear and have caused tremendous confusion in the historical circle. Thus, they need to be examined herein in chronological order as per the date their specific work was written. First, is the closest to Christ in time, dated at the end of the 1st century AD, while the three others were in the first quarter of the 2nd century AD:

Josephus

The first historian to mention Jesus herein is the Romano-Jewish historian, Flavius Josephus, known simply as Josephus (c. 37 AD–100 AD). Although his three references to Jesus and the origin of Christianity in the surviving manuscripts attributed to him have raised many doubts amongst the general scholarly view —especially the text they termed *Testimonium Flavianum* (Testimony of Flavius) that some consider to be not authentic in its entirety, others, partially—it is still a source we need to tackle here and is the first one among the three penned by Josephus in one of his works.

Therefore, in his *Antiquities of the Jews*, probably written around the years 93–94 AD, he mentioned Jesus twice, James his cousin once, and John the Baptist one time. He wrote[487]:

> Now there was about this time Jesus, a wise man, if it be lawful to call him a man; for he was a doer of wonderful works, a teacher of such men as receive the truth with pleasure. He drew over to him both many of the Jews and many of the Gentiles. He was [the] Christ. And when Pilate, at the suggestion of the principal men amongst us, had condemned him to the cross, those that loved him at the first did not forsake him; for he appeared to them alive again the third day; as the divine prophets had foretold these and ten thousand other wonderful things concerning him. And the tribe of Christians, so named from him, are not extinct at this day.

Reading this *Testimonium Flavianum* carefully, it does not necessarily relate Jesus or the Christ to the Jews, or to any of the three Jewish sects that Josephus mentioned earlier in his book, and the notion that Jesus was thence followed by both Jews and Gentiles confirms our analysis. However, it reports very well that the Roman authorities, at the suggestion of the Jewish chiefs, condemned Jesus to the Cross, similar to what appears in the New Testament. It was thus not on the suggestion of the Gentiles that the condemnation of Jesus by the Romans occurred. In truth, the Gentiles basically followed him, for they believed he was one of them; he truly was. His appearance to them, alive, after three days suggests a Phoenician-Galilean system of belief that matches exactly the Rise of the Phoenix from his ashes after three days and the Resurrection of Adon (Adonis) in the spring, in conjunction with the month Jesus is said to have resurrected, in April. In addition, it is unlikely that Josephus would have used the sentence "He was [the] Christ" in the confirmative when talking about Jesus. If Jesus was the Jewish Messiah and if Josephus believed he was, he would certainly talk about him, and even more fervently, in his other writings, perhaps in his reputed

---

work, the *War of Jews*, as well. Yet, Jesus was only cited another time later on in the same book as the brother of James, the death of whom was reported by Josephus, as we shall see in a bit.

Before we read what he had to say about James and Jesus together in one paragraph, his words on John the Baptist seem to be the only recorded reference of John outside the Church New Testament. Josephus wrote[488]:

> Now some of the Jews thought that the destruction of Herod's army came from God, and that very justly, as a punishment of what he did against John, that was called the Baptist: for Herod slew him, who was a good man, and commanded the Jews to exercise virtue, both as to righteousness towards one another, and piety towards God, and so to come to baptism ... Now when [many] others came in crowds about him, for they were very greatly moved [or pleased] by hearing his words, Herod, who feared lest the great influence John had over the people might put it into his power and inclination to raise a rebellion ... Accordingly he was sent a prisoner, out of Herod's suspicious temper, to Macherus, the castle I before mentioned, and was there put to death.

And concerning James and Jesus, he wrote[489]:

> And now Caesar, upon hearing the death of Festus, sent Albinus into Judea, as procurator. But the king deprived Joseph of the high priesthood, and bestowed the succession to that dignity on the son of Ananus, who was also himself called Ananus ... . But this younger Ananus, who, as we have told you already, took the high priesthood, was a bold man in his temper, and very insolent; he was also of the sect of the Sadducees, who are very rigid in judging offenders, above all the rest of the Jews, as we have already observed; when, therefore, Ananus was of this disposition, he thought he had now a proper opportunity [to exercise his authority]. Festus was now dead, and Albinus was but upon the road; so he assembled the Sanhedrin of judges, and brought before them the brother of Jesus, who was called Christ, whose name was James, and some others, [or, some of his companions]; and when he had formed an accusation against them as breakers of the law, he delivered them to be stoned.

---

488 Ibid., Book 18, Chapter 5, Paragraph 2.
489 Ibid., Book 20, Chapter 9, Paragraph 1.

These are the three passages that mention Jesus or Christ, John, and James. It is important to note, however, that the Jews didn't keep any of Josephus' writings due to the fact that they considered him a traitor, therefore, all knowledge about him and his so-called extant manuscripts comes from Christians, particularly Origen and Eusebius, who seemed to have had access to the Greek versions of his texts. All three paragraphs have been greatly studied by Biblical scholars and history specialists. A great number of them believe the texts to have been interpolated at some point in time by Christian monks who had preserved them.

In fact, under the patronage of Vespasian, the Flavian Emperor, Josephus began writing once he got established in Rome around 71 AD. However, all of his surviving manuscripts in Greek fail to be dated before the 11th century AD, and the oldest of these are tiny fragments that were hand-copied by Christian monastic scribes afterward. Some of the Latin translations of his work originally done in the 4th century AD might have survived from the 6th century AD. Although the following important Christian figures, Justin Martyr (c.100 AD–165 AD), Irenaeus (c.130 AD–202 AD), and Clement (c. 150 AD–215 AD) seem to have referred to Josephus in general terms, the first known comprehensive reference to his work is found in the writings of Origen in the 3rd century AD. Origen cites Josephus's *Antiquities of the Jews* concerning "John the Baptist, baptizing for the remission of sins," and "the death of James the Just, who was a brother of Jesus (called Christ)—the Jews having put him to death, although he was a man most distinguished for his justice."[490]

The second known comprehensive reference to Joseph's work is found in the writings of Eusebius. While penning his *Historia Ecclesiastica* in the 4th century AD, Eusebius mentioned "the condemnation of James the Just by the Jews to be stoned,"[491] preceded by "the beheading of John the Baptist by the younger Herod." He also quoted the passage known as "the Testimony of Flavius"[492] exactly in the same manner as the one found in Josephus' surviving work kept by the Christians. This discovery by itself has caused the scholarly circle to debate the matter further. While some have suggested that part of the passage may have been interpolated by Eusebius, or even before, since the time of Origen, or perhaps sometime before the latter, or maybe in between both, others believe that the passage in its totality may

---

490 Origen, *Against Celsus*, Book 1, Chapter 47.
491 Eusebius, *Church History*, Book 2, Chapter 23:20-22.
492 Ibid., Book 1, Chapter 11.

have been a creation of Christian writers, specifically Eusebius, perhaps in an attempt to exhibit an extra-New Testament reference, mainly *Jewish*, for the life of Christ.

That being said, we shall see in the section that deals with the "Christian Writings and the Formation of the Church New Testament" in the next chapter, the possibility of such tampering with the texts related to Jesus and his origin by the early Church authorities. As for now, let us examine the three other *Roman* extra-New Testament sources about Jesus.

Pliny the Younger

The second text we will examine comes from Gaius Caecilius Cilo or Gaius Plinius Caecilius Secundus, better known as Pliny the Younger, a Roman lawyer, author, magistrate, and senator who lived approximately between 61/62 AD and 112/113 AD. He seems to have been a friend of the historian Tacitus that we will come to mention next, as well as Suetonius, whom he employed among his staff.

In one of his letters to Emperor Trajan residing in Rome at the time he was on a mission around 111 AD in Bithynia, a Roman province in Asia Minor, Pliny sounded a bit anxious concerning his actions against the followers of Christ living there. In the letter he asked the emperor for guidance and instructions in order to know how to deal with them after forcing them to curse Christ under excruciating severe interrogation. Pliny, who didn't mention the name "Jesus," only "Christ," in his letter, wrote[493]:

> It is my invariable rule, Sir, to refer to you in all matters where I feel doubtful; for who is more capable of removing my scruples, or informing my ignorance? Having never been present at any trials concerning those who profess Christianity, I am unacquainted not only with the nature of their crimes, or the measure of their punishment, but how far it is proper to enter into an examination concerning them ... .
>
> In the meanwhile, the method I have observed towards those who have been brought before me as Christians is this: I asked them whether they were Christians; if they admitted it, I repeated the question twice, and threatened them with punishment; if they persisted, I ordered them to be at once punished: for I was persuaded, whatever the nature of their opinions might be, a contumacious and inflexible obstinacy certainly deserved correction ... .

493 Pliny the Younger, *Letters of Pliny*, Book 10, Letter 96.

They affirmed the whole of their guilt, or their error, was, that they met on a stated day before it was light, and addressed a form of prayer to Christ, as to a divinity, binding themselves by a solemn oath, not for the purposes of any wicked design, but never to commit any fraud, theft, or adultery, never to falsify their word, nor deny a trust when they should be called upon to deliver it up; after which it was their custom to separate, and then reassemble, to eat in common a harmless meal. From this custom, however, they desisted after the publication of my edict, by which, according to your commands, I forbade the meeting of any assemblies. After receiving this account, I judged it so much the more necessary to endeavor to extort the real truth, by putting two female slaves to the torture, who were said to officiate' in their religious rites: but all I could discover was evidence of an absurd and extravagant superstition ... .

Pliny didn't link the Christians to the Jews, and his clear description about them as people of good social behavior who meet at dawn, addresses a prayer to Christ as God, and bind themselves by a solemn oath, greatly resembles the description offered about the Essens of Qumran Community, although we know that such a ritual was practiced by all ascetic groups of Phoenicia-Galilee and Palestine, collectively named Essenes, as we have seen in Chapter 8. Like Suetonius, who we shall cite after Tacitus, Pliny judged the Christian faith as a superstition.

Tacitus

The third text is by Publius (Gaius) Cornelius Tacitus, a senator and historian of the Roman Empire who lived sometime between 56 AD and 117 AD and was thus a contemporary to Suetonius and seems to have been a friend of Pliny. In his *Annals*, probably written around 116 AD, he reported the execution of Christians by Nero after the six-day fire he inflicted on Rome in 64 AD. In the quoted passage, he recalled the story of Jesus Christ and his judgment by Pilate. Tacitus wrote[494]:

Consequently, to get rid of the report, Nero fastened the guilt and inflicted the most exquisite tortures on a class hated for their abominations, called Christians by the populace. Christus, from whom the name had its origin, suffered the extreme penalty during the reign of Tiberius at the hands of

---

494 Tacitus, *Annals*, Book 15, Chapter 44.

one of our procurators, Pontius Pilatus, and a most mischievous superstition, thus checked for the moment, again broke out not only in Judæa, the first source of the evil, but even in Rome, where all things hideous and shameful from every part of the world find their centre and become popular. Accordingly, an arrest was first made of all who pleaded guilty; then, upon their information, an immense multitude was convicted, not so much of the crime of firing the city, as of hatred against mankind. Mockery of every sort was added to their deaths. Covered with the skins of beasts, they were torn by dogs and perished, or were nailed to crosses, or were doomed to the flames and burnt, to serve as a nightly illumination, when daylight had expired.

Again, like his coeval and friend, Pliny, Tacitus didn't connect the Christians to the Jews and considered them a class of people of wicked superstition who took their name from Christus. Also, like Pliny, he exposed the persecution of the Christians by the Romans.

Suetonius

The last historian to mention was also a Roman, a biographer by the name of Suetonius (c. 69 AD–after 122 AD). In his work, known as *De vita Caesarum* (The Lives of the Twelve Caesars), most likely written in around 121 AD during the reign of the Emperor Hadrian, for whom he worked as a secretary, some scholars thought Suetonius had made reference to Christ, the founder of Christianity. In the part when he narrates the life of Claudius, he wrote[495]:

He banished from Rome all the Jews, who were continually making disturbances at the instigation of one Chrestus.

It is highly unlikely that the name "Chrestus," cited here would mean and refer to Jesus Christ for two reasons actually. The first is that it would be impossible to place Jesus the Christos in Rome around 49 AD at the time of Claudius, since he is reported to have existed during the time of Tiberius. The second reason would be that Jesus Christ was never considered a threat and troublemaker (as were the Zealots in Jerusalem) to Rome

---

495 Suetonius, *The Lives of the Twelve* Caesars, Book 5, CLAUDIUS, Chapter 25.

even during his ministerial life, as cited in the New Testament[496]. In addition, early Christians were not the ones who caused disturbances; on the contrary, they were the ones who were persecuted for their beliefs.

Therefore, we conclude that this phrase penned here by Suetonius does not refer to Christ. Suetonius, however, refers to a prior expulsion of the Jews from Rome at the time of Tiberius, when he wrote[497]:

> He suppressed all foreign religions, and the Egyptian and Jewish rites, obliging those who practised that kind of superstition, to burn their vestments, and all their sacred utensils. He distributed the Jewish youths, under the pretence of military service, among the provinces noted for an unhealthy climate; and dismissed from the city all the rest of that nation as well as those who were proselytes to that religion, under pain of slavery for life, unless they complied. He also expelled the astrologers; but upon their suing for pardon, and promising to renounce their profession, he revoked his decree.

We believe that at the time of Tiberius, when Christianity was still in its infant stages in the course of history, the Jews and their practices were not accepted in Rome. When Christians gained their identity less than fifty years later in Rome at the time of Claudius, as followers of Jesus Christ—whose Messianic mission and life had caused much trouble to Judaism at the heart of Jerusalem—the tension between Jews and Christians became evident and seems to have resulted in a commotion, which first led the authorities in Rome to intervene. Only in that perspective we can understand the above phrase used by Suetonius in Claudius, as such (italics mine)—

> He banished from Rome all the Jews, who were continually making disturbances at the instigation of *the Christians*.

---

496 Matthew 27:23-24, "And the governor said, Why, what evil hath he done? But they cried out the more, saying, Let him be crucified. When Pilate saw that he could prevail nothing, but that rather a tumult was made, he took water, and washed his hands before the multitude, saying, I am innocent of the blood of this just person: see ye to it."

497 Suetonius, *The Lives of the Twelve* Caesars, Book 3, TIBERIUS, Chapter 36.

Moreover, in Suetonius's narration of the life of Nero, he mentioned the Christians as people of a new religion definitely apart from Jews and Judaism when he wrote[498]:

He (Nero) likewise inflicted punishments on the Christians, a sort of people who held a new and impious superstition.

Similar to both authors that preceded him here, Pliny and Tacitus, Suetonius' opinion about Christians as people of superstitious beliefs, using the following words in Latin, *Superstitionis novae et maleficae*, meaning, "novel malefic superstition," is simply rejected by myself as well and does not concern us in today's perception of Christianity as a religion of Love, Peace, and Grace, nor in its primary original conception by Christ. What really matters here is citing Christians as people distinct from Jews.

We have previously reported that the Talmud also cited Jesus in person but presented him and his mother in a very disgraceful manner, as we have seen in both the Introduction and in Chapter 3.

---

498 Ibid., Book 6, NERO, Chapter 16.

Chapter 11

The Church New Testament

Having finished the exposé of the most important extra-New Testament sources we have found, let us now have a look at how things actually developed and then formed since the Crucifixion of Yāwshu and his Glorious Resurrection until the time of Eusebius, the Church's first historian and Roma's first theologian.

The Development of the Church New Testament

As traditionally defined, the Book or Canon that was called the New Testament, and which has been accepted by the majority of Christians worldwide, is a set of 27 books. They are divided into: the four Gospels, which explore the Good News of the Life, Teachings, Death, and Resurrection of Jesus Christ; one Acts of the Apostles, narrating the Apostles' ministries in the early Church period; 21 Letters of the Apostles that describe the Christian doctrine and teachings; and, finally, one Book of Revelation or the Apocalypse, which closes with a text of prophecy, symbols, and the end of times. The New Testament has been *ipso facto* regarded as a divinely inspired work.

First thing first, it seems that these early Christian writings, canonized later in the 4th century AD by the Church as the "Church New Testament," were written in Koine Greek in the 1st and 2nd centuries AD, starting from around 51-52 AD (with Paul) and ending between 90-110 AD (with John). However, it appears there was an interesting source that was not canonized and which had actually inspired both the canonized gospels of Luke and Matthew. A source that came into existence no more than 50 AD, surely before Mark, and known as the Q Source, we will tackle later on in the last chapter of the book.

At any rate, the authors of these 27 canonized books are divided as follows:

- Gospels: Matthew, Mark, Luke, John.
- Acts of the Apostles: Luke.

- Letters of the Apostles: of which eight were written directly by Paul (including the Letter to the Hebrews) and six were indirectly penned by him yet through his disciples, one by James and one by Jude (the cousins and not blood-brothers of Jesus), two by Peter, and three by John.
- Book of Revelation: John.

That being briefly presented, we shall move now to the part that would undoubtedly shed an important light on the approximate timing when the writings were executed. We shall begin with Paul.

Paul

Paul was the only one amongst the writers of the Church New Testament who was not one of the Twelve Disciples and/or Seventy Apostles of Jesus whom we have mentioned in Chapter 6. It is traditionally believed, based on the Church New Testament, precisely from the Letters of Paul and the Acts written by Luke, his companion, that Paul (Paulus), originally named Saul (Šā'ûl), was a native of the city of Tarsus, the capital of the Roman province of Cilicia[499]. He was a Hebrew born of Hebrews, a Pharisee[500], who during his youth, was sent to Jerusalem to receive his education at the school of Gamaliel[501], a famous Rabbi at the time[502]. So, a fervent or fanatic Jew, Saul seemed to have zealously persecuted the early Christians in hope of destroying the newly born religion and the Church. However, on the road to

---

499 According to Canaanite/Phoenician tradition, Cilicia was founded by Cilix, the brother of Kadmus and Europa, being all children of Agenor, King of Tyre, or children of Phoenix, who is sometimes pictured as their brother. Tradition says that when Kadmus failed to find in Greece his sister Europa kidnapped by Zeus, Cilix went to search for her in Asia Minor where he settled. Thus, the land was named Cilicia after him.

500 Philippians 3:3-5, "For we are the circumcision, who worship God in the Spirit, rejoice in Christ Jesus, and have no confidence in the flesh, though I also might have confidence in the flesh. If anyone else thinks he may have confidence in the flesh, I more so: circumcised the eighth day, of the stock of Israel, [of] the tribe of Benjamin, a Hebrew of the Hebrews; concerning the law, a Pharisee."

501 Acts 22:3, "I am indeed a Jew, born in Tarsus of Cilicia, but brought up in this city at the feet of Gamaliel, taught according to the strictness of our fathers' law, and was zealous toward God as you all are today."

502 Prominent Scholars like the German Helmut Koester have expressed their doubts concerning this issue. It is not determined if Paul either was in Jerusalem at the time the New Testament says he was or had been taught by this Jewish Rabbi.

Damascus one day, Paul had a vision of Christ calling him to stop persecuting him (Acts 9:3-6; 22:6-10; 26:12-16). It was this spiritual encounter with Christ that made Paul change his life completely. He converted and became one of the most religious personalities of the early Apostolic Age of the Church. Indeed, he was the most important figure attributed for the foundation of many churches in Asia Minor and Europe.

This is the general view agreed upon by the Church regarding Paul: his Jewish origin, his conversion by Christ, and his great role in the foundation of Christianity. However, the contradiction begins immediately from the New Testament itself, for we learn that Paul was a Roman citizen[503] by birth, as was his father[504]. A native Roman citizen of Tarsus, Paul might have learned Koine Greek, the official language of the Roman Empire, and encountered Greek philosophy, especially Stoicism, which was very dominant there; he seems to have used the philosophy's terms and metaphors in his letters.

Now, the question that scholars have raised is whether Paul actually obtained Roman citizenship, since such a privilege was uncommon at the time. Yet, according to Roman laws inscribed in the self-governing city of Tarsus, where citizenship had not been offered to every citizen there, Paul could have then only obtained such honor if he had been indeed a member of a family with high social status that had been living there for four or more generations past. If that was the case, and we think it was, then Paul could have been given Roman citizenship by birth from his father, who had been given it in turn from his father, etc., a privilege he stood up for, defending his right when the law had been broken by Roman centurions and commanders (as we have just seen in the footnotes 692 and 693).

It would be then very probable that Paul was in fact a Roman Gentile citizen who had converted to Christianity, not Judaism. His ministry was always performed among the Gentiles and not

---

503 Acts 16:37-38, "But Paul said to them, They have beaten us openly, uncondemned Romans, [and] have thrown [us] into prison. And now do they put us out secretly? No indeed! Let them come themselves and get us out. And the officers told these words to the magistrates, and they were afraid when they heard that they were Romans."
504 Acts 22:25-28, "And as they bound him with thongs, Paul said to the centurion who stood by, Is it lawful for you to scourge a man who is a Roman, and uncondemned? When the centurion heard [that], he went and told the commander, saying, Take care what you do, for this man is a Roman. Then the commander came and said to him, Tell me, are you a Roman? He said, Yes. The commander answered, With a large sum I obtained this citizenship. And Paul said, But I was born [a citizen]."

among the Jews[505], and he is best known as "Apostle to the Gentiles,"[506] hence, "Paul of the Gentiles." Therefore, while some scholars see him in opposition to 1st century AD Judaism because of his "Theology of the Gospel" that sped up the separation of Christian religion from Judaism, we find the development of his teachings taking the very logical path since its conception by Yāwshu, for it has nothing to do with Judaism. In the same manner, while scholars still believe that his writings regarding Faith in Christ were alone vital in the salvation for both Gentiles and Jews as the main cause that made the schism between the followers of Christ and mainstream Jews unavoidable and enduring, he in fact, preached the non-Jew Yāwshu he knew and comprehended because the belief in him would grant Salvation to the whole world. It is not though by coincidence that the Gentiles were converted easily and in great numbers in comparison to Jews, who were difficult and had but very few converts. Thus, his clear argument exposed in the New Testament that Gentile converts did not need to become Jews, get circumcised, or even observe the law of Moses as requisite to be Saved, is another piece of evidence that Paul speaks in Gentile Christian tongue, not Jewish.

Having said that, it would also be inconceivable for us to consider that Paul, who had been presented as having such a powerful religious character after his conversion by Christ—a glorious event that inspired and helped him in his mission to change the world and build many churches in both Asia Minor and Europe—to present himself as a Jewish Pharisee[507]. According to the New Testament and the Church's belief, when Paul experienced his spiritual meeting with Christ on the road to Damascus, he became a dedicated and devout Christian, and thus, his later statement of being a Pharisee would not be suitable for the Church or his conversion.

This second contradiction compels us to believe that any Jewish connection given to Paul by both authors of the Acts and Pauline Letters (Philippians), mainly, in the following way, "I more so: circumcised the eighth day, of the stock of Israel, [of] the tribe of Benjamin, a Hebrew of the Hebrews; concerning the law, a Pharisee," is nothing but a deliberate attempt to show that at the

---

505 Acts 22:18, "and saw Him saying to me, Make haste and get out of Jerusalem quickly, for they will not receive your testimony concerning Me."
506 Romans 1:5-6; 11:13; Galatians 2:8; Acts 22:21, etc ...
507 Acts 23:6, "But when Paul perceived that one part were Sadducees and the other Pharisees, he cried out in the council, Men [and] brethren, I am a Pharisee, the son of a Pharisee; concerning the hope and resurrection of the dead I am being judged!"

time of his circumcision he was given the name of Saul—which must have been a Jewish custom—in memory of Saul (Sha'ul), the first king of the Israelites. In fact, this was only a part of the rhetoric used by authors or copiers of the texts that formed the Church New Testament and related it to the Old Testament. Conclusively, what had been falsely written about the Jewish origin of Paul, who succeeded Jesus on the throne of Christianity and founded many churches, is greatly identical to what has been penned, especially by Matthew, about Jesus, the founder of Christianity, and his genetic ties to King David, who succeeded Saul on the throne of Israel. The formula Saul–David–Jesus–Saul (Paul) is then exposed in its entirety as a fabrication.

Thus, we strongly believe that this was not the case in factual history, and in the same method we have determined that Yāwshu and his Disciples—except for two—were all Galilean-Phoenicians, we thus ascertain that Paul, most likely, was a Roman Gentile that converted to Christianity. Yet, was he Galilean? St. Jerome, one of the Church Fathers, believes so. In his work, *On Illustrious Men*, he wrote[508] in the same Church rhetoric:

> Paul, formerly called Saul, an apostle outside the number of the twelve apostles, was of the tribe of Benjamin and the town of Giscalis in Judea. When this was taken by the Romans he removed with his parents to Tarsus in Cilicia.

Should we look at the maps, we would find that Giscala (Gischala or Giscalis) is located in the Galilean-Phoenician region, and very close to the Ladder of Tyre, as a matter of fact. If Jerome's report proved to be true, then Paul would be another Galilean-Phoenician Apostle of Yāwshu. In the *Catholic Encyclopedia*, the Galilean origin of Paul's family is not at all improbable. Perhaps Paul's Galilean origin would explain what came in Acts (24:5):

> For we have found this man a pestilent fellow, and a mover of sedition among all the Jews throughout the world, and a ringleader of the sect of the Nazarenes.

However, even if Paul was indeed a Gentile Roman from Tarsus, he could have been *enlightened* into the sect of the Nazarenes by Yāwshu when he appeared to him on the road to Damascus and got *Initiated* thereafter by an unknown Christian Teacher who might have met him. Definitely, the sect of the

---

508 St. Jerome, *On Illustrious Men*, Chapter 5.

Nazarenes here mentioned were not the Jewish-Christians of Judea that had been related to the writing of the hypothetical Gospel of the Nazoraeans in the 2nd century AD as we shall note in one of the coming footnotes. The Nazarenes, of whom Paul was probably a member, were essentially active in both Galilee and Mt. Carmel; they formed the ascetic branch of the Ashayas (or Asayas) of whom Yāwshu, Yāwhanan, and Maryām were prominent members, as we have previously related on different occasions.

After this challenging exposé on the true origin of Paul, let us start now with the Christian writings that have been canonized. The earliest of these appears to have been the First Letter to the Thessalonians that was surely written by the Apostle Paul while during his ministry in Athens or Corinth (Kórinthos in Greece), around 51-52 AD.

Although we know that Paul began his first mission a few years earlier in c. 45 AD when he departed to Ephesus in Asia Minor (Turkey), passing by Antioch (in Syria today)[509], we believe that this particular first Christian writing, which would have opened the way for the others to follow suit, might have been the result of the first *official* Christian Assembly convened by James (the cousin of Jesus) in the city of Jerusalem sometime between 49 AD and 52 AD, and attended by Paul, John, and Peter.[510]

It should be noticed, however, that before this first *official* Christian Assembly, the Inner Circle of Yāwshu had most probably, if not certainly, gathered many times after his Death, mainly at Maryām's (his mother's) house in the Galilean Cana of Lebanon and in both Phoenician coastal cities of Sūr (Tyre) and Saydoun (Sidon).[511] We have tackled this issue before in Chapter 6.

---

509 We don't have to forget that Yāwsep of Rameh (Joseph of Arimathea), the great uncle of Yāwshu, was the first Christian missionary. He preached the Lord in Glastonbury, Britain, as early as 35 AD-37 AD. It is said that Maryām of Mejdel (Mary Magdalene) accompanied him during his voyage to the west and landed in France where she is said to have preached the Lord in Marseille. Both Glastonbury and Marseille stood as important places to the Phoenicians.

510 Lenoir, Frédéric, et, Tardan-Masquelier, Ysé (Sous la Direction), *Encyclopédie Des Religions*, Tome 1, page 379.

511 Acts 21:3-5, "When we had sighted Cyprus, we passed it on the left, sailed to Syria (Phoenicia), and landed at Tyre; for there the ship was to unload her cargo. And finding the disciples, we stayed there seven days. They told Paul through the Spirit not to go up to Jerusalem. When we had come to the end of those days, we departed and went on our way; and they all accompanied us, with wives and children, till [we were] out of the city. And we knelt down on the shore and prayed."

That was, however, not the only letter Paul wrote during his preaching ministry. There were also his following Epistles: the First and Second Letters to the Corinthians (the first written in Ephesus, the second in Philippi or Thessalonica in Macedonia), Letter to the Galatians (probably written during his stay in Macedonia), Letter to the Romans (it was most likely written in Corinth), Letter to the Philippians (it was most probably written in Corinth), and finally, Letter to Philemon (it was most likely penned in Rome when Paul was in prison). All six were written sometime between 53/54 AD and 60 AD. Although a matter of great debate, we believe the Letter to the Hebrews[512] was written by him in c. 58 AD to 60 AD, either addressing the Jews in Jerusalem or those living in Rome. The other known six Letters that have been attributed to him—the Second Letter to the Thessalonians, Letter to the Colossians, Letter to the Ephesians, Letter to Titus, and the First and Second Letters to Timothy—were argued by scholars to have been penned by his inspired followers and/or Disciples, sometime around 80 AD and 100 AD. Whatever the case may be, we would not linger on the question of who actually wrote them. We are only exhibiting the fact that they were amongst the books that constituted the Church Canon.

The Pauline Letters were religious and spiritual in their very essence and were mainly addressed to the Gentiles living particularly in Greece, Syria, and Asia Minor. They preached salvation through Jesus Christ and belief in his Father who resides in Heaven, yet also in every human heart, a God of universal Love and Mercy. This theological approach is way too far from the Jewish concept of the Old Testament's deity, portrayed as Yahweh and described as having chosen the people of Israel as his own while discrediting the existence of other world nations and gods, considering them all enemies of the Hebrew Israel and Yahweh, and calling them Goyim.

It was certainly because the Pauline Letters do not take into consideration the already existing Jewish custom, religion, and theology that pushed the Jews at the time to hate and persecute Paul tremendously, and the later Jews to accuse him of anti-Semitism. Yet, the Apostle Paul was in fact orbiting around a

---

512 Other than the Apostle Paul, a few names have been proposed concerning the authorship of this epistle, like Clement of Rome, Barnabas, Luke the Evangelist and Apollos—all four being named among the Seventy Apostles listed in Table 2. Others suggest that the author of this work was a woman called Priscilla, known to have been one of the very first few Jews who were converted to Christianity. The New Testament cites her (Acts, Romans, 1Corinthians, 2 Timothy) as accompanying Paul in his travels along with her husband, Aquila.

different cosmic sphere, for he said in Romans (14:17), "for the Kingdom of God is not eating and drinking, but righteousness and peace and joy in the Holy Spirit."

James:

James was the cousin of Yāwshu and son of Klôpas, also known as Alphaeus, as we have seen in Chapter 3. He was made an Apostle. After Paul's epistles comes the Epistle of James. Following the success of the First (official) Assembly in Jerusalem, which had most probably and ultimately culminated in the assignment of James as Bishop of Jerusalem and most importantly envisioned a road map that they had put together (James, Paul, John and Peter) for the already existing Christian Communities and for the ones to create worldwide, James, like Paul, decided to write an epistle, which might have been revised and polished by a later writer of the 2nd century AD.

It is most probable that James became Bishop of Jerusalem after the Assembly was convened in 49 AD–52 AD, and stayed in his position until his death by lapidation around 62 AD. On his position as head of the Church in Jerusalem, we may refer to the *Church History* by Eusebius, who wrote[513]:

Then James, whom the ancients surnamed the Just on account of the excellence of his virtue, is recorded to have been the first to be made bishop of the church of Jerusalem. This James was called the brother of the Lord because he was known as a son of Joseph, and Joseph was supposed to be the father of Christ, because the Virgin, being betrothed to him, was found with child by the Holy Ghost[514] before they came together, as the account of the holy Gospels shows.

Although we believe that Eusebius made the mistake of considering James as brother of the Lord in this paragraph—an issue which we have dealt with before and have connected them as cousins[515]—he seems to have quoted Clement of Alexandria (c.

---

513 Eusebius, *Church History*, Book 2, Chapter 1:2.
514 It should be Holy Spirit.
515 In chapter 2 of his *De Viris Illustribus* (On Illustrious Men), Jerome (c. 347AD–420 AD) argued that James was not the brother of Jesus but rather his cousin, the son of Mary of Cleophas. Jerome wrote, "James, who is called the brother of the Lord, surnamed the Just, the son of Joseph by another wife, as some think, but, as appears to me, the son of Mary sister of the mother of our Lord of whom John makes mention in his book."

150AD–215 AD) on the date James became Bishop of Jerusalem. Eusebius added[516]:

> But Clement in the sixth book of his Hypotyposes writes thus: For they say that Peter and James and John after the ascension of our Saviour, as if also preferred by our Lord, strove not after honor, but chose James the Just bishop of Jerusalem[517].

Of course, Clement was definitely mistaken when he related the Ordination of James as Bishop of Jerusalem immediately after the Ascension of Christ. We think this would not have happened in around 30AD–33 AD after the Crucifixion of Yāwshu by the Romans, provoked by the Jewish Priests and Pharisees in the manner mentioned in the New Testament.[518] In fact, following his Crucifixion and Resurrection, the Christians were not only rejected and persecuted by the Jews because of the threat they felt coming from Christians on all levels, especially on the theological level as stated in Acts[519], but also by the Romans, who felt unable to control the situation in Jerusalem if the Christians were to retaliate and seek vengeance in the name of Christ. However, early Christians did not cause trouble, for they actually formed a society filled with Love, Peace, and Grace, as taught by their beloved Lord who had conquered Death and had risen.

It is thus historically recorded that the first act of persecution against the Christians in Jerusalem by the Jews was to be connected with the martyrdom of Stephen, stoned to death around 34/35 AD. Within all that dangerous ambiance, it would have been impossible back then for James to organize the Christians in a Church. We believe this vision had to wait for some fifteen years or so until the time the Assembly had been convened, and during a time which James (along with Peter and John) would have found some fertile ground in a very small

---

516 Eusebius, *Church History*, Book 2, Chapter 1:3.

517 On choosing of James Bishop of Jerusalem, Clement could have learned it from the Christian chronicler of the early Church, Hegesippus (c. 110AD–180 AD) whose account of James the Just comes from the fifth and last volume of his now lost five-books work entitled *hypomnemata* (Memoirs), where he is quoted saying, "After the apostles, James the brother of the Lord surnamed the Just was made head of the Church at Jerusalem." Hegesippus was probably known to Jerome through Eusebius, and this piece of information is also cited in his *De Viris Illustribus*.

518 Mark 15:14, "Then Pilate said to them, Why, what evil has He done? But they cried out all the more, Crucify Him!" And in Luke 23:21; John 19:6, 15.

519 Acts 8:1, "… At that time a great persecution arose against the church which was at Jerusalem …"

number of Jews wanting to be converted to Christianity. Meanwhile, Paul, Barnabas, and Peter (as written in his First Epistle) were active among the non-Jews ever since Paul started his mission a few years earlier in around 45 AD, as we have seen above.

This plan for the missionaries laid by the Apostles was mentioned in Paul's Letter to the Galatians (2:7-9) as follows:

> But on the contrary, when they saw that the gospel for the uncircumcised had been committed to me, as [the gospel] for the circumcised [was] to Peter, (for He who worked effectively in Peter for the apostleship to the circumcised also worked effectively in me toward the Gentiles), and when James, Cephas, and John, who seemed to be pillars, perceived the grace that had been given to me, they gave me and Barnabas the right hand of fellowship, that we [should go] to the Gentiles and they to the circumcised.

During his bishopric office, probably between 52 AD and 58 AD, James might have written his letter, focusing on the act of patience and perseverance during trials and temptations, while condemning various sins such as religious fanaticism, evil speaking, fatalism, boasting, falsehood, and oppression, as well as placing warning against vices like ritual formalism that should be replaced by an active love and purity. It calls on his Christian brothers to be patient while awaiting the Second Coming of the Lord Christ and shows the way that enforces the practical duties of the Christian life.

Since we may agree that the First Official Christian Assembly, known also as the Council of Jerusalem, set forth the rules for the Christian life, we may strongly debate on what was the real aim of such Council. The Church New Testament in both books—Paul's Letter to the Galatians (Chapter 2) and Luke's Acts of the Apostles (Chapter 15)—reveals that the Council actually took place to debate whether or not male Gentiles who were to become Christians (followers of Jesus Christ) by converting were required to become circumcised, a system-belief prescribed in the Jewish Law (for an eight days old child) in accordance with the Old Testament's book of Genesis[520]—a Law given by Yahweh to Moses

---

520 Genesis 17:10-11, "This [is] My covenant which you shall keep, between Me and you and your descendants after you: Every male child among you shall be circumcised; and you shall be circumcised in the flesh of your foreskins, and it shall be a sign of the covenant between Me and you."

that unless one is circumcised, one cannot be Saved[521], and which proves to be an "everlasting" sign of the Abrahamic Covenant[522].

It thus became known by reading the Old Testament and therefore the teachings of the Torah that this was the way Abraham signed the covenant with YHWH, setting down the foundation of Judaism. This everlasting signature of the Abrahamic/Mosaic Law by which Hebrew/Jewish men were ordered to sign in blood the covenant with their God in order to live as the Chosen People, was subject to Yahweh's protection as long as they keep it, and his curse, when they break it.

With all due respect to the Church New Testament that considered for a moment in the past a debate occurring between Christian Apostles over the possibility that this Jewish Law should be applicable to the followers of Christ whether they were converted Gentiles or converted Jews, I say it has been totally mistaken, not only on the basis of this low covenant that should be made between Christian men and God, but also on the basis that would demean the Divinity of Yāwshu, the Son of God, and his relationship with His Father in Heaven who has no resemblance whatsoever with Yahweh of the Old Testament. Can anyone, especially Christians, imagine that Christ with all His Spiritual Glory as the Son of God, is connected to his Father in Heaven through a cut in his genitals! What an ignominious thought that would be.

Though the New Testament reveals that the Apostolic Decree reached by James at the Council after hearing Paul, Barnabas, and Peter, retained the prohibitions against the Gentiles from eating meat containing blood or meat of animals not properly slain and against acts of fornication and idol worship, it definitely decided that most of the Mosaic Law, including the requisite for circumcision of their males, was not obligatory in their conversion to Christianity.[523] Yes, according to Biblical scholars, this announcement by itself may have caused a major act of

---

521 Acts 15:1, "And certain [men] came down from Judea and taught the brethren, Unless you are circumcised according to the custom of Moses, you cannot be saved."

522 Genesis 17:13-14, "He who is born in your house and he who is bought with your money must be circumcised, and My covenant shall be in your flesh for an everlasting covenant. And the uncircumcised male child, who is not circumcised in the flesh of his foreskin, that person shall be cut off from his people; he has broken My covenant."

523 Acts 15:19-20, "Therefore I judge that we should not trouble those from among the Gentiles who are turning to God, but that we write to them to abstain from things polluted by idols, [from] sexual immorality, [from] things strangled, and [from] blood."

distinction of the Church from its Jewish roots at a time when the officials of Rabbinic Judaism (the Pharisees) made their circumcision prerequisites even stricter than before.

We, however, believe that there was no actual link between the Church and the Synagogue in the first place to have a split up at any moment in time later on. They are two different religions founded by two different cultures as we have been proving all along in the pages of this book. And should we put it once again in the implicit tongue of the New Testament, we would then quote from the Letter to the Galatians (2:16-19. New Living Translation):

Yet we know that a person is made right with God by faith in Jesus Christ, not by obeying the law. And we have believed in Christ Jesus, so that we might be made right with God because of our faith in Christ, not because we have obeyed the law. For no one will ever be made right with God by obeying the law. But suppose we seek to be made right with God through faith in Christ and then we are found guilty because we have abandoned the law. Would that mean Christ has led us into sin? Absolutely not! Rather, I am a sinner if I rebuild the old system of law I already tore down. For when I tried to keep the law, it condemned me. So I died to the law—I stopped trying to meet all its requirements—so that I might live for God.

The absolute and total dissimilarities at the very core of the human life itself between both Judaic and Christian systems were what resulted in the Crucifixion of Jesus, the stoning to death of Stephen and that of James because he confessed that Jesus is the Savior and Son of God, refusing in his clear voice to renounce his faith in Christ in the presence of the Jews in Jerusalem, and who, according to Eusebius quoting Clement, "was thrown from the pinnacle of the temple, and was beaten to death with a club."[524] Eusebius, furthermore, reported the account of Hegesippus, who is said to have lived immediately after the Apostles from c. 110 AD to 180 AD—an account which Eusebius deemed accurate, taking it from the author's fifth book of his five-book work called *Memoirs*. Eusebius, who had previously described the fact that the Jews, frustrated now since they failed to entrap Paul before he was sent to Rome, turned against James, whom the Apostles had entrusted with the Episcopal seat at Jerusalem, wrote[525]:

---

524 Eusebius, *Church History*, Book 2, Chapter 23:3.
525 Ibid., Chapter 23:16.

So they went up and threw down the just man, and said to each other, 'Let us stone James the Just.' And they began to stone him, for he was not killed by the fall; but he turned and knelt down and said, 'I entreat you, Lord God our Father, forgive them, for they know not what they do.'[526]

Peter (Simon Peter)

Peter was a disciple from the Phoenician-Galilean town of Bethsaida; he was made an Apostle (Cephas). After James' Letter comes the First Epistle of Peter. Although the work is disputed among scholars to be that of the Apostle Peter, suggesting different authors and later timing, we believe it could have been written in the same period during which Paul addressed his Letters to the Gentiles of Asia Minor, around 54 AD and 60 AD, in either Antioch, where Peter stood as bishop, or later in Rome before he died. This letter was mainly addressed to the Gentile Christians of the various churches spreading throughout the regions of Pontus, Galatia, Cappadocia, Asia, and Bithynia, which constituted the five geographical areas that were grounded as Roman provinces in Asia Minor. It seems it has probably inspired —because of the similarities in many of the same features—the later epistles attributed to Paul, which were most probably written by his followers, particularly, the Letter to the Ephesians, Letter to the Colossians, and the Pastoral Epistles (Letter to Titus, First and Second Letters to Timothy).

The Second Epistle of Peter comes directly after Jude (see next). It quotes Jude and considers his text largely, as it clearly identifies Jesus the Son with God the Father. It warns about a threatening heresy to Christians that had arisen because the anticipated Second Coming of Christ had not yet occurred. However, if the author explains that God actually delayed the Second Coming of Christ so that people would have the courage to refuse evil and find Salvation in Christ, it is because sometimes, the Second Coming of Christ also called *Parousia*, which would mean Christ's Physical Resurrection and appearance on Earth, was on the third day, Sunday. It is important to note that the Jews never regarded Jesus Christ as the Messiah they were waiting for. This is simply because he did not accomplish any of their prophesies or Yahweh's promises for his Chosen People, but

---

526 It seems, according to Eusebius, James used the same words uttered by his cousin Jesus when he was on the Cross, as cited in Luke 23:34, "Then Jesus said, Father, forgive them, for they do not know what they do. And they divided His garments and cast lots."

rather fulfilled the prophesy of another people, the people who believed in him first, the Phoenician-Galileans. Like Jude, who remembered the words uttered by Jesus while addressing the Pharisees and Sadducees as "brood of vipers, hypocrites, and blind guides," the letter also indicates the wrongness of "false teachers," who may twist the authentic Apostolic tradition, and forecasts judgment unto them. We have clearly related the matter of how Jews in Jerusalem persecuted the early Christians because they strongly believed in Yāwshu the Meshiha, stoning them to death, as stated in Acts[527]. Consequently, the letter addresses the Christians in all churches and could have been written by Peter around 60 AD to 67 AD since it refers to the Pauline Epistles and quotes Jude. Others suggest it was penned around 80 AD to 90 AD, and still others place the date between 100 AD and 160 AD, considering the work a Pseudepigrapha, and a "disputed writing" as determined by Eusebius, maybe because it calls on Christians to wait patiently for the *Parousia* yet to occur. Christ, however, came first as a Son of Man and appeared a second time through his Glorious Resurrection as God.

Jude

Jude was the cousin of Yāwshu and brother of James. Between the First and Second Epistles of Peter, and after Paul's Letter to the Hebrews, as we have seen earlier, comes in time the Epistle of Jude. It is very probable that during his position as Bishop of Jerusalem, James asked his brother Jude to write a letter in the memory of their beloved cousin, Jesus. It is a short text of 25 verses having some similarities with the Second Letter of Peter (as stated above) and quotes the Apocryphal Book of Enoch. It could have been written in Jerusalem when James was still alive and head of the Church, or a few years after his death, sometime between 60 AD and 90 AD. Others suggest it was penned in the first quarter of the 2nd century AD, thus being a pseudonymous work and a "disputed writing," being part of the *Antilegomena*, as classified by Eusebius. It addresses Christians in general and seems to have been destined to be circulated and read in all churches. In it, the cousin of Jesus exhorts the faithful to defend the Christian Doctrine and the Teachings of Christ, remember the words of the Apostles, and warns his readers about

---

527 Acts 7:59, "And they stoned Stephen as he was calling on God and saying, "Lord Jesus, receive my spirit."
It is said that Stephen, with two thousand other Christians, were all slain in the name of Christ on the same day he was martyred.

the beliefs of errant teachers to whom they may be exposed, probably recalling during the writing of it the words uttered by Jesus to the Pharisees and Sadducees.

Then comes the first gospel in time, contrary to the manner in which the three Synoptic texts were organized and presented in the Church New Testament (Matthew, Mark, Luke). We have already presented a brief summary about all four gospels in the Introduction; however, it is beneficial to present here additional information concerning them. We shall start with Mark.

Mark (John Mark)

It seems that the Gospel of Mark was the first gospel. There are some different theories about the origin of Mark. While the Coptic Church believes he was born in Cyrene, a city of North Africa (known today as Libya), others believe he was the cousin of Barnabas, a Cypriot. We, on the other hand, believe that Mark was a son of one of the Maryāms[528] who followed Yāwshu in Galilee, and thus he could be from any of the following Phoenician-Galilean villages: Bethsaida, Capernaum, an unknown village if he was related to Thomas, or perhaps a native of the Lebanese village of Kana (Qana), tasting and serving the wine at the wedding ceremony. In the list of the Apostles (Table 2), Mark was made an Apostle, probably by Peter, who ordained him Bishop of Alexandria in Egypt, and later, Bishop of Byblos (Gebel) in Phoenicia-Lebanon.

Mark the Evangelist began his narration with the description of the Ministry of Yāwshu from the time he was baptized by his Great Cousin Yāwhanan the Baptist until the time he died, was buried, and resurrected[529]. In fact, for unknown reasons, Mark seems to have abstained from giving his readers information about the origin of Jesus before these two events—Baptism and Resurrection. Unlike Luke and Matthew, both the story of Nativity and the genealogy are absent in Mark. In the Gospel of Mark, we learn about the last week of Jesus' life in Jerusalem and the many characteristics that shaped him as a person of principles and daring actions, an Ashaya (Healer), exorcist, miracle worker, and

---

528 Acts 12:12, "So, when he had considered [this], he came to the house of Mary, the mother of John whose surname was Mark, where many were gathered together praying."

529 Mark 16:6-7, "But he said to them, Do not be alarmed. You seek Jesus of Nazareth, who was crucified. He is risen! He is not here. See the place where they laid Him. But go, tell His disciples—and Peter—that He is going before you into Galilee; there you will see Him, as He said to you."

most importantly an enigmatic Man in White. Mark also portrays Him as the Son of God coming "out of Galilee" with a great hidden secret related directly to his real identity as the Meshiha who exorcises demons and heals the sick, telling his patients to keep it secret while speaking in parables that were sometimes confusing to his Disciples. It is very probable that when writing his gospel later on, Mark worked under the direction of Peter and relied on his preaching since he was his companion, and depended mainly on his memory, although we feel that Mark's account may be the closest to reality amongst all the others. It could have been written in c. 60/64 AD and 68/70 AD in Greek and addressed to Gentile Greek speaking people of the Roman Empire. However, the excessive use of Aramaic words and phrases, such as 'Talitha," "Kumi,"[530] "Korban,"[531] "Abba,"[532] etc., suggests that the Synoptic was probably penned somewhere in Phoenicia (Kana or Byblos), Antioch, or Palestine—in a Gentile Christian atmosphere.

Luke

The Gospel of Luke comes next. It is generally believed that Luke the Evangelist, a young companion and disciple of Paul, who seemed to have probably chosen him as an Apostle, was a Gentile Christian, most likely a physician, educated, well connected, and originating from the Hellenistic city of Antioch in Syria or Phoenicia. Luke wrote his gospel in Greek—although it has some Hamito-Semitic feeling throughout it—around 80 AD–85 AD, addressing the Gentile world of Christians wherever they existed, and assuring them that Christianity is indeed an international religion. His synoptic narrates the Life and Ministry of Yāwshu with a good many historical details from the moment of Birth until Resurrection. While Luke undoubtedly presented Yāwshu as Son of God, he exposed him as a complete Son of Man, having great compassion for the weak, for those who suffer, and those who are regarded as outcasts.

What differentiated Luke from the other three gospels is his clear attention to the role of women in the life of Yāwshu and early Christianity. This is a very important characterization. He appeared to have focused on the important role they played as

530 Mark 5:41, "Then He took the child by the hand, and said to her, *Talitha, cumi*, which is translated, Little girl, I say to you, arise."
531 Mark 7:11, "But you say, If a man says to his father or mother, Whatever profit you might have received from me [is] *Corban*—(that is, a gift [to God])."
532 Mark 14:36, "And He said, *Abba*, Father, all things [are] possible for You. Take this cup away from Me; nevertheless, not what I will, but what You [will]."

followers of Yāwshu, precisely the role of Maryām of El-Mejdel (Mary Magdalene). In fact, the Gospel of Luke, like the Apocryphal Gospel of Bartholomew, is the only one of the Canonical texts that narrates the Great Annunciation of the Divine Birth of Yāwshu to the Virgin Lady Maryām.

We, like the large opinion of scholars, believe in a conclusive manner, that Luke, who was not present with Yāwshu at the time of his ministry, copied or used some of the important materials, particularly when writing his chronology, from the Gospel of Mark, which preceded his work. The Gospel of Luke might have been written under the guidance of Paul, either in Antioch or somewhere in Phoenicia, in Ephesus, or even in Salonika where he may have served as bishop. He might have had access to the *Quelle* documents as well, the Galilean work known also as the Q Source, hypothetical sayings for many of the Teachings of Yāwshu, the existence of which we shall prove later on in the next chapter. Some others even suggest that Luke may have also been informed of a hypothetical unknown hidden written document and/or an oral tradition called the L Source[533], which he incorporated in his gospel like the *Magnificat*, in which Maryām praises God the Savior, the "Prodigal Son," and the "Good Samaritan" stories.

The Gospel of Luke was not the only work written by the Syrian or Phoenician Apostle Luke. His second work, the Acts of the Apostles, which outlines the history of the Apostolic Age, has been always read and examined along with the gospel, so as if forming a single work by the same author. Similarly to his gospel, the Acts was written in Koine Greek, although it has some Hamito-Semitic feel to it, and was addressed to an international Gentile Christian audience. That being said, we believe the Acts is a vital continuation of the Gospel of Luke. It does not reflect, however, any work done by Yāwshu after his Resurrection and Ascension with a prophecy to return, but instead narrates the missionary work of the Disciples and Apostles of the early Christian Church, Greatly Commissioned by Yāwshu to spread his teachings to all nations of the world—the teachings that they carried out so powerfully and faithfully under the guidance of the Holy Spirit. The Acts also emphasizes in a particular manner the life of Paul, starting with his conversion, ministry, arrest, and imprisonment, and finally, his trip to Rome.

While the gospel clearly exhibits the motion of the ministry of Yāwshu from Galilee to Samaria and Judea, then to Jerusalem

---

533 The L Source or "Luke Source" was an early Christian hypothetical oral source only known to Luke.

where the Crucifixion took place, followed by his Glorious Resurrection and Ascension into the Abode of the Father, the Acts begins at that focal point and then goes backward from Jerusalem to Judea and Samaria, Phoenicia-Galilee, Syria, Asia Minor, and Europe towards Rome. Therefore, since it was perceived as a sequel to the gospel, the Acts could then be dated between 85 AD– 100 AD, maybe a few years later. It could have been penned either in Antioch or in an unknown place in Phoenicia, in Ephesus or Salonika, and/or Rome, being the last option.

Matthew

After the Lukan Gospel comes the Gospel of Matthew. Again, as we have seen before, Matthew came from the Phoenician-Galilean town of Capernaum, thus not originated in a Jewish-Christian community as theorized by scholars. He was chosen by Yāwshu to be among his Disciples. We have referred to Matthew in many places throughout this book, explaining that he might have penned his gospel to convince the Jews at the time that Jesus was fulfilling a Jewish prophecy, being the Son of David, a direct descent from Abraham, and born in Judaic Bethlehem, the place where David was said to have been born. Yet, in his gospel, Matthew seems to have exhibited numerous contradictions to his sayings, as we have previously shown. Whatever the case, Matthew narrates the Life, Ministry, Death, and Glorious Resurrection of Yāwshu of Nazareth. He appears to have drawn his knowledge about Yāwshu from his direct connection to him, yet, like Luke, he depended on the Gospel of Mark, on the Q Source, and on some other materials unique to him, a hypothetical oral tradition called the M Source[534]. Thus, it is believed that Matthew could have copied Luke and added to his sayings of Yāwshu from his M Source.

It is traditionally believed that Matthew wrote the original version of his gospel sometime between 80 AD and 90 AD in Hebrew or Aramaic before it was translated into Koine Greek, the version the Church New Testament has. However, it is thought that Matthew could have written two versions by himself; one in Hebrew, which is meant to refer an Aramaic dialect, now lost, and the other, in Greek. There are three additional gospels that have shown some close relation to each other, and which Biblical scholars believe have some connection to the Gospel of Matthew but are not identical to it. They are listed as follows: the Gospel of

---

534 The M Source or "Matthew Source" was an early Christian hypothetical oral source only known to Matthew.

the Hebrews[535], which was considered by Eusebius as one of the "disputed writings"; the Gospel of the Nazoraeans;[536] and the Gospel of the Ebionites[537]. All three have survived only as fragments quoted by early Church Fathers.

Matthew, who most probably wrote his gospel in the region of Galilee, narrates that the hypothetical Jewish Messiah, called Immanuel and who had been rejected by the God's Chosen People of Israel, the Jews, turned his mind and heart away from them, Jerusalem and Judea, after judging them everlastingly. Therefore, Matthew's narration failed to convert the Jews to the new faith, something that made Yāwshu send his Disciples and Apostles to preach amongst the nations around the Mediterranean Basin, in Galilee-Phoenicia towards Antioch, where his teachings were highly accepted, naturally.

John

Next in order comes the Gospel of John. John, the Disciple whom Jesus loved, was from the Galilean town of Bethsaida or its neighboring town, Capernaum. His work is the most mystical and the most spiritually inspired of all that has been written about Yāwshu in the Church New Testament. It strongly differs from the other three Synoptic texts authored by Mark, Luke, and Matthew, which are best described as historical records and recollections of events. That being said, John presents Yāwshu as the incarnation of the Divine Logos, the Eternal Word, through whom all things were made. While focusing on the relationship of the Son to the

---

535 The Gospel of the Hebrews was used among Greek-speaking Jewish Christians in Egypt, where it was composed in Greek in the early 2nd century AD. It has been classified a Jewish Christian gospel yet with various contradictory beliefs, merging Jewish, Gnostic, and Christian thoughts. References to it come first from early Alexandrian Church Fathers, Clement and Origen; it was later known to Jerome who called it the Hebrew Gospel.

536 The Gospel of the Nazoraeans, a hypothetical gospel, probably written in the 2nd century AD in Hebrew for the Hebrew-speaking Jewish Christian communities in Judea, Palestine and Syria. Its hypothetical name, not mentioned by any one of the Church Fathers, was given to some quotations cited by Hegesippus, Origen, Eusebius, and Jerome, perhaps in reference to the Sect of the Nazarenes who soon transformed into Christians or to "men from Nazareth."

537 The Gospel of the Ebionites, which survived only in seven brief quotations by Epiphanius (c. 310/320 AD–403 AD), Bishop of Salamis, Cyprus, in chapter 30 of his work, the *Panarion* (Against Heresies), is regarded as an Apocryphal work thought to have been written in around the middle of the 2nd century AD in Greek and used by a Jewish Christian sect known as the Ebionites who might have lived around the Jordan River.

Father, Yāwshu is then the Word become flesh, the Son of God, and even more explicitly, God incarnate, to whom veneration is required, for he is "the bread of life,"[538] "the light of the world,"[539] "the good shepherd,"[540] "the resurrection and the life,"[541] "the way, the truth, and the life,"[542] and "the real vine."[543]

The Gospel of John exhibits Yāwshu as being a Galilean, relates his public ministry in a very unique way, and gives witness of John the Baptist, making their encounter a blessed moment when the Baptist recognized him as the Lamb of God. It then emphasizes the Seven Miracles of Yāwshu (the Seven Signs), including the most powerful of them, the Raising of Lazarus. John portrays Yāwshu as a Teacher with a Divine role, sharing his secret knowledge with his Disciples only, where a major part of his theological teaching seems to show a major discrepancy with those of the Jews. The Gospel of John gives the reader a strong and affirmative feeling that both ministries are totally in conflict with each other. Thus, the Church and the Synagogue do not match at all. The gospel finishes with the Passion of Christ, his Crucifixion, Death, Burial, Glorious Resurrection, and finally, his appearances to his Disciples in a post-resurrection scene, where he is portrayed as immortal and his spirit remains ever-present in the hearts and minds of faithful Christians.

While some scholars believe it was not John alone who could have written the whole gospel, linking it to a "Johannine Community" that continued the writing process, we shall linger on that matter for only a moment to add that there are many non-Jewish elements within it, and some other non-dualist Christian Gnostic influences, as well. It was probably written in Ephesus, in c. 90 AD–100 AD.

Then follows the Book of Revelation. It opens with these words, "The Revelation of Jesus Christ." In fact, John explains that the Revelation was given by God to Jesus, who in turn gave it to John through an angel. John then resumes with an epistolary

538 John 6:35, "And Jesus said to them, I am the bread of life. He who comes to Me shall never hunger, and he who believes in Me shall never thirst."
539 John 8:12, "Then Jesus spoke to them again, saying, I am the light of the world. He who follows Me shall not walk in darkness, but have the light of life."
540 John 10:11, "I am the good shepherd. The good shepherd gives His life for the sheep."
541 John 11:25, "Jesus said to her, I am the resurrection and the life. He who believes in Me, though he may die, he shall live."
542 John 14:6, "Jesus said to him, I am the way, the truth, and the life. No one comes to the Father except through Me."
543 John 15:1, "I am the true vine, and My Father is the vinedresser."

271

note addressed to his readers, the Christians responsible for the Seven Churches of Asia, before he continues with an apocalyptic depiction of different sorts of events complicated in their structure, probably evoked from prophetic visionary dreams about the coming future that he saw unfolding in front of his inner eye. The book also contains narratives of elementary images, strange figures and creatures that he might have encountered along his spiritual journey to the heavenly realm. All these important symbols in their chronological order—Seven Churches, Throne of God, Seven Seals, Horses, Seven Trumpets, Fire, Blood, Stars, Locusts, Four Angels, Little Scroll, Woman, Dragon, Child, Beasts, Lamb, Seven Bowls, Great Harlot of Babylon, Destruction of Babylon, Judgment of the Beast, the Devil and the False Prophet, End of the Old Jerusalem, Rising of the New Jerusalem on a New Earth under a New Heaven where God and Humanity dwell together after the curse is ended where both the river and tree of life appear for the healing of the nations—could probably be explained in a Kabalistic sense. However, it is not by coincidence that John related the end of the Old Jewish Jerusalem with the destruction of Babylon that had preceded it, and thus, his Revelation would be understood through the correct historical accounts of the people (the Babylonian origin of the *Aebirou-al-naher* of the Jewish Jerusalem) to whom Christ and Christianity have been tied so erroneously. With Immanuēl, the Rising of the New Jerusalem is indeed tied to the ancient Canaanite/Phoenician city of Urušalim, the city of Šalim, Son of Ēl.

At any rate, the work could have been penned in Ephesus, but tradition has it that while being exiled on the Isle of Patmos in the Aegean Sea during the reign of Domitian, John heard the great voice of Yāwshu, as he noted, and began immediately after, the writing of his *Apokalypsis*, his "unveiling of the truth" (in Greek), perhaps originally in Aramaic, around 95 AD–96 AD. He ends it with the promise of the Second Coming of Jesus Christ.

These two books were not the only work attributed to John the Apostle. He also seems to have penned three epistles, one after the other, while in Ephesus, sometime between 96 AD and 110 AD.

The First Epistle of John is the most important. It was written to oppose what Christianity termed as heresy, especially Docetism —a system of belief that claims that Jesus did not come in the flesh, but only in spirit—which might have begun at the time, although it is recorded to have started in the middle of the 2nd century AD. Along with its opposition to heresies, the epistle also illuminates the path for Christians to identify true teachers from the wrong ones by perceiving their sense of ethics, their declaration that Jesus came in the flesh, and their embracement of *Agape*—Love. John opened his letter to his audience with a clear declaration that the Word of Life (Yāwshu), the Eternal Life that was with the Father and was manifested to us (John and the Disciples), can also be heard by them so that they may be united in fellowship with the Father and his Son Jesus Christ.[544] Thus, an eternal union with God is possible through the belief in Christ, his atoning work and advocacy, while living a fully joyful life, without sin, experiencing a life of holiness, obedience, purity, faith, and love.

The Second Epistle of John was addressed to "the elect lady and her children," perhaps he meant, the Church and the faithful, and appears also to defend the Christian belief against Docetism and Gnosticism by condemning their doctrines. Though, like Docetism, Christian Gnostic belief appeared in the 2nd century AD and prospered in the following century and seems to have been in existence at the time John was writing his epistles. Like Docetism, the general belief of Gnostics is that Yāwshu, who resembles the Divine, would not appear in the flesh and associate Himself so closely with the manifested and incomplete low and defiled world of matter; instead, his appearance looked as if in the flesh, and thus his resurrection was only in spirit and not in body.

The Third Epistle of John does not treat any of the Christian doctrinal issues and has been only classified as social and personal, describing a recommendation letter sent by a man calling himself "the Elder"[545] to another one, Gaius[546], asking him to show his loyalty and hospitality to a group of journeying brothers sent to spread the gospel in that part of the world, most probably, Asia Minor.

Having now finished examining the authors and their work, the 27 early Christian books, we shall hence observe as much possible how these books were written as a testimony to the words and teachings of Yāwshu in the Judaic environment of Jerusalem in order to appear alongside the already existing Old Testament—books that were later selected by the Church Fathers, particularly Origen and Eusebius, in their shaping of the Church

---

544 1John 1:1-3.
545 He was most likely John, or perhaps Paul in the pen of John.
546 He was probably the same Gaius, who resided in Corinth and was baptized by Paul, becoming his host, a close friend, and supporter of the Church.

New Testament. In the same context, Adolf Harnack, the German theologian, believed that the Old Testament was not yet closed in the 1st century AD, even among the Jews, and that the Church had added in time some other writings to it, which it held fast[547]. So true, for the Church intentionally connected the Old Testament to her own book, the Church New Testament. He then wrote[548], "Lastly, judging from the standpoint of the Apostolic Age, we should not have been surprised if in the near future the Old Testament had been rejected or set aside by the Gentile Churches."

Indeed it was rejected because the Old Testament was never revered as a Holy Book by the Gentiles, neither before nor after their conversion to Christianity. Thus, its use—conceived and programmed by early Christian authors since the famous Council of Jerusalem was only intended for the Jews to become Christians so that they would become part of the New Covenant through Christ who has the Divine plan of Salvation—and reference to a plan, however, ends the Law of Moses, the Old Covenant, the Old Testament, and replaces it completely.[549] With all that being said, time has proved that the Church failed in her plan—but, so far, Yāwshu has not. Yet, the time has come to say the truth on his behalf.

Christian Writings and the Formation of the Church New Testament

To begin with, we know for sure that the original Christian writings were established for two audiences: the Gentiles who believed in Christ immediately and the Jews who rejected him instantly and still even today. There is so much logical evidence that suggests that the original writings, meant for a Jewish audience, mainly in Jerusalem, were penned in what I term, the "rhetoric of the Church," probably in consequence to the Crucifixion of Yāwshu in 30/33 AD in the city of Jerusalem, the protomartyr of Stephen in 34/35 AD also in Jerusalem, and the continuous persecution of the followers of Christ thereafter.

Although these same writings contained elements like "Christ is the end of the Law,"[550] they were mainly approved at the Council of Jerusalem organized in 49 AD-52 AD by James and

---

547 Harnack Adolf, *The Origin of the New Testament*, page 4.
548 Ibid., page 5.
549 John 1:17, "For the law was given through Moses, [but] grace and truth came through Jesus Christ."
550 Romans 10:4.

attended by Paul, John, and Peter,[551] to convince the Jews at the time that Jesus was one of them, the Messiah fulfilling their prophesies. Thus, persecuting Christians would be wrong and would bring Divine wrath[552] upon them and the Holy City, as reported by Eusebius following the murder of James[553], whereas, believing in Him would be an essential task for their Salvation, something that deemed conversion to Christianity a necessary step on their behalf.

This "rhetoric of the Church" continued to be promoted—in the same manner it was first conceived at the Council of Jerusalem—by the early Fathers, theologians, and historians of the Church, ever since the writings began in the 1st century AD until the formation of the Church New Testament in the 4th century AD. The most prominent of them were: Justin Martyr[554]

---

551 That explains why the first Christian writing, the First Letter to the Thessalonians, by the Apostle Paul, was written thereafter in Athens or Corinth around 50 AD–52 AD. In fact, it would not be a coincidence to notice that the four Apostles who convened at that Council that year had their writings canonized in the Church New Testament.

552 1Thessalonians 2:14-16, "For you, brethren, became imitators of the churches of God which are in Judea in Christ Jesus. For you also suffered the same things from your own countrymen, just as they [did] from the Judeans, who killed both the Lord Jesus and their own prophets, and have persecuted us; and they do not please God and are contrary to all men, forbidding us to speak to the Gentiles that they may be saved, so as always to fill up [the measure of] their sins; but wrath has come upon them to the uttermost."

553 Eusebius, *Church History*, Book 2, Chapter 23:19, "These things are related at length by Hegesippus, who is in agreement with Clement. James was so admirable a man and so celebrated among all for his justice, that the more sensible even of the Jews were of the opinion that this was the cause of the siege of Jerusalem, which happened to them immediately after his martyrdom for no other reason than their daring act against him."

554 Justin Martyr was born a Gentile in Palestine and converted to Christianity by an old Phoenician Christian man probably on the road from Palestine to Rome, but as agreed upon by the first *official* Church Council in Jerusalem, he seemed to have referred to a Christian-Jewish connection in the middle of the 2nd century AD in his two accredited works; *Fisrt Apology* (c. 155/157 AD) where he emphasized the connection between the historical testimony of the gospels and the Old Testament prophecies most likely in a challenging tone to contemporary Marcion who rejected totally that connection, and *Dialogue with Trypho* (c. 160/161 AD) where he had created a dialogue with probably a fictitious Jew (Trypho) he met in Ephesus to convince him that Jesus was the Jewish Messiah and thus conversion was necessary for him. This has all been done to accommodate the Church plan of converting Jews through faith in Christ as the Son of God, although Justin appeared to have attacked Judaism and only had a little knowledge of the Old Testament.

(c. 100 AD–165 AD), Hegesippus (c. 110–180 AD), Irenaeus (c.130 AD–202 AD), Clement (c. 150 AD–215 AD), Tertullian (c. 160 AD–225 AD), Hippolytus Romanus (c. 170 AD–236 AD), Origen (c. 184/185 AD–253/254 AD), Eusebius (c. 260/263 AD–339/340 AD), Athanasius (c. 296-298 AD–373 AD), and instantly after, Jerome (c. 347 AD–420 AD). However, the writings, meant to address the Gentiles and which had no original reference to Christ having a Jewish Messianic role as agreed at the Council, were later tampered with by the Church for the same reason of convincing the Jews that Christ is the Son of God and the only Savior of the world. The reason for this was the fact that Jews formed the most difficult hitch for the world Christian Preaching Mission when compared to Gentiles, who immediately believed Yāwshu as Son of God; the fastest among all nations to accept Him were the people of Galilee-Phoenicia, naturally.

In that sense, Harnack, commenting on one of the works of Justin, wrote[555]:

No one that reads Justin's Dialogue with Trypho but can receive the liveliest impression that the author is simply crying for a New Testament; but, seeing that he cannot produce it *directly as a fundamental document* he is compelled to write endless chapters and laboriously to construct it himself from the Old Testament and the history of Jesus (the Gospels)!

Yet, Justin, being one of the most influential early Christian authorities, speaks—with an undoubted Christian confidence, so as to say—not only of "our doctrines" but also of "our writings,"[556] side by side with the Old Testament, but as yet, he knew nothing of the Scriptures of the New Covenant. He knew though, as he stated, of weekly worship of the Christians on Sunday in the early churches, which comprises of reading aloud in public worship "the memoirs of the Apostles" (the Gospels), or "the writings of the prophets"[557] (the Old Testament). To this Harnack commented[558]:

---

555 Harnack, Adolf, *The Origin of the New Testament*, page 16.
556 Martyr, Justin, *First Apology*, Chapter 28.
557 Ibid., Chapter 67.
558 Harnack, Adolf, *The Origin of the New Testament*, page 26-27. Note the *or*, remarks Harnack, and we may add that the Christians had the choice to decide what to read in the churches on condition that the "memoirs of the Apostles," say the gospels, comes first, and that the "writings of the prophets" comes second, for reasons we have tackled and which had been agreed upon at

Above all, it was because Christian writings were in public worship actually treated like the Old Testament, without being simply included in the body of the old Canon, that the idea of a second sacred collection could be realized. This was the case in the first place with the Gospels.

Harnack, who believed that behind the public reading of the Apostolic memoirs lay not only the "historical" motive (that would eventually preamble the physical existence of the Church New Testament) but also the motive of "moral and religious edification" (that would stamp Christianity as a New Religion of Salvation in the course of history), later added[559]:

Christians took upon themselves to correct the Old Testament and even to interpolate whole verses. It was accordingly to be expected that, as the simplest way of developing the *litera scripta* given in the Old Testament, the ancient Canon would be enlarged by the addition of new works[560], and that thus in the most obvious way the whole Canon (Old & New) might have been declared to be the property of Christians and not of Jews.

In fact, all this *modus operandi* of collecting the Christian New Testament (with falsified history of Jesus as a Jew, along with the truth of his Teachings, Commands, Crucifixion, and Resurrection)

the Council of Jerusalem.

559 Harnack, Adolf, *The Origin of the New Testament*, page 170-171.

560 Examples of such tendencies are found with Tertullian, who, at the end of the 2nd century AD, opted to add the Book of Enoch to the Old Testament, among other works. Even later, in the Middle Ages, Christians decided to add the *Shepherd of Hermas* to many western exemplars of the Old Testament. The possibility of such inclusion, noticed Harnack, was considered even in the Muratorian Fragment (7th century AD Latin manuscript, copy of perhaps the oldest known list of the New Testament books, originally written in Greek, and dated from the 4th century AD), but was rejected because the "Old Testament was closed for the Church" in 397 AD. Please note that the Hebrew version of the Old Testament was most probably closed for nearly all Jews in around 90/95 AD at the Council of Jamnia; maybe in response to the early Christian writings that were taking form and attempting to link Jesus to the Jews.

side by side with the ancient Jewish Scriptures in the hope of coming up with one whole Canon (*Holy Bible*), has been in process from as early as the end of the 2nd century AD, most likely after the challenge caused by the writings of Marcion, which we shall tackle in the following chapter, and until the formation of the Church New Testament, mainly by Eusebius, as exposed in his *Church History*, 326 AD. Eusebius' work has been essentially inspired by Origen, who might have been using a primitive form of them as early as 200s AD, then, followed by Athanasius, as revealed in his famous 39th Easter Letter, 367 AD, and finally, its binding with the Old Testament at the Third Council (Synod) of Carthage in 397 AD.

In his *Church History*, Eusebius wrote[561] on the Divine Scriptures that are accepted and those that are not (italics mine):

... First then must be put *the holy quaternion of the Gospels*; following them the *Acts of the Apostles*. After this must be reckoned the *epistles of Paul*; next in order the extant former *epistle of John*, and likewise the *epistle of Peter*, must be maintained. After them is to be placed, if it really seem proper, the *Apocalypse of John*, concerning which we shall give the different opinions at the proper time. These then belong among the accepted writings. Among the disputed writings, which are nevertheless recognized by many, are extant the so-called *epistle of James and that of Jude*, also the *second epistle of Peter*, and those that are called the whether they belong to the evangelist or to another person of the same name. Among the rejected writings must be reckoned also the Acts of Paul, and the so-called Shepherd, and the Apocalypse of Peter, and in addition to these the extant epistle of Barnabas, and the so-called Teachings of the Apostles; and besides, as I said, the Apocalypse of John, if it seem proper, which some, as I said, reject, but which others class with the accepted books. And among these some have placed also the Gospel according to the Hebrews, with which those of the Hebrews that have accepted Christ are especially delighted. And all these may be reckoned among the disputed books ... We have felt compelled to give this catalogue in order that we might be able to know both these works and those that are cited by the heretics under the name of the apostles, including, for instance, such books as the Gospels of Peter, of Thomas, of Matthias, or of any others besides them, and the Acts of Andrew and John and the other apostles, which no one belonging to the

---

561 Eusebius, *Church History*, Book 3, Chapter 25.

succession of ecclesiastical writers has deemed worthy of mention in his writings. And further, the character of the style is at variance with apostolic usage, and both the thoughts and the purpose of the things that are related in them are so completely out of accord with true orthodoxy that they clearly show themselves to be the fictions of heretics. Wherefore they are not to be placed even among the rejected writings, but are all of them to be cast aside as absurd and impious.

The Third Council of Carthage held in 397 AD, approved the following Christian Biblical Canon:

Genesis, Exodus, Leviticus, Numbers, Deuteronomy, Joshua son of Nun, Judges, Ruth, 4 books of Kingdoms, 2 books of Chronicles, Job, the Davidic Psalter, 5 books of Solomon, 12 books of Prophets, Isaiah, Jeremiah, Daniel, Ezekiel, Tobias, Judith, Esther, 2 books of Ezra[562], 2 books of Maccabees, and in the New Testament: 4 books of Gospels, 1 book of Acts of the Apostles, 13 letters of the Apostle Paul, 1 letter of his to the Hebrews, 2 of Peter, 3 of John, 1 of James, 1 of Jude, and one book of the Apocalypse of John.

That being said, and since history always gets written by the winners, the Official Church finally succeeded in canonizing the 27 books of the Church New Testament and determined the Christian faith accordingly, after being satisfied: first, in overcoming the many socio-political difficulties at the time, and second, after winning chiefly over Marcion, and to a certain extent over Paul, having denounced other early Christian groups like the Gnostics, as heretics. It considered the significance of its New Testament Canon in the following manner, as presented by Harnack[563]: first, it is the authentic because it was written by the Apostles with authority on the history of Salvation through Jesus Christ and thus this brings about the belief in him as Son of God (in agreement with Marcion on the Salvation through Jesus as the Son of God). Second, it completes what was thence indicated in the Old Testament, and while it recognizes the Divine origin of the Jewish Bible, it only designates to it a kind of preparative importance (in absolute disagreement with Marcion). And third, it is the Divine Instrument of laws and ordinances—the Gospels and

---

562 It could most probably be 1Esdras and Ezra-Nehemiah as appeared in the Septuagint version, since the Vulgate version of Jerome, which has Ezra and Nehemiah, was not completed until a few years later, in 405 AD.
563 Harnack, Adolf, *The Origin of the New Testament*, page 178,179.

Apostolus—that should be observed by the Church and the Community of faithful, giving equal importance to both the Word of Christ and that of the Apostles. Yet, it exercises a certain "sifting criticism" on the laws and ordinances of the *instrumentum divinum* of the Old Testament (in accordance with Marcion only in what concerns the authenticity of the word of Christ and that of Paul, and in disaccord with Marcion, since he rejected the Old Testament, totally).

At any rate, when Eusebius was commissioned by Constantine in around 331 AD to deliver fifty Bibles for the Church of Constantinople, he was more than happy to do that. These Bibles (the Christian Biblical Canon: Old Testament & New Testament) written in Greek may have added the additional need for the formation of the Church New Testament, where both Codex Sinaiticus and Codex Vaticanus are possible extant examples. However, it is important to note that a few years earlier, at the First Christian Ecumenical Council of Nicaea in Bythinia (Turkey, nowadays), attended by Christian bishops from almost all over the world and which was convened by Emperor Constantine in c. 325 AD, we have no evidence among the available records of the time that such a determination on the Christian Biblical Canon was approved.

According to surviving records, Eusebius, who occupied the first seat on the right of the emperor and delivered the opening introduction of that Council on his behalf, seemed open to do almost anything that pleased the powerful emperor. Having been surely elected as the official theologian of the Roman Christian Empire and accepted as the first official Christian historian of the Church, Eusebius appeared, as we believe, to have insisted in an official term, on both theological and historical levels, to describe Christianity as being an extension of Judaism. Most likely, his insistency on that matter was driven by the early Christian accord at the Council of Jerusalem as well as the *supposed* writings of Judeo-Christians (Jews who began to believe, after the Death of Jesus Christ, that he may have originally been the Messiah and Savior of the Jewish nation in regards to the Old Testament literature), and definitely according to his wish and that of Constantine.

How's that? One may ask. We will explain that in the following paragraph. In the meantime, we should not avoid the fact that when Eusebius quoted Porphyry for the paragraph we cited in the prior chapter, he accused him of writing against Christianity[564], considering him to be part of the pagan threat to all that he now

---

564 Please refer to Note 1 at the end of the book.

stood for as a newly converted Gentile[565] to Christianity. Eusebius would also bear false witness against Porphyry in an attempt to present himself a faithful Christian—especially after denying he was one in order to escape torture during the last Roman Persecution[566]. In fact, he would do that in regret, not only to the Church itself, but also to the persecuted Christian community in Ceasaria and the erudite circle of Pamphilus to which he was in debt for all his theological and religious knowledge. Yet, what concerned him the most was the fact that Emperor Constantine, who adopted Christianity after many years of being an adept of the solar Roman deity and made it—Christianity—the "Official and only Religion of the Empire," became the first Christian emperor to rule the world in the 4th century AD—and that suited Eusebius very well. Constantine believed himself to be the Elected One by God to protect the Church, and so he did, especially, on the political level. Not only that, he also interfered in disciplinary and doctrinal affairs, behaving as if on a holy mission representing God on earth.[567] Meanwhile, Eusebius stood firm at his right hand.

In fact, Eusebius followed Origen, who was basically the man responsible for the collective information to be used regarding the texts that became the Church New Testament since these 27 texts, written in the 1st and 2nd century AD, were not majorly circulated as a one complete published work but as separated texts. These canonized texts, along with other Christian writings that were rejected or considered Apocrypha, were most probably preserved at the library of Pamphilus, who seemed to have occupied himself, joined by Eusebius, with the textual criticism of the Septuagint text of the Old Testament[568], and to a great extent,

---

565 Please refer to Note 2.
566 Please refer to Note 3.
567 Lenoir, Frédéric, et, Tardan-Masquelier, Ysé (Sous la Direction), *Encyclopédie Des Religions*, Tome 1, page 403.
568 According to legend, 70 or 72 Jewish elders and scholars were asked by the Greek King of Egypt Ptolemy II Philadelphus who reigned from 283 BC to 246 BC, to translate the Torah of Moses and some related texts from the Hebrew Biblr into Koine Greek, for inclusion in the Library of Alexandria. Thus, the Septuagint, derives its name from the Latin *versio septuaginta interpretum*, or "translation of the 70 interpreters" or "72 of the Jewish Elders." As the translation began in the 3rd century BC, it was completed sometime around 132 BC. This Greek version (not the Hebrew one) of the Old Testament is quoted in the New Testament, not only in the writings of St. Paul but also by the Apostolic fathers (A fact that shows that they had not been in contact with Jewish texts. We wonder why!) The order in which the Geek version of the texts was displayed is plain in the earliest Christian Bibles of the 4th century AD.

the texts of the New Testament. It is to be noted that this edition of the Septuagint, adopted by Christians, had been already and first of all prepared by Origen, and which, according to Jerome, was "revised or rewritten" and circulated by Eusebius (and Pamphilus). From this rich library, and the many texts he had access to, Eusebius prepared his fifty Bibles to Constantine.

What has been just said drives us to suggest that the information used to create the late 4th century Easter Letter[569], and which declared the accepted Christian writings, was most probably based on the *Historia Ecclesiastica* (Ecclesiastical History or Church History, probably finished around 324 AD) of Eusebius of Caesarea. He, we believe—after the death of Pamphilus and the imprisonment of the Christian Circle of Scholars and his acquisition of the famous library—began to change the reality of things for a few important reasons. First, he thought of breaking the essential relation between Jesus and the Gentile world, particularly his relation to the Phoenicians—although he seemed unable to ignore it fully as we shall see in a bit—who were always a challenging nation not only to the Assyrians, Babylonians, Persians, Jews, and Greeks, but also to the Romans ever since the time of the Punic Wars. Second, while doing just that, he would give the newly Gentile converted Roman emperor a justified reason for his conversion and a legitimate divine power as the head of the Christian Roman Empire. Third, while linking Jesus directly to the Jews and addressing Christians as a newborn nation having their roots in the Jewish nation, he would then be on the same brain frequency with Matthew, who wrote to the Jews trying to convince them that Jesus was the Son of David, born in

---

569 It was in the year 367 AD when Egyptian born Athanasius bishop of Alexandria (c. 296/298 AD–373 AD) wrote the 39th Easter Letter (Festal Letter), which was approved at the Quinisext Council (often known as the Council in Trullo held in 692 AD at Constantinople). Athanasius, considered a great Eastern Doctor of the Church in the Roman Catholic Church and in Eastern Orthodoxy, and venerated as a saint, listed the same 27 books of the Church New Testament in use today. His list that includes the Letter to the Hebrews was declared dogmatically at the Council of Trent (Trento, Italy, between December 13, 1545, and December 4, 1563 in twenty-five sessions for three periods). His 39th Easter Letter along with the New Testament writings of the Codex Vaticanus (one of the oldest surviving manuscripts of the Greek Bible in its Old and New Testaments, dated in c. 325 AD–350 AD), constituted one of the early Christian writings that had been considered essential in the formation of the Roman Catholic New Testament that is said to have been determined—yet still disputed—under the authority of Damasus 1, bishop of Rome, at the Council of Rome (382 AD). It seems, however, that the determination of the New Testament along with the Old one has been confirmed by the Third Council (Synod) of Carthage (397 AD).

the Bethlehem of Judea; an event also cited by Eusebius, for that sole reason. However, by accusing[570] them for the crimes they dared to commit against Christ the Savior while crying out that they had no other king than Caesar[571], he would then have indirectly indicated to them the kingship of David through Jesus and not that of Caesar. That had to change with Christian Emperor Constantine anyway.

Having said that, I would like to share two important texts from Eusebius' book, *Church History*. The first text comes from Chapter 4, which opens with the following title, "The Religion Proclaimed by Him (he meant Jesus) to All Nations Was Neither New Nor Strange." He wrote[572]:

> But that no one may suppose that his doctrine is new and strange, as if it were framed by a man of recent origin, differing in no respect from other men, let us now briefly consider this point also. It is admitted that when in recent times the appearance of our Saviour Jesus Christ had become known to all men there immediately made its appearance a new nation; a nation confessedly not small, and not dwelling in some corner of the earth, but the most numerous and pious of all nations, indestructible and unconquerable, because it always receives assistance from God. This nation, thus suddenly appearing at the time appointed by the inscrutable Counsel of God, is the one which has been honored by all with the name of Christ. One of the prophets, when he saw beforehand with the eyes of the Divine Spirit that which was to be, was so astonished at it that he cried out, 'Who hath heard of such things, and who hath spoken thus? Hath the earth brought forth in one day, and hath a nation been born at once?'[573] And the same prophet gives a hint also of the name by which the nation was to be called, when he says, 'Those that serve me shall be called by a new name, which shall be blessed upon the earth.'[574] But although it is clear that we are new and this new name of Christians has really but recently been known

---

570 Eusebius, *Church History*, Book 2, Chapter 6:3, 5, 8.

571 John 19:14-15, "Now it was the Preparation Day of the Passover, and about the sixth hour. And he said to the Jews, Behold your King! But they cried out, Away with [Him], away with [Him]! Crucify Him! Pilate said to them, Shall I crucify your King? The chief priests answered, We have no king but Caesar!"

572 Eusebius, *Church History*, Book 1, Chapter 4:1-9.

573 Isaiah 66:8, "Who has heard such a thing? Who has seen such things? Shall the earth be made to give birth in one day? [Or] shall a nation be born at once? For as soon as Zion was in labor, She gave birth to her children."

among all nations, nevertheless our life and our conduct, with our doctrines of Religion, have not been lately invented by us, but from the first creation of man, so to speak, have been established by the natural understanding of divinely favored men of old. That this is so we shall show in the following way. That the Hebrew nation is not new, but is universally honored on account of its antiquity, is known to all. The books and writings of this people contain accounts of ancient men, rare indeed and few in number, but nevertheless distinguished for piety and righteousness and every other virtue. Of these, some excellent men lived before the flood, others of the sons and descendants of Noah lived after it, among them Abraham, whom the Hebrews celebrate as their own founder and forefather. If anyone should assert that all those who have enjoyed the testimony of righteousness, from Abraham himself back to the first man, were Christians in fact if not in name, he would not go beyond the truth. For that which the name indicates, that the Christian man, through the knowledge and the teaching of Christ, is distinguished for temperance and righteousness, for patience in life and manly virtue, and for a profession of piety toward the one and only God over all—all that was zealously practiced by them not less than by us. They did not care about circumcision of the body, neither do we. They did not care about observing the Sabbaths, nor do we. They did not avoid certain kinds of food, neither did they regard the other distinctions which Moses first delivered to their posterity to be observed as symbols; nor do Christians of the present day do such things. But they also clearly knew the very Christ of God; for it has already been shown that he appeared unto Abraham, that he imparted revelations to Isaac, that he talked with Jacob, that he held converse with Moses and with the prophets that came after. Hence you will find those divinely favored men honored with the name of Christ, according to the passage which say of them, 'Touch not my Christs, and do my prophets no harm.'[575]

---

574 Isaiah 65:15-16, "You shall leave your name as a curse to My chosen; For the Lord GOD will slay you, And call His servants by another name; So that he who blesses himself in the earth Shall bless himself in the God of truth; And he who swears in the earth Shall swear by the God of truth; Because the former troubles are forgotten, And because they are hidden from My eyes."

575 1Chronicles 16:22, "[Saying], Touch not mine anointed, and do my prophets no harm."

This text is so important because it shows that Eusebius wanted by all means to prove that every pious and righteous man, whether a Gentile in an indirect matter when he said words like "from the first creation of man and accounts of ancient men,"[576] or a Jew in a direct matter when he cited "Abraham, Isaac, Jacob and Moses," had known the very spirit of the Christ of God and became by that a divinely favored man by the natural understanding of God. Although he seemed to tend more toward connecting the new Christian nation with the old Jewish nation, he succeeded in showing the differences between the two, especially in matters of temperance, righteousness, virtue, piety, circumcision, and the observation of the Sabbaths. While doing that, he kept the Christ that had incarnated in Jesus at that time always above all men. In a different work, moreover, Eusebius seems to have considered the story of Moses and the Hebrew struggle against a race of tyrants (he meant the Egyptians) and how the God of the Hebrews saved them from bondage, as fabulous.[577]

At any rate, the second text that I would like to share herein comes from Chapter 3 of *Church History*, which opens with the following title, "The Name Jesus and also the Name Christ were known from the Beginning, and were honored by the Inspired Prophets." The first Church historian wrote[578] (italics mine):

He, although he received no symbols and types of high priesthood from any one, although he was not born of a race of priests, although he was not elevated to a kingdom by military guards, *although he was not a prophet like those of old, although he obtained no honor nor pre-eminence among the Jews*, nevertheless was adorned by the Father with all, if not with the symbols, yet with the truth itself. And therefore, although he did not possess like honors with those whom we have mentioned, he is called Christ more than all of them. And as himself the true and only Christ of God, he has filled the whole earth with the truly august and sacred name of Christians, committing to his followers no longer types and images, but the uncovered virtues themselves, and a heavenly life in the very doctrines of truth. And he was not anointed

---

576 If the Church historian by the reputation of Eusebius could well have mistaken or even believed that ancient men or the man that appears before Abraham, as he showed it here in the text, was a Jew or Hebrew, he would then be labeled too naive for us to even consider his writings. Of course, he meant the Gentile man.

577 Eusebius, *Life of Constantine*, Book 1, Chapter 12.

578 Eusebius, *Church History*, Book 1, Chapter 3:11-19.

with oil prepared from material substances, but, as befits divinity, with the divine Spirit himself, by participation in the unbegotten deity of the Father. And this is taught also again by Isaiah, who exclaims, as if in the person of Christ himself, 'The Spirit of the Lord is upon me; therefore hath he anointed me. He hath sent me to preach the Gospel to the poor, to proclaim deliverance to captives, and recovery of sight to the blind.'[579] And not only Isaiah, but also David addresses him, saying, 'Thy throne, O God, is forever and ever. A scepter of equity is the scepter of thy kingdom. Thou hast loved righteousness and hast hated iniquity. Therefore God, thy God, hath anointed thee with the oil of gladness above thy fellows.'[580] Here the Scripture calls him God in the first verse, in the second it honors him with a royal scepter. Then a little farther on, after the divine and royal power, it represents him in the third place as having become Christ, being anointed not with oil made of material substances, but with the divine oil of gladness. It thus indicates his especial honor, far superior to and different from that of those who, as types, were of old anointed in a more material way. And elsewhere the same writer speaks of him as follows: 'The Lord said unto my Lord, Sit thou at my right hand until I make thine enemies thy footstool';[581] and, 'Out of the womb, before the morning star, have I begotten thee. The Lord hath sworn and he will not repent. *Thou art a priest forever after the order of Melchizedec.*[582] *But this Melchizedec is introduced in the Holy Scriptures as a priest of the most high God,*[583] *not consecrated by any anointing oil, especially prepared, and not even belonging by descent to the priesthood of the Jews. Wherefore after his order, but not after the order of the others, who received symbols and types, was our Saviour proclaimed, with an appeal to an oath, Christ and priest.*[584] History, therefore,

---

579 Isaiah 61:1, "The Spirit of the Lord GOD [is] upon Me, Because the LORD has anointed Me To preach good tidings to the poor; He has sent Me to heal the brokenhearted, To proclaim liberty to the captives, And the opening of the prison to [those who are] bound."
580 Psalm 45:6-7.
581 Psalm 110:1.
582 Psalm 110:3-4, "Your people [shall be] volunteers In the day of Your power; In the beauties of holiness, from the womb of the morning, You have the dew of Your youth. The LORD has sworn And will not relent, You [are] a priest forever According to the order of Melchizedek."
583 Genesis 14:18, "Then Melchizedek king of Salem brought out bread and wine; he [was] the priest of God Most High."
584 Hebrews 5:6, "As [He] also says in another [place]: You [are] a priest forever According to the order of Melchizedek." And, Hebrews 5:10, "called by

does not relate that he was anointed corporeally by the Jews, nor that he belonged to the lineage of priests, but that he came into existence from God himself before the morning star, that is before the organization of the world, and that he obtained an immortal and undecaying priesthood for eternal ages.[585] But it is a great and convincing proof of his incorporeal and divine unction that he alone of all those who have ever existed is even to the present day called Christ by all men throughout the world, and is confessed and witnessed to under this name, and is commemorated both by Greeks and Barbarians and even to this day is honored as a King by his followers throughout the world, and is admired as more than a prophet, and is glorified as the true and only high priest of God. And besides all this, as the pre-existent Word of God, called into being before all ages, he has received august honor from the Father, and is worshiped as God.

Any reference to Milki-Sedek in the Hebrew Bible whether linking David to him as we've just seen in Psalm, or Abraham as in Genesis[586], is nothing but a later attempt by the editors of the Bible as a whole to tie them together with Jesus Christ as one special race of humanity different than others, one holy family, or one Chosen People. This has been suggested by many scholars and many have already proven that the existence of Milki-Sedek in Genesis could not be considered but an informal insertion into the narration, since his sudden appearance interrupts the meeting of Abraham with the king of Sodom.[587] In addition, we may find other critics of the biblical texts who even proposed that this particular narration was not derived from any of the common pentateuchal (the Torah or what is known as the totality of Jewish teaching and practice) sources.[588]

God as High Priest according to the order of Melchizedek."
585 Hebrews 6:20, "Where the forerunner has entered for us, [even] Jesus, having become High Priest forever according to the order of Melchizedek." And, Hebrews 7:11, "Therefore, if perfection were through the Levitical priesthood (for under it the people received the law), what further need [was there] that another priest should rise according to the order of Melchizedek, and not be called according to the order of Aaron?"
586 Genesis 14:18-20, "Then Melchizedek king of Salem brought out bread and wine; he was the priest of God Most High. And he blessed him and said: Blessed be Abram of God Most High, Possessor of heaven and earth; And blessed be God Most High, Who has delivered your enemies into your hand. And he gave him a tithe of all."
587 Gunkel, Hermann, *Genesis*, page 284-285.
588 Scholars like Speiser E. A., *Genesis. Introduction, Translation, and Notes*, (1964); Noth Martin. *A History of Pentateuchal Traditions*, (1972); and Von

Besides, the insertion of Melki-Sedek, King of Urušalim—identified primarily as Rušalim, and which was later developed into the city of Shalim or *Shalam* ("Šalam" meaning "peace")—and High Priest of the Most High God Ēl-Ēlyon, could not have any meaning in a spiritual-priestly sense when linked to an event related to war in the Christian-Jewish Biblical story that tells how Abraham (Abram) returned from defeating king Chedorlaomer (Kedorlaomer) of Elam before meeting Bera, king of Sodom. Milki-Sedek, a representative of the Kingdom of Peace here on Earth, could not have blessed Abraham on his return from bloodshed. This definitely contradicts the Order of Priesthood to which Jesus Christ, the King of Peace, belonged.

The notion of Eusebius in the text we just quoted is thus clear, for Jesus does not belong by descent to the priesthood of the Jews, but rather, proclaimed a Savior, with an appeal to an oath, Christ and Priest, belonging by descent to the Order of Priesthood of Milki-Sedek, the Canaanite/Phoenician King and High Priest. Once more, maybe recalling Immanuēl, named after Ēl and meaning "Ēl with us," will refresh our memory.

Yet, with all the clarity Eusebius showed above, he also seems to have decided—for strange reasons that could perhaps only be understood from the political point of view at the time—to link to the Jews the Christ that came in the personality of Jesus, especially to Abraham and David, although we have shared numerous important quotes that clearly show essential distinctions between Yāwshu and the Jews; examples of such are what came in the New Testament, particularly in John, Paul, and Matthew. Along with that, we, humanity as a whole, and Christians in particular, would be totally misguided should we continue—for the same political reasons that drove Eusebius and were agreed upon before at the First Official Council in Jerusalem —denying the Canaanite/Phoenician genetics of Jesus, and the spiritual, theological, and religious inspiration they had on his missionary life.

Chapter 12

Rad Gerhard, *Genesis*, (1973).

The Religion and Theology of Jesus the Phoenician

The collection of the Christian writings gathered by Origen and passed down to Pamphilus and then to Eusebius was the only collection we have of the Church New Testament in its earliest virgin form. Of course, there were other Christian writings that we believe were not revised or even interpolated by the Church Fathers, especially Eusebius, hence, they were rejected and considered Apocrypha. The most important, ancient, first, and complete of all the Canons is the one of Marcion, which we will tackle right away. However, before we do that, let's have a look at the lost gospel, known as the Q Source. Please check Table 3 in the Appendix for the New Testament timeline.

The Q Source

We have noted briefly that the Q Source known also as the *Quelle* Document—*Quelle* being the German word for "source"—has been identified as an important literary work of the sayings for many of the teachings of Yāwshu. While some scholars say it is hypothetical, the majority believe it is true because the evidence of its existence is enormous. It was the original source from which both Luke and Matthew drew their knowledge for the construction of their own gospels, besides taking from Mark, whose gospel has been considered to be the first. Studies show that Mark and the Q Source are not linked, but both generated the essential materials for both Luke and Matthew. While the narrative of Mark held the story of the Passion of Christ, his Trial and Death, as central, followed by Luke and Matthew, there is no supportive evidence that such material was included in the sayings of Gospel Q.

In his inspiring book, *Jesus in History*, Howard Clark Kee, American Professor of Biblical Studies Emeritus at Boston University and Visiting Faculty at the University of Pennsylvania, assumed that Luke and Matthew used Mark as a basic source, but also noticed that more than one-fourth (1/4) of Luke and one-third (1/3) of Matthew consist of common material that is not found in Mark. He adds[589] in an interesting annotation:

---

589 Clark Kee, Howard, *Jesus in History*, page 79.

This common material is characterized by a high degree of verbal similarity and by a close correspondence in order, from the baptismal sayings through the Beatitudes to the final eschatological sayings. Remembering that the preliterary language of the tradition would have been Aramaic rather than the Greek of the gospels, we can best account for the verbal similarity by postulating Matthew and Luke's use of a single Greek source. And both the verbal similarity and the similarity in the order of the sayings suggest that the source was written.

Burton L. Mack, American Professor of New Testament at the School of Theology at Claremont, California, confirmed the existence of the Q Source, and thus wrote[590], "But once Q was recognized as a source for these gospels, it could be studied on its own. And so the book of the first followers of Jesus has come to light after being lost for almost eighteen hundred years." Burton believes it was lost to the historical memory of the Christian Church because the narrative gospels—which showed Jesus as the Jewish Messiah who appeared to reform Judaism, challenging the teachings of the Pharisees and Sadducees, etc., and which were penned later than the Q Source, first by Mark then by both Matthew and Luke who used Mark as their basic source for the New Testament plot—eventually prevailed.[591]

We certainly approve Burton's rejection, based on his analysis of the Q Source, of the Church New Testament plot that describes Jesus as a Jewish Messiah who came to reform Judaism. We have stated clearly that Yāwshu was not a Jew in the first place to march to Jerusalem and reform its Jewish religion. We have shown that Yāwshu and his followers were not at all in that frame of mind since their socio-religious system was not related to Judaism, but rather to the Phoenician-Galilean religious code that had long prophesied the coming of a Savior in a troubled time—a Savior who would die and resurrect for the Salvation of the people, exactly like their previous Son of God, Adon (Adonis). However, the knowledge about Yāwshu's movement in Galilee that began to spread powerfully yet peacefully in neighboring regions, greatly agitated the curiosity of the Jews in Judea, mainly the Sadducees and Pharisees, who decided to investigate him thoroughly, sending spies and agents of the temple to Galilee; the most famous was Judas, as we learned in Chapter 6.

---

590 Mack, Burton L., *The Lost Gospel*, page 4.
591 Ibid., page 3,4,5.

Although the Q Source was first theorized as a hypothetical document, it seems it gained ground in due time as an official logia of Yāwshu based on the tradition of an unknown Christian body within the early unofficially established Church. It has been formed in two disciplines; the first, a physical document maintained in a series of short writings, and probably penned in Greek, and the second, simply an oral hidden teaching, probably in Aramaic.

What is really interesting in the Q Source is that it gives us a great feeling since it fits very well with our understanding of Yāwshu and who he was in reality. Reading the text in both Luke and Matthew[592] definitely adds more value and grandeur to Jesus the Galilean-Phoenician while it extremely diminishes Jesus the Jew to a point that he loses his already fake reputation that was given to him by the Church New Testament.

For that reason, Frederic Amsler, one of the most prominent Christian historians and teachers who has dealt with the Q Source, beautifully explained in his book[593]:

As surprising as it may seem, nowhere does Jesus textually quote the Hebraic Bible. According to the Q Document, Jesus draws his inspiration from other sources than the Bible and the few allusions he has made create even room for doubt that he has a direct knowledge.

In addition to that sharp differentiation between the Q Document and the Jewish Bible, Clark Kee exhibited some major difficulties in approving the theorists who advanced that there might have existed a kind of similarity between the Q Document and 1st century Jewish wisdom literature. He affirms[594], "But in the extensive wisdom literature of Judaism, there is nothing that really resembles the Q Material."

This is crystal clear; it directly answers those who still want to connect Jesus to Judaism. In fact, what Amsler, Kee, and many others have observed while studying the Q Document, simply matches what we have been concluding from only reading the Church New Testament itself, after finding its many flaws and contradictions on historical, geographical, cultural, and theological levels. In short, the Q Source reveals that Yāwshu had no connections whatsoever with the Jewish teachings.

---

592 It seems that Luke more often preserves the original order of the text than Matthew.
593 Amsler, Frederic, *L'Évengile Inconnu*, page 34.
594 Clark Kee, Howard, *Jesus in History*, page 80.

Thus, Burton shares also the same conviction as ours through his discoveries that led him to believe that the people of Q, the followers of Jesus, did not think of him as the Jewish Messiah. "Instead," he continued[595], "they thought of him as a teacher whose teachings made it possible to live with verve in troubled times."

While Burton, who seems to have denied the narrative of the New Testament almost completely, suggests that the "Jesus People" were not similar in their factual way of life to the early Christians as described by the Church in the New Testament, were not forming a new religion of salvation with a preaching mission to both Jews and Gentiles, and did not take his teachings as an indictment of Judaism[596], Amsler, on the other hand, appears to have located the origin of the Q Source, as well, explaining[597], "The few geographical indications move towards the conclusion that the Source of the sayings of Jesus is a document carried by a group rooted in Galilee and in conflict with Jerusalem."

That being said, we, like Amsler, tend to affirm an already existing conflict between the Phoenician Galilee and the Judean Jerusalem. Of course, it is a conflict not to be termed in the military sense, since neither Yāwshu and his followers nor the people he descended from were in any way partisans of war, but rather, it was more of a cultural and theological conflict. Thus, we tend to confirm that the *Quelle* Document, the Q Source, which is still yet considered the earliest written text and oral tradition on Yāwshu's sayings and teachings, was carried by a Phoenician-Galilean group none other than the Nazarenes; the ascetic branch of the Ashayas, or Asayas—the Galilean Essenes. This Galilean-Phoenician group is not related at all to the Jewish-Christian group also known as the Nazoraeans or Nazarenes, accredited for the writing of the Gospel of the Nazoraeans, as we have seen in the previous chapter.

Hence, we conclude that the Galilean sect of the Nazarenes are the Q People of Yāwshu. While history has showed and still shows even today that all Jewish groups such as the old Pharisees,

---

595 Mack, Burton L., *The Lost Gospel*, page 4.
596 We certainly agree on few points raised by Burton in regards to the fabricated plot of the New Testament and disagree on few others. The New Testament is therefore not rejected by us in terms of the spiritual and universal religious awareness that it conveys; it is only rejected in terms of the historical narration and the identity of Jesus, his family, and his early followers. And so, while Burton may think Jesus was Jew, but not a Jewish Messiah, we believe Jesus was neither a Jewish Messiah, nor a Jew, entirely.
597 Amsler, Frederic, *L'Évengile Inconnu*, page 34.

Sadducees, Essens of the Qumran Community, etc., were closed groups, strict and rigorous in the choices they often undertook in accepting members within their sects and communities, of course, restricting them to the people who obey the Law of Moses. Thus, purely of Jewish blood, the Q People on the other hand, were open to all nations, including Gentiles if they wished to follow Christ, and/or Jews, if they desired by their own free will, or had been activated clandestinely to infiltrate the early Christian Circle[598]. As a matter of fact, the Galilean Essenes congregation of Yāwshu was open to just about anybody who recognized Him as Son of God.

This universal approach by itself is not Judaic by nature but Canaanite/Phoenician, and the way it has been envisioned by the Q People or the Sect of the Nazarenes was said explicitly by Paul who was one of them, as we have seen previously. Paul tried to convey the message that both Gentiles and Jews could be united through faith as the people of God in Christ Jesus.[599] He also taught that the "strange" Jewish tradition of circumcision that had been a signature of the Covenant that linked them to their God meant nothing for the New Creation of Christ[600], and therefore, what counts in the sight of God is pure love[601].

This universal approach of envisioning Christ and his followers as being blessed by the Father has also been mentioned by Luke[602], and beautifully placed[603] by Clark Kee, "It is this knowledge of God's purpose, esoteric in essence and yet evangelistic in thrust, that constitutes the wisdom set forth in Q."

The Doctrine of Marcion

598 The only two Jewish disciples of Yāwshu were Judas who betrayed him and Nathanael who rejected him as the son of God. We don't know exactly the hidden role of Nathanael, but we're absolutely certain that Judas was an agent of the Temple, as we have seen before.

599 Galatians 3:28, "There is neither Jew nor Greek, there is neither slave nor free, there is neither male nor female; for you are all one in Christ Jesus."

600 Galatians 6:15, "For in Christ Jesus neither circumcision nor uncircumcision avails anything, but a new creation."

601 1Corinthians 2:9, "But as it is written: Eye has not seen, nor ear heard, Nor have entered into the heart of man The things which God has prepared for those who love Him."

602 Luke 10:21-22, "In that hour Jesus rejoiced in the Spirit and said, I thank You, Father, Lord of heaven and earth, that You have hidden these things from [the] wise and prudent and revealed them to babes. Even so, Father, for so it seemed good in Your sight. All things have been delivered to Me by My Father, and no one knows who the Son is except the Father, and who the Father is except the Son, and [the one] to whom the Son wills to reveal [Him]."

603 Clark Kee, Howard, *Jesus in History*, page 82.

It was not until the first half of the 2nd century AD that the Christian historical and theological truth was said. Marcion was probably born around the year 85 AD[604], at the time both Matthew and Luke were penning their gospels. He was the son of the Bishop of Sinope in Pontus, one of the most important Greek commercial cities on the south coast of the Black Sea (it is known today as a region in the northeast of Turkey). He took his Christian authority from his father, became bishop himself, and decided to change the course of things. His main aim became focused on freeing Christianity from Judaism, and thus, returning it to its original form. How to do that was not as simple as he might have thought, but Marcion had a plan in mind—a plan that would counteract the plan once proposed by James, Paul, John, and Peter at the Council of Jerusalem, which he might have heard of from his father and learned who Yāwshu was in reality and who his Father was.

During his time, Marcion had most likely observed the fact that two broad parties in the early Church were at work. Quite understandably so; there were strong voices within Christianity standing against the notion that Jesus was a Jew ever since the beginnings of the Christian Church. These voices, led by Paul, mainly outside Jerusalem, regarded Christianity as a prologue of a new spiritual system, applicable to all, and replacing the Mosaic privilege of the Law with a Universal dispensation of Grace. The other voices were led by Peter, principally in the city of Jerusalem, as agreed at the Council—who sketched Christianity as just a simple continuation of the purported Law, enclosing it into an Israelite institution, or better said: a narrow sect of Judaism; and their antagonism is faintly revealed in the Epistle to the Galatians[605]. Indeed, it was the voice of Paul that was heard by Marcion, who in his turn started to shout aloud, yet, peacefully against the voices of Peter, James, and John.

Marcion began first working on the early Christian texts he had with. Whether he knew of the other texts that later formed the Church New Testament or not, since they were not compiled as one book at this time, we can't really know. However, he might have known about them but for a reason only he knew. Marcion chose the Gospel of Luke, omitting its first two chapters, and ten of the epistles attributed to Paul. Of them, he selected, first of all, Galatians, which he considered the charter of Marcionism, then Corinthians I and II, Romans I and II, Thessalonians, Ephesians

---

604 Some suggest he was born around 100 AD.
605 Blavatsky, H.P., *Isis Unveiled*, Volume 2, page 161.

(which he knew under the name of Laodicians), Colossians, Philippians, and Philemon.[606]

Marcion might have chosen both Luke and Paul as his inspiration for he probably deemed their work sufficient for his upcoming work, although, we may find one important theological notion in his work that has similarity with John and another one that counters him. Therefore, Marcion would surely agree with John (1:1-2), who began his gospel with, "In the beginning was the Word, and the Word was with God, and the Word was God. He was in the beginning with God." He would disagree with John in dealing with the idea revealed in the following sentence when he continued[607] (italics mine), *"And the Word became flesh and dwelt among us*, and we beheld His glory, the glory as of the only begotten of the Father, full of grace and truth." This theological approach presented by John in regard to the Father and Son is quite similar to Marcion's view of Yāwshu and his Father, yet, the disagreement falls only in the way Christ appeared on Earth, since Marcion believed that Christ was God Manifest, meaning he had nothing about him that was earthly and was not God Incarnate, as expressed by John. To Marcion, this Supreme God that had manifested in Christ from the beginning of time was the Invisible, Indescribable, and Good God that had nothing to do with Jehovah[608], the Jewish God, and that which he defined as the Demiurgus[609] (the Demiurge), the creator of the material world (world-maker) and who by special choice elected the Jewish people as his own and thus became the god of the Jews.

Thus, having fully realized that, Marcion began writing his Canon in opposition to the Old Testament, while focusing his mind also on the shameful Council of Jerusalem which had been planned to convince the Jews that Christ was one of them in order to convert them. Therefore, it is not by coincidence that Marcion regarded the pure Pauline Letters as having been corrupted and

---

606 The Catholic Encyclopedia, *Marcionites*.
607 John 1:14.
608 YHWH, say, Jehovah, is Kabalistically described as Yod-Heva (Adam & Eve). He represents the androgynous principles of creation, as we have seen before.
609 According to the *Catholic Encyclopedia, Demiurge*. The Gnostics consider the Demiurge a personification of the inferior creative power in the Universe, being the offspring of a union that had gathered Achamoth (lower wisdom) and matter. Since Achamoth herself was only the daughter of Sophía the last of the thirty Æons, the Demiurge was distant by many emanations from the Supreme God. Later on, the Demiurge was looked upon as personifying the power of evil, Satan, who, some of the Gnostics had identified with Jehovah, the Jewish God that sometimes was made identical to the great tyrant Yaltabaoth or Ialdabaoth, Son of Chaos.

that the three pillar Apostles, Peter, James, and John had betrayed their trust. Why he would have alluded to that? At any rate, Marcion's doctrine had been greatly announced in his great, now lost work, known as *Antitheses*, and his Canon of eleven books, the *Gospel of the Lord*, considered to be the most ancient Canon we have of the New Testament. In the process, he efficiently and sufficiently relied on the writings of Paul and Luke with slight modifications he had cleverly implemented on the original texts, in favor of his doctrine. While he was a great follower of Paul, remaining always faithful to him, Marcion was probably the first one who used the term "gospel" in reference to a Christian written document, basically that of Luke. He might have chosen Luke maybe because Luke was a companion of the Apostle Paul, or probably because it showed the greatest concern for Gentiles in the ministry of Jesus, or perhaps more likely, because it was the gospel he was raised on in his home church of Sinope.[610]

To Marcion, however, Christ was indeed the Son of God, but he was also simply "God" without any further qualification. Like the majority of the Christian Gnostics who were blossoming at the time, he believed that the main purpose of the coming of Christ as the Savior of humanity and Redeemer of their sins was to rescue them from the power of the Demiurge, the lord of the world of this darkness, and bring them to the light of the Good God, His Father in Heaven.

Although this may be the main concept Marcion adopted in his doctrine, he nevertheless was not dualist[611] like some Christian Gnostic systems who believed that the Demiurge was the personification of evil itself, thus Satan, identified with Jehovah, the god of the Jews presented in the Old Testament, brought in opposition to Christ of the New Testament. Accordingly, the faithful in Christ had to wage war against the Demiurge till the end. Doing that would please the Supreme and Good God whose Christ is the Only-Begotten Son. Marcion, on the other hand, was not that extreme or complex in his theological views, for he didn't care much about the metaphysical explanation or the abstract questions on the origin of evil and its eternal fight against the principle of good. He believed though that the Demiurge was in fact a secondary deity, a god, in a sense, or a quasi-god, but not at all the Supreme God, a just god, yet rigidly or severely just and having few good qualities (only in regard to

610 Ehrman, Bart D., *Lost Christianities*, page 108.
611 Harnack, Adolf, *Marcion the Gospel of the Alien God*, page 14.

the Jews), but he was not the Good God who was the Father of the Lord Jesus Christ.

Now, having finished conceiving his work—the prospect of his teachings—Marcion probably discussed it with his father who refused them, most likely on the basis that he would not want to oppose the mainstream Church that had already been set at the Council of Jerusalem. Having fallen out with his father and been excommunicated by him, Marcion traveled first to Asia Minor[612] mainly for purposes of propaganda, impressing the people there while seeking recognition from the leaders of the churches, laying before them his interpretation of the gospel, but was countered back fast with rejection.[613] It was then that he decided to move to Rome and to set sail aboard his own ship sometime shortly after the death of Hyginus, before the accession of Pius I as Pope of Rome in 140 AD, and coinciding with the first year of reign of Roman Emperor Antoninus Pius, in c. 138–139 AD.

As Adolf Harnack has suggested, Marcion might have chosen his trip to Rome after clearly considering the fact that there the Church's break with Judaism was more complete than in Asia. People (Christians) did not fast on the Sabbath or celebrate Passover together with the Jews.[614] We agree on the suggestion proposed by Harnack, especially after he was totally refused in Pontus by his father—although he seemed to have had some followers there—and by the leaders of the churches in Asia Minor. Yet, even that the Christian Church in Rome was established as a totally separate entity from Judaism, and that's essentially natural, Marcion had to play it right this time. He had one goal. Therefore, he would not allow his enthusiasm to rescue Christianity and his thrust to liberate it from Judaism, as did Paul before him, failing at the doors of Rome. He had a new plan. Although Paul, as the scriptures at hand allow—for much has been tampered with—had definitely deleted much of the old Jewish ideas of God and a number of other intolerable teachings, was pictured to have only broken with the Law, whereas Marcion went much further than that, and in his special faith in Christ, he totally rejected not only the Law as described in the Old Testament, but the Jewish lawgiver himself.

Considering himself still a member of the Christian Community, he accepted the gospel as it was given to the Church and represented it without changes as he joined the Christian

---

612 His main visit was to Ephesus, but he might have also visited Smyrna and perhaps Hierapolis.
613 Harnack, Adolf, *Marcion the Gospel of the Alien God*, page 16-17.
614 Ibid., page 148 (fn.9)

group in Rome after offering them a donation of 200,000 sesterces for the Church's missionaries. The Christian Community in Rome, which had accepted his gift of money, and him as a brother, did not probably know of his earlier history and teachings. Yet, when they soon became acquainted with little part of it, since Marcion was at the very beginning extremely cautious in laying the foundations of his doctrine, acting on a low profile, and conducting himself discreetly yet seriously, they didn't seem to react to the point of excluding him. It was not until four to five years later, in c. 144 AD, when Marcion had completed his New Testament, his "authentic" Canon, the Gospel of the Lord, which he based on the Gospel of Luke and ten epistles of Paul after purging them of the Judaistic interpolations, along with the composition of his great critical work, *Antitheses*, based on demonstrating the irreconcilability of the Old Testament with the gospel, contrasting the Demiurge with the Heavenly Father, that the break with the Church in Rome truly happened.[615]

Even when the break with the official Church in Rome occurred, Marcion didn't show any anger towards it, considering the Church to be a victim of a seduction, but became only hostile to the original Apostles and Judaistic evangelists.[616] In fact, Marcion tried his best to reform the Church, nothing more than that, and because he believed his understanding of the true meaning of the words of Jesus and his teachings in his gospel to be the Truth, he called for a Council of Church leaders in Rome to convene so that he could present his views[617], and probably as counterpoint to the First Official Council of Jerusalem that had been convened by James, Paul, John, and Peter almost a century before. However, after hearing his daring and revolutionary thesis, the Church elders felt compelled to reject them, deeming them very dangerous. At once, they refunded him and sent him away after excommunicating him from a community he thought would accept him as successor of Paul, whom he considered the Chief Apostle and whom he credited correctly for transmitting the universal message of Jesus Christ, the Savior sent by God.

His powerful sense of logic and the truth he said about the flaws in the Church's doctrine as Christendom ought to represent it, frightened them. In fact, they were bewildered by his intellect and defiance, while, in truth, the battle with the Catholic Church seemed to be a battle with texts, mainly on the theological front, nothing more. To Marcion, the Old Testament was true enough.

615 Ibid., page 17.
616 Ibid., page 148 (fn.11)
617 Ehrman, Bart D., *Lost Christianities*, page 108.

Moses and the Jewish Prophets were all messengers of God, but not the Supreme Good God, rather, the Demiurge, and the Jewish Messias were sure to come in order to establish a millennial kingdom for the Jews on earth, but the Jewish Messias had nothing to do whatsoever with the Christ of God.[618]

Surely, Marcion must have read *The Song of Moses* in the Old Testament, *The Voice of the Jealous Yahweh*[619]:

> They shall be burnt with hunger, and devoured with burning heat, and with bitter destruction: I will also send the teeth of beasts upon them, with the poison of serpents of the dust. The sword without, and terror within, shall destroy both the young man and the virgin, the suckling also with the man of gray hairs.

Marcion, a devoted Christian, took the words of Paul for granted, especially those that had not been forged or corrupted, as he stated, and felt obliged so confidently to restore the truth in them. Words like when the Apostle said that a person is justified, thus, made right with God, only by faith in Christ, not by doing the works of the Law[620]. This stood as an essential fact to Marcion, who never actually believed in the authentic and divine origin of the Old Testament. The point of contrast between the Law and the Gospel was extremely important to Marcion, and in that perspective D. Ehrman wrote[621]:

> This distinction became fundamental to Marcion, and he made it absolute. The Gospel is the good news of deliverance; it involves love, mercy, grace, forgiveness, reconciliation, redemption, and life. The Law, however, is the bad news that makes the Gospel necessary in the first place; it involves harsh commandments, guilt, judgment, enmity, punishment, and death. The Law is given to the Jews. The Gospel is given by Christ.

Marcion was not able to understand the notion that there is one God, the same God who could be responsible for all the contradictory attributes given in the Old Testament like hatred,

---

618 *The Catholic Encyclopedia, Marcionites.*
619 Deuteronomy 32:24-25.
620 Galatians 2:16, "Knowing that a man is not justified by the works of the law but by faith in Jesus Christ, even we have believed in Christ Jesus, that we might be justified by faith in Christ and not by the works of the law; for by the works of the law no flesh shall be justified."
621 Ehrman, Bart D., *Lost Christianities*, page 104.

vengeance, and judgment, and in the New Testament like love, mercy, and grace. This obvious confusion in the perception of the metaphysical divine world made him reach a conclusion that there must be in reality two Gods, the Demiurge of the Jews and the Father of Jesus. And thus the opposition between the Old Testament and the gospel demanded the acceptance of two Gods.[622]

To Marcion, Jesus Christ was not the Son of David, nor was he the Messiah of the Jews, and not even a king, but a Divine Being sent to reveal the divine truth, preach the glad tidings, and bring reconciliation and Salvation to all men—a wholly new spiritual religion.[623] Jesus Christ was called God—the Father of goodness and grace—a Loving and Merciful God, whereas the Jewish God, as shown in the Hebrew Bible, was very distinct from the Father; he was unjust, unmerciful, angry, jealous, tribal, and a God of war. And therefore, to Marcion, Christ had pretended to be the Messiah of the Demiurge in a skilled way only to spread the truth concerning his Heavenly Father, whereas the true believers in him would enter the Father's Kingdom, and the unbelievers would thus remain forever slaves of the Demiurge. Eventually, Marcion found it just irrational and impossible to think that Yahweh could be the God of Jesus, hence, Jesus Christ came to abrogate the Jewish Lord, who was opposed to his God and Father, as "matter is to spirit, impurity to purity."[624]

In that sense, H.P. Blavatsky wrote[625]:

Jesus *the initiate*—the type from whom the 'historical' Jesus was copied—was not of pure Jewish blood, and thus recognized no Jehovah[626]; nor did he worship any planetary god beside his own 'Father,' whom he knew, and with whom he communed as every high initiate does, 'Spirit to Spirit and Soul to Soul.'

While she seemed totally correct in drawing a line of demarcation between the Father of Yāwshu and the God of the Jews, she sounded halfway right concerning the true historical identity of Jesus. Not only he was not of pure Jewish blood, he was not of Jewish blood at all.

---

622 Harnack, Adolf, *Marcion the Gospel of the Alien God*, page148 (fn.12)
623 Blavatsky, H.P., *Isis Unveiled*, Volume 2, page 162.
624 Ibid., page 163.
625 Blavatsky, H.P., *The Secret Doctrine*, Volume 1, page 577-578.
626 John 8 (especially John 8:38-47).

At any rate, although Marcion felt defeated at the hearing despite all that he had offered as proofs, he nevertheless left Rome and the Church with more determination than before and continued preaching his gospel and his doctrine on a broader scale, starting anew in Asia Minor to which he returned safely. It was there where he found victory indeed, as he experienced unparalleled success on his mission in propagating his "authentic" version of the faith in Christ the Savior and Redeemer of the world. In fact, Marcion succeeded in establishing churches wherever he went, like his predecessor Paul, in all the provinces of the Roman Empire. The extraordinary spread of his churches, which in some parts of Asia Minor were the original form of Christianity and continued for many years to come to incorporate the greatest number of Christians, certainly extended towards the late 5th century AD.[627]

That being said, the Church of Marcion proved itself extremely powerful and in that perspective, Harnack wrote[628], "Marcion, conscious of being the called successor of Paul, established, not unstable sects, but *one* great Church, consisting of ordered and well-established congregations, *the* church of Jesus Christ." In fact, Marcion wanted a universal Christianity, the same one conceived by Yāwshu and expanded by Paul, not confined or undefiled by association to Judaism. To him, Christianity was the New Covenant between the Father and the Son, pure and simple, with no complexities. Thus, the "Unknown Alien Good God" he proclaimed was a graceful, merciful, and redeeming love, primarily and eventually. Following his obvious views of God, Harnack continued[629], "All else is rigidly to be excluded; God is not the creator, not the lawgiver, not the judge; he does not become wrathful and does not punish but is exclusively love incarnate, redeeming, and blessing."

At any rate, many of the traditional Christian Church authorities in fact related anti-Marcionic literature in their writings, accusing Marcion of dangerous heresy, like Justin Martyr (in his *1st Apology*), Ireneaus (in his *Adversus Haereses*, or Against Heresies), Tertullian (in his *Adversus Marcionem*, or Against Marcion, and other works), Hippolytus (in his *Kata Pason Aireseon Elegchos*, or A Refutation of All Heresies), and Epiphanius (in his *Panarion*, where he offers remedies against heresies). Following that line of the Official Church attack on Marcion and against his reformist, revisionist church, Harnack

---

627 Ehrman, Bart D., *Lost Christianities*, page 109.
628 Harnack, Adolf, *Marcion the Gospel of the Alien God*, page 19.
629 Ibid., page 13.

also noticed that Marcion viewed the Official Church at the time as being an Old Testament Church, one that "follows the Testament of the Creator-God," the Demiurge, and not the Church that should follow the New Testament of the Supreme Good God. He also made notice that the Official Church might have gradually begun to formulate its New Testament canon in response to the many various challenges posed by Marcion, since it seems it had not yet one in its hand.[630] Other scholars and authors went even further than Harnack. In *History of the Christian Religion to the Year Two-Hundred*, published in 1881, Charles B. Waite suggested that Marcion's gospel may have actually preceded the Gospel of Luke. John Knox in *Marcion and the New Testament*, written in 1942, also believes this theory as true. And just recently, in *Marcion and Luke-Acts: A Defining Struggle*, authored in 2006, Joseph B. Tyson believes that not only the Gospel of Luke but also the Acts of the Apostles, both attributed to Luke, were formulated in response to Marcion, rather than the Gospel of Marcion being a rewrite of Luke.[631]

Whatever the case, we will not confirm or deny what gospel came first in time, for our concern now is directed solely towards Marcion's doctrine. We believe his only flaw was his proposed concept—aligning well with Gnostic thought—that Jesus was mainly a divine spirit or being who appeared to men in the shape of a human form and not in a true physical body. Therefore, everything related to this Docetic idea, which we have seen before when tackling the First and Second Epistles of John, is deemed wrong because we believe that the Resurrection of the Body that Marcion denied, probably drawing his belief literally from the words he read in Paul[632], actually occurred.

Despite this flaw in Marcionite thinking, one cannot but pay homage to this great man who proclaimed the Unknown Alien Good God on probably three basic characteristics; *Unknown*, because He cannot be recognized in the World or in man in any possible sense; *Alien*, because He is not connected to the world or to man by any bond or obligation; *Good*, because He is absolutely the Redeemer that became manifest for the first time in the history of the world and man in the person of Christ, prompted by an act of love, mercy, and grace.[633]

---

630 Harnack, Adolf, *The Origin of the New Testament*, page 223.
631 Wikipedia, *Gospel of Marcion*.
632 1Corinthians 15:50, "Now this I say, brethren, that flesh and blood cannot inherit the kingdom of God; nor does corruption inherit incorruption."
633 Harnack, Adolf, *Marcion the Gospel of the Alien God*, page 3.

In fact, there would be no other God in the history of the Earth that would fit to a certain high degree the God proclaimed by Marcion as the Father of Jesus but the Most High God, Ēl-Ēlyon, unknown to the ancient world and men of Babylon, Judea, Athena, and Rome, yet, very much known to the Canaanite/Phoenicians as the Supreme God from ancient times. And, as we have said before, it couldn't have been just a coincidence to have actually found the Divine connection in the Church New Testament itself when it clearly linked Immanuēl to Ēl, hence, "Ēl is with us," manifested in Christ and incarnated in Jesus, for the salvation of men—*all* men.

Truth be said, the great epic of Baal and Anat discovered in Ugarit and dated back to the 14th century BC, stands still as a witness to the Divine declaration of the Canaanite/Phoenicians. It is written that Ēl had addressed his daughter Anat with the following words, "War is against my will; plant in the soil seeds of peace, and multiply the seeds of love in the heart of the fields."

If Marcion thought of the Canaanite/Phoenician God the Most High, Al-Ēlyon, when he proclaimed the Unknown Alien Good God as the Father of Jesus Christ, or not, we can't really affirm, since Marcion stated that this God was unknown in the old world and in the old era, was not revealed before Christ, and exists nowhere but in the gospel. However, he most certainly knew who the God Ēl was and what He represented when reading the Old Testament in the Church at Sinope. He might have reached a conclusive comparison between Him and the Jewish God, Yahweh, and this knowledge might have led him to think of Him as the Father in Heaven, and the quality he gave Him as the "lofty one" or "higher," matches exactly with the attribute given by Canaano-Phoenician priests to Ēl as *Ēlyon*.

If he knew of the true Phoenician origin of Jesus Christ or not we don't really know, but his total rejection that the Jewish God of the Old Testament is the God of the New Testament, the Father of Christ, suggests that he had certain knowledge, at least, on the theological and religious levels. This is exactly what concerns us herein. Marcion was a true believer in Christ and his Father, and according to Epiphanius (Haeres., XLII, ii), he, in his youth, professed to lead a life of chastity and asceticism[634]. Thus, the way of life he led may very well coincide with the life chosen by Paul, who had been one of the Nazarenes, and undoubtedly fits with the lives of Yāwshu, Yāwhanan the Baptist, and Maryām El-Mejdel. It seems after all that Marcion thought of himself a Nazarene, an ascetic member of the Ashayas.

---

634 The Catholic Encyclopedia, *Marcionites*.

Yāwshu, an Ashaya, Member of the Galilean Community? YES

In fact, we have tackled a few times before that the term *Essenes* has been given to all ascetic, mystic, and messianic groups appearing in the region that spread from Nabatea-Jordan, Judea-Palestine, Galilee-Phoenicia, perhaps Asia Minor, and elsewhere in Egypt under the name of *Therapeuts*, or Healers. These groups were not identical with each other on the basis of ethnicity, but they all shared, each in their own way, a special spiritual experience and a similar belief that a Savior would come to their rescue in a world filled with troubles and uncertainties. While the Essens of the Qumran Desert or the Qumran Community who were Orthodox Jews were waiting for their Savior in the form of a divine warrior that would conquer lands and defeat the Goyim, the Essenes of Galilee-Phoenicia (the Ashayas or Asayas), on the other hand, were waiting for a Savior that would redeem the world from sin, and join humanity by an act of Love to the Most High God whom they called Ēl-Ēlyon. We have expeditiously proved them to be Galilean-Phoenicians, not Jewish at all. It is to this community that Yāwshu belonged.

It is worth it, however, to remind the readers of a few things that have added some light to our study. With the advent of Jesus Christ in the course of physical history, Christianity promptly took root in the city of Melkart in Sūr (Tyre), and most likely, the first Church ever to exist was built there as early as 54 AD. A mere 12 kilometers southeast of Sūr, the famous wedding of Kana remains still engraved in a rock, picturing people, Disciples, the bride, and the faces of Yāwshu and Yāwhanan the Baptist. It was at that particular wedding that Maryām, the Mother of Yāwshu, had asked him for the miracle of wine. Not far from there, beyond the ancient boundaries of the city of Saydoun, in a small village called Makdoushi, people can still see the ancient grotto of "Sayadet al-Mantara" or "Our Lady of Mantara," translated into English as "Our Lady of the Awaiting," standing on a hill above the sea. It was in that particular place where Maryām used to wait for her son to return from his travels, Tradition says[635]. No wonder we still find the notion that Jesus used to retreat to his homeland after preaching in Jerusalem, as mentioned in Matthew (15:21), "Then Jesus went out from there (Jerusalem) and withdrew into the region of Tyre and Sidon." The grotto has recently been converted into a small church dedicated to the Virgin Holy Mother.

---

635 Please see picture of the grotto in the Appendix.

It was there, as well, on the peak of Mt. Hermon, known as Jabal al-sheikh, and called "the Mountain of the Meetings" by Anak or Enoch, that Yāwshu professed his divinity through transfiguration to Peter, James, and John. It was there where they had recognized Him as the only beloved Son of God, and as a result of this, Yāwshu entrusted them with the spiritual secret key to his Church, as mentioned in Matthew[636]. Unquestionably, the Phoenicians of Sūr and Saydoun constituted the first group of believers in Yāwshu the Meshiha, whom they had previously worshiped through Al-Ēlyon as the Son, Adon, who sacrificed himself with his Death, and then Resurrected. Yāwshu undoubtedly expressed happiness in retreating to the place where he had first felt "accepted."

As a reminder, we have seen that at the time of Jesus, both Galilee and Mt. Carmel were part of Phoenicia, belonging to the city of Tyre. This area remained a Phoenician-Lebanese territory until the end of the Ottoman era. However, in 1920 AD, it became part of Palestine, and later, in 1948, of Israel. History reveals that the Canaanite/Phoenicians dedicated Temples to Al and Adon on Mt. Carmel, hence the name Carmel, *Krm-Ēl*, the "Generous Vine of Ēl." In conjunction to that, the grotto of Bet-Lahem (Bethlehem), located on the Northeastern base of Mt. Carmel, meant the "House of Bread," in the Phoenician language. Adon (Adonis), who represented the spirit of the corn, that young and beautiful god of Gebel who also incarnated the cycle of nature and symbolized the spring as well—the resurrection of every atom in the kingdom of life—might well have dwelt and later worshiped in this Bet-Lahem. At Mt. Carmel and Galilee, the Ashayas (Asayas, Healers) believed in the God Ēl represented by an inscription of his name on medallions they wore on their chests, close to their hearts.

We have also learned that the first Church that rose near the grotto of Mt. Carmel was in devotion to Maryām—still living

---

636 Matthew 17:1-8, "Now after six days Jesus took Peter, James, and John his brother, led them up on a high mountain by themselves; and He was transfigured before them. His face shone like the sun, and His clothes became as white as the light. And behold, Moses and Elijah appeared to them, talking with Him. Then Peter answered and said to Jesus, Lord, it is good for us to be here; if You wish, let us make here three tabernacles: one for You, one for Moses, and one for Elijah. While he was still speaking, behold, a bright cloud overshadowed them; and suddenly a voice came out of the cloud, saying, This is My beloved Son, in whom I am well pleased. Hear Him! And when the disciples heard [it], they fell on their faces and were greatly afraid. But Jesus came and touched them and said, Arise, and do not be afraid. When they had lifted up their eyes, they saw no one but Jesus only."

among them. Some say the grotto was changed into a chapel. Others say it was probably built from the stones of a Temple dedicated to Ashirai (Asherah)—the Mother-Goddess of the Phoenicians; she is the Virgin Lady Anat herself—Queen of Heaven. It is also said that the Galilean-Essenes or Phoenician-Asayan hermits became Christians after being properly prepared, ever since the day of the Whitsuntide. Hence, Mt. Carmel—cradle of the monastic life—became a place for the veneration of the Virgin Maryām and a sanctuary of the spiritual contemplative life that characterized the Carmelite Order.

The Galilean Essenes were very different from the Qumran Community that appeared by the Dead Sea as a closed religious community strongly rejecting the mainstream Jewish Law of the time. They were Orthodox Jews who refused to live in Jewish territory, taking the caves in the Qumran Desert as their homes. The law within their male community was very strict towards women, whom they considered impure.

Yāwshu was not at all one of them, as we have previously seen. He instead was an adept of the Asayan society who feasted the Last Supper on Thursday[637]—a healer of mind, spirit, and body. The Phoenician-Galilean Asayas respected women greatly, and Yāwshu had many female disciples and followers like Maryām el-Mejdel—the most famous among them. In truth, after his baptism by Yāwhanan, he became a *Nazarene*, an adept of the ascetic branch of the Ashayas that counted but a few members; Yāwhanan the Baptist, Maryām Magdalene, Paul, and a few others. They all knew at once that Yāwshu was the long awaited Meshiha, and followed him faithfully ever since.

It was the Galilean Essenes, and not the Essens of the Qumran Community of Orthodox Judaism, that Robert Charoux mentioned as not Jewish. He wrote[638], "The Essenes are not of Jewish origin but of Pythagorean origin." The same note has been expressed by H.P. Blavatsky, where she asserted that the Essenes were Pythagoreans in all their doctrines and habits, and on Iamblichus' assertion, he (Pythagoras) spent a certain time at Carmel with them.[639] Of course, the Pythagoreans were Enochians (from Enoch-Thor) or Hermetists in all their doctrines and habits, since Pythagoras himself was Phoenician.[640]

The Book of Isaiah is in fact the book of *Asaya*, a Galilean book; the same stands for the Q Source: two books that talked

637 All Jews feasted their holidays on Saturdays.
638 Charoux, Robert, *Forgotten Worlds*, page 278.
639 Blavatsky, H.P., *Isis Unveiled*, Volume 2, page 130,145.
640 Please refer to *Pythagoras the Mathemagician* by Sunbury Press, 2010.

about Galilean Prophecy and Prophets. Isaiah was not a Jewish Prophet, nor was his book a Jewish book as we have learned before. Rooted in Galilee with the Phoenician-Ashayas (Galilean-Essenes) since the 4th and 3rd century BC, the book was considered sacred to them, who, were in a continuous socio-religious conflict with the Judeans of Jerusalem at the time. Thus, the famous citation from Isaiah[641] proves it and copes very well with the verse in Matthew (1:23).

This is surely not Hebrew-Jewish, for Immanuēl, "Ēl with us," describes Jesus Christ as a man manifesting the will and incarnating the spirit of Ēl, the Canaanite/Phoenician Most High God. This is how Yāwshu became the Divine Son of God, whispering ethereal hymns of Love and Peace, and Son of Man, speaking Aramaic, not Hebrew.

From that perspective, the Lebanese researcher and author, Alfred Murr, has a clear say in his book, *El, Yahvé et Jésus*. In a reply to poet and philosopher, Said Akl, who wrote the preface, "wondering" if Jesus was the son of the Israelite Yahweh or the son of the Phoenician Ēl[642], Murr concludes[643]:

> Jesus then completes the Canaanite Religion and abolishes everything that is not in concordance with the perfection of his Father in the Jewish Religion. He then completes El, re-animates his Priesthood and declares it eternally solid, while abolishing Yahweh in everything he has of cruelty, chauvinism and vengeance.

To us, of course, and many other thinkers like Alfred Murr, Jesus would then stand as a continuation of the Priestly Order of Milki-Sedek, and a completion of the Phoenician religion and theological system, as thus understood.

There is no doubt that the New Testament clearly portrays Jesus as being born from God the Father and the Virgin Lady Maryām, and so was Adon (Baal) portrayed in Phoenician historical and theological literature, born from the Virgin Lady Anat and the Most High God Ēl. The Phoenician-Galileans were longing for a Savior, and to them, Adon was a Savior sent by the God Ēl; now, Jesus is Immanuēl himself, "Ēl with us." In fact, the connection of Adon—the Phoenician Savior—with Jesus—the Christian Savior—is undeniable. Just as the God Ēl was clearly

---

641 Isaiah 7:14, "Therefore, the Lord himself shall give you a sign: Behold a virgin shall conceive, and bear a son, and shall call his name Immanuel."
642 Murr, Alfred, *El, Yahvé et Jésus*, page 10.
643 Ibid., page 111.

portrayed as the Father of Adon in the Phoenician religion, so did the Church New Testament portray God as Father of Yāwshu or *Immanu-Ēl*—the incarnation and representation of the God Ēl on Earth.

Epilogue

The language Clement of Alexandria used to address his brother coreligionists does really suggest that even the seals they had to engrave upon the gem of their rings should not be in any way related to Judaism. He advised his brothers in his *Paedagogus*[644]—

And let our seals be either a dove, or a fish, or a ship scudding before the wind, or a musical lyre, which Polycrates used, or a ship's anchor, which Seleucus got engraved as a device; and if there be one fishing, he will remember the apostle, and the children drawn out of the water.

His words were not totally heeded by early Christians who had only adopted one emblem of his five suggestions, and that was the fish; add to it the Lamb of God, and the Good Shepherd. However, one may definitely ask why the early Church father made his suggestion in this manner. Why the sailing ship running before the wind? Was it because he was a converted pagan or was it because he knew very well the Phoenician origin of Yāwshu and the majority of his Phoenician-Galilean Disciples as fishermen? Though, for reasons still unknown, no one of the Christian clergy but a very few have dared to say the truth about the true identity of Jesus Christ, their Lord and Savior, who strongly rebuked liars, lies, and the father of lies, in all forms and shapes. They could have said the truth, and only the truth, so help them God, *Ēl and his son Immanu-Ēl*, but not all the hearts and minds of the Christian clergy are as strong and resolute as the heart and mind of the Good Shepherd.

We have spoken plainly in this book about who the true historical and theological Jesus was, though it would take us eternity to know him. What concerns us here on Earth, finally, is the message of Love and Peace he conveyed to us, which would add more meaning to our lives and ample power to our conviction in the truth about the Man who changed the world so beautifully.

These are briefly the seven main characteristics and features of Christianity as depicted by Father Youssef (Yāwsēp̄) Yammine,

---

644 Clement of Alexandria, *Paedagogus*, Book 3, Chapter 11.

author of *The Messiah was Born in Lebanon not in Judea*. In an easy yet constructive dialogue with him he answered as such—

1- How do you define God? I mean, who is God? – God is Love: absolute Love. God is the Father of all mankind, and man is Son of God. He is their creator and their reason for being. Christianity is essentially Love.

2- How do you define the Christian trinity? – God is Trinity: three Entities—the Father, the Son, and the Holy Spirit—in one Being. They are distinct, yet they are one in essence and nature. The Father is the creator, the Son is the image of God, and the Holy Spirit is the bond of Love between the Father and the Son.

3- Who is the Son? I mean, how God had incarnated in the Son? – The second Entity of the Trinity is the Son that became flesh. He is both absolute God and absolute man. He has two natures, one Divine and the other Human, and thus, he has two wills, respectively. The Sacrament of the Eucharist emphasizes on the Incarnation of Jesus Christ, who represents God, becoming flesh, to raise Humanity up towards Divinity. Christ is all things and is in everything ... . By whom all things were created ... the universe was made through him and to him. He is the essence of all things.

4- How does salvation happen then? -- This is the Sacrament of Redemption where the second Entity of the Trinity, Jesus Christ, saved the world and humanity from evil and sin. He gave them eternal life and raised them to Heaven where their happiness resides.

5- What is the Church? – The Church is the mystical body of Christ; it is his living extension at all times and in all places until the end of time.

6- What is the Mystery of Christianity? Its unique feature? Its absolute secret? – Its mystery is the Love of Neighbors, where Christians should concentrate on the love to all people with no discrimination, for Christ has said, "Love one another as I have loved you." Its unique feature is the love of enemies, for Christ has said, "love your enemies." Finally, its absolute secret resides in the great concept that the Kingdom of Heaven is inside man, all men.

7- What is the purpose of man, all men? – The ultimate purpose of man is thus the search for happiness, which consists of participating in the Divine Nature.

Appendix

Maps

Authentic Maps of the Phoenician Bethlehem
Bet(h)-Lahem (House of Bread)

Map 1
Section of "Palestine"

Map 2
Section of ancient "Soria"
This is a section of the first scientific map of Syria (meaning
Phoenicia). It was drawn by the geographer Ptolemy around 150
AD, basing it on the work of Arastonis and Marinos of Tyre.

Map 3
Section of "Bird's Eye View of the Holy Land"

Map 4
Section of "Israel"

Pictures

The Grotto of Makadoushi where Virgin Lady Maryām waited for
her son to return from his missionary journeys in Jerusalem

The Lebanese Kana or Qana
the place of origin of the Virgin Lady Maryām
the famous wedding of Kana where the first miracle of turning
water into wine occurred

Tables

Table 1
Yāwshu Family Tree

Table 2
The Apostles

Table 3
The Approximate Timeline of the Most Important Christian Events
and the Development of the Church New Testament

Map 1 - Section of "Palestine"

Map 2 - Section of ancient "Soria"

29	Jezzin.	56	Achzib.	83	Suweideh.	111	Haifa.	139	
30	Castle Shuḥif.	57	Accho.	84	Derat.	112	Athlit.	140	
31	Ijon.	58	Beth Emik.	85	Kamh.	113	Dor.	141	
32	Abel.	59	Rehob.	86	Try.	114	Cæsarea.	142	
33	Hasbeiya.	60	Gabara.	87	Bozra.	115	Megiduo.	143	
34	Dan.	61	Cana.	88	Kureiyeh.	116	Hadad Rimmon	144	
35	Banias.	61½	Jotapata.	89	Beth Gamul.	117	Dothan.	145	
36	Castle.	62	Hazor.	90	Richab.	118	Jenin.	146	
37	Lake Phials.	63	Seffurieh.	91	Abila.	119	Samaria.	147	
38	Jubata.	64	Hukkok.	92	Gadara.	120	Shechem.	147½	
39	Rimeh.	65	Bethsaida.	93	Jabesh Gilead.	121	Joseph's Tomb.	148	
40	Kautana	66	Chorazin.	94	Abel Mehola.	122	Jacob's Well.	149	
41	Kaukab.	67	Capernaum.	95	Succoth.	123	Shalim.	150	
42	Kesweh.	68	Magdala.	96	Rehob.	124	Akabeh.	151	
43	Hurjilleh.	69	Tiberias.	97	Bethshean.	125	Archelais	152	
44	Kuneiterah.	70	Kerak.	98	Endor.	126	Pennel.	153	
45	Nowaran.	71	Hippos.	99	Deburieh.	127	Gerasa.	154	
46	Golan.	72	Gamala.	100	Nain.	128	Rabbath Ammon	155	
47	Kedesh.	73	Apek.	101	Chesulloth.	129	Heshbon.	156	
48	Safed.	74	Gerasa.	102	Nazareth.	130	Mashita.	157	
49	Castle Hunin.	75	Khastin.	103	Japhia.	131	Zophim.	158	
49½	Giscala.	76	Nawa.	104	Shunem.	132	Beth Peor.	159	
50	Castle Tibnin.	77	Ederi.	105	Jezrell.	133	Beth Nimra.	160	
51	Iron.	78	Nejran.	106	Tasnach.	134	Beth Haran.	161	
52	Rameh.	79	Zebriskin.	107	Gabatha.	135	Beth Jesimoth.	162	
53	Kanah.	80	Shukkah.	108	Bethlehem.	136	Beth Roglah.	163	
54	Hiram's Tomb.	81	Shubba.	109	Jeffa.	137	Gilgal.	164	
55	Tyre.	82	Kunawat.	110	Shefa Omar.	138	Jericho.	165	

Map 3 - Section of "Bird's Eye View of the Holy Land"

314

PHENICIE

Tyr

Qana

Beth-Anath

Simon Pierre c
en Jésus le Mes
(Mt 16,16)

Domicile de Jean de Giscala,
qui contesta l'autorité de
Flavius Josèphe en Galilée,
devint le chef des Zélotes et
dirigea en partie la défense
de Jérusalem.

Qèdesh, Kédès

Jésus guérit la fille d'une
femme phénicienne après
avoir tout d'abord refusé de
l'entendre.

Lac Semac

mmôn

Yiréon

The

Meroth

Haç

Mafshata

Beth-Shemesh

Gouch Halav (Giscala)

Yamnith

Ces trois
TRIANGLE
la grande
de Jésus.
Capiarn
souvent.

Avdén

La Galilée produisait
l'huile la plus fine

Merôn

Yanoah

Baqa

Teqoa

Cefat, Sepph (Safed)

Beth-Dagan

Huile

Achbera (Akabaron)

Beth-Emeq

Principale forteresse de
Galilée contre l'armée de
Vespasien. Elle tomba
après in long siège.
Flavius Josèphe y fut fait
prisonnier.

Rama

Bersabe

Chorazin

Sermon sur la
Montagne
(Mt 5,1-7,29)

Me'araja

Houqoq

Néiel

Houqoq

Calamin (Selame)

Ki
Ge

Akko

Rehov

Mimle

Magd
Taric

Mishèal

Kavoul

Sachne

Arav

Lieu de naissance
de Marie Madeleine

Arbela

Raqqat

Afiq

Yodfat, Yotapata

Cana

Les Noces de Cana (Jn 2,1-11)

Adama

GALILEE

Beth-Ma'on

Hama

Shefar'am

Uosh:

Hannatôn Shichin

Rouma

Rimmôn

Tétrarchie d'Hérode Antipas

Hali

Sepphoris (Cippori)

Garis

Aznoth-
Tabor

Hélef

Ein-Gannim

Bèen

Gath-Héfer

Damin

Y

Akshaf

Daverath,
Dabaritha

Ein-Hadda

Beth-S

Gaba

Bethléem

Domicile de Joseph et Marie
où Jésus passa son enfance

Nazareth

Kisloth-Tabor

Shimrôn Simonia

Shahacima

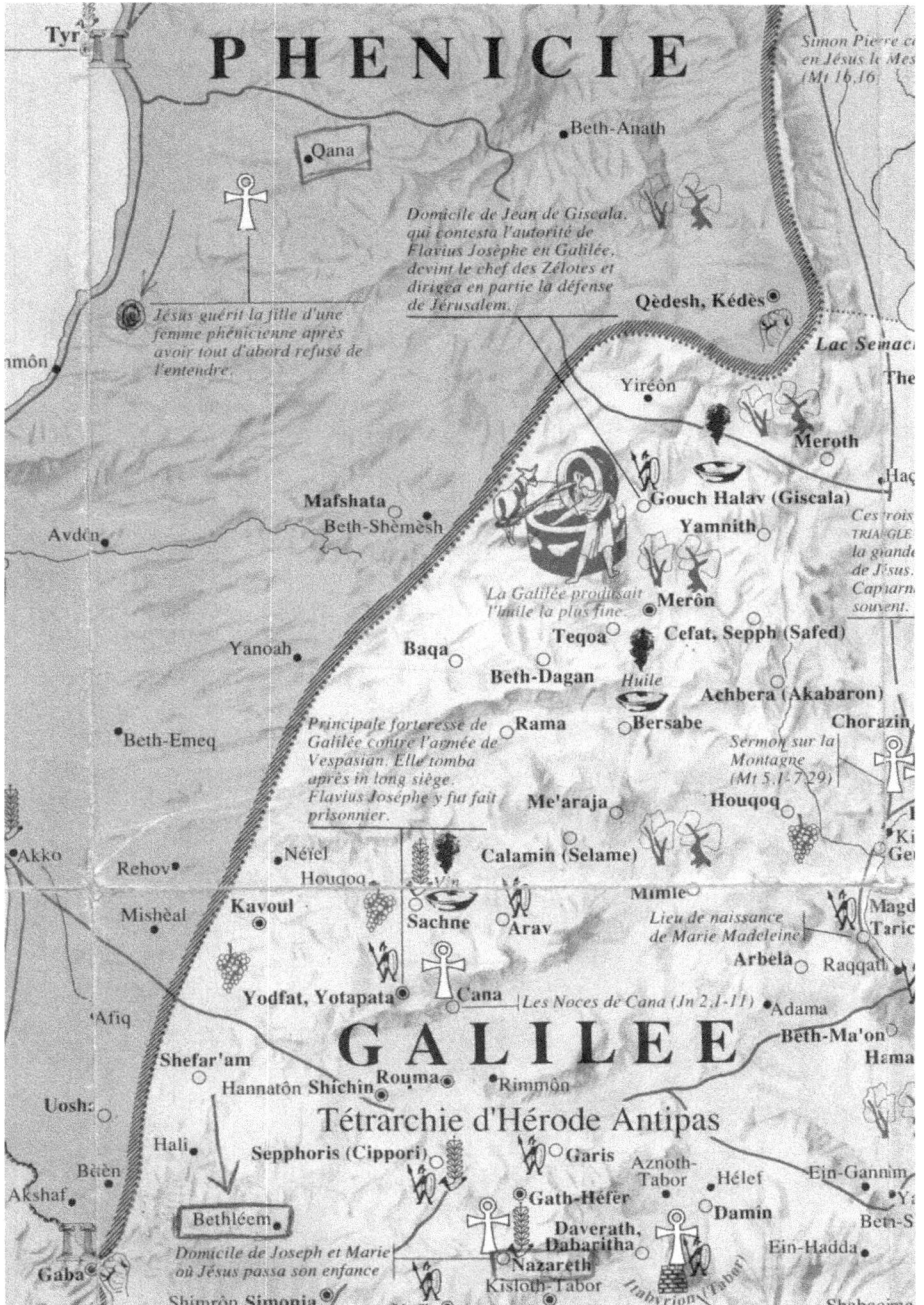

Map 4 - Section of "Israel"

Grotto of Makadoshi turned into a chapel. It was there where Virgin Lady Maryām waited for her son Yāwshu to return from his missionary journeys in Jerusalem.(Source=Khoury Hareb, Antoine, The Christian Roots in Lebanon, page 57)

Jesus and his twelve disciples at the wedding of Kana. (by Samih Zaatar)

Part 1 of the audience at the wedding of Kana. (by Samih Zaatar)

Part 2 of the audience at the wedding of Kana.(by Samih Zaatar)

Probably the two seats reserved for officials at the wedding where we can see the statue of one of them. (by Samih Zaatar)

The waterpots of stone used for turning water into wine at the wedding of Kana. Here, in this photo, we can see five out of six, mentioned in John (2=1-13). (by Samih Zaatar)

The Bride at the wedding of Kana. (by Samih Zaatar)

The statue of Maryām (Our Lady of the Awaiting) waiting for her son to return

(Source=Khoury Hareb, Antoine, The Christian Roots in Lebanon, page 57)

Table 1

Yāwshu Family Tree		
Yāwsēp̄ (of Ramah or Rameh, also known as Joseph of Arimathea) He was brother of **Yāwqim**	**Yāwqim (Yāw-yāqîm)** married **Anna**	**Elizabeth** married **Zakaria** She was sister of **Anna**
And uncle of **Maryām**	They gave birth to **Maryām**	They gave birth to **Yāwhanan the Baptist**
And great uncle of **Yāwshu**	**Maryām** married **Yāwsēp̄**	**Klôpas** married **Maryām** He was brother of **Yāwsēp̄** , the adoptive father of **Yāwshu** She was sister of **Maryām**, the mother of **Yāwshu**
	They gave birth to **Yāwshu** (Jesus)	They gave birth to **James** (Jacob), **Joses** (Justus or Yāwsep), **Simon** (Symeon) and **Jude**

Table 2

The Apostles	Position & Condition	List 1 Hippolytus Romanus (170 AD–236 AD)	List 2 St. Dorotheus, Bishop of Tyre (255 AD–362 AD)	List 3 Mâr Solomon (13th century AD)	List 4 St. Dimitri of Rostov (17th century AD)	N.T. References
Yawsēp̄ (of Ramah, or Rameh, also known as Joseph of Arimathea, Great Uncle of Yāwshu)	**1st Bishop of Britain** (Britannia) We prefer not to number him as a Disciple or as one of the Apostles. We believe he was more than that.	Omitted	Omitted	Mentioned (As Joseph the Senator)	Omitted	
Paul (of Tarsus, having Roman origin by birth, which suggests that he might have been a Gentile. He could have also originated from Galilee)	**Not a Bishop of any Church but founder of many** (he played an important role in spreading Christianity across the world from Jerusalem to Rome and beyond)	Omitted	Omitted	Omitted	Omitted	
-1- James (also Jacob, cousin to Yāwshu, not his brother)	**1st Bishop of Jerusalem** (he died by lapidation in Jerusalem in c. 62 AD)	Mentioned	Mentioned	Mentioned	Mentioned	Matthew 27:55-56 Mark 15: 40-41 Luke 24:10
-2- Klôpas (Clopas, Cleopas or Cleophas, also called Alphaeus, Alphaios or Alphee, younger brother of Joseph the betrothed, and father of James, Joses, Jude, and Simeon)	**2nd Bishop of Jerusalem** (he died a martyr, slain by the Jews for preaching Christ)	Mentioned	Mentioned	Mentioned	Mentioned	Luke 24:18
-3- Simeon (also Symeon, brother of James, Yāwshu's cousin)	**3rd Bishop of Jerusalem** (some say he was the 2nd)	Omitted	Omitted	Mentioned	Mentioned	
-4- Justus (also Joses, Joseph or Jesus, from the Aramaic roots Yawsēp̄ . He is brother of James, Yāwshu's cousin)	**Bishop of Eleutheropolis** (Israel) (originally Known in Aramaic as Bet-Gabra: House of the Powerful)	Mentioned	Mentioned (As Jesus)	Mentioned (Also as Joseph and Barshabbâ)	Mentioned	Matthew 27:55-56 Mark 15:40-41 Acts 1:23 Col 4:11
-5- Matthias	He replaced Judas Iscariot.	Mentioned	Omitted	Mentioned (As 1 of the 12)	Omitted	

The Apostles	Position & Condition	List 1 Hippolytus Romanus (170 AD–236 AD)	List 2 St. Dorotheus, Bishop of Tyre (255 AD–362 AD)	List 3 Mâr Solomon (13th century AD)	List 4 St. Dimitri of Rostov (17th century AD)	N.T. References
-6- **Thaddeus** (Thaddeus of Edessa, also called Addai)	He is said to have cured Avgar or Augarus in Edessa of his illness. He died in the Phoenician city of Berytus.	Mentioned	Mentioned	Mentioned (As Thaddaeus)	Mentioned	
-7- **Ananias**	**Bishop of Damascus** (Syria)	Mentioned	Mentioned	Mentioned	Mentioned	Acts 9:10,17; 22:12
-8- **Stephen** (the Protomartyr. One of the 7)	He was stoned to death by the Jews in Jerusalem in c. 34/35 AD marking the first martyrdom.	Mentioned	Mentioned	Mentioned	Mentioned	Acts 6:5; 6:8-9 7:59 11:19
-9- **Philip** (also Philip the Evangelist. One of the 7)	**Bishop of Tralles** (Asia Minor)	Mentioned	Mentioned	Mentioned	Mentioned	Acts 6:5; 8:6 8:26-40 21:8-9
-10- **Prochorus** (One of the 7)	**Bishop of Nicomedia** (Bithynia) He died a martyr in Antioch.	Mentioned	Mentioned	Mentioned	Mentioned	Acts 6:5
-11- **Nicanor** (One of the 7)	He was slain for Christ on the same day Stephen fell as a protomartyr.	Mentioned	Mentioned	Mentioned	Mentioned	Acts 6:5
-12- **Timon** (One of the 7 deacons who suffered greatly)	**Bishop of Bostra** (Island of Arabia) He was persecuted by the Jews for preaching Christ	Mentioned	Mentioned	Mentioned	Mentioned	Acts 6:5
-13- **Parmenas** (One of the 7)	**Bishop of Soli** He preached many years in Asia Minor before he settled in Macedonia. He died a martyr in Philippi, Macedonia in c. 98 AD	Mentioned	Mentioned	Mentioned	Mentioned	Acts 6:5

The Apostles	Position & Condition	List 1 Hippolytus Romanus (170 AD–236 AD)	List 2 St. Dorotheus, Bishop of Tyre (255 AD–362 AD)	List 3 Mâr Solomon (13th century AD)	List 4 St. Dimitri of Rostov (17th century AD)	N.T. References
-14- Nicolaus (also Nicolas. One of the 7)	Bishop of Samaria	Mentioned	Mentioned (As having deviated from the true faith together with Simon)	Mentioned (As the proselyte Antiochian)	Omitted	Acts 6:5
-15- Barnabas (also Joses or Yāwsẽp̄, Joseph)	Bishop of Milan He was stoned to death by Greeks and Jews and died in his homeland on the island of Cyprus	Mentioned	Mentioned	Mentioned	Mentioned	Acts 4:36; 9:27 1Cr 9:6 Gal 2:1 Col 4:10
Barnabas (another one!)	He could be identical to the 1st Barnabas cited above.	Mentioned (As Bishop of Heraclea or Heraklion)	Omitted	Omitted	Omitted	
-16- Mark (also John & Mark the Evangelist)	Bishop of Alexandria (Egypt) & Gebel-Byblos (Phoenicia-Lebanon)	Mentioned (As Bishop of Bibloupolis)	Mentioned	Mentioned	Mentioned	Acts 12:12,25 15:37-41 1Pe 5:13 Col 4:10 2Ti 4:11
-17- Luke (also Luke the Evangelist, & author of the Acts)	Bishop of Salonika (Turkey)	Mentioned	Mentioned (As coming from the Phoenician city of Antioch)	Mentioned (As a Physician)	Mentioned	Col 4:14
-18- Silas (like Luke, preached the Gospel all over the world together with Paul)	Bishop of Corinth	Mentioned	Mentioned	Mentioned	Mentioned	Acts 15:22
-19- Silvanus	Bishop of Thessalonica	Mentioned	Mentioned (As Bishop of Salonika)	Omitted	Mentioned	1Pe 5:12 2Cr 1:19
-20- Crisces (also Criscus or Crescens)	Bishop of Galatia & later of Carchedon (Gaul) after preaching Christ for many years. It is said he appointed his disciple Zacharias as Bishop of Vienne.	Mentioned	Omitted	Mentioned	Mentioned	2Ti 4:10

The Apostles	Position & Condition	List 1 Hippolytus Romanus (170 AD–236 AD)	List 2 St. Dorotheus, Bishop of Tyre (255 AD–362 AD)	List 3 Mâr Solomon (13th century AD)	List 4 St. Dimitri of Rostov (17th century AD)	N.T. References
-21- Epænetus (also Epenetus)	Bishop of Carthage (Tunisia - Phoenician city)	Mentioned	Mentioned	Omitted	Mentioned	Romans 16:5
-22- Andronicus	Bishop of Pannonia	Mentioned	Mentioned	Mentioned (As the Greek)	Mentioned	Romans 16:7
-23- Amplias (also Ampelius)	Bishop of Odyssus or Odissa (Diospolis, Lydda of Odyssopolis)	Mentioned	Mentioned	Mentioned	Mentioned	Romans 16:8
-24- Urban (also Urbanus)	Bishop of Macedonia (Died a Martyr)	Mentioned	Mentioned	Mentioned	Mentioned	Romans 16:9
-25- Stachys	Bishop of Byzantium	Mentioned	Mentioned	Mentioned	Mentioned	Romans 16:9
-26- Phygellus	Bishop of Ephesus (Turkey)	Mentioned	Mentioned	Omitted	Omitted	
-27- Hermogenes	Bishop of Megara (Thrace)	Mentioned	Mentioned	Omitted	Omitted	
-28- Demas	It is said he opposed the teachings of the Christian God just like Phygellus & Hermogenes.	Mentioned	Mentioned	Mentioned	Omitted	1Jo 2:19 2Cr 11:13
-29- Apelles (also Apollos)	Bishop of Heraclea (Heraklion)	Mentioned (As Bishop of Smyrna)	Mentioned	Mentioned (As Apollos)	Mentioned	Romans 16:10
-30- Aristobulus	Bishop of Britain (Britannia) He could be the 2nd Bishop after Yāwsēp̄ of Ramah.	Mentioned	Mentioned	Mentioned (As preaching in Isauria in Asia Minor where he died and buried)	Mentioned	Romans 16:10
-31- Narcissus	,Bishop of Athens (Greece)	Mentioned	Mentioned	Mentioned (As having been rejected from among the 70)	Mentioned	Romans 16:11

The Apostles	Position & Condition	List 1 Hippolytus Romanus (170 AD–236 AD)	List 2 St. Dorotheus, Bishop of Tyre (255 AD–362 AD)	List 3 Mâr Solomon (13th century AD)	List 4 St. Dimitri of Rostov (17th century AD)	N.T. References
-32- Herodion (also Rodion or Rhodion, martyred in Rome)	Bishop of Patfas (Patras) or Neopatras (He died with Peter and Olympus in Rome executed by Nero)	Mentioned (As Bishop of Tarsus)	Mentioned	Mentioned (As the son of Narcissus)	Mentioned	Romans 16:11
-33- Agabus	He possessed the gift of Prophecy, and was called, the Prophet.	Mentioned	Mentioned	Omitted	Mentioned	Acts 11:27-28
-34- Rufus	Bishop of Thebes (Greece)	Mentioned	Mentioned	Mentioned	Mentioned	Mark 15:21 Romans 16:13
-35- Asyncritus	Bishop of Hyrcania (Asia)	Mentioned	Mentioned	Mentioned	Mentioned	Romans 16:14
-36- Phlegon (also Plïgtâ)	Bishop of Marathon (Thrace)	Mentioned	Mentioned	Mentioned (As Plïgtâ)	Mentioned	Romans 16:14
-37- Hermes	Bishop of Dalmatia	Mentioned	Mentioned (As Bishop of Philippi or Philipopolis)	Mentioned (As Hermas)	Mentioned	Romans 16:14
-38- Patrobulus (also Patrobas)	Bishop of Neapolis (Naples) & Puteoli (Pottole) (Italy)	Mentioned	Mentioned	Mentioned	Mentioned	Romans 16:14
-39- Hermas	Bishop of Philippi (Philipopolis)	Mentioned	Mentioned (As Bishop of Dalmatia)	Mentioned	Mentioned	Romans 16:14
-40- Linus (a disciple of Paul)	Bishop of Rome (after Peter, which makes him the 2nd Bishop of Rome)	Mentioned	Mentioned	Omitted	Mentioned	2Ti 4:21
-41- Timothy	1st Bishop of Ephesus	Omitted	Omitted	Mentioned	Mentioned	
-42- Caius (also Gaius)	2nd Bishop of Ephesus (after Timothy or Timotheus)	Mentioned	Mentioned	Mentioned	Mentioned	Acts 19:29 20:4 1Cr 1:14 Romans 16:23

The Apostles	Position & Condition	List 1 Hippolytus Romanus (170 AD–236 AD)	List 2 St. Dorotheus , Bishop of Tyre (255 AD–362 AD)	List 3 Mâr Solomon (13th century AD)	List 4 St. Dimitri of Rostov (17th century AD)	N.T. Referenc es
-43- Philologus (also Philogogus or Philologos)	Bishop of Sinope (Turkey) He was ordained by the Apostle Andrew)	Mentioned	Mentioned (As Philogogu s)	Omitted	Mentioned (As Philologos)	Romans 16:15
-44- Olympus (also Olympas)	He was martyred for Christ in Rome along with Rhodion and Peter from a death penalty executed by Nero.	Mentioned	Omitted	Mentioned (As Olympas)	Mentioned (As Olympas)	Romans 16:15
-45- Lucius (Of Cyrene)	Bishop of Laodicea (Syria) He was one of the founders of the Christian Church in Antioch	Mentioned	Mentioned	Mentioned	Mentioned	Acts 13:1
-46- Jason (Of Tarsus)	Bishop of Tarsus (Tarsis) (Turkey) He was ordained by the Apostle Paul	Mentioned	Mentioned	Mentioned	Mentioned	Acts 17:5-9
-47- Sosipater	1st Bishop of Iconium He was appointed by his relative Paul, the Apostle.	Mentioned	Mentioned	Omitted	Mentioned	Romans 16:21
-48- Tertius	2nd Bishop of Iconium	Mentioned	Mentioned	Omitted	Mentioned	Romans 16:22
-49- Erastus	Bishop of Panellas (Paneas, Baneas) (Caesarea Philippi, Palestine) He was chamberlain of the Church in Jerusalem before	Mentioned	Mentioned	Omitted	Mentioned	Acts 19:22 Romans 16:23 2Ti 4:20
-50- Quartus	Bishop of Berytus (Beirut) (Phoenicia-Lebanon)	Mentioned	Mentioned	Omitted	Mentioned	Romans 16:23

The Apostles	Position & Condition	List 1 Hippolytus Romanus (170 AD–236 AD)	List 2 St. Dorotheus, Bishop of Tyre (255 AD–362 AD)	List 3 Mâr Solomon (13th century AD)	List 4 St. Dimitri of Rostov (17th century AD)	N.T. References
-51- Apollo (also Apollos)	Bishop of Cæsarea (Phoenicia-Galilee)	Mentioned	Mentioned (Yet another one as Bishop of Smyrna)	Mentioned (As the Elect)	Mentioned (As Bishop of Corinth)	Acts 18:24 19:1 1Cr 1:12; 3:4-6; 4:6; 16:12 Titus 3:13
-52- Cephas (could be Simon-Peter, 1 of the 12)	1st Bishop of Antioch	Mentioned	Mentioned (As Bishop of Iconium, perhaps after Sosipater and Tertius)	Mentioned (As Preacher at Antioch)	Omitted	1Cr 9:5
-53- Evodus (also Euodius)	2nd Bishop of Antioch (after St. Peter)	Mentioned	Mentioned	Omitted	Mentioned	Phl 4:2
-54- Sosthenes	1st Bishop of Colophonia or Colophon. (Ionia)	Mentioned	Mentioned	Omitted	Mentioned	1Cr 1:1 Acts 18:17
-55- Tychicus	2nd Bishop of Colophonia or Colophon. (Ionia)	Mentioned	Mentioned	Omitted	Mentioned	Acts 20:4 Eph 6:21 Col 4:7
-56- Tychicus (another one!)	Bishop of Chalcedon (Bithynia, Asia Minor)	Mentioned	Mentioned	Omitted	Omitted	
-57- Epaphroditus (also Epaphras)	Bishop of Andriace (Andriaca or Hadriacus) (Turkey)	Mentioned	Mentioned	Omitted	Mentioned (As different from Epaphras, Bishop of Colossae)	Phl 2:25-30 4:18
-58- Cæsar	Bishop of Dyrr(h)achium	Mentioned	Mentioned	Omitted	Omitted	
-59- Mark (also Marcus, the nephew of Barnabas. Not to be confused with the Evangelist)	Bishop of Apollonia(s)	Mentioned	Mentioned	Omitted	Mentioned	Col 4:10
-60- Artemas (also Artemus)	Bishop of Lystra (Turkey)	Mentioned	Mentioned	Omitted	Mentioned	Titus 3:12

The Apostles	Position & Condition	List 1 Hippolytus Romanus (170 AD–236 AD)	List 2 St. Dorotheus, Bishop of Tyre (255 AD–362 AD)	List 3 Mâr Solomon (13th century AD)	List 4 St. Dimitri of Rostov (17th century AD)	N.T. References
-61- Clement	Bishop of Sardinia (Sardice or Sardis) (Turkey)	Mentioned	Mentioned	Omitted	Mentioned	Phl 4:3
-62- Onesiphorus	Bishop of Cyrene (Libya) & Bishop of Colophon (Ionia) He could be the 3rd after Sosthenes and Tychicus.	Mentioned (As Bishop of Corone, yet there is no such place)	Mentioned	Omitted	Mentioned (As Bishop of both Colophon & Cyrene)	2Ti 1:16
-63- Carpus	Bishop of Beroea (Berroia or Berrhoe (Thrace, Macedonia, in Greece)	Mentioned (As Bishop of Berytus in Thrace, yet Berytus is in Lebanon!	Mentioned	Omitted	Mentioned	2Ti 4:13
-64- Aristarchus	Bishop of Apamea (Syria)	Mentioned	Mentioned	Omitted	Mentioned	Acts 19:29 20:4; 27:2 Col 4:10 Phm 1:24
Aristarchus (another one!)	He could be identical to the 1st Aristarchus cited above.	Mentioned	Mentioned	Omitted	Omitted	
-65- Zenas	Bishop of Diospolis (Israel)	Mentioned	Mentioned (As the Lawyer)	Omitted	Mentioned	Titus 3:13
-66- Philemon	Bishop of Gaza (Palestine)	Mentioned	Mentioned	Omitted	Mentioned	Phm 1
-67- Pudes (also Pudens)	He was a pious Roman Senator who sheltered Peter & Paul in his house, known as 'the Shepherd's Church'	Mentioned	Mentioned	Omitted	Mentioned	2Ti 4:21
-68- Trophimus (the Ephesian)	He fell a martyr in Rome along with Aristarchus, Pudens and Paul. All were beheaded by Nero.	Mentioned	Mentioned	Omitted	Mentioned	Acts 20:4 21:29 2Ti 4:20

The Apostles	Position & Condition	List 1 Hippolytus Romanus (170 AD–236 AD)	List 2 St. Dorotheus, Bishop of Tyre (255 AD–362 AD)	List 3 Mâr Solomon (13th century AD)	List 4 St. Dimitri of Rostov (17th century AD)	N.T. References
-69- Crispus	He was cited in the Acts as *the chief ruler of the synagogue.* We very much doubt this. His *Gentile* name does not support this position.	Omitted	Mentioned (As Bishop of Chalcedon in Galilee)	Omitted	Mentioned (As Bishop of Aegina, an island near Peloponnesus)	
-70- Onesimus	**Bishop of Byzantium** He died in Potiole or Puteoli.	Omitted	Mentioned	Omitted	Mentioned	
-71- Titus	**Bishop of Gortyna** (Crete)	Omitted	Omitted	Mentioned	Mentioned	
-72- Simon Niger (also Simeon called Niger)	He was mentioned by Luke in the Acts of the Apostles.	Omitted	Omitted	Mentioned	Mentioned	

Table 3

The Approximate Timeline of the Most Important Christian Events and the Development of the Church New Testament		
Event	Location	Time
Divine Conception of **Christ**	- Temple of Mt. Carmel in Galilee	9 months before
Birth of **Christ**	- Bet-Lahem in Galilee	C. 6-4 BC
Ministry of **Christ**	- Mainly Galilee - Occasionally Judah	C. 27-28 AD
Crucifixion of **Christ**	- Golgotha, Jerusalem	C. 30-33 AD
Missionary of **Yāwsep of Rameh**	- Britain	C. 35-37 AD
Missionary of **Paul**	- Antioch - Asia Minor	C. 45 AD
First *Official* Christian Assembly: **James, Paul, John, Peter**	- Jerusalem	C. 49-52 AD
The Galilean Nazarenes of the Ashayas, most probably writing the *Q Source*	- Galilee	C. 50 AD
Paul writing his *1st Letter to the Thessalonians*	- Athens or Corinth in Greece	C. 51-52 AD
Paul writing his *1st & 2nd Letter to the Corinthians, Letter to the Galatians, Letter to the Romans, Letter to the Philippians, and Letter to Philemon*	- Ephesus - Philippi or Thessalonica in Macedonia - Corinth - Rome	C. 53/54-60 AD
James writing his *Letter*	- Jerusalem	C. 49/52-62 AD
Peter writing his *1st Letter*	- Antioch - Rome	C. 54-60 AD
Paul writing his *Letter to the Hebrews*	- Jerusalem (or) - Rome	C. 58-60 AD
Jude writing his *Letter*	- Jerusalem (most probably)	C. 60-90 AD

The Approximate Timeline of the Most Important Christian Events and the Development of the Church New Testament		
Event	**Location**	**Time**
Peter writing his *2nd Letter*	- Jerusalem (or) - Rome	C. 60-67 AD
Mark writing his *Gospel*	- Cana or Byblos in Phoenicia (or) - Antioch (or) - Palestine	C. 60/64-68/70 AD
Luke writing his *Gospel*	- Antioch - Unknown place in Phoenicia - Ephesus - Salonika	C. 80-85 AD
Matthew writing his *Gospel*	- Galilee (most probably)	C. 80-90 AD
Paul's Disciples writing the *2nd Letter to the Thessalonians, Letter to the Colossians, Letter to the Ephesians, Letter to Titus,* and the *1st and 2nd Letter to Timothy*	- Ephesus - Corinth - Rome	C. 80-100 AD
Luke writing his *Acts of the Apostles*	- Antioch - Unknown place in Phoenicia - Ephesus - Salonika - Rome	C. 85-100 AD
John writing his *Gospel*	- Ephesus	C. 90-100 AD
John writing his *Revelation*	- Patmos in the Aegean Sea - Ephesus	C. 95-96 AD
John writing his *3 Letters*	- Ephesus	C. 96-110 AD
Marcion writing his *Gospel of the Lord* (as the New Testament) and his *Antitheses*	- Sinope (Pontus) in Asia Minor - Rome	C. 130-144 AD
Justin Martyr writing his *First Apology* among others	- Rome	C. 155-157 AD (c. 147-161 AD)
Hegesippus writing his *Memoirs*	- Rome	C. 174-189 AD

The Approximate Timeline of the Most Important Christian Events and the Development of the Church New Testament		
Event	**Location**	**Time**
Irenaeus writing his most important work; *Adversus Haereses* (Against Heresies)	- Smyrna in Asia Minor - Lugdunum in Gaul	C. 180 AD
Clement writing his most important works; *Protrepticus* (Exhortation), *Paedagogus* (Tutor) and *Stromata* (Miscellanies)	- Alexandria in Egypt	C. 195 AD C. 198 AD C. 198–203 AD
Tertullian writing many Theological, Dogmatic, On Morality, Apologetic and Polemical works including his *Adversus Marcionem*	- Carthage in Africa	C. 204–220 AD C. 208 AD
Hippolytus Romanus writing his *A Refutation of all Heresies* among a few other works; *On Christ and the Antichrist*, *On the Seventy Disciples...*	- Rome	C. 200–? AD
Origen writing many works characterized as Textual Criticism, Exegesis, Systematic, Dogmatic, Practical and Apologetic Theology, and Letters, besides certain spurious works. His most vital work on Textual Criticism was the *Hexapla*, a comparative study of various translations of the Old Testament. He was largely responsible for gathering the information concerning the texts that became the 'Church New Testament'.	- Alexandria - Jerusalem - Caesarea in Palestine - Athens	C. 211–245 AD
Eusebius writing his most important works; *Proof of the Gospel, Preparation for the Gospel, Chronicle, Church History, Life of Constantine, On the Place-Names in the Holy Scripture*, among many other writings on Biblical Text Criticism, Apologetic and Dogmatic works, Exegetical and Miscellaneous works. His work depended greatly on the Library of Pamphilus of Beirut in Caesarea Maritima. It was his *Church History* that paved the way for the late 4th century Easter Letter which declared the accepted Christian writings that eventually formed the 'Church New Testament'.	- Caesarea in Palestine	C. 291–339 AD

The Approximate Timeline of the Most Important Christian Events and the Development of the Church New Testament		
Event	**Location**	**Time**
Athanasius writing his *Against the Heathen*, *The Incarnation of the Word of God*, among many other Biblical Exegesis. His vital *39th Easter Letter (Festal Letter)* which included the 27 books of the 'Church New Testament' was also approved at the Council in Trullo at Constantinople	- Alexandria	C. 316-319 AD C. 367 AD C. 692 AD (Council)
Jerome writing his *Chronicle*, *On Illustrious Men*, and many other Theological writings and works like his translation of the Old Testament, called the *Vulgate*. A Scholar and Historian, whose most of his work were mainly based on both, Origen and Eusebius.	- Antioch - Chalcis (in what is known today as Anjar in Lebanon) - Constantinople - Rome - Alexandria & Nitria in Egypt - Jerusalem	C. 373–415AD
Third Council (Synod) of Carthage confirmed the 'Church New Testament' & the Old Testament as one Holy Bible for Christians.	- Carthage	C. 397 AD

Bibliography

English:

Allegro, J.M, *The Dead Sea Scrolls*, Penguin Books Ltd, Made and printed in Great Britain by C. Nicholls & Company Ltd, Reprinted, 1959.

Ballou, Robert O., *The Portable World Bible*, Edited by Robert O. Ballou, Published by the Penguin Group, Penguin Books USA Inc., Printed in the United States of America, Reprinted Edition, 1976.

Baring-Gould, Sabine, *A Book of Cornwall*,

Baronius, Caesar, *Annales Ecclesiatici*, 16th century AD.

Bartholomew, *the Gospel*, 2nd century AD.

Bernal, Martin, *Black Athena: The Afroasiatic Roots of Classical Civilization, Volume I: The Fabrication of Ancient Greece*, Vintage Books, Random House UK, Printed and bound in Great Britain by Cox & Wyman Ltd, 1991.

Blavatsky, H.P., *Isis Unveiled*, The Theosophical Publishing House, First Quest Edition, Printed in the United States of America by Versa Press, 1993, Volume I & II.

Blavatsky, H.P., *The Secret Doctrine*, The Theosophical Publishing House, First Quest Edition, Printed in the United States of America by Versa Press, 1993, Volume I, II & III.

Bock, Darrell L., PH.D., *Breaking The Da Vinci Code*, Published in Nashville, Tennessee, by Thomas Nelson Inc., Nelson Books, A Division of Thomas Nelson Publishers, Printed in the United States of America, 2004.

Capt E. Raymond (M.A., A.I.A, F.S.A. Scot.), *The Traditions of Glastonbury*, Published by Artisan Sales, 1983, 1987, California, USA.

Charoux Robert, *Forgotten Worlds*, Popular Library Edition, Printed in the USA, New York, 1973.

Clark Kee, Howard, *Evolution of the Synagogue: Problems and Progress*, 1999

Clark Kee, Howard, *Jesus in History - An Approach to the Study of the Gospels*, Harcourt Brace Jovanovich, Inc., Printed in the United States of America, Second Edition, 1970, 1977.

Clement (of Alexandria), *Paedagogus*.

Crossan, John Dominic & Reed, Jonathan L., *Excavating Jesus - Beneath the Stones, Behind the Texts*, First published by HarperCollins Publisher, Inc. New York, Printed in the United States of America, 2001.

Cyril (of Jerusalem), *Catechetical Lectures*.

Dobson, C.C., *Did Our Lord Visit Britain as They Say in Cornwall and Somerset?*,

Ehrman, Bart D., *Lost Christianities - The Battles for Scripture and the Faiths We Never Knew*, Fist Published by Oxford University Press, Inc., 2003, 2005, New York, Printed in the United States of America.

Eusebius (of Caesarea), *Demonstratio Evangelica* (Proof of the Gospel)

Eusebius (of Caesarea), *Historia Ecclesiastica* (Church History).

Eusebius (of Caesarea), *Martyrs of Palestine.*

Eusebius (of Caesarea), *Praeparatio Evangelica* (Preparation for the Gospel).

Eusebius (of Caesarea), *Vita Constantini* (Life of Constantine).

Finkelstein, Israel & Silberman, Neil Asher, *The Bible Unearthed - Archaeology's new vision of ancient Israel and the origin of its sacred texts*, A Touchstone Book, Published by Simon & Schuster, New York, Manufactured in the United States of America, 2002.

Frazer, Sir James, *The Golden Bough* (A Study in Religion and Magic), An Abridged Edition, Dover Publications, Inc., Mineola, New York, Manufactured in the United States of America, 2002.

James, *the Gospel*, 2nd century AD.

Jerome, *De Viris Illustribus* (On Illustrious Men)

Jerome, *Epistles.*

Jerome, *Isaiah* (The Prologue to the Prophet)

Josephus, Flavius, *The Antiquities of the Jews.*

Josephus, Flavius, *The Wars of the Jews; or the history of the destruction of Jerusalem*, translated by William Whiston.

Justin (Martyr), *First Apology.*

Harnack, Adolf Von, *The Origin of the New Testament and the most important consequences of the New Creation*, Translated by J. R. Wilkinson, Wipf & Stock Publishers, Eugene, Oregon, USA, 2004. (Previously published by Williams and Norgate, 1925)

Harnack, Adolf Von, *Marcion the Gospel of the Alien God*, Translated by John E. Steely and Lyle D. Bierma, Wipf & Stock Publishers, Eugene, Oregon, USA, 2007. (Previously published by the Labyrinth Press, 1990)

Herodotus, *The Histories*, Printed in the United States of America, Published by Barnes & Noble Books, 2005, New York, USA Press Inc.

Hippolytus Romanus, *On the Seventy Disciples.*

Hippolytus Romanus, *A Refutation of all Heresies.*

Irenaeus, *Adversus Haereses* (Against Heresies)

Gunkel, Hermann, *Genesis,*

Knox, John, *Marcion and the New Testament*, 1942

Lemche, Niels Peter, *The Israelites in History and Tradition*, First Published in the United States by Westminster John Knox Press, Louisville Kentucky, USA, 1998.

Lewis, Glynn S., *Did Jesus Come to Britain? An Investigation into the Traditions That Christ Visited Cornwall and Somerset,*

Luther, Martin, *On Christian Liberty*, Edited by Harold J. Grimm, Fortress Press, Philadelphia, PA, USA, 2003.

Mack, Burton L., *The Lost Gospel - The Book of Q & Christian Origins*, HarperOne, An Imprint of HarperCollinsPublishers, New York, USA, 1994.

Malmesbury, William of, *Chronicle of the English Kings*, 12th century AD.

Maurus, Rhabanus, *Life of Mary Magdalene*, 9th century AD.

Origen, *Against Celsus*.

Philo of Alexandria, *Quod Omnis Probus Liber Sit* (Every Good Man is Free).

Pliny the Elder, *History of Nature*.

Pliny the Younger, *Letters of Pliny*.

Ratzinger, Joseph (Pope Benedict XVI), *Jesus of Nazareth*, first published in Great Britain by Bloomsbury Publishing, 2007, Printed in Great Britain by Clays Limited, St Ives plc.

Rawlinson, George, *History of Phoenicia*, The Project Gutenberg EBook, 2006. First Published 1889 by Longmans, Green, and Co.

Reed, Jonathan L., *Archeology and the Galilean Jesus - A Re-examination of the Evidence*, Trinity Press International, an imprint of Continuum Publishing, Harrisburg, PA, 2002, Printed in the United States of America.

Roncaglia, Martiniano Pellegrino, *Cana*, 1995

Roncaglia, Martiniano Pellegrino, *In the Footsteps of Jesus, the Messiah, in Phoenicia/Lebanon*, 2004

Smith, Mark S., *The Origins of Biblical Monotheism: Israel's Polytheistic Background and the Ugaritic Texts*, Oxford University Press, USA, 2001.

Solomon, Mâr, *The Book of the Bee*, edited and translated by Earnest A. Wallis Budge, M.A., Oxford, the Clarendon Press, 1886.

Strabo, *Geography*.

Strobel, Lee, *The Case for Christ: A Journalist's Personal Investigation of the Evidence for Jesus*, Published by Zondervan, part of HarperCollins Publishers, 1998, printed in the United States of America.

Suetonius (Gaius Suetonius Tranquillus), *The Lives of the Twelve Caesars*, translated by Alexander Thompson and edited by T. Forester, Dodo Press, United Kingdom, 2007

Tacitus, *Annals*.

Tertullian, *Adversus Judaeos* (An Answer to the Jews)

Tertullian, *Adversus Marcionem* (Against Marcion)

Theophanes, *Chronography*.

Thompson, Thomas L., *The Historicity of the Patriarchal Narratives*, 1974

Thompson, Thomas L., *The Mythic Past - Biblical Archaeology and the Myth of Israel*, Published by Basic Books, a Member of the Perseus Books Group, 1999, Printed in the United States of America.

Tyson, Joseph B., *Marcion and Luke-Acts: a defining struggle*, 2006

Waddell, L.A., *The Phoenician Origin of Britons, Scots, & Anglo-Saxons*, First Published 1924 by The Christian Book Club of America, Hawthorne, California, Printed in the USA.

Wait, Charles B., *History of the Christian Religion to the year Two Hundred*, 1881.

Whitelam, Keith W., *The Invention of Ancient Israel - The Silencing of Palestinian History*, First Published by Routledge, Taylor & Francis Group, London, Great Britain, 1996

French:

Amsler, Frederic (Traduction, Introduction et Annotation), *L' évangile Inconnu - La Source Des Paroles De Jésus (Q)*, Essais Bibliques, Éditions Labor et Fides, Imprimé en France, 2001.

De Bizemont, Dorothée Koechlin, *L'univers D'Edgar Cayce*, Tome 1, Edgar Cayce Foundation, Éditions Robert Laffont, (Éditions J'ai lu, Paris, France, 1985

Duquesne, Jacques, *Jésus*, Tirage Spécial Liban-Syrie-Egypte. Coédition Flammarion, Desclee de Brouwer, FMA. Cet ouvrage a été imprimé sur les presses de la SIEL (Beyrouth) pour le compte des Éditions Flammarion et des éditions FMA en Decembre 1994.

Giordano, Silvano (Sous la Direction), *Le Carmel en Terre Sainte - des origines à nos jours*, Éditions Le Messagger de L'Enfant Jésus, Arenzano, 1995.

La Sainte Bible, traduite en français sous la direction de L'école Biblique De Jérusalem, Les Éditions Du Cerf, Paris, France, 1961.

Lenoir, Frédéric, et, Tardan-Masquelier, Ysé (Sous la Direction), *Encyclopédie Des Religions*, Nouvelle Édition, Revue, Augmentée et Mise a Jour, Bayard Éditions, Achevé d'imprimé en CEE, Août, 2000.

Markale, Jean, *L'enigme du Saint Graal*, Éditions J'ai Lu, Aventure Secrète, Achevé d'imprimé en France, Octobre, 2009.

Mordillat, Gerard, Prieur Jerome, *Corpus Christi*, Enquête sur L'écriture des Évangiles, Éditions Mille et une nuits/ ARTE Éditions, Mars, 1997.

Murr, Alfred, *El, Yahvé Et Jésus*, Deuxième Édition, Éditions Cadmus, Beyrouth, Liban, 1966.

Renan, Ernest, *Vie de Jésus*, Édition établie, présentée et annotée par Jean Gaulmier, Éditions Gallimard, Imprimé en France, Août, 1974.

Schuré, Édouard, *Les Grands Initiés - Rama, Krishna, Hermès, Moïse, Orphee, Pythagore, Platon, Jésus*, Esquise de L'histoire secrète des Religions, Librairie Académique Perrin, Imprimé en France, Avril, 1997.

Quere, France (Réunis et Présentés), *Évangiles Apocryphes*, Éditions du Seuil, Imprimé en France, Novembre, 1983.

Arabic:

Hourany, Youssef, *Lebanon in the value of its History / Phoenician Era*, (Arabic Title: Loubnan fi Qiyam tarikhihi / Al-ahed Al-finiki— لبنان في قيم تاريخه / العهـد الفينيقـي), Published by Dar El-Mashreq Publishers, Beirut, Lebanon, 1972.

Hourany, Youssef, *Cana of Galilee in South Lebanon,* (Arabic title: Kana Al-Jalil fi Jounoub Loubnan—قانا الجليل في جنوب لبنان), Published by the Ministry of Tourism, Lebanon, 1995.

Hourany, Youssef, *The Cosmogonic Theory of the Phoenicians* and its Impact on the Greek Civilisation, (Arabic title: Nazariat Al Takween Al Finikia wa

نظرية التكوين الفينيقية وأثارها في حضارة الإغريق), —Athariha fi Hadarat Al Ighreek, Published by Dar Al Nahar, Beirut, Lebanon, 1970.

Khoury Hareb, Antoine, *The Christian Roots in Lebanon*, (Arabic Title: Jouzour Al Massihia fi Loubnan—جذور المسيحية في لبنان), Published by the Lebanese Heritage Institute—مؤسسة الـتراث اللبناني, Printed in Lebanon by Raiidy Group, 2008.

The Jesuit, Martin Rev., *History of Lebanon*, (Arabic Title: Tarikh Loubnan—تاريخ لبنان), Printed in Lebanon and published by Dar Maroun Aboud, second edition, 1986.

Yammine, Youssef Rev., *The Messiah was born in Lebanon not in Judea*, (Arabic Title: Al Massih woulida fi Loubnan la fi al-Yahoudia— المسيح ولد في لبنان لا في اليهودية), An Abridged Version, El-Loubnanioun Editions, Printed in Lebanon by Kareh Printing Press, Ehden, Lebanon, 2010.

Yammine, Youssef Rev., *The Galilean Kana in Lebanon*, (Arabic Title: Kana Al-Jalil fi Loubnan—قانا الجليل في لبنان), El-Loubnanioun Editions, Printed in Lebanon by Kareh Printing Press, Ehden, Lebanon, 1994

Digital & Online:

Catholic Encyclopedia: *Acta Pilati*; *Cana*; *Demiurge*; *Marcionites*; *Paul*.

The Encyclopædia Britannica: *Zion*.

Wikipedia: *Canaan*; *Chaldea*; *Gospel of Marcion*.

Documentaries:

Marisa, Larson, *Bethlehem*, National Geographic, 2008-JUN-17.

Nasr, George, *If Lebanon Told its Story*, Lebanese Ministry of Tourism, 1997.

Notes

1- Porphyry was accused of writing against Christianity in the following works that have been wrongly attributed to him: *De Philosophia ex Oraculis Haurienda* (Philosophy from Oracles), and *Adversus Christianos* (Against the Christians) in fifteen books, yet, only very few fragments remain. We believe this accusation has no historical basis, but rather, a political one raised by Constantine and Eusebius. It was leveled against Porphyry after the death of Pamphilus in 309 AD and that of Porphyry in 304/5 AD. The English theologian of the 18th century AD, Dr Nathaniel Lardner, refused to attribute *Philosophy from Oracles* to Porphyry. In addition, both fathers of the Church, St. Augustine of the 4th/5th century AD and his contemporary Christian Church historian, Socrates of Constantinople, assert that Porphyry was once a Christian. At any rate, we believe both Pamphilus and Porphyry could have identified the forgery of Eusebius if they were still alive when he began writing his book around 313 AD, in an attempt to prove the excellence and uniqueness of Christianity over the so-called "pagan" religions and philosophies, especially that of the Phoenicians, and maybe, just maybe, for very important reasons he wished to hide!

2- The origin of Eusebius is still unknown to this day and his birthplace, not determined with absolute certainty, yet, is suggested to be Ceasaria where he was raised and lived most of his adult life. It is most probable, however, that he belonged originally to the Gentile community that constituted the largest amongst Jewish and Samaritan minorities. The Gentile population retained control of the city ever since the time of Pompey and Herod the Great afterwards, taking its name from Augustus Ceasar. Being of Gentile origin in the most probable case, (probably "Palestinian," as written by Marcellus (*Euseb. lib. adv. Marcell.* I. 4), Basil (*Lib. ad. Amphil. de Spir. Sancto*, c. 29) and Theodorus Metochita of the 14th century AD, in his *Cap. Miscell.* 17; *Migne, Patr. Lat.* CXLIV. 949), he may have been baptized (as attested in his epistle to the church of Cæsarea where he says that he was taught the creed of the Cæsarean church in his childhood, or at least at the beginning of his Christian life: *en te katechesei*, and that he accepted it at baptism) and trained by Bishop Agapius of Ceasaria who ordained him a priest before succeeding him on the Bishopric See in the city. [Part of this analytical note has been taken from the work of the 19th century German-American theologian and Church historian, Philip Schaff. Eusebius Pamphilius: *Church History, Life of Constantine, Oration in Praise of Constantine.* Translated and commented with Prolegomena and notes by Rev. Arthur Cushman McGiffert, Ph.D. and Dr. Ernest C. Richardson. Under the editorial supervision of Philip Schaff, D.D., LL.D., Professor of Church History in the Union Theological Seminary, New York, and Henry Wace, D.D., Principal of King's College, London, Published in 1890 by Philip Schaff, New York: Christian Literature Publishing Co.]

3- It is perfectly legitimate to ask how it was that Pamphilus and many of his Christian followers were imprisoned, while Eusebius had indeed the freedom to come and go so frequently without being arrested and condemned? It is very possible that he possessed some friends among the Roman or Gentile authorities whose influence could have secured his safety. In fact, this suggestion finds lots of support, for his acquaintance with Constantine (as attested by him in his *Life of Constantine*, I. 19) some years before, in Cæsarea, could not have happened without him having connections with probably high officials and/or influential families of the city. The position of prominence which he later acquired at the imperial court of Constantine presents itself as enough evidence, yet, not only then, but also before, during the persecution of the Christian community in Ceasaria. His connection with Rome definitely secured him from imprisonment and martyrdom, although it has been suggested that he denied his faith during the Diocletian persecution to keep himself from harm and torture, but he didn't need to do that, or compromise or concede for that matter, if he had the connections —unless it was a theatrical show that made him appear guilty and not guilty at the same time. However, it is reported that during the Council of Tyre in c. 335 AD, Potamo, Bishop of Heraclea, in Egypt, accused Eusebius in the following words: "Dost thou sit as judge, O Eusebius; and is Athanasius, innocent as he is, judged by thee? Who can bear such things? Pray tell me, wast thou not with me in prison during the persecution? And I lost an eye in behalf of the truth, but thou appearest to have received no bodily injury, neither hast thou suffered martyrdom, but thou hast remained alive with no mutilation. How wast thou released from prison unless thou didst promise those that put upon us the pressure of persecution to do that which is unlawful, or didst actually do it?" On hearing that, Eusebius seems not to have denied the charge, but simply dismissed the Council in anger. (Epiphan. Hær. LXVIII. 8). Was it after all some kind of a theatrical act that would show Eusebius guilty as a Christian and not guilty as a Roman Christian, at the same time?! [Part of this analytical note has been taken from the work of the 19th century German-American theologian and church historian, Philip Schaff. Eusebius Pamphilius: *Church History, Life of Constantine, Oration in Praise of Constantine.* Translated and commented with Prolegomena and notes by Rev. Arthur Cushman McGiffert, Ph.D., and Dr. Ernest C. Richardson. Under the editorial supervision of Philip Schaff, D.D., LL.D., Professor of Church History in the Union Theological Seminary, New York, and Henry Wace, D.D., Principal of King's College, London, Published in 1890 by Philip Schaff, New York: Christian Literature Publishing Co.]